ASYLUM BETWEEN NATIONS

ASYLUM BETWEEN NATIONS

Refugees in a Revolutionary Era

JANET POLASKY

Yale
UNIVERSITY PRESS
New Haven and London

Published with assistance from the foundation established
in memory of Amasa Stone Mather of the Class of 1907,
Yale College.

Yale University Press books may be purchased in quantity for
educational, business, or promotional use. For information, please
e-mail sales.press@yale.edu (U.S. office) or sales@yaleup.co.uk
(U.K. office).

Set in Janson type by Integrated Publishing Solutions.
Printed in the United States of America.

Library of Congress Control Number: 2022942893
ISBN 978-0-300-25656-7 (hardcover : alk. paper)

A catalogue record for this book is available from the British Library.

This paper meets the requirements of ANSI/NISO Z39.48-1992
(Permanence of Paper).

10 9 8 7 6 5 4 3 2 1

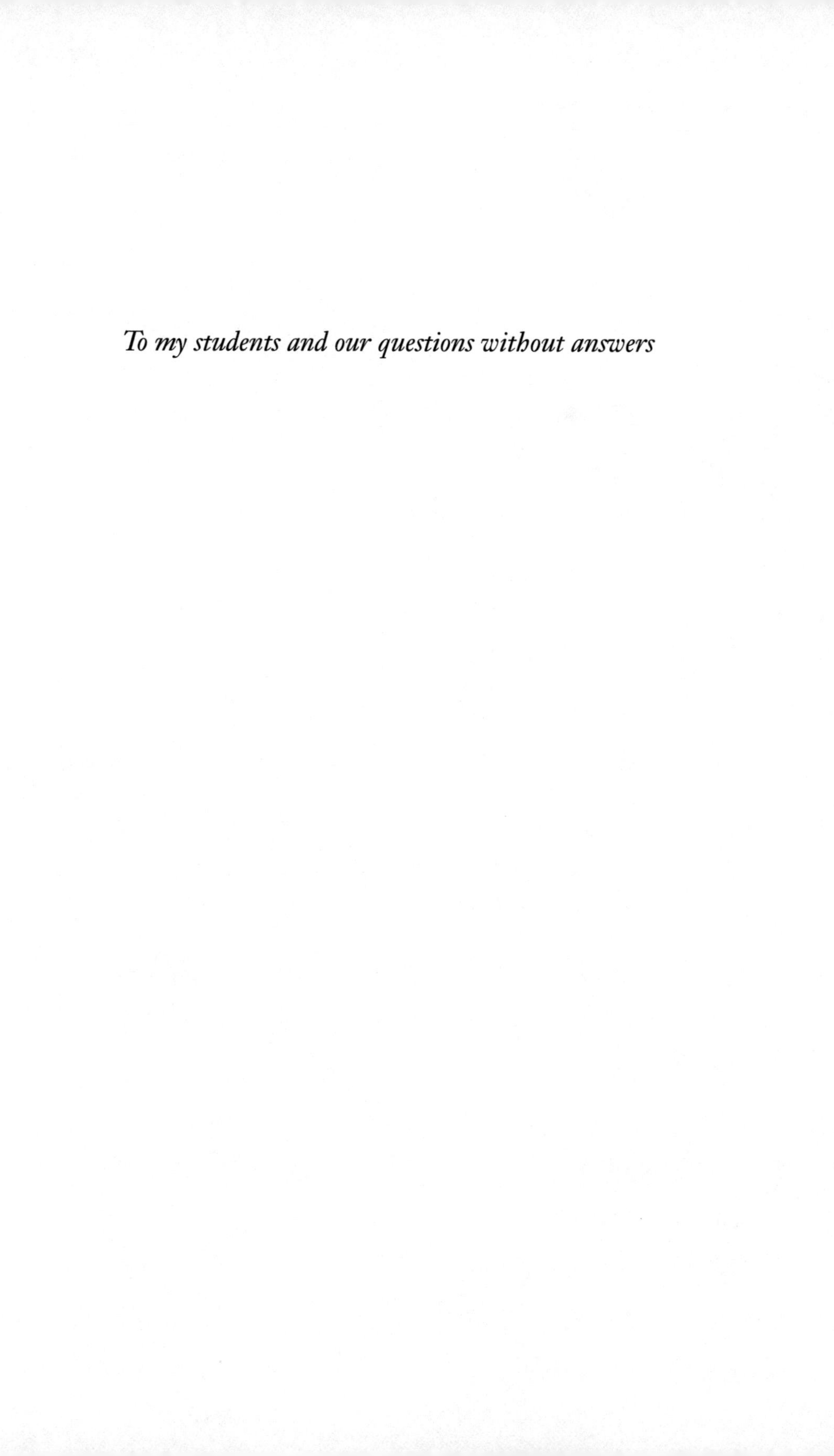

To my students and our questions without answers

Contents

Introduction
Asylum between Nations

THE PHILOSOPHER HANNAH ARENDT, herself a refugee, described the stark reality of being adrift between nations in a world at war. The night in 1933 when Hitler's supporters burned the Reichstag, twenty-six-year-old Hannah Arendt had just completed her doctoral studies. She was taking a break for lunch from her research on anti-Semitism in Berlin when the Gestapo arrested her, along with her mother, in a café. Released after a week, mother and daughter realized they were no longer safe at home as Jews in Germany. Hannah Arendt fled to Paris by way of Prague and Switzerland, the first stops on her route into an exile that would last a lifetime. Unmoored from any sense of belonging, deprived of national citizenship, Arendt lost what she called the "right to have rights."[1]

Hannah Arendt was again arrested in 1940, this time by French fascists for her work helping Jewish children to escape to Palestine. Imprisoned in the internment camp at Gurs in southwestern France, she escaped as part of a massive break by the women of the camp and found her way to Montauban, a crossroads for refugees in unoccupied France. There she secured exit papers with the help of a well-placed friend and eventually made her way to the United States through Spain and Portugal. She was fortunate. Two years earlier, both the United States and Cuba had refused entry to the ship *Saint Louis*, crossing the Atlantic with over nine hundred Jewish refugees from Germany on board. Turned back, most of the passengers died in the Holocaust.

Hannah Arendt as a student in Germany, circa 1930.
Courtesy of the Hannah Arendt Bluecher Literary
Trust/Art Resource, NY.

Hannah Arendt arrived in New York speaking no English, a not uncommon predicament for a refugee. A relief organization helped her to secure work as a housekeeper in Massachusetts, where she learned English. In characteristically stark terms, Arendt summed up the age-old universal experience of refugees: "We lost our home, which means the familiarity of daily life. We lost our occupation, which means the confidence that we are of some use in this world. We lost our language, which means the naturalness of reactions, the simplicity of gestures, the unaffected expression of feelings."[2] Exile begins with loss.

That loss is compounded by the confusion of the journey, shedding one identity and language before finding another. The Pulitzer Prize–winning poet Charles Simic, another refugee who made his way to the United States, began his account of his family's memorable journey from Belgrade in 1945 by downplaying its noteworthiness. "Mine is an old, familiar story by now," he wrote. "So many people have been displaced in this century, their numbers so large, their collective and individual destinies so varied, it's impossible for me or anyone else, if we are honest, to claim any special status as a victim." The Simic family's leaving was set in motion by Hitler's wars and Stalin's takeover of Eastern Europe, although, Simic explained, his family "had no intention to stray far beyond our neighborhood." Once they made it to Paris, their lives consisted of standing in lines to serve up documents to bureaucrats intent on verifying their identity. "Everyone we met asked us who we were the moment we opened our mouths, and they heard the accent." Simic and his family had no ready answer to the question. "Being rattled around in freight trains, open trucks, and ratty ocean liners," he recounts, "we ended up being a puzzle even to ourselves."[3] Displaced, they were outsiders forced to reinvent themselves.

"Displaced" is how both Hannah Arendt and Charles Simic pictured modern refugees caught between nations. A "post-war expression," Arendt commented, "'displaced persons' has been expressly invented in order to make disappear from the world the disturbing fact of 'statelessness' by ignoring it."[4] Refugees who did not go on to write books as philosophers and poets have been displaced not only by governments and their bureaucrats, but also by historians. They fall between national histories. Having left one nation, refugees are routinely dismissed from its history. Only exceptional immigrants who have fully integrated as citizens or who have notoriously disrupted their new nation make it over the bar of significance warranting consideration. More often, the national frame of reference leaves them outside. Border crossers, like the many transnational movements they organize, refugees do not readily fit the conventions of sedentary national histories.[5]

Asylum between Nations reclaims the lost story of political refugees and of the cities that sheltered them in the turbulence between the American and French revolutions at the end of the eighteenth century and the Revolutions of 1848. It is a transnational history of the doors willingly opened wide between 1789 and 1848 and of the people who passed through them. During one of the most turbulent periods in modern history, in the midst of hostile states jostling against each other as regimes changed radically, cities, federated cantons, monarchies, and new republics offered asylum to refugees. A century before the codification by international organizations of individual rights to movement, these communities recognized the inalienability of the human rights defined in the American and French revolutions. They offered asylum between nations.

Cast off from homelands, refugees from ancient times to the present have sought asylum in worlds turned upside down. The United Nations set legal parameters defining refugees as a special category of the displaced only after the unprecedented cataclysm of two world wars. The 1951 Geneva Convention, drafted by the UN Commission on Human Rights, and the 1967 Protocol that followed defined refugees as persons with a well-founded fear of persecution for reasons of race, religion, nationality, or membership in a particular social group or political opinion. Refugees found themselves outside the country of their nationality and unable to return. As opposed to migrants, according to the Convention and Protocol, they were not motivated by economic needs. As explicated by Oxford professor Andrew Shacknove, refugees are "persons whose basic needs are unprotected by their country of origin, who have no remaining recourse other than to seek international restitution of their needs."[6] Unable to return home, refugees are dependent on others to provide shelter and to secure their human rights.

Two hundred years before the United Nations set stringent parameters for the legal category of "refugee," the term was more commonly deployed to describe the men, women, and children set adrift by political revolutions and economic crises. In what has been identified as the first modern refugee crisis, at the turn of the nineteenth century, "refugee" as a generic term encompassed all those who were forced to take to the road "without passports, having broken off all connections to their home state," historians Sylvie Aprile and Delphine Diaz explain. Whether aristocrats fleeing the Terror of the French Revolution or German artisans down on their luck, this more inclusive definition of refugees takes in all who fled their homelands and sought "the help of their host country in order to survive."[7]

"Migrants" is the more generic term adopted by the United Nations High Commission on Refugees (UNHCR) at the turn of the twenty-first century to refer to people forced to flee but excluded from the legal definition of a refugee. A century earlier, Victor Hugo, banished to the rocky island of Jersey off the coast of France, complained that "migrant" was too neutral a term and denied agency to those who traveled across borders in the midst of revolutions. In search of a label that bore witness to the struggles of the many fellow exiles who shared his fate in the middle of the nineteenth century, the author of *Les Misérables* suggested the term "*les éprouvés*," or "those who have been tested."[8]

Perhaps moved by similar reflections, in acknowledgement of the fatal consequences for many "migrants" of their institutional attempt to delimit their definition of "refugees," in 2016, the United Nations and assembled heads of state resolved that going forward, "Refugees and migrants [will] have the same universal human rights and fundamental freedoms."[9] They declared their "profound solidarity" with the millions of people uprooted from their homelands through no fault of their own, whether the cause was economic, ecological, religious, or political. They recognized that the uprooted had all undertaken equally perilous journeys across national borders, mountains, deserts, and seas. There was no line to be drawn in terms of guaranteeing universal human rights in the modern world between forced and voluntary migration. Against the advice of family and friends, these refugees, broadly defined, had all risked their lives in search of the shelter of a new home.

For all of these reasons, "refugee" will be the term most commonly used here to include the range of people who left their homes in search of safety and a better life in the midst of a revolutionary age.[10] It is inclusive, encompassing political poets dabbling in commerce, revolutionary insurgents under death sentences, and marginalized laborers seeking work in expanding industries. The range in refugees then was as wide as it is now, even if in our unthinking categorization, we habitually refer only to desperate migrants fleeing unrest in Honduras or Afghanistan or rising oceans on Pacific islands and coastal reefs. We assign another, more respectful, set of labels to the German engineers fleeing the Holocaust, Indian chemists studying for advanced degrees, or high-tech innovators migrating to the Silicon Valley. All of them, though, were border crossers who had to redefine themselves abroad. This history of refugees in the first period of mass migration purposefully follows immigrants in all their varieties, arguing that in the end they all contributed to the societies that offered them asylum.

In contrast to refugees arriving at national border crossings in numbers that figure prominently in today's news, refugees at the end of the eighteenth and the beginning of the nineteenth century were more likely to travel as isolated individuals or in family groups. They included aristocrats who left behind sumptuous estates confiscated by revolutionary governments, enterprising merchants seeking new business opportunities, destitute artisans and their families, and revolutionaries pursued by regimes intent on restoring the status quo. They often bore little resemblance to the immigrants camped on the Mexican border with the United States or arriving in rubber rafts and leaky dinghies on European shores. These revolutionary refugees, however, were no less adrift two hundred years ago between vigilant nation-states than the refugees set in motion by civil unrest and seeking shelter and a better life in our own time.

Contemporary novelist and literary critic André Aciman, born and raised in Egypt before moving to New York, opened his collection of essays written by contemporary refugees with three questions: "What does it mean to be an exile? How does exile alter someone? How does it reinvent one?"[11] There is another dimension. *Asylum between Nations* looks at the story of refugees as an evolving dialogue between those who fled their homelands and the places that offered asylum. Focused on the first modern refugee crisis, it asks about the communities that have welcomed refugees throughout history. Why do nations or cities open their doors rather than fortify their borders? What are the consequences of integration or assimilation of potentially disruptive newcomers for the citizens who reside in nations and neighborhoods? How does the offer of asylum alter not only the community that offers shelter, but also the world beyond? *Asylum between Nations* is a dialectical history of relationships that developed between refugees, broadly defined, and the societies that offered them shelter.

The term "asylum" can be as restrictive in its modern usage as "refugee." Since ancient times, "asylum" has encompassed places of sanctuary offered to those who, Arendt explains, "were forced to become outlaws through circumstances beyond their control."[12] From the Greek *a-sylas*, it has described a place free of violence and safeguarded from incursion. Adopted by modern states offering protection to individuals fleeing persecution in their countries, it, too has been given a precise legal definition based on the experience of the world wars, when the numbers of asylum seekers overwhelmed nations. The UNHCR recognized 4.2 million people in 2021 around the world awaiting decision on their claims to "the grant, by a State, of protection on its territory to persons from another State who are fleeing persecution or serious danger." These asylum seekers were given "permission to remain on the territory of the asylum country" and afforded "humane standards of treatment."[13] As opposed to a refugee seeking entry, in legal terms, an asylee already resided within the host country. In the eighteenth and nineteenth centuries, however, "asylum" had no formal definition or international legal guarantees. Nor was it always limited to legally defined refugees without economic claims, as it was at the end of the twentieth century.

Refugees throughout history have shared a perspective as outsiders that differed decisively from that of their neighbors who remained settled in place with a claim to citizenship. The writer Edward Said, born in Jerusalem, who had come to the United States by way of a childhood in Egypt, observed that exiles came to see "the entire world as a foreign land."[14]

Knowing multiple homes, they learned to adapt, to reconstruct their lives away from their past. V. S. Naipaul in *The Enigma of Arrival*, published in 1987, recounting his "insecure past—peasant India, colonial Trinidad," similarly explained that his "uprooting" had given him "an especially tender or raw sense of an unaccommodating world."[15] And yet, Naipaul noted that with the passage of time "in that unlikely setting, in the ancient heart of England, a place where I was truly an alien," he began to heal. He was "given a second chance, a new life, richer and fuller than any I had had anywhere else." Naipaul, walking every afternoon through the valley around his cottage concludes, "The life around me changed. I changed."[16] The influence of his neighbors and the new landscape transformed his life, but he also altered theirs.

The experience derisively labeled "displacement" is perennial, ebbing and flowing in waves through human history. It has changed in dialogue with the places that have opened their doors, offering asylum to strangers. At one of the most critical junctures, just as revolutions drove unprecedented numbers of refugees out in search of safer harbors, the cosmopolitanism that inspired communities to welcome outsiders into their midst ran into the walls of an emerging nationalism unleashed by those same revolutions.

"We the People": Cosmopolitanism and Nationalism

The parameters of this dialogue between refugees and sites of asylum were set long before the two world wars and the proclamations of the United Nations. Two and a half centuries earlier, philosopher Immanuel Kant defined the hospitality owed a visiting foreigner as universal. All people have a right to visit, he argued, to travel and "to offer themselves as potential members of any society." As long as newcomers to a community behaved peacefully, they were not to be treated with hostility as foreigners. In his essay, *Perpetual Peace*, Kant justified his claim to hospitality as a universal right "by virtue of their common possession of the surface of the earth."[17] A philosopher of the Enlightenment, Kant pointedly stayed in one place, Königsberg, a city that he believed to be outward looking and well connected to the world.

Other Enlightenment philosophers roamed more widely, boldly defining themselves as cosmopolitans in the tradition of Diogenes the Cynic, the ancient Greek who identified as "a citizen of the world."[18] At home across the world themselves, concurrently they acknowledged a responsi-

Immanuel Kant at his desk. Eighteenth-century engraving by Birck. Public domain. Photograph by Eleta Exline.

bility to welcome outsiders into their homes. Taken together, these early modern proclamations of the right of all individuals to visit (but not to invade) across the globe and the corresponding obligations of universal hospitality have bolstered the claims of political refugees seeking asylum ever since.

In 1646, Hugo Grotius, a prolific Dutch humanist whose interests in sovereignty, international commerce, and war took him to France, Germany, and Sweden, affirmed the natural right of exiles to reside abroad. "A permanent residence ought not be denied to foreigners who, expelled from their homes, are seeking a refuge," Grotius asserted.[19] Simply stated, refugees innocent of any crime deserved asylum. Over a century later, after the Treaty of Westphalia of 1648 had laid down the doctrine of the law of nations, German philosopher Christian von Wolff added the seemingly obvious but often ignored fact that "exiles do not cease to be men because they are driven into exile."[20] Wolff's pupil Emer de Vattel argued even more emphatically for the right to emigration and immigration as long as it did not harm the interests of the state, and even then, if the journey was compelled by danger to the immigrant.

In the decades before the establishment of the American and French republics, Enlightenment philosophers aspired, as did the French editor of the monumental *Encyclopédie*, Denis Diderot, to be "strangers nowhere in the world."[21] In their universalism, they envisioned themselves as open-minded spokesmen for the values of mankind. Scottish philosopher David Hume, known widely for his tracts on history, politics, and economics, described their vision as "not limited by any narrow bounds, either of place or time," extending "into the most distant regions of this globe, and beyond this globe, to the planets and heavenly bodies."[22] Diderot wrote to his friend Hume: "My dear David, you belong to all nations. . . . I am proud to be like you, a citizen of the big universal city."[23] Their networks of ideas and friendships transcended language and geography. They did not, however, bridge the yawning racial divide of a century that trafficked in slaves.

Nor were their assertions of universal hospitality the most sweeping early modern definitions of refugee rights in a world before rigid national boundaries.[24] After all, Kant, who advocated for hospitality, extended the offer only "until there is a favorable opportunity to leave."[25] The question of accepting visitors as permanent citizens necessarily entailed more complex negotiation between states, he recognized. Those provisions of international law would come much later, as would challenges to exclusions based on race. Finally, Kant also granted societies the right to refuse entry to travelers if sending them away would not cause substantial harm.

Over the course of the nineteenth century, the right to hospitality evolved in relationship with the emergence of the modern nation-state. Their history is complementary and intertwined. Hannah Arendt exposed the interworking of cosmopolitanism and nationalism at the dawn of the modern era. The Enlightenment gave humanity an "'abstract' human being who seemed to exist nowhere," she suggested. The newly independent states that emerged from the eighteenth-century revolutions then appropriated the rights of this abstract individual for their own citizens.[26] Founding fathers in America and France secured what they declared to be the natural rights of man for some of their own people within territorially bound republics.

With the words "we the people" on one side of the Atlantic and "the representatives of the French people" on the other, the Americans and the French proclaimed the rights of man to liberty and equality. Their declarations have framed our understanding of the universal rights of man ever since. Revolutionaries in Philadelphia, Paris, Port au Prince, Brussels, Warsaw, Dublin, and other places, many of whom would become refugees, shared an assumption, derived from the Enlightenment, that these rights would be universal the world over, anchored by nation-states that would launch their own revolutions. What they did not realize, and what we forget, is that the founding fathers on both sides of the Atlantic guaranteed rights of their people within the borders of their sovereign nation. In a revolutionary era when the cosmopolitanism of the Enlightenment promised all individuals the right to move freely across the earth, the new republics consciously set "the people" and their representatives apart from others, from outsiders or foreigners. These borders have endured into our own time.

The quest for liberty, begun in America, seemed to be unstoppable at the end of the eighteenth century. Claims to the rights of man spread as "a general fermentation." The Marquis de Condorcet, one of the rare Enlightenment philosophers to live long enough to see the American and French revolutions, enthusiastically predicted: "The more free people that exist in the world, the more the liberty of each individual is assured."[27] American poet, sometime diplomat, and aspiring entrepreneur Joel Barlow, in a speech to the French National Convention, acknowledged the "intense light" of the American Revolution but declared that it was not until the French Revolution that "the sun at its zenith revealed the practical results of that philosophy whose principles had been sown in the dark."[28] Revolutionary ideals radiated from France. News of the French Revolution reached Mauritius in the Indian Ocean in January 1790, and within four days, hundreds of men and women donned revolutionary cockades as placards invited citizens to national assemblies thousands of miles from Paris.[29]

These revolutionaries roamed as freely as the philosophers who inspired them, trading ideas and goods not only across the Atlantic, but also beyond. They did not recognize limits or borders. Thomas Paine, an enthusiastic American revolutionary newly arrived in Philadelphia from London, announced in his widely distributed pamphlet, *Common Sense:* "My country is the world, my countrymen mankind."[30] In 1789, revolutionaries, including Paine, came from across the globe to Paris to join in the French Revolution. They dismissed off-hand references to themselves as "foreigners." It was "a barbarous expression" not in keeping with the universalism of the French Revolution. Instead, they savored the promise of a universal citizenship that transcended borders.[31] Dubbing himself the "orator of the human race," the Prussian-born Dutch revolutionary Anacharsis Cloots introduced a delegation of Arab, Prussian, Belgian, British, Spanish, Swedish, Italian, and Dutch refugees to the French National Assembly, many bedecked in stereotypical versions of their native dress.[32] "Sovereignty resides essentially in the whole human race," Cloots proclaimed. "It is one, indivisible, imprescriptible, immutable, inalienable, imperishable, unlimited, absolute, without boundaries and all mighty."[33] He looked around the world, starting with Boston and Charlestown, and extending to Pondicherry, the Île de Bourbon, Saint Domingue, Jamaica, and Guyana.[34] In the summer of 1792, two weeks after the French king had been toppled from his throne, a delegation of Parisian citizens, led by Marie-Joseph Chénier, petitioned the French Legislative Assembly, asking that eighteen foreigners, "courageous philosophers who have sapped the foundations of tyranny," including Cloots and Paine, be granted full French citizenship.[35] Hailing from elsewhere, they "had dared to speak the language of liberty and equality."[36] After debate, they were proclaimed French citizens with full political rights. Three of them, including Paine and Cloots, won election to the new National Convention, the self-proclaimed "congress of the whole world."[37]

The revolutionary French defined their universal nation as something completely novel, without precedent in global history. Perhaps they had been inspired by the Americans, but a deputy to the Constituent Assembly, Jean-Pierre Rabaut, proclaimed the French were "made not to follow examples, but to give them."[38] The Jacobin leader, Maximilien Robespierre, called for a "complete regeneration . . . to create a new people."[39] Not tied to their past, the revolutionary French looked to the future. So did their revolutionary adherents, steeped in the promise of Enlightenment rhetoric.

The French harnessed the rhetoric of Enlightenment cosmopolitanism, adapted to their dream of a universal republic to wage war in the name of liberty and equality for all. The revolutionary regime declared war on tyrants scattered across neighboring empires and oppressing their peoples. In the name of cosmopolitanism, they launched military campaigns that would come to define modern nationalism.

By the end of the eighteenth century, within decades of their conception, the freedom-loving republics were restricting the rights of all who were not their citizens. Embroiled in wars across the continent, the embattled French National Convention called for the arrest or expulsion of all foreigners from countries at war with France. Those supporters from abroad who had been drawn to Paris in the early days of the revolution were required to don a tricolor ribbon as a sign of their eligibility for hospitality. Now far from the cosmopolitan definition of "*patrie*," Jean-Lambert Tallien, secretary to the Insurrectional Commune of Paris, formulated the clear dichotomy between outsiders and French citizens: "The only foreigners in France are bad citizens."[40] Henceforth, "foreign" would carry negative connotations. Both Paine and Cloots were hastily imprisoned; while Paine escaped with his life to return to the United States, Cloots lost his at the guillotine.

Even as the Americans decried the escalating violence of the French Revolution, they also turned defensively inward. Thomas Paine, who had in 1776 voiced his aspiration that one day the revolutionary American republic would "receive the fugitive and prepare in time an asylum for mankind," was denied the right to vote when he finally settled in New York.[41] Paine fared better than the loyalists, Black and white, who fled the new United States, a diaspora dispersed across the Atlantic world. They would never return home.[42]

The French Revolution, like the American Revolution before it, created the modern nation-state. Nationalism implied loyalty to the nation: You are either with us or against us. The nineteenth-century French philosopher and historian Ernest Renan defined a nation as a spiritual principle, a soul, explaining: "The essence of a nation is that all individuals have many things in common; and also that they have forgotten many things."[43] A quintessentially modern concept, a nation enforced boundaries, including the drawing of lines between citizens with rights and foreigners on the outside. Empires had frontiers, but democracies have borders. These borders defined the parameters of the modern world for refugees seeking asylum and forced to find their way between nations.

Although America and France claim a long heritage of liberal immigration policies and generous rights for immigrants who arrive on their shores, that has not always been the case. The new republics spurned refugees at the turn of the nineteenth century within decades of their celebrated founding. The half-century of chaotic nation building following the late eighteenth-century revolutions spun a plethora of definitions of citizenship designed to determine membership in political communities conferring rights and of frameworks for exacting responsibilities. Citizenship came to be associated with residence within a nation that was imbued with the responsibility for distributing goods, including rights to its citizens who dwelled within.[44] Outsiders had none of the rights of man. The revolutionary nation-states had claimed the rights for their own citizens and closed their gates. The revolutions meant to guarantee liberty ironically excluded the neediest among them from "the right to have rights."

What happened to Kant's universal hospitality in a world of nation-states? Without legitimate claims to citizenship, refugees seeking to reside abroad posed a challenge to the nascent nation-states. Even the most community-minded of all Enlightenment philosophers, Genevan Jean-Jacques Rousseau, writing a constitution for Poland in 1772, bluntly called for borders, characterizing a foreigner as the ultimate outsider who "no longer has a *patrie*, no longer exists and is better off dead."[45] This dark view of the plight of outsiders posed questions for his eighteenth-century readers that remain as urgent now as then. Who is responsible for those excluded in the new world of nation-states? Does a nation have obligations beyond the boundaries of its community?[46]

What follows is a history of the independent city-states, cantons, and monarchies that answered "yes" during this age of revolution and nation building. These smaller spaces stepped up to the challenge in this, the first modern refugee crisis. They did not let their own, or more often their powerful neighbors', fears of refugees deter them. The conundrum of protective nationalism in the age of revolution that began with such cosmopolitan promise has been highlighted by historians. The stories of asylum for refugees offer an alternative to this narrative of national fortification.

"Small Places": Asylum in "a World Loudly Turned Upside Down"

Asylum between Nations focuses on the small spaces that not only welcomed refugees, but also prospered during the turbulent decades between the eighteenth-century Atlantic revolutions and the Revolutions of 1848. Many of the refugees who found shelter in the independent German city-state of Hamburg and the neighboring Danish port of Altona in the 1790s, in the Swiss cantons in the 1820s and 1830s, and in the Belgian capital in the 1840s viewed their asylum as a critical interlude between revolutions. It was a time when everyone seemed to be on the move, and societies were on edge.

In this revolutionary era, the foundations of both sides of contemporary debates over immigration and of the policies that reflect them can be found. In these turbulent decades, the idealism of the cosmopolitan Enlightenment encountered the security concerns of the nascent and not yet stable nation-states. The threats posed by possibly disruptive foreigners arriving in numbers with the potential to overwhelm their hosts and their housing were no less real then than now. The foreign policies and immigration practices of these ports in a storm reflected the tension of what contemporaries named a migration crisis. Hamburg and Altona, the Swiss cantons, and the small Belgian nation found a different balance than their neighbors as they weighed the natural right of free movement for individuals and the principle of territorial sovereignty enforced by national governments.

Most histories of exile focus on the immigration policies and practices of the largest modern nations, in particular the countries that took in the majority of refugees—France, Great Britain, and the United States. They track the flow of migrants against the changing laws of these countries. Moreover, most studies of forced migration concentrate on the decades since the world wars. Year zero for refugee and migration studies is often 1951, the year the UNHCR was institutionalized and the Convention on the Status of Refugees was signed. The displacement of individuals, families, and populations has a history longer and broader than that.

Undetected in such studies are the smaller doors opened wide in earlier decades, doors that refugees themselves found in the eighteenth and nineteenth centuries. These overlooked enclaves at the diplomatic and commercial hubs of the Atlantic world have encouraged free trade and welcomed strangers for at least two hundred and fifty years. Some traditional city-states and others new nations, they offered a remarkably broad asylum even as their neighbors protected their borders with aggressive foreign policies and threatened them with standing armies. Their hospitality predated the international conventions defined by the United Nations in the twentieth century.

The new Belgian regime consciously kept the national borders open to all travelers at the same time that its larger neighbors were reinforcing their claims to territorial sovereignty with regimes of passport and border controls. One of the national founders, Alexandre Gendebien, a self-declared "*grand patriote*" and Freemason, mused a decade into independence along lines suggested by Immanuel Kant at the beginning of the project of nation founding about the need for another, more far-reaching, revolution to break down national borders. "It would make sense in the end to go back to my project for a federation of peoples," he wrote, remembering the projects of his own youth. He added: "It may seem utopian, but I am convinced more each day that it alone is realizable."[47] Any reforms short of that were an invitation to neighboring absolutist powers to overrun the small country.

To ignore these small spaces that offered asylum during dangerous periods of the past, when governments sought to balance individual liberties and "the right to have rights" with national security, is to come up short in our understanding not only of the historic plight of refugees, but also of the possibilities of asylum now and in the future. Writing at the beginning of the twenty-first century, Turkish American political scientist Seyla Benhabib reminds us that "the virtues of liberal democracies do not consist in their capacities to close their borders, but in their capacities to hear the claims of those who, for whatever reasons, knock at our doors."[48] The vulnerable cosmopolitan communities overcame the multiple voices of fear within their societies to offer shelter in this revolutionary era of nation building that followed the American Revolution.

In 1796, an aspiring young lawyer from Bremen, Ferdinand Beneke, marveled as he sailed into the harbor of the independent German city-state of Hamburg at "the countless rows of ships . . . thronging this cosmopolitan port."[49] It was so different from the closed German cities inland. No merchant himself, Beneke was in awe of the panoply of ships, sails set, coming and going from the busy harbor on the Elbe. Of the two thousand ships that docked over the course of Beneke's first year in Hamburg, few were owned by residents. Immigrants were investing heavily in the shipping fleets of Hamburg and the adjoining Danish municipality of Altona.

Hamburg and Altona flourished in a period when war laid waste to vast swathes of Europe. At the end of the eighteenth century, without a princely court but harboring a thicket of sailing ships and barges, Hamburg was governed by a prosperous and well-read middle class. The chief town of the Duchy of Holstein under the Danish crown, Altona was a short walk along the banks of the Elbe River and through the city gates from the larger municipality of Hamburg. It featured an open gate on its city seal. Both widely known for their press freedom and tolerance, the cities stood prominently as symbols of liberty for their burghers but also for their neighbors.

The legendary openness of Altona and Hamburg to outsiders drew a wave of French émigrés to their shores. These displaced aristocrats were seeking refuge close to their ancestral estates; they expected to return home at the end of what they all wrongly assumed would be a short-lived revolution. For them, exile was a stage poised between what they envisioned as a traumatic past and a promising future.

Hamburg and Altona promised not only the security of asylum while armies marched over the rest of Europe and navies skirmished all the way to the Caribbean, but they also offered an economic livelihood to refugees prepared to take advantage of opportunities in the last decade of the eighteenth century. A steady stream of merchants, diplomats, philosophers, and journalists, among others, sought a safe haven where their families might not only thrive, but also prosper. Commercial ventures departing from the two harbors linked American merchants, prominent Hamburg senators, and French diplomats in schemes to skirt the blockades of a continent at war.

In the early nineteenth century, the French invaded and occupied Hamburg, but despite the best efforts of security-conscious governments, borders remained porous. Increasingly during this revolutionary era of shifting borders and tightening passport regulations, nationalism and cosmopolitanism seemed destined to collide. Nevertheless, a plethora of small states, including the Swiss cantons, deliberately opened their doors to all manner of refugees, from Italian supporters of Napoleon to down-on-their-luck German radicals. Some just passed through these renowned places of asylum, but others put down roots. In some of the cantons, refugees enjoyed almost full political rights, including the right to publish political tracts. These cantons responded to pressure from neighboring states to roll back their liberal policies by simply naturalizing refugees. *Asylum between Nations* examines the changes introduced with the implementation of passport controls and border surveillance and the threat of extradition, differentiating the experiences of Altona and Hamburg from those of Belgium half a century later.

In the decade leading up to the revolutions that would sweep through Europe in 1848, the newly independent kingdom of Belgium welcomed a steady stream of immigrants to stoke its precocious industrialization. The quintessentially liberal Belgian constitution of 1831 extended liberties to all who resided within its territory. Neutral in foreign affairs and connected to its neighbors by the densest railway network on the European continent, Belgium drew more than its share of refugees from neighboring countries.

Legend has it that Karl Marx, a German exile, sat down to write the *Communist Manifesto* in a café on the Grand Place of Brussels.[50] Police agents made regular rounds through the cafés in the center of the Belgian capital, but Marx, expelled from both his native Prussia and France, had no real cause for alarm. The German refugee who would call on the workers of the world to unite had permission to reside with his family in the heart of the new Belgian nation. He had signed a perfunctory pledge not to overthrow the king. He turned his attention elsewhere. That assurance was enough for some but certainly not for all Belgian authorities at the federal level, nor for Belgium's neighbors, who foresaw trouble.

Marx's imagined community of revolutionaries materialized in Brussels, the forerunner of the socialist internationals. German communists, French socialists, Polish revolutionaries, and others in smaller numbers associated in the cafés, cabarets, and dance halls of the Belgian capital. They were joined by the leaders of Belgian workers' associations, as well as by Liberals from the government, in a collaboration that escaped the gaze not only of the police, but of many historians as well. Only when demonstrations spilled into the streets of Brussels in the days after the February 1848 uprising in Paris did the Belgian government bow to Prussian pressure to expel foreigners from its capital. Even then, Marx's ally Friedrich Engels showed no hard feelings toward the Belgians who, he wrote, "saw in us not foreigners but democrats."[51]

From our vantage point, it seems unimaginable that the most powerful call to revolution of all time was written by a political refugee in plain view of the authorities. Today, rumors of such a gathering of foreign incendiaries would be more than enough to convince even the country that sees itself as the world's leading democracy to secure its borders, perhaps by building a wall. And yet, in the midst of an era that historian Sarah Knott aptly describes as "a world loudly turned upside down and rearranged," Altona, Hamburg, the Swiss cantons, and Belgium offered hospitality to refugees, quite often over the vigorous objections of their larger neighbors' governments.[52] They found a balance that recognized the natural right of individuals to move freely and to dwell somewhere in the world as other emerging revolutionary nations were ever more aggressively asserting control over their territories. These decades between revolutions marked a critical period for new nation-states as they defined citizenship and legislated their outlook on foreigners. *Asylum between Nations* traces the dialogue between refugees and the communities that offered them asylum at the crossroads of an interconnected world in times as roiled as our own. The difference is one of scale.

Asylum between Nations is an exploration of the people and places that opened their doors to strangers. It begins in the 1790s in the glades along the Elbe River just west of Altona, where the Sievekings and Poels invited eighty guests, give or take a dozen, to their summer house. It examines the diplomatic pressure exerted by larger, more powerful states on the Swiss cantons to expel foreign insurgents, leaders, and laborers, in the 1830s. A decade later, in Brussels neighborhoods inhabited by artisans and workers, Germans, Poles, and Belgians, Jenny Marx shopped the local markets to feed not only her family of five, but also all of the communists who passed through the Belgian capital. Only later, in the United States, would revolutionary refugees make a claim to national citizenship. For them "the loss of home and political status" did not mean, as it would for Hannah Arendt a century later, the loss of "the right to have rights," an "expulsion from humanity itself."[53]

National histories of subsequent waves of exclusion from the United States and elsewhere are well documented and recounted by historians; it is indisputable that nationalism has dominated the world stage over the last two centuries. *Asylum between Nations*, however, suggests that more than the original foundations of their border walls can be found embedded in the revolutionary era of nation building. Hamburg, Altona, the Swiss cantons, and Belgium illuminate a path less traveled. They are just a few of the seemingly hidden cosmopolitan spaces with histories waiting to be told across the globe. A humane tradition of open doors has persisted if we but know where to look for it. There are alternatives to building ever higher border walls.

Hannah Arendt sat next to me at lunch many years ago. I was just an undergraduate student at Carleton College. I had read *Eichmann in Jerusalem* the previous year and was in the midst of *The Origins of Totalitarianism*, thinking specifically about the ninth chapter, "The Decline of the Nation-State and the End of the Rights of Man." I remember the questions she asked me over lunch. I have been thinking about them ever since. Those questions launched this book. I don't remember her answers. This might be a richer book for her insights offered to a curious student.

Last year, Kwame Anthony Appiah, a philosopher raised in England and Ghana and author of *Cosmopolitanism: Ethics in a World of Strangers*, asked students in my freshman seminar questions that I doubt they will forget. We came together on Zoom in the midst of the pandemic, so there was no lunch to be shared with our visiting scholar. He engaged them in a discussion of his experiences abroad in the world. Together they pondered the question, "What do we owe a stranger?" It is fitting, then, that this book, beginning with Hannah Arendt's assertion of "the right to have rights," asks readers to consider the same question: What do we owe a stranger?

This book is dedicated to my students, who have challenged me to pose the big questions in my scholarship that we ask in our classroom.

CHAPTER ONE

Aristocratic Émigrés and Luxurious Temptations in Hamburg and Altona

Aristocrats fleeing revolutionary France in 1792 were among the first refugees to arrive in Altona and Hamburg, on either side of the Danish-German border. Some traveled with sizeable retinues of servants and boasted the means to maintain their aristocratic lifestyles for years in exile. Others, in their haste to escape the guillotine, had left their wealth behind and were reduced to foraging by dabbling in commercial ventures: a marquis as a wholesaler in soap and candles, a count as a distiller, one duke as a dance master and another as a guitar teacher. Regardless of their newly adopted daytime occupations, however, evenings in the neighboring port cities were given over to sumptuous dinners that reminded them of all they had lost.

The assault on the Bastille in July 1789, the French declaration of war against Austria in April 1792, the fall of the monarchy later that year, and the Terror of 1793–94 convinced first royalists and then moderate republicans to leave revolutionary France. Between 100,000 and 150,000 emigrants left France for the relative safety offered by England, the Netherlands, Germany, Russia, Switzerland, and the United States in what has been called the first mass migration in modern history.

At least ten thousand of these emigrants alighted in the independent Germany city-state of Hamburg and four thousand in the neighboring

Danish city of Altona.[1] In 1795, at the peak of the immigration, the wife of a Hamburg physician commented with exasperation that one of every three people she met walking between Hamburg and Altona on the high banks above the Elbe River could be overheard speaking French.[2] Seeking each other's company in the cafés and shops of their compatriots, they flaunted the latest fashions, standing apart and standing out from the merchants and artisans who populated the port cities.

Aristocrats made up less than 20 percent of the emigrants from revolutionary France, but they left behind voluminous memoirs and reams of correspondence addressed to friends scattered over Europe. Their stories of harrowing escapes from the guillotine and of struggles to regain Old Regime privileges are told and retold in histories of the French Revolution and the emigration that ensued. The colorful collection of literary émigrés in London and of counterrevolutionary troops drilling in the shadow of the massive fortress in Koblenz provide the standard pictures of eighteenth-century asylum. A resident in Koblenz complained of these émigrés: "There is no more inept creature on earth. . . . Proud and puffed up like the frog in the fable, they disdain everything that is not French and noble—like them."[3]

The entanglement of these aristocrats in the counterrevolution has made the terms "émigré" and "counterrevolution" almost synonymous. How different, at first glance, these eighteenth-century aristocrats seem from refugees in the twenty-first century. Nevertheless, they too had been forced to flee, many fearing for their lives. Not infrequently, the friends and family left behind lost theirs. Together with the approximately sixty thousand loyalists, Black and white, who left revolutionary America, and later the slave-holding refugees abandoning a turbulent Caribbean, they formed what historians characterize as a "multi-national political diaspora of refugees of revolution," inhabiting and defining "a transnational space of political exile."[4] Their politics were diverse, as wide-ranging as the places offering them asylum.

Britain served as the undisputed anchor for revolutionary emigrants. Upward of 12,500 émigrés arrived on British shores every year of the French Revolution, with a peak of 25,000 in 1795.[5] French aristocrats joined Black loyalists from America, many in correspondence with British leaders. Religious and political differences cut across the communities of refugees. Veritable Catholic corners existed among the narrow streets of Soho. The British government not only did not close its doors, at least not until the Alien Act of 1905, but it also provided limited subsistence to many of the immigrants.

Other French emigrants found closer retreats where they could more easily transport their households intact, including retinues of servants, their horses, and their wardrobes. One of these centers near at hand was Brussels, with its French-speaking cultural scene. Even as Austrian minister plenipotentiary Klemens von Metternich lavishly and openly entertained the French émigrés at his official Brussels residence, he worried that their vociferous support of counterrevolution would antagonize the French regime next door. The Austrians hoped they would not stay long.[6] As it turned out, France annexed the Belgian provinces, driving the émigrés and their entourages back onto the road in search of refuge. Rapidly changing politics scattered aristocrats across Europe. For many of these émigrés, crossing the French border was just the beginning of a sojourn that would last longer than they had expected, with many stops among different gatherings. Marginality defined their experiences as foreigners abroad in a tumultuous world.

For decades, aristocrats had moved freely around Europe; many traced their education to a grand tour. Their flight from revolutionary France, after tumbrils started rolling to the guillotine in Paris and the National Convention condemned the king to die, followed well-worn routes. Émigrés called on connections, secured over generations by intermarriage, to borrow funds and secure temporary lodging. Where they did not travel personally, their correspondence did, linking the privileged displaced across the continent.

Why choose Hamburg and Altona in particular? Hamburg and Altona offered safe alternatives to the larger refugee centers that lay farther away from home, should it be possible one day to return. The neighboring port cities were not only close by, but they had traditionally been open to outsiders. Hamburg was governed by a particularly liberal constitution. Next door, the Danish government's policy, promoted by its foreign minister and the provincial governor, was to welcome refugees without regard to their political or religious affiliations. Prosperous and cultured, the cities promised émigrés the society they had missed since leaving Paris. In addition, word on the street noted that it was possible to earn a living in these cities.

Situated near the mouth of the Elbe River, inland from the North Sea, both Hamburg, with a population approaching 120,000, and Altona, with 24,000 people, were well connected, not only with the rest of Europe, but with the world.[7] Both had reputations for tolerance, Altona even more than Hamburg. Contemporaries described the cities as bastions of freedom. One new arrival dubbed the region "this happy earth, virgin among the horrors of war."[8] The cities offered an island of peace in a turbulent world.

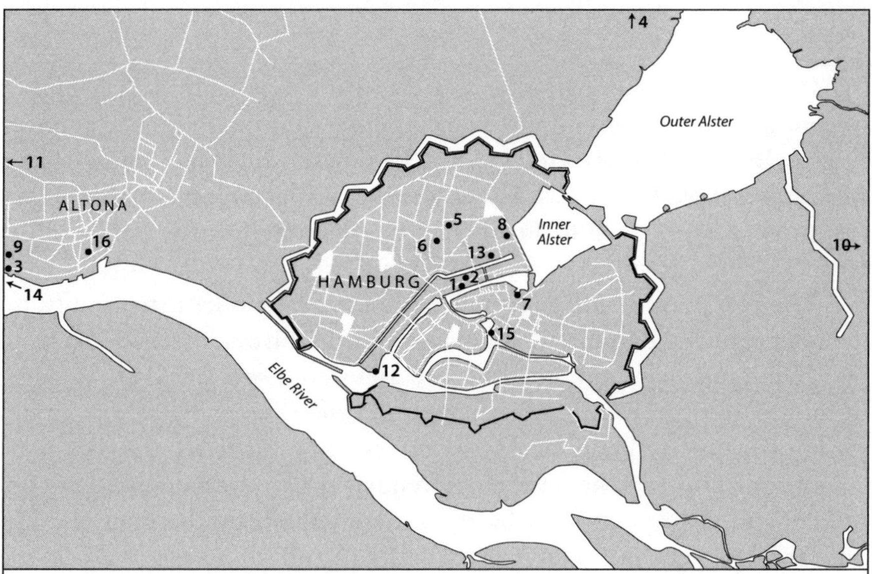

1 Georg Heinrich and Johanna Sieveking, Neuenwall 149
Winter house in town for Sievekings from 1788 to 1811 across from the Görtz palace. Their warehouse was located 7-8 houses to the northeast on the North side of the street. Note the canal at the back.

2 Georg Heinrich Sieveking's business offices. Neuenwall 158. Elise Reimarus and her foster daughter resided in the living quarters of the warehouse, 1788-1794.

3 Neumühlen (now Donner's Park)
Summer residence of the Sievekings and Poels

4 Rented garden house of Sieveking family and site of 14 July 1790 festivities, Harvestehude, 2 km north of Hamburg

5 Johann Albert Hinrich Reimarus, Fühlentwierte 122
Residence of Reimarus and his family beginning in 1783

6 Johann Georg Büsch, Fühlentwiete 94
Residence not only of Büsche, but also of Christophe Ebeling and their salon

7 Akademisches Gymnasium, school founded in 1613

8 Charlotte Sophie Bentinck, Jungfernstieg 3
Summer residence in Eimsbüttel to the north

9 Caspar Voght Estate at Klein Flottbeck
Designed as gardens and a model farm

10 Jacques Chapeaurouge, Hammerhof, house and gardens in Hamm, 5 km east of Hamburg
Known to garden lovers for the paths among English style gardens, complete with an artificial spring

11 John Parish Estate at Nienstedten
A palatial estate renowned for its lavish entertainment

12 Patriotic Society meeting room in the Baumhaus or toll station. Built in 1662, it featured commanding views of the Harbor and the Elbe.The Patriotic Society met here, beginning in 1765.

13 Harmonie, Grosse Bleichen 19
Meeting rooms for club

14 Rainville's Garden, Ottensee (currently Rainvilleterrasse 4), 250 meters downstream from the Altona Balcony

15 Rathaus, seat of the City Council and Senate (Rat/Senat)

16 Grund 98, Rathhausmarkt, Pflock's Lodging house where Madame de Genlis resided in 1794.
It is in Altona across from what is now the Rathaus.

Hamburg 1791. Map drawn by Bill Nelson, based on Friedrich August Von Lawrence and T. A. Pingeling. Grundriss Der Kayserl. Freien Reichs Und Handels Stadt Hamburg Nebst Dem Auf Königl.: Danischen Gebiet Daran Liegenden Altona Einen Hochpreislichen Senat. Harvard Map Collection Digital Maps, Imaging the Urban Environment.

Hamburg's traditional status as a Hanseatic diplomatic seat facilitated its commercial relations. Ministers came and went from Prussia, Hannover, France, England, Russia, Holland, and Denmark while Spain and Portugal were represented by consuls. Altona was the second largest city in bilingual Denmark; Copenhagen had two chancelleries, one Danish and the other German, and was linked by a common king with Norway.

The two ports assiduously maintained their diplomatic neutrality, remaining connected to foreign ministers but aloof from international troubles. Diplomatically nimble, the cities adjusted more quickly to changes in international political fortunes than did their larger neighbors entangled in alliances and burdened with armies deployed across the continent. "Cosmopolitan" was the term most frequently used by contemporary observers and visitors to describe the refuge chosen by the émigrés. The outward-looking vantage points of Hamburg and Altona evolved with the expansion of world trade anchored in the two ports. This municipal cosmopolitanism had a somewhat different meaning than it did for arriving aristocrats, though it also implied being at home in the world.

One of the earliest of the traveling aristocrats to alight in the neighboring port cities, Countess Charlotte Sophie Bentinck, a friend of Voltaire and Frederick the Great, arrived in Hamburg in 1767, seeking refuge from her complicated familial relations. She personified aristocratic cosmopolitanism; she was not tethered to any one place. She had been married to a Dutch nobleman at seventeen; the father of her two illegitimate sons was the husband of her cousin. Separated from her husband, she emigrated first to Copenhagen, then to Leipzig, Berlin, Vienna, and finally Hamburg. She confided in her granddaughter, "You know that your old grandmother is a German and an aristocrat from the crown of my head to the soles of my feet."[9] In correspondence with monarchs throughout Europe, Countess Bentinck avowed that she was especially loyal to "the noble House of Austria," but as a good cosmopolitan, she was at home in her travels and among worldly companions who had also settled in Hamburg.[10]

These two definitions of cosmopolitanism, embodied by the well-traveled émigrés and the free-trading entrepreneurial neutrality, were not readily compatible. That was a problem in Hamburg and Altona. Merchants governed the port cities, neither of which had a noticeable native aristocracy. Consequently, very few of the émigrés settled permanently. They viewed exile as transitory and expected to wait out the end of the revolution that had driven them into exile. For all of the aristocrats, as for the priests, bishops, and cardinals who were part of the mix, exile was a period to be endured between a traumatic past and a promising future.

The exiles' request for asylum in Hamburg and Altona was in strict keeping with Immanuel Kant's maxims of universal hospitality. In *Perpetual Peace*, Kant asserted the "right of a stranger not to be treated as an enemy when he arrives in the land of another." All refugees "by virtue of their shared humanity" deserve asylum, defined as "a temporary sojourn, a right to associate," Kant argued in terms that the United Nations would later adopt.[11] In contrast to their larger and more xenophobic neighbors in the midst of revolutions, the lawmakers and citizens of Altona and Hamburg recognized their responsibility to extend hospitality to foreigners arriving on their doorstep. The rest of the world would come around to that recognition only after World War II.

Hamburg and Altona: "A Hospitable Plot of Ground under a Foreign Sky"

Émigrés inundated Hamburg and Altona by the thousands in the 1790s.[12] They included Countess Adélaïde Flahaut, who had traveled to Hamburg with future king of France Louis Philippe; was being courted by wealthy Portuguese Baron de Souza; and feared the arrival of her former lover, former French foreign minister Charles Maurice de Talleyrand. Talleyrand arrived in Hamburg a few months later, returning from a voyage to the United States, but he sought the company of Stéphanie Félicité de Genlis instead. She was busy entertaining her former ward, Pamela, the new bride of Irish lord Edward Fitzgerald. It was rumored that Irish revolutionaries had the run of the house. Theirs were entangled lives.

Travelers complained that the roads of northern Europe were clogged with carriages and people fleeing on foot ahead of French armies spreading revolution. "Some [of the refugees] crossed the border to Maastricht, others to the Hague, Germany, England, Italy, the United States," one observer remembered. "Everyone was fleeing further from their patrie, in the middle of winter, without money or exile, under the fire of cannon and flames."[13] They often came to Hamburg and Altona by way of the Belgian provinces or the Netherlands or made stops along the German border at Koblenz or Worms, clustering in transit around figures such as the Comte d'Artois and the Prince de Condé. Their stories of flight were quite terrifying, probably becoming more so with each retelling.

The Marquis de Lally-Tollendal recounted how they had all traversed "barbarous regions in search of a hospitable plot of ground under a foreign sky."[14] Renowned royalists allegedly crossed the French border disguised as peasants, hid out in forests, and were assisted by sympathetic families who smuggled them across other borders disguised as market women.[15] Once they arrived in the port cities on the Elbe, after weeks of impassable roads necessitating carriage repairs and stays in loathsome inns with scanty provisions, they sought out aid from those already established in Hamburg and Altona. Some continued to testify to unrelenting hunger. "Suicides were common this winter," Madame de Neuilly commented after the frigid weather of 1794–95.[16] Although they carried more possessions and provisions than contemporary migrants, their plight was perilous.

In the spring of 1795, en route to Hamburg and Altona from the Swiss cantons, Louis Philippe and Madame de Flahaut solicited funds from Gouverneur Morris, the former American consul in France, now in residence in Hamburg, for a proposed passage to America. Having started out in Britain, Madame de Flahaut had been on the road, traveling incognito, for months. Morris, who had been romantically involved with her in prerevolutionary Paris, found the pair apartments under the name of Mr. Muller. Eventually, Madame de Flahaut moved out of what she disparaged as a pitiable auberge in the center of Altona to better lodgings in Hamburg.[17] The fall of the former salonnière and the duke had been precipitous into a world they barely recognized. In Hamburg, though, they worried that one of the many émigrés strolling the streets would recognize the duke and expose him as an enemy of the revolution. Never, they moaned in a plea to their benefactor for additional funds, were prisoners in a dungeon treated worse. Other refugees might disagree.

Madame de Flahaut took up the fabrication of elegant hats, but she also wrote novels and contributed articles to the counterrevolutionary newspaper *Le Spectateur du Nord* (Northern Spectator). In her widely read novels, Flahaut described the humiliations suffered by exiles and the pity that awaited them abroad. In one of the most well-known, *Eugénie et Mathilde*, Eugénie is forced to leave the convent and to live by her embroidery. Nevertheless, she recoils from negotiating prices and is overcome when she presents her first earnings to her father. Commerce did not come easily to countesses and princesses accustomed to their generous inheritances and patrons.

Morris, known for his generous purse, had himself taken leave of France under a cloud when the French revolutionaries convinced President Washington to recall his diplomatic envoy. Morris had too often voiced his hostility to the revolution and seemed to feel more at ease in the company of aristocrats, especially women, than of revolutionaries. After the revolutionary French Committee of Public Safety detained Morris for questioning, the American diplomat left for Switzerland. From there, he was quite content to wander aimlessly through Europe, not eager to return either to France or to America.

The forty-four-year-old author of some of the more memorable phrases in the American Constitution, including "we the people," Morris traveled with a large carriage and driver, a baggage wagon, a valet, and postillions, concealing what he declared to be a significant fortune in his trunk.[18] Without set plans, he reveled in his nomadic life. Expenses posed no problem for this wealthy American abroad. En route, he advised George Washington; dabbled in bonds, shipping, and real estate; and visited now scattered Parisian acquaintances, including the former minister of French finance, Jacques Necker, and his daughter, Germaine de Staël. Morris found the gathering of French émigrés in Lausanne, and Madame de Staël herself, boring, confiding that he would rather have his pillow for company. He ended up in Hamburg.

Accustomed to court manners, aristocratic émigrés were particularly ill prepared for life in the port cities. They did not fit in. A prime example is Madame de Genlis. A former governess to the French royal household and royal favorite, she fled France just after the king was stopped at the border trying to flee France himself. Madame de Genlis adopted the pseudonym and persona of Miss Clarke, an Irish woman educated in France waiting to return to her own country. She lived in a modest lodging house in Altona, where she had to adjust to the shared meals of a pension. The other residents, she lamented, were the last people on earth she would have chosen as dining companions.[19] Incognito, she felt marginalized. She complained that she was forced to listen to their political gossip, including the rumor that Madame de Genlis had taken up residence in the neighborhood with the disgraced French military hero General Dumouriez. She also watched English theater troupes putting on translations of her plays, biting her tongue rather than revealing her identity. Finally, after nine months, when her landlady, known for her revolutionary sympathies, tried to fix her up with a local baker, an indignant Madame de Genlis revealed her identity and promptly moved to a country house outside of Hamburg with General de Vailence. She had just sold a novel, so she could afford to pay half of the rent.

Fortunately, there was sufficient wealth in the cities to support the luxury trades plied by the aristocrats who needed to earn a living. New French shops sprung up, most specializing in gourmet delicacies and fine

Stéphanie Félicité Ducrest, Marquise de Sillery, ci-devant Comtesse de Genlis. Collection générale alphabétique des portraits français et étrangers. Courtesy of Bibliothèque Nationale de France.

fashions. Some aristocrats painted portraits, and others gave piano lessons or opened schools. The Comte de Neuilly recounts that the Chevalier de Montmorency opened a patisserie; Mssrs. de Langeac and de Saint-Hilaire established themselves as interior decorators; Madame de Biencourt assisted a tobacco merchant; the Count de Gimel was employed as a distiller;

M. du Vivier took up commerce as a music merchant and M. de Laenière as a *maître d'armes*. Meanwhile, the Countess de Neuilly kept a store stocked with frivolities and her daughter made embroidered works, while the Marquise de Romance together with the Countess d'Asfeld opened a wine shop and delicatessen. One young émigré even played the role of a learned bear for the new Altona theater. For the sake of their honor, some hid their identities behind pseudonyms, adding to their disorientation.

By 1798, it was said that everything sought in Paris could be found in Hamburg, if only on a smaller scale. Three French nobles bought a country house together and opened a café-restaurant. The personal adjunct to General Dumouriez, César Claude Lubin Rainville, who arrived in Altona in 1794, married another refugee and opened several hotels and restaurants. "Rainville's Garten" in Ottensen, with its two levels of terrace overlooking the Elbe, ornamental gardens, music, fireworks, and what was billed as the very finest French cuisine, attracted Sunday strollers. The preponderance of émigrés gathered with Hamburgers drew the attention of anxious authorities. What were they up to?

In the center of Hamburg, M. de Quatrebarbe founded the Alster Pavilion, an elegant café serving refreshments and ice cream on the Jungfernstieg, a wide, shaded avenue along the inner Alster. Aristocrats parading along the Jungfernstieg attracted attention from the local residents, lending an outsized presence to the French émigrés, who openly displayed their penchant for luxuries. Down the street, the Marquis de Chastenet opened a café in a self-styled Chinese temple. A former French council in Tunis and envoy to Geneva opened a bookstore. Theirs are familiar stories. So too are the apocryphal tales of the bishop working as a tanner, priests become barbers, and a marquis laboring as a cobbler. They did not garner much pity among the local residents, even if they felt estranged from their former lives.

"I've acted as a merchant all day long, now I'm going to be a lady for a while," the Countess de Neuilly told her children.[20] During the day, the Princess de Vaudémont sold books, but in the evening, she gathered the nobility of France around her in Altona. There was no shortage of possibilities for recreating the Old Regime, with its elegant dinners and mistresses, although it was done without whalebone dresses or towering hairdos. The "Emigrantenball" was a particular highlight, drawing the elite to the Hôtel Delvaux. The pursuit of pleasure continued during the winter, described by one visitor witness to Carnival as "the great pleasure hunt."[21]

Doors were also opened to soirees hosted by the minister of Denmark, the Count Schulenburg, the minister of Russia, the Count Mouraviev, and Mr. Raser, the minister of England, as well as a former favorite of Catherine II and a rich Dutchman. Diplomats, especially those dispatched by the imperial courts of central Europe had never mixed easily with the "rich and well-educated négociants," a leading merchant noted.[22] But neither the émigrés nor the diplomats could rely on established nobles in either Hamburg or Altona. The republican atmosphere there was set by the governing merchants. The outsiders, nevertheless, had no trouble creating their own world of salons, suppers, and comedy.

Countess Bentinck routinely entertained newcomers as well as old friends in her salon on the Jungfernstieg, described as "the great house of Western Europe," beginning at six in the evening. She worried, nevertheless, about the inadequacy of her hospitality when faced with a visit from Prince Henry of Prussia, the uncle of the Prussian monarch.[23] Receiving the French royal family, Countess Bentinck caught a glimpse of the former life she longed to rediscover. "They entered the room, not as exiles, not as despised fugitives, but with all the pomp of a ruling Court, in a grand cortege, preceded by an army of retainers and a troop of high military dignitaries, adjutants, and officers of the Guard," she noted. Other guests included aristocrats, resident and passing diplomats, and a few well-connected merchants and well-traveled scholars. It was reported that champagne flowed and conversations were learned, venturing into archaeology and philosophy. Cards were also played and a supper served at nine. Otherwise, she commented, "One eats, one dances, one kills the time!"[24] Their suffering was relative.

Merchants and Aristocrats: "Economic Interest Decides Everything"

A few of the merchants who presided over the governments of Hamburg and Altona welcomed émigrés into their homes, sometimes even staging elegant balls and sumptuous dinners. For example, Madame de Chapeaurouge, the wife of a merchant who had himself immigrated from Geneva a decade earlier, served a dinner that showcased pheasants from Bohemia, huge fish speared through the ice of the Elbe, and champagne. It was evidence one émigré noted, not only of good taste, but of their comestible relations with all of Europe.[25] "The nobles and merchants give each other parties," an English visitor observed in 1786, concluding, "In these two society classes there is a cheerful attitude and sincerity everywhere."[26] Such intermingling was more the exception than the rule when the aristocrats threatened to overwhelm their welcome after 1792.

Constitutional monarchists, who made up much of the second wave of aristocrats, enjoyed more invitations. Their politics were more congenial to the wholesale merchants like Georg Heinrich Sieveking and his wife Johanna, the daughter of Johann Albert Heinrich Reimarus, a well-known physician and scholar. The Sievekings entertained as many as eighty guests at their magnificent house at Neumühlen, along the banks of the Elbe, every Sunday afternoon. There, foreigners, including French émigrés, mixed with leaders of the Hamburg Senate, prosperous merchants, and scientists. An Englishman in his journal described the gatherings as a "clearing house for intelligence."[27] Poets and philosophers held forth, as did family members.

Sieveking's business partner, Caspar Voght, a close friend of Madame de Staël's, also received guests at his architecturally renowned house in Flotbek. The son of a senator and leading merchant, Voght was at ease in noble circles in Hamburg and throughout Europe. Through his father's diplomatic connections, on his grand tour in 1775, Caspar Voght had dined with foreign ministers at Versailles, been presented to the royal family in Spain, and listened to music in the smaller Italian courts. When he returned to Hamburg, he found not only Countess Bentinck's door open to him, but also the doors of the diplomatic circle of the nobility resident in Hamburg.

Gouverneur Morris acted occasionally as a go-between, visiting both aristocrats, whose lifestyle he had adopted, and merchants and lawyers. One particular favorite was the successful entrepreneurial British merchant John Parish, who invited Morris and others who had fallen out with the Jacobins or were just seeking their fortunes in Hamburg to frequent gatherings on Sundays at his country house. Other evenings, Morris often dined with one person and then spent the evening with another. He probably should have stayed home with a cold one evening, he wrote in his memoirs, but went out as was his custom after a day's correspondence. "I am better Company than I suspected," he mused. "Sitting up so late, however, is not useful and Supping must be pernicious but what can one do? It is impossible to change the Customs of a Country and absurd to attempt it. One must therefore comply and submit and suffer."[28] He dined frequently with Countess Bentinck, both at large functions and in intimate company, the two displaced persons consoling each other on the latest political news. In February 1795, he moved to Altona to better entertain. In June 1796, he was again looking for lodging, complaining of the expensive rates charged by inns given the influx of visitors.

Different sectors crossed paths in public spaces throughout the two cities. Merchants and diplomats met when the venerable Hamburg Exchange, founded in 1558, closed and trading stopped midday for two hours. They shared news and small talk. There were more than twenty coffee houses, and in the evenings, they featured conversation, billiards, and cards. Although the local merchants and visiting aristocrats made strange political bedfellows, as would the progressive local lawyers and visiting German communists half a century later in Brussels, in each case, theirs was an alchemy that sometimes worked.

A testament to their integration were the not infrequent intermarriages among social circles, sometimes with political ramifications. Henriette, the niece of Madame de Genlis, married a wealthy Hamburg banker, with the wedding celebrated in both the Protestant and Catholic churches. The revolutionary Irishman, Lord Fitzgerald, was one of the witnesses. He then traveled on to Basel to secure arms for the United Irishmen and to meet French diplomats and the general who would lead the next French expedition to spark revolution in Ireland. On the trip back to Hamburg, Fitzgerald discussed his secret journey with a fellow traveler who turned out to be a former mistress of William Pitt. She promptly passed Fitzgerald's information along, leading to the uncovering of the plot and the discovery of a cache of arms in Hamburg. Henriette, meanwhile, immersed herself in Hamburg society, entertaining from her new house on the Speersort. Pamela, Fitzgerald's wife and Madame de Genlis's daughter, gave birth shortly after her arrival in the city, before joining Henriette in Hamburg society.

Morris helped the American sons of the French aristocrat-turned-American-farmer St. John de Crèvecoeur, the author of *Letters from an American Farmer*, flee revolutionary France, where they had been educated after being raised in New York. One of the sons, Ally, ended up in Altona. However, Morris could not help Crèvecoeur himself because Crèvecoeur was a French citizen. So Crèvecoeur, who had profited from his account of a homespun idyll among the farmers of upstate New York, made his way to Altona alone in early 1795, staying for a year, during which he complained in letters to friends about boredom and the meager hospitality of the merchants.

Crèvecoeur's stay was typical of that of the émigrés in that he laid down shallow roots and stayed but a short time. In the words of Immanuel Kant, who made the time-honored case for asylum as the right of universal hospitality, Crèvecoeur visited, rather than staked claims to citizenship. Few of the aristocratic refugees remained in Altona or Hamburg for more than a couple of years. Some were literally passing through, as did Madame Lafayette, among others. The English author Mary Wollstonecraft, who stayed for just a few months and was a dining companion of Crèvecoeur's, was stunned to hear that Adrienne Lafayette "lived in a lodging up two pair of stairs, without a servant, her two daughters cheerfully assisting."[29] The Marquis de Lafayette's wife was quickly helped on her way by John Parish, then serving as American consul in Hamburg. Parish gave her funds and traveling papers in the name of a Mrs. Motier of Hartford, Connecticut, so that she could go to Vienna to free her husband.

Merchants and aristocrats alike rallied to help free Lafayette, taken prisoner by the Austrians after his defection from the French army. They included Johann Wilhelm von Archenholz, the Hamburg editor of *Minerva,* who smuggled information to Lafayette and then passed along information from him to allies in London. Even the English consul stationed in Hamburg, William Hanbury, whose wife was a close friend of Johanna Sieveking, got involved in the effort to win Lafayette's release. The assistance fanned out by correspondence through trade, banking, and diplomatic connections across Europe and the Atlantic.[30]

Freed from his Austrian prison in 1797, Lafayette found refuge in Danish Holstein, to the north of Altona. Lafayette called it "the most tranquil place in Europe," removed from powerful rulers and their armies and surrounded as it was by sympathetic aristocrats and proponents of liberty.[31] Morris and Parish both worried about Lafayette's lavish expenses, incurred while traveling, and wondered if he would keep his promise to remain aloof from French politics. Dinner conversations at Lafayette's wife's aunt's estate at Wittmold, where he was surrounded by his family and former aides de camp, of course dipped frequently into politics, dwelling especially on the past mistakes of various leaders. Morris, among others, traveled to visit him there, trying to convince the former war hero to emigrate to America.

Instead, Lafayette seemed content to pass his time working on a model farm, tending the merino sheep and gardening. For the time being, at least, at his spacious house on a peninsula jutting out into Small Plön Lake, without substantial funds himself, he was able to depend on loans and gifts from John Parish, as well as from Americans scattered throughout Europe. He counted on good relations with the Hamburg circles that had worked together to spring him from prison. Lafayette continued to correspond with George Washington and Alexander Hamilton in America, with Talleyrand, and with the leading British Whigs, including Charles James Fox. With all of the comings and goings, Hamburg and Altona functioned as vibrant centers of communications.

Although he was living in what others around him considered relative comfort, Lafayette's financial and political situation was nevertheless dependent on others. The French government had seized his property when it declared him an émigré and counterrevolutionary. Lafayette, like the other émigrés, was all too aware that many of his friends had perished and that others still in France lived under constant threat. Even in his tolerant, tranquil asylum, he was heckled from time to time by hostile local residents. When his wife and daughters were able to return to France, he had to remain behind and complained of his "insupportable estrangement."[32]

Lafayette had limited options for other places to reside. He was effectively caught by the changing politics on both sides of the Atlantic. His participation in the American Revolution meant that he was less than welcome in England; French officials did not want him to return and requested that he prolong his exile; and the passage of the Alien Enemies Act in America rendered a transatlantic crossing potentially politically dangerous. Lafayette lamented in a letter to a friend, "The monarchical governments detest me, as you well know, and all the Republican governments of Europe are provisionally submissive to a single government [France's] that is not in a hurry to see me again."[33] He was fortunate to have found a small space willing to offer him asylum. In this era of emerging nationalism and tightening borders, it is all too easy for historians to overlook the open possibilities of these smaller spaces.

Eventually, the long-serving French foreign minister, Charles Talleyrand, and the Batavian minister resident in Hamburg secured Lafayette a passport to travel incognito to the Netherlands, then into the Batavian Republic. He crossed the border through British Hanoverian territory under the name of "Mottier." There he would stay, in the small town of Vianen, south of Utrecht, and close enough to France to return to his native land at the first sign that it was safe to do so.

"So Inundated . . . One Can Hardly Turn Round": Short Stays and Long-Lasting Luxury

If the exiles lodging in Hamburg, London, and Geneva assumed they would move on before the end of the revolutionary decade, established citizens feared the aristocrats' assumptions of privilege and love of luxury would linger long after they had departed, corrupting the solid, respectable citizenry. By the winter of 1794–95, even the more established émigrés were complaining that they felt completely overwhelmed, "so inundated were they with French emigrants, Brabançois, Dutch, and [emigrants] from the borders of the Rhine, that one can hardly turn round."[34] The displaced aristocrats came in such numbers to her dinners expecting to be well fed, Countess Bentinck complained, that they might as well all starve together.

Apparently, the political dissension had also grown tiresome, even among émigrés. A third wave of refugees, chased out of the Netherlands by advancing French troops, was out of step with the previous two. At stake in their discussions were questions of life and death that had raged in revolutionary France over the last decade. By the summer of 1795, the politics of the refugees covered the spectrum from liberal monarchists to die-hard royalists. These royalists were not eager to entertain moderates who sympathized with the French republic. Worse yet, the new Swedish minister was said to harbor democratic sympathies. Madame de Flahaut informed Gouverneur Morris that she was aching to find "a little retreat, quite secluded" where she could be "retired, the more incognito."[35] Another countess complained about having to tolerate "raging democrats" just because they were wealthy merchants, and money in Altona and Hamburg permitted everything.[36]

The Sievekings were known throughout Europe for their July 1790 celebration toasting the French Revolution, complete with poetry and fireworks in the garden of their home in Harvestehude, along the Alster, just north of Hamburg. They invited a few aristocrats. Countess Bentinck subsequently made sure on 14 July to invite "gallant knights" to preoccupy her while "the Jacobins" celebrated in other parts of the city.[37] The countess, who had closely followed news of the French Revolution, bemoaned the "idolatry of liberty" and "insane Equality," which she feared had come to prevail everywhere but in Germany.[38] She was troubled about the fate of friends and acquaintances, especially as retold in letters and visits. Their accustomed world was ending. Reading the newspapers just presented more stories of violence and torrents of blood, she complained.[39]

Much of the press read by the émigrés came from counterrevolutionary newspapers, including *Le Spectateur du Nord*, which was read throughout Europe. Letters claiming to be from Paris appearing in the paper heralded a future that would bring an end to revolution and reintroduce morals, good faith, and humanity.[40] The newspaper also published letters addressed specifically to French expatriates. The newspaper celebrated the virtues of émigré families as it reported on wars and treaty negotiations, and it featured commentary on the ramifications of neutrality as practiced by the Danish ports and Hamburg.

Antoine Rivarol, the editor of *Le Spectateur*, enlivened the social scene with his cynical journalism. Rivarol was not enamored of Madame de Genlis, whom he dismissed as a Jacobin, reporting on her residence with General Dumouriez, her visit to the theater disguised as a jockey, and her presence in a Protestant church. He condemned her as an "instigator and apologist of crimes and corrupter of her children."[41] His sarcasm was so scathing that other émigrés hesitated to be seen entering or leaving the salon of Madame de Genlis. Rivarol was drawn, however, to Madame de Flahaut, who, he wrote, "made velvet paws with her eyes."[42] He appreciated Hamburg in general because it had taken in so many émigrés; for him it was indeed "the consoler of the afflicted and the refuge of the sinners."[43] The independent German city-state was generous in its hospitality, no matter the political persuasion of the arrivals.

The merchants, though, grew weary of the dukes and countesses, whose politics and values were so different from their own. The "follies of fashions" especially prompted discussions among citizens in the ports.[44] For decades, moral weeklies such as *Der Patriot* (The Patriot) had warned burghers against the pretensions of a court culture. They branded aristocrats as immoral social climbers awash in conspicuous consumption. Even if there was social mobility in the ports, with newcomers moving up relatively quickly, they did not seek ennoblement. They remained merchants, grounded in hard work, with its economic opportunities. Nobles were barred from owning property in Hamburg and so could not become citizens. The merchants' values of frugality, reason, and honesty contrasted sharply in the 1790s with the luxurious lasciviousness of the aristocracy.

Hamburgers cherished their reputation as "sober, temperate, and level-headed northerners." Without a local aristocracy, the blame for the introduction of luxury in Hamburg and Altona naturally fell on the foreigners. Friedrich Johann Lorenz Meyer, cathedral canon in Hamburg, complained about the "fashionable hair artists in their cabriolets, the bacchanal feasts and banquets in each city and town." He noted the obvious French influences: "the vulgar pomp of slovenly maids; the fragrances from the perfume shops, the garlic from restaurant kitchens," asking, "Is not all that and more 'Parisian Civilization!' "[45] Would the émigrés' penchant for privileges corrupt the legendary civic spirit of Hamburg and Altona?

Countess Bentinck blamed the bad reputation of aristocrats among the merchants on a few badly behaved Frenchmen who repeatedly alarmed the stodgier citizens of the ports. French exiles reportedly left any place they rented in shambles, so wild and ostentatious were their lives. The problem was the Hamburgers' imitation of the foreigners, the growing "prejudice for things foreign."[46] Rather than joining the conversations of reading circles, it was said, merchants could be found promenading with the aristocrats along the Jungfernstieg or playing cards. No longer did learned people discuss world affairs, but instead they prattled away at lavish banquets.

Even for the tolerant cities whose cosmopolitanism was firmly rooted in a tradition of welcoming all who came to their shores, the aristocrats had strained their welcome. The influx of aristocrats had dramatically increased rents and food prices and lowered wages. Over the longer term, rather than adapting to the republican virtues of the commercial centers, these "spoiled nobles, fanatic immoral priests, and swindling gamblers" were attempting a "physical-moral transformation" of the cities, threatening to destroy "civic virtue" in their wake.[47] The Hamburg Senate responded with regulations limiting the freedom of the émigrés and requiring them to register with local authorities.

The discontent was mutual. Foreigners were welcomed, émigrés noted, as long as their name was connected to a large trading house, "thanks to this rampant inbreeding of money, which comprises the family of Europe's capitalists and bankers."[48] Aristocrats complained about the undue influence of money in Hamburg and Altona. They commented with disapproval that women, even the mistresses of grand houses, seemed at home with accounting ledgers. "Today everything is permitted to people with money and impudence," one aristocrat alleged.[49] They were not used to the inversion of power relations, with merchants determining their fate. Countess Bentinck remarked in a letter, "Since it is a trading city, economic interest decides everything."[50] In the ports at the end of the 1790s, the émigrés were definitely the interlopers.

However, identities and politics had shifted on both sides of the social divide over the decade, in part as a result of the limited mingling between aristocrats and merchants. The aristocrats dabbled in commerce; the merchants conversed in their salons. Even Madame de Genlis cast herself in exile as a completely different character from the former governess to the children of the royal court. She claimed that she now had come alive as an author. Still, she longed someday to return to France. She had heard through friends that under the Directory the life of the salons had resumed.

The march of revolutionary armies into the Belgian provinces and the Netherlands dashed those hopes and for some, the assumptions that they would soon be able to return home.

Countess Bentinck mused: "I do not know which nation to place first and by which to get myself adopted, finding neither character nor virtue anywhere."[51] A German married to a Dutchman, she had lived all over, having befriended Frederick the Great in Prussia and Empress Maria Theresa in Vienna, but she complained, in this era of revolution, that she felt at home nowhere.

These émigrés had not been involved in the sensational plots of the counterrevolution, of which myths have been made. Most of them had left by 1800, trickling back to France in small groups when it seemed safe. "In effect, what is emigration," one marquis asked. "It means leaving your country to go settle in another; but is it emigration to make a temporary voyage seeking shelter from the danger that threatens?"[52] They saw their stay as temporary, identifying as travelers rather than residents. "It's now the fashion to return, just as it used to be to leave. There are now only Hamburgers in Hamburg. The French society is reduced to nothing," Madame de Neuilly observed with disappointment at the turn of the century.[53] Had they really left the port cities unchanged? Was their influence that ephemeral? The next immigrants to come through the gates of the two cities would find out. Decidedly less flamboyant, they adapted upon arrival.

CHAPTER TWO

"A Temple Always Open to Peace"

Poets and Ports

WHEREVER FREE TRADE FLOWED, as in Hamburg and Altona, true liberty flourished, Johanna Sieveking told a friend in July 1794 to introduce the newcomer to the city of open borders that was her home.[1] Merchants from far and near docked in these ports up river from the mouth of the Elbe on the North Sea. Many middle-class immigrants settled in; there were profits to be made here.

Hannchen, as Johanna Sieveking's family knew her, contributed to that cosmopolitan hospitality. Together with her husband and their friends the Poels, she welcomed as many as eighty guests for dinner every Sunday. The guests found a place at makeshift tables spread throughout the salons and drawing rooms of the summer house the Sievekings and Poels shared on the banks of the Elbe River. Visitors remembered a cacophony of foreign tongues mixing together as the party broke into conversation after dining, with newspapers read aloud and card games and chess played in adjoining rooms. At the end of the evening, a few guests would stake out a spot to sleep while others took care to depart before the Hamburg city gates closed for the night. Otherwise, there were no borders limiting access to the city. The gates opened every morning as shipping resumed up and down the Elbe.

Ferdinand Beneke, a young lawyer from nearby Bremen, was excited to sail into the teeming harbor in February 1796. Echoing the Sievekings' and Poels' guests, Beneke remarked on all of the different languages calling to him as he sprang from his ship "onto land—republican soil!" Soon a regular himself at the gatherings hosted by Hannchen, in contrast to the émigrés, Beneke came to identify "this little cosmopolitan place" as his "fatherland."[2] He felt more at home than he had inland in Prussia, where he had just completed an apprenticeship. Beneke assimilated readily, like other lawyers, scholars, and merchants, many with their families. Unlike the aristocrats, many of these newcomers expected to prosper and to stay. In contrast to the émigrés, and to most modern refugees, they could return home, although their livelihoods would have been imperiled by the ongoing wars.

Only a newcomer like Beneke would have been surprised that wherever one looked, "one found the most heterogeneous things inconspicuously placed next to one another."[3] For longtime residents like the Sievekings, the conglomeration of differences introduced by such a mix of peoples had become commonplace. The bookstores were stocked with books in English and French as well as German, and the abundant coffeehouses subscribed to Dutch, French, and English, as well as German, newspapers.

Burghers resident in the two cities frequented the coffee houses and bookstores but rarely joined in the salons hosted by French émigrés and their diplomatic friends. Christine Reimarus, whose half-sister Johanna Sieveking hosted Sunday dinners, wrote a friend in Lübeck describing a rare evening spent at a ball given by Countess Bentinck. She was relieved at 10:30 to have an excuse to leave the "noblesse" behind. She returned to the more familiar company of fellow burghers, whom she described as the democrats of the third estate, to celebrate Georg Heinrich Sieveking's birthday.[4] The two worlds did not mix easily, making it easier for burghers to integrate into the port cities and more difficult for the aristocrats, especially those clinging to their memories of the Old Regime, to assimilate.

Unlike the aristocrats, most of the middle-class immigrants seeking economic opportunities and tolerance of their politics and religion assimilated into the port cities so fluidly that they escaped notice not only by contemporaries, but also by historians of revolutionary emigration. Perhaps that is why no one at the time complained publicly about the arrival of lawyers like Beneke or merchants from across the Atlantic world. Residents had come to view middle-class refugees from landlocked entrepots and neighboring states at war as just more of the "heterogeneous things." They not only fit in, but they also contributed to the prosperity of the cities. Without the discord that earns a place in history books, social change passes unnoticed by contemporaries and by historians because it is so readily absorbed into the passage of daily life.

The merchants, philosophers, artisans, and writers arriving in 1794 and 1795 must have found the French aristocrats who had come a year or two earlier with their counterrevolutionary convictions strange bedfellows in the inns and lodging houses they often shared in what sociologists describe as a "zone of contact."[5] The diversity of the foreigners who sailed up the Elbe into the two harbors or traveled on foot or by carriage overland through the German territories or the Netherlands contributed to the cosmopolitanism of the two centers of trade and diplomacy.

Strolling from the city hall in the center of Hamburg to the harbor just a few kilometers upstream from Altona, Beneke "delighted in the tumult of water, the arriving and departing vessels, the seeming confusion of the immense rigging."[6] The diplomatic neutrality and open economy of the ports attracted shipping firms from across Europe and beyond. At a time when war had laid waste to vast swathes of Europe, the two cities continued to trade and flourished.

Altona and Hamburg functioned as hubs for river, land, and oceanic trade. Only London and Amsterdam had more active ports at the end of the eighteenth century.[7] Their location made them an ideal entrepôt for transferring and shipping sugar, textiles, coffee, grains, wine, wood, iron, and tobacco to and from West European ports, the Americas, the Mediterranean, the West Indies, and northern Europe. Altona, with its textile mills and sugar refineries, had the advantage of proximity to the sea, but Hamburg's low-lying grounds, crisscrossed by canals facilitating transit to warehouses, gave it an edge in shipping grains and exchanging Silesian textiles for colonial coffee and sugar, as well as wines from France. The ties to the slave trade were well worn but not widely discussed.

Hamburg's shipping grew erratically during this volatile period. Shipping between France and Hamburg had slumped during the financial crisis of 1769 but then increased steadily over the decade leading up to the French Revolution from 1780 to 1790, before it fell off again. It reached another high point in 1795, followed by a precipitous decline. These were not times for the faint of heart, especially with the additional question of how to collect funds in France at the end of a completed transaction. At the same time, by way of contrast, shipping from France to Lübeck, a neighboring but less important Hanseatic harbor, continued without substantial variation at a much lower rate throughout the period.

A view of the Elbe River taken from Altona and looking toward Hamburg. "Prospect der Elbe gegen Altona zu Hamburg," Georg Balthasar, 1770, SHMH-Altonaer Museum, AB02692. Courtesy of Altonaer Museum.

Hamburg and Altona had traditionally been oriented toward commercial relations with England, but as soon as the American Revolution broke out, Hamburg merchants began sending out feelers for trade with merchants throughout the colonies. Surreptitiously, a number of Hamburg firms opened trading relations with Americans in anticipation of their independence. In 1782, the size of the fleet docked in Altona doubled, from 81 to 165 ships, thanks to trans-Atlantic shipping. Commercial freedom and diplomatic neutrality went hand in hand; both encouraged peace on a war-torn continent, or so the citizens of the two cities claimed.

In 1789, 247 ships arrived in Hamburg; 101 of them came from Bordeaux.[8] Things got more complicated in the 1790s, when the French revolutionary regime declared war on most of Hamburg's and Altona's shipping partners. In 1794, French revolutionary troops occupied Amsterdam, a traditional center of commerce and finance, closing off access to its ports. Hamburg's and Altona's merchants and bankers picked up contracts dropped by others. By 1795, Altona's fleet outnumbered that of Hamburg, with 283 ships to Hamburg's 193. In 1797, Altona was home to 423 ships, many of them owned by immigrants.[9]

The neighboring port cities were accessible not only to goods at the end of the eighteenth century, but also to thousands of refugees from the wars and revolutions that roiled the European continent, spilling into the Americas. The prosperous municipalities afforded newcomers a lucrative shelter from the wars engulfing the rest of Europe. The number of immigrants swelled—an influx related in part to the opportunities opened by the new commercial activity. Jacques Chapeaurouge, who had arrived from Geneva in 1764, strategically joined a large trading house focused on France. Not atypical, as his family prospered over subsequent generations, its members married into local governing circles.

Many of the senators who governed the city of Hamburg were descended from families of recent immigrants, while others could trace earlier generations' journeys from neighboring lands. Visitors committed to the free trade in goods and ideas were as readily absorbed in the 1790s as they had been for generations. These middle-class immigrants fit into the existing social fabric that boasted steady growth and no revolutionary unrest.

Religious struggles throughout Europe had brought Dutch, English, and Flemish merchants and Sephardic Jews in the early seventeenth century and, later, political and economic immigrants from Italy, Spain, Portugal, France, Bohemia, Moravia, the Rhineland, and southern Germany to Hamburg. In particular, the Dutch had developed a special relationship with Hamburg dating back to 1605, and the English had been accommodated as "merchant-adventurers" since 1611.[10] Altona, the smaller and less congested of the two cities, was predominantly Lutheran, like Hamburg, but it extended religious toleration to Calvinists, Catholics, Jews, and Mennonites. At the end of the eighteenth century, 9 percent of the Danish city's populace were Jews.

Hamburg and Altona, with their strong civic culture of republicanism, stood out among overwhelmed hosts as examples of patriotic societies without walls. Until Napoleon occupied them, the two port cities quietly found a balance that worked between guaranteeing the individual rights of refugees and assuring the security of citizens.

The immigrants may have come in the hundreds, totaling in the thousands by the end of the 1790s, but contemporaries on both sides of the Atlantic, in Philadelphia as well as in Paris, anxiously pointed to the 1790s as the first modern refugee crisis. Granted, the influx of outsiders in the 1790s was not on the scale of the mass migration experienced after the world wars of the modern world, nor did these immigrants make a claim on public assistance. In their time, the merchants were not unlike the highly educated scientists, engineers, and entrepreneurs who arrive as individuals in the United States today; both sets of immigrants were drawn by opportunities. Their hosts facilitated their assimilation, reserving the derogatory label of "refugee" for the others, the aristocratic émigrés in the eighteenth century and poorer migrants in the twenty-first century, both fleeing unrest.

Inner Circles

Society in Hamburg and Altona centered around its merchants, to the exclusion of the aristocrats, who held sway elsewhere in Europe. The 1712 Hamburg constitution, or *Hauptrezess*, shared governance between the Senate, made up of the forty wealthiest and most powerful lawyers and merchants, who served life terms, and the Citizen Board (*Bürgerliche Kollegien*) representing non-noble Lutheran men over thirty years of age with substantial land holdings.[11] A visiting Englishman observed: "Persons of rank here are merchants, many of them are at the same time senators, men well inform'd, scholars and gentlemen."[12] Together, republican political culture and commercial dynamism assured Hamburg's continued independence as the largest city-state in the complicated political conglomeration known as the Holy Roman Empire. Altona, the city of the open gates and one of Denmark's most important harbors, garnered its municipal rights from the king of Denmark and Norway.

Bürgerstadt meant belonging to a republic—that is, residing in an independent, self-governing state. Not unlike other societies that considered themselves democratic, only four thousand men out of the more than one hundred thousand residents of Hamburg counted themselves as burghers or citizens with full political rights. A circumscribed set of families controlled political and economic decisions in the two cities, but the inner circles of Hamburg and Altona shifted and were permeable. Newcomers folded neatly into the civic republicanism of the cities, occasionally rising to leadership roles within a generation.

To become a citizen, as Beneke did, an immigrant who met the criteria of wealth, property, and religion had to disavow allegiance to another state. Alternatively, resident immigrants paid an annual fee for "protection" to the city, giving them the right to work and to marry in the city. Jewish residents were assessed an additional tax in Hamburg but attained citizenship in Altona.[13] In Hamburg, the *Fremdenkontrakt* (foreign contract) gave wealthy foreigners the same economic privileges as did citizenship, even if it did not formally convey political rights to participate in the government.

Outward looking, the cosmopolitans of Hamburg and Altona were solidly anchored in the domesticity of their homes. Johanna Sieveking was carrying on a tradition of hospitality from earlier generations. Few days passed at the table set for her family by Sophie Reimarus, the second wife of Johann Albert Heinrich Reimarus, without the additional company of "local scholars and young people eager to learn."[14] On Friday evenings, guests were often invited for punch and sandwiches to share their writing and to discuss the latest news of the world. Sophie suggested that Hamburg and Altona needed congenial spaces of sociability because "in a world where everything is in anxious anticipation, one must at least make one's inner circles as quiet as one can."[15] For Sophie, as for the procession of guests who passed through her house and its gardens, "quiet" did not mean isolation from that outside world, but rather a place of respite from the anxieties of speculative commerce during a war-torn decade. The gatherings around tea tables served as a congregation of friends of like minds.

Sophie Reimarus herself was cognizant of all that happened, from the port to the seats of government in Altona and Hamburg; she not only knew who had newly arrived, but she also read their books and treatises before meeting them.[16] Studies of immigration often render women invisible because they were not directly involved in the international commercial speculation or diplomatic maneuvering. In the two port cities at the end of the eighteenth century, the women were not far removed from either. Women, like men, congregated and conversed at the tables hosted by Sophie Reimarus and Johanna Sieveking.

In preparation for the Sunday gatherings of poets, philosophers, theater directors, authors, and businessmen at Neumühlen, Frederieke Poel assembled a digest of the week's news for her husband, Piter, a widely traveled diplomat and newspaper editor and son of a Dutch merchant, to peruse before everyone arrived. That spared him the trouble of reading all the papers. When she was living with her brother's family, Doctor Reimarus's unmarried sister, Elise, helped host guests. Raised by parents who believed in girls' education, Elise Reimarus had pursued her own education through correspondence with her brother after he left for university, a path denied her. She also corresponded with many leading literary figures, including the poet Friedrich Gottlieb Klopstock, the philosopher Moses Mendels-

Georg Heinrich Sieveking, by Martin Ferdinand Quachi, 1796. Public domain. https://commons.wikimedia.org/wiki/File:Georg_H_Sieveking.jpg.

sohn, the writer Gotthold Ephraim Lessing, and the economics professor Johann Georg Büsch from the Hamburg Gymnasium. Rare was a letter from her that did not mention a book she was reading.

When one of her close friends married, Elise lamented: "Her education and talents seemed to predestine her for a wider circle, but she had to follow her fate. A lonely landscape, where her husband is a local magistrate, and human souls as arid as the ground, plus a toilsome household were what was granted to her."[17] In short, her friend had been forced to leave Hamburg, where intellectual interchange was open to women as well as men. Elise never married and continued to pass her days sitting by the window reading, drawing, sewing, and corresponding. Although Elise had

Johanna M. Sieveking. Historic Images/
Alamy Stock Photo.

no children of her own, she raised the youngest child of a cousin who had died in a pauper's institution.

Georg Heinrich Sieveking later professed that after a week filled with business, he was happy on the weekends to welcome the "enlightened" into their home.[18] An archaeologist visiting from Dresden remarked that also sitting at his table at the Sievekings', he met "the last descendent of the house of Gonzaga, a prince without a land but with much understanding." Across from the prince, next to the hostess, and outshining her, he glimpsed "two rich Dutch women who glittered with jewels. There sat an Englishman from Liverpool next to a republican from Bordeaux, . . . a Swedish Consul returning from Morocco talking to a pair of English Jews from Santo Domingo, and an American from New Jersey," just to complete the varied assortment. "Nothing is happier and more enjoyable than a tea table conversation in the circle of the [Reimarus-Sieveking] family," the visitor concluded.[19] Historians have described these Sunday evenings at the Sievekings as the very center of the German Enlightenment, where "strangers" and their ideas were received with "hospitality and courtesy."[20] The gatherings socialized willing immigrants to the civic values of the Hamburg burghers.

The Sievekings wintered in town. Their luxuriously furnished residence on Neuenwall, across from the fashionable Görtz Palace, was just down the street from their warehouse. Summers, though, were spent at Neumühlen, the country house that they shared with Frederieke and Piter Poel.

Sunday afternoon brought coaches to Neumühlen carrying friends, family, and assorted guests. A frequent visitor, one of the first German women to receive a doctorate in philosophy, Dorothea Rodde-Schlöze, described walking at her leisure through the English gardens with their tranquil grottos and ponds, the landscape dotted with small kiosks where groups paused in conversation. After a simple dinner, relishing the heat from the warm oven and the friendship, the guests retired to the salon. There the interplay of different languages continued as some guests played cards and others read newspapers. A guest recounted, "An emigrant was applauded as a virtuoso on the piano, there was no end to the colorful turmoil."[21] Newcomers felt truly at home at Neumühlen among the assembled guests.

Caspar Voght, Sieveking's business partner and a frequent visitor, lived nearby on an experimental farm in Flottbek. Voght reminisced about afternoons spent when he and Sieveking were younger, reading Klopstock's odes together on the shores of the Alster. They were joined by another senator, who was a merchant trading in whale and fish oils, and a diplomat visiting from Basel who would go on to write the first constitution of the Helvetic Republic. Voght emphasized the lack of separation between the world of commerce and culture. Ideas came from near and far. A devoted lifelong friend of Johanna Sieveking, Voght was romantically involved with Magdalena Pauli, Piter Poel's sister and wife of Adrian Pauli.[22]

Wealthy Hamburg families purchased summer houses outside of the city along the banks of the Elbe at Blankenese, Altona, and Flottbek. Leading Danish statesmen owned estates in the neighborhood, further enhancing the connection between Hamburg and the Danish territories. One of the most renowned houses for its English gardens belonged to Jacques Chapeaurouge in Hamm, to the east of Hamburg; it featured shady paths that wound their way across grassy meadows and flowerbeds to an artificial spring.[23] The Chapeaurouges staged comedies at home in the winter for the extended Reimarus-Sieveking circle.

The households at the center of Hamburg and Altona were intertwined, some through marriage, others through friendship. Often, they brought recently arrived merchants into more established circles. In one

The banks of the Elbe River below the Sieveking country house. Elbufer bei Neumühlen-Landhaus Sieveking, Jens Bundsen, 1797, SHMH-Altonaer Museum, 1937–167, 2. Courtesy of Altonaer Museum.

example of the integration over generations, the son of Jacques Chapeaurouge, Jean, married Elisabeth Dorothea Glashoff, a ward of Adrien Pauli, her uncle. Jean's courtship involved daily letters attesting to "my impatience" as he awaited approval from her uncle while trying to humor her grandmother, who thought Elisabeth too young for marriage.[24] The Chapeaurouge family had a prosperous trading company to which Elisabeth contributed financially on their marriage.[25] Jean would become first deputy mayor of Hamburg, and their daughter would marry into the Sieveking family. A cousin, Jacob Chapeaurouge, would become president of the Hamburg Chamber of Commerce.

The Wednesday evening gatherings in the Reimarus household spawned one of the oldest associations, the Patrotische Gesellschaft, or Patriotic Society, which still meets today. Hermann Samuel Reimarus, Sophie's father-in-law, initially assembled the first members of the Patriotic Society in his house in 1765 "to discuss philanthropy, and through a closer union of men of insight from different backgrounds, of different ages and professions, to secure a deeper bond of friendship and patriotism through the exchange of useful knowledge and experience."[26] Once the club moved its meetings to the Baumhaus, or tree house, overlooking the harbor, it excluded the women who had played such an active role in informal gatherings at home. Otherwise, the Patriotic Society served the same function as the tea tables, bringing together merchants and scholars, citizens and visitors for reading and discussion.

In his inaugural speech to the Patriotic Society, Reimarus called upon the assembled merchants, lawyers, and scholars to propose and pursue urban reforms that lay beyond the purview of the government. He argued that the policies of free trade that allowed merchants to pursue profits without restraint in the port cities obliged them to be attentive to the welfare of the community. That was Reimarus's definition of civic republicanism. The Patriotic Society, whose membership grew from 154 members in 1790 to 514 members and 66 associates in 1805, consciously linked civility and commerce, trade and enlightenment, and civic engagement and open borders.[27] Many of the members also sat in the Senate, the seat of municipal judicial and executive power in Hamburg. A number, including Sieveking, were also Freemasons, another of the connections sealing the civic republicanism of the ports.

The expansion of Harmonie, another club founded in 1789, soon outpaced that of the Patriotic Society. When it outgrew the room it rented above a coffee house, Harmonie moved in 1793 to a new building complete with an assembly hall seating two hundred, a library, and a reading room. The library subscribed to at least fifty journals from all over Europe. From one hundred members in 1794, the club mushroomed to include about five hundred male members at the turn of the nineteenth century, with upward of seven hundred visitors in any given year. Evenings at Harmonie, devoted to reading or billiards or cards, were enjoyed by residents and newcomers alike.

Like the informal gatherings, but without women, the clubs socialized and integrated immigrants unobtrusively. Newspapers, ranging from the three major Hamburg papers and the *Altonaer Merkur* to the English *Morning Chronicle*, the *Gazette de France*, and the *Nouvelles politiques de Leyde*, were in high demand. Harmonie was a gathering place for men of all nationalities and all political persuasions from republicans to royalists. Sieveking noted that individuals who had fought on opposite sides of recent wars came together, as did Hungarian magnates; Frankfurt merchants; Dutch ministers; Irish, English, and Russian lords; and American congressmen, in addition to the Italians and the Swiss. A guest one evening marveled at the variety he encountered: "generals, adventurers, statesmen, country pastors, ambassadors, spies, officers, bishops, sailors, farmers, actors, princes, numerous merchants, French dukes, monks, deported émigrés, royalists, and republicans."[28] Men from Calcutta and Senegal, the West Indies and Siberia, met over books or chamber music.

A convener of one of the many reading societies that gathered merchants and scholars into discussion justified the formation of yet another club in Hamburg by explaining, "Humanity has always reaped benefits from meeting together."[29] That sums up the sociability of the two port cities that attracted so many members of the middle classes. Expansive commerce, republican tolerance, and diplomatic neutrality all intertwined to build cosmopolitanism as territorially based sovereignty strengthened its hold in new nations all around them.

"Pocket a Clear Commission"

Civic republicanism complemented commercial prosperity in the port cities, facilitating the assimilation of foreigners arriving to share in an open exchange of goods and ideas. This cosmopolitan stance contrasted starkly with merchant guilds elsewhere in Europe that counted on regulations distinguishing local from foreign merchants to protect their trade.[30] "Hamburg was always and still is largely inhabited by foreigners," a geographer newly arrived from Pomerania, on the shores of the Baltic Sea, explained in his three-volume topography of Hamburg. "Either these new, naturalized men or their sons and grandsons are merchants," he observed, and by the first or second generation, "they adopt all the inclinations, desires, and cares of Hamburg merchants."[31] They adapted to the civic values of the entrepôts where entrepreneurial daring was key to community prosperity as well as individual fortunes.

Hamburg and Altona citizens traveled as readily to other cities as they welcomed visitors. Georg Heinrich Sieveking frequently visited Paris for business, dining with Enlightenment philosophers and business leaders alike. Sieveking's visits mixed talk of credit and foreign demand with philosophy. Voght was more likely to head to England than France, befriending members of the Committee for the Abolition of the Slave Trade and the United Irishmen. As taken with English liberty as Sieveking was with the French Revolution, Voght brought home the ideas of the English supporters of the American Revolution and plans for planting potatoes.

Merchants from Altona and Hamburg, including Sieveking, frequently functioned as mediators of Atlantic trade because they were free agents. Caspar Voght and Company, with G. H. Sieveking as a new partner, was among the earliest Hamburg enterprises to take advantage of the opportunities opened by American independence. "I was the first Hamburg merchant who took coffee from Mocha, tobacco from Baltimore, coffee from Surinam, and rubber from Africa," Voght would later boast.[32] A New York Quaker, Isaac Hicks, started trading with Voght in 1794, when the Hamburg firm decided to add linens to its food-importing business. Hicks professed that he preferred doing business with Hamburgers because they steered clear of the rapidly shifting European politics. Backed by the neutral diplomacy of the government, they just wanted to do business.

Younger Hamburg merchants were especially drawn to the new Atlantic markets, as were newcomers. Charles Buck opened a trading firm in 1797, beginning by befriending American entrepreneurs residing in Hamburg and Altona. Buck specialized in exporting German linens in one direction and importing American sugar and cotton in the other. Another American, Stephen Girard, ran two ships back and forth between Philadelphia and Hamburg. Vessels launched in Hamburg and Altona frequently sailed to America by way of other European ports. Some of the trade was illicit. Hamburg merchants also looked south, initiating trade with Central and South America and the West Indies for sugar. By the end of the decade, four hundred sugar refineries were operating in the port cities.

Robert Oliver's trade in pewter and tableware from Baltimore grew so steadily that he sent his brother to set up a branch in Hamburg in 1799. He was not alone. It was a common practice for a business partner to emigrate and set up branches in Hamburg. By 1796, more than twenty-six merchants from New York, Philadelphia, Boston, Charleston, Baltimore, Savannah, and Salem did business in Hamburg. Trade with America continued to accelerate through the 1790s; tobacco traveled east, and finished goods and luxury items such as linens and glass traveled west to America.

Rapidly assimilated Hamburg and Altona shipping entrepreneurs, such as Gouverneur Morris's friend John Parish, upheld "what we Merchants call, and what it really is, the most solid of Business: namely receiving Goods for Sale, and against which to make liberal Advances so eventually [to] pocket a clear Commission."[33] Parish's daring repelled the British but attracted friends and gathered business associates among the more congenial and like-minded residents of Hamburg, making him one of the wealthiest men in the port cities. The profits to be made by brokering and reflagging ships as neutral vessels in times of naval blockades were substantial, even if the risks were great. From a family of Scottish merchants, John's father, George Parish, had participated in the smuggling trade and moved his children and wife to Hamburg during the Seven Years War. While John was apprenticed, he witnessed his father's mistreatment as a foreigner by the "little minds" of his father's timid countrymen, who ran the English factory in Hamburg.[34]

Although Great Britain had traditionally been Hamburg's major trading partner, Parish did not hesitate to spurn them and to jump into trading ventures with the insurrectionary Americans. He traded rice from South Carolina for armaments procured in the Danish and German territories. Even after the English consul in Hamburg pressured the Hamburg Senate to declare its disapproval, Parish continued openly to ship saddles, tents, uniforms, blankets, gunpowder pouches, guns, ammunition, and textiles to George Washington's troops. Morris helped him through his French and American connections. Parish's American trade was too profitable to abandon, no matter the challenges.

Parish recounted one of his many adventures: the untimely arrival of one of his ships, the *Patty*, in the Hamburg harbor right under the nose of the English consul. Before the ship could dock, Parish led twelve men down to the harbor, and together they towed it, under cover of darkness, back up the river to Altona.[35] An angry consul tried to interrupt the Hamburgers' illicit trade by impounding two ships, the *Jamaica Packet* and the *Clementine*, allegedly bound for Nantes, Cadiz, Madeira, and the Canaries. The proceedings created such public outrage against the British that the Hamburg Senate had to intervene. The ships were released and sailed, not, as advertised, for European ports, but, as everyone knew they would, for their true destinations in America. In recognition of his commercial connections, the Second Continental Congress appointed Parish as consul for the United States in Hamburg, a post that promised to be lucrative for the merchant and to confer additional prestige.[36]

Parish proceeded, full sail, from the American into the French Revolution, as did many others, profiting from the grain shortage in revolutionary France. Sieveking and Voght, for example, negotiated directly with the city of Paris for shipments of wheat.[37] "I kept launching out the full length of my tether—at home & abroad, I perceive people giving me credit to the full, & perhaps more than I deserved," Parish commented in his memoirs. He negotiated and conspired "with a set of wild & extravagant born speculators who [were] not content with selling their grain on the spot"—merchants, that is, like him.[38] If he suspected failure, Parish pulled away, always, it seems, in time to avoid disaster.

Parish invested his ever-accumulating profits in his adopted homeland, purchasing a large estate in Danish Nienstedten, near Hamburg.[39] He poured massive sums into the renovation and expansion of the palatial house for his growing family. His entertaining there was legendary. Gouverneur Morris, who lodged with him from time to time, commented: "A week in Nienstedten is more companionable than a year in England."[40] Parish's children, especially his five sons, all educated at the Johanneum with members of the Reimarus-Sieveking circle, inherited his tastes for fine living as well as business. They traveled widely: one son, George, moved to India with the British East India Company, and the favorite son, David, to Antwerp and then Philadelphia, where he settled in an elegant house on Washington Square.

The diaries that John Parish left for his daughter, Henriette or Henny, boasted on page after page of the opportunities he had exploited, of the reversals of fortune he had weathered, and of the optimistic confidence that sustained him as he partnered with French, American, British, and Hamburg bankers and merchants to trade goods with plantations in the West Indies and vineyards in Bordeaux.[41] He recounted for her all of the bankruptcies of associates and his assiduous work, day and night, to avoid their fate.

Parish had married in 1768, becoming, he claimed, "as serious & sober a citizen as the best of them." This early marriage, he told his daughter was "one of the lucky circumstances attending my life" because as his expenses increased with the birth of each additional child, he dedicated himself yet more doggedly to his business. He understood that domestic happiness for Hamburg and Altona merchants meant "one fine child following another."[42] Parish asserted in his memoirs that he separated business from his domestic household, never sharing his worries with his wife, chatting calmly through dinners, and then, after the household had gone to bed, returning to his desk to work through the night. He protected his family from the knowledge of the risks of his speculative trade, he claimed. It is curious, then, that he left his memoirs with their detailed business advice to his daughter rather than his sons.

Where many entrepreneurs in this speculative climate prospered, still more failed. Shipping in wartime had become a risky business as merchants relied increasingly not on accumulated family funds, but on external capital accessed on the basis of thin claims to security. Even well-connected and enormously wealthy individuals, such as the banker of the House of Nettine, Edouard de Walckiers, lost their fortunes in these tumultuous times. Walckiers arrived in Hamburg from Brussels by way of revolutionary Paris in 1794. He had been forced to sell off his personal effects when the Jacobins issued a warrant for his arrest in France. Like many other merchants and a few aristocrats at the end of the eighteenth century, and refugees now, his motives were mixed. Politics had forced him to flee France, and economics drew him to Hamburg. There is no definitive line separating motivations to immigrate.

In Hamburg, Walckiers resurrected his banking ties through Parish and the London-based Boyd & Cie, just in time to jump into the shipping of rice and wheat to France through a Belgian intermediary.[43] With North America as the stated destination of the neutral vessels, Walckiers contracted to ship a sizeable quantity of grain every month to provision Paris. Together with seasoned Hamburg merchants, including Jacques Chapeaurouge, Walckiers also offered uniforms for the French army at rates that both made a sizeable profit for the Hamburg merchants and appeared to be advantageous to the French. They all rode the wave of prosperity and good fortune for two years. Then it collapsed again. Walckiers returned to Paris in 1796, financially ruined for a second time.

Parish had sufficient reserves by the time of the French revolutionary wars to ride out these downturns. Referring to his "lucrative business," Parish commented that he had always been interested in the long haul with the goal of accumulating capital. "Was this patriotism, or self-Interest?" he asked his daughter Henny. Perhaps, he suggested, it was a happy mixture of both.[44] They easily coexisted in the port city. The free trade that favored speculative risk taking encouraged these entrepreneurial, cosmopolitan patriots.

Identities in this era of migration and mobility were far from fixed, for merchants as for aristocrats, especially in neutral ports. By 1793, Parish was referring in his journal to the French declaring war on "us." By "us," this one-time American consul in Hamburg now meant England. On the side of the British, whom he had spurned as a young man, he purchased ships to transport troops to the West Indies. Hamburg senators raised an alarm when Parish's actions were so extensive that they threatened to endanger the neutrality of the city. Undeterred, Parish simply hoisted a transport sack instead of the Hamburg flag up the poles of his sixteen ships. A former advocate of revolution, whether American or French, he then switched sides, transferring silver from Britain to Prussia via Hamburg.

That realignment, he wrote in his journal, "never occasioned me an hour's uneasiness."[45] Parish personified the other side of the ready assimilation of foreign merchants: the shifting identities of rootless refugees dictated by conditions on the ground and motivated by their commercial interests.

In response to the Holocaust, Hannah Arendt, in her often-cited essay "We Refugees" describes the tension experienced by refugees pressured to forget the land they have left behind, all the while remembering that it was there that they had once been "somebodies." They had been chased from the place where they had been somebody to a new land where they were nobody. They had to reinvent themselves, as Parish did, often more than once. "Very few individuals have the strength to conserve their own integrity if their social, political and legal status is completely confused," Arendt explained. These wanderers were encouraged to "adjust in principle to everything and everybody," and, she concludes, in the end, unlike Ulysses, they "don't know who they are."[46]

Parish, like many of the other merchants from the Americas and Europe, prospered, settled, and raised a family, becoming "a somebody" in Hamburg and Altona. Over time in this revolutionary era, though, he shifted political identities as a reptile sheds its skin. The constant was his sense of himself as a man of business, just as Countess Bentinck was an aristocrat first. Social class was more important than nationality. The French occupation of Hamburg in 1807 caused Parish to flee, first to Eastern Frisia, then Copenhagen, and finally to Bath in the west of England. Identifying at the end of his life as British, Parish nevertheless fondly looked back to what he then remembered as "that happy spot" where he had prospered and his family had grown. But Parish never did go back. He was content, entertaining society at his elegant house in Bath. As in Hamburg, the world continued to come to him.[47]

"The Thronging of This Cosmopolitan Port"

Not all those who came to Hamburg and Altona chasing opportunity adapted so readily to the port cities or assimilated as easily as the Chapeaurouge or Parish families. One couple who never felt at home in Hamburg and Altona was Ruth and Joel Barlow. Joel was a Connecticut poet, merchant, and diplomat. Ruth, in particular, was always thinking of going home to Connecticut, while her husband, like Jacques Chapeaurouge and John Parish, was intent on pursuing his economic and diplomatic fortunes in Europe. She was not unlike Madame de Genlis or Madame de Flahaut, who had left home against their will, assuming their time abroad would pass quickly.

Joel had struggled mightily to convince Ruth to leave her friends and family behind in Connecticut to join him in Europe. Before embarking, she sought advice from Abigail Adams about transatlantic travel and packing. When she finally arrived in London in 1790, after what seemed to her an endless crossing, she found her husband had just left for revolutionary Paris. Alone in a strange city, she was not happy, subsisting on strange food and on letters delivered intermittently and sent on circuitous routes to escape wartime censure. Would they ever see each other again, she asked, with "all the ports blocked up with fleets & the frontiers surrounded with armies."[48] Exile tested couples.

Ruth finally joined Joel in Paris, only to discover that the Jacobins were interrogating, detaining, and guillotining their friends, French and foreign alike. The final blow came in the middle of a December night, when their friend Thomas Paine asked the police conveying him to prison to stop at the Barlows' lodging, leading the agents up four winding flights of stairs to the apartment above a casino. Out of breath, Paine slipped the just-roused Barlow the first part of his manuscript of *The Age of Reason* for safekeeping before he was dragged away to await his fate in the Luxembourg prison. The Barlows, fearing for their own lives, left, with a French government commission for shipping grain in their baggage. On the French coast, they negotiated a series of business deals for the French and met their friend Mary Wollstonecraft. From there, they traveled to the safety of the ports of Hamburg and Altona.

The Barlows arrived in Altona just before the frigid winter of 1794–95, when winds blowing from Siberia froze the Elbe solid, closing down the harbor for months. Gouverneur Morris, wintering in Altona, claimed that foolhardy men who did venture out of doors in January froze to death. The rare souls who reached their destination rushed inside, coming back outside a few hours later, only to find their waiting horses keeled over, victims of the bitter cold. Morris still apparently gave little thought to returning to the United States until 1799.

Joel Barlow opened a brokerage house in Hamburg, within easy walking distance of the living quarters he and Ruth secured in Altona. He had failed spectacularly at every business deal he had tried, so Ruth was skeptical. In Hamburg, Barlow's luck changed. Here, he could buy goods cheaply and ship them under the American flag to beleaguered ports at substantial profits. Hoisting a neutral flag and claiming Spain as a destination, the ships could dodge British blockades before landing instead at a French Atlantic port. Many ships kept several flags aboard that could be swapped out as circumstances demanded.[49] In a single year, the Barlows accumulated sufficient funds to support them for the rest of their lives. Barlow justified the sizeable profits made through speculation by convincing himself he was contributing to the French Revolution by provisioning a starving country.

In a typical venture, Chapeaurouge pretended to sell a brig to Barlow, thus allowing it to sail under the neutral American flag. In fact, an Englishman purchased the ship, and Barlow, as the broker, was just paid a commission. It happened that the British seized the ship as soon as it set off and impounded it, necessitating further deception on Barlow's part in a British vice-admiralty court. None of that was uncommon.

The Barlows would look back on their year's asylum in Altona as a welcome domestic idyll, sandwiched as it was between the periods of revolutionary chaos that separated husband from wife for long periods of time. Memories can be deceptive. At least in Altona in 1794–95, they were together, sharing rooms in one house. Neither of them spoke a word of German, which made them more dependent on each other. Ruth often complained about the lack of reasonable female companionship. During the frigid winter months, they scorned what they dismissed as the shallow amusement of the residents of Hamburg, who took unfathomable pleasure, when temperatures dipped, in "lighting large fires, eating, dancing, skating, and roasting oxen whole on the ice."[50] They do not seem to have been included in the Sievekings' gatherings, and they complained about the mundane quality of the verses of the renowned German poet Klopstock. But at least business was booming.

Lonely though they complained to be, the Barlows were not without German friends. They were befriended by the erudite librarian Christoph Daniel Ebeling, who shared a house with the leading Hamburg economist, Professor Johann Georg Büsch, the founder and director of Hamburg's acclaimed commercial academy. Many of Büsch's and Ebeling's guests were Freemasons, visiting the oldest German lodge, Absalom zu den drei Nesseln, founded in 1737, and located nearby.

Ebeling was a student of everything American; Büsch was the author of one of the most widely read treatises on the importance of free trade for a republic, arguing that the major aim of the city's economic policy should be to assure the greatest happiness of its residents. That could best be achieved in a society where there was work for all, putting money into circulation. At issue were the widely discussed questions of the interrelation of diplomacy and finances in causing war and bringing peace, of commercial freedom and the independence of states in a world dominated by empires, and of free trade as a means of stabilizing international relations. Büsch chronicled the payoff from Hamburg's decades-long investment in international trade and diplomatic neutrality; Ebeling extended the picture to America. Linked by trade, American ideals were spreading freely to Europe, he argued.

The Barlows especially enjoyed the company of one of the founders of the Sheffield Society for Constitutional Information, the radical British editor Joseph Gales, and his wife Winifred, a novelist and student of the classics. The Galeses had sought temporary exile in Altona. Gales faced charges of treason in England for his unabashed support of the French Revolution and his criticism of the British government. Arriving in September 1794 with their four children and a young apprentice, the Galeses intended Altona to be just a place to board a ship for America, but they ended up staying long enough for Winifred to give birth to a fifth child, a daughter named Altona, and, unlike the Barlows, to learn German as well as French. During the frigid winter, they toyed with the idea of returning home to their "native land," but as political exiles, they concluded that Britain was no safer than France, although for the opposite political reasons. Hamburg and Altona offered safety that was in short supply on the European continent during the revolutionary wars.

The Galeses rented a furnished apartment in Altona. "Considering that we were in a Country perfectly strange to us, and that we were in other Respects uncomfortably situated," Gales wrote in his diary, "the Time passed as agreeably as we could expect."[51] Winifred Gales commented on the surprising friendliness of the people they encountered, even though she initially spoke no German. After treatment by a doctor and a nurse, she thought their bill too low and reminded the physician how often he had visited her during her convalescence. He answered: "I remember the Lady is a stranger, and in a strange Land, and has many dear little children," so he had reduced his bill.[52] When the Galeses were ready to leave for the United States in June 1795, the Barlows took a Gales daughter into their care.

The Barlows left shortly thereafter, finally returning to what Ruth embraced as home. Neither the Galeses nor the Barlows ever returned to Altona. For them, unlike the Parish, Chapeaurouge, and so many other merchant families, the port cities offered a safe respite from a tumultuous decade, nothing more. They were more like the aristocrats who never intended to settle and were intent on returning home.

"A Deeper Bond of Friendship and Patriotism"

The Barlows left just as Mary Wollstonecraft arrived. Unwelcome at home in England and insecure in revolutionary France, Wollstonecraft had secured lodgings in September 1795 for herself and her infant daughter, Fanny, in Altona. Like many other newcomers during this revolutionary era, she had made the rounds of northern Europe. She had also been engaged in commercial ventures, though the speculative adventures of her friends had left her unsympathetic to the commercial ethos of the two ports.

Wollstonecraft might not have been too happy to encounter the Barlows. Joel had been involved in a business arrangement with Gilbert Imlay, her former lover and father of her child. As Imlay's proxy, Wollstonecraft had overseen the loading of French silver on a ship in Le Havre, reregistered as a neutral Norwegian vessel.[53] Barlow and Imlay probably intended to trade the silver for naval construction materials in Scandinavia to be used in the French revolutionary wars. Bound for Gothenburg, the ship and its silver mysteriously disappeared somewhere off the Norwegian coast. Imlay sent Wollstonecraft north to investigate the mystery. Unable to make any headway with their business associates or with the justices investigating the case, Wollstonecraft, her daughter, and her nursemaid traveled to Copenhagen to plead with the Danish prime minister on Imlay's behalf, ending what turned out to be a fruitless chase in Hamburg. Rumor had it that the ship might have landed there.

Wollstonecraft counted the days until she could leave Altona. She felt betrayed by Imlay, who had apparently taken a new lover, and alone in a strange place where she, like the Barlows, did not speak the language. In letters to her friends, Wollstonecraft derided the "mushroom fortunes" amassed by speculators in what she characterized as an evil "whirlpool of gain." In the ports of Hamburg and Altona, she complained, "the interests of nations are bartered by speculating merchants."[54] She spurned the company of merchants and financiers from across the Atlantic world who, like her former lover, made their fortunes through what she derided as the "muddy channels" of commerce.[55]

Wollstonecraft instead took solace in the company of St. John de Crèvecoeur. The author of the immensely popular *Letters from an American Farmer*, Crèvecoeur had fled revolutionary France, seeking a more tolerant asylum. He expected to join his son Ally, who was profitably engaged in business in Altona, except when he arrived, his son was absent, having traveled to London on business. Crèvecoeur complained of his loneliness despite all of the invitations from Ally's business associates to Sunday dinners, which he described as sad affairs given by pale, small, and sickly hosts. Had he encountered these associates at the Sievekings' country house? He preferred dinner in the boarding house where Wollstonecraft had taken up residence. The two writers railed against commerce and the merchants who dominated the neighboring cities.

Neither Wollstonecraft nor Crèvecoeur would have echoed Ferdinand Beneke, who saw a causal connection among free trade, cosmopolitanism, and the liberty of an independent city-state. Unlike many of the other middle-class asylum seekers who flooded Altona and Hamburg, investing in the burgeoning shipping fleet, they did not stand directly to profit from trade in grain and armaments.

In the end, though, even Wollstonecraft benefitted, if only indirectly. She made a sizeable profit from the sales of her book describing her trip to northern Europe. John Quincy Adams, who read Wollstonecraft's book when he visited Hamburg two years later, challenged her "canting, whining, sickly style of complaint."[56] Mary Wollstonecraft, like Ruth Barlow, was probably just tired of traveling during this revolutionary era. It is interesting that in the conclusion to her book about her Scandinavian travels, Wollstonecraft derided her timorous British compatriots who never dared to leave home. And if they did, she complained, they imagined that every other place should resemble what they knew at home. Claiming to have "no home—no resting place to look to," Wollstonecraft called on her readers to imagine a future when "the factitious national characters which have been supposed permanent" would yield to a more cosmopolitan outlook.[57] She did not realize that the outward-looking society of the ports that so readily welcomed outsiders like her was intertwined with the freewheeling capitalism that she disparaged.

Patriotism in Hamburg and Altona presupposed openness to the world. Hamburg senators recognized that the city prospered because of its unfettered commerce and the influx of adventurous merchants. In Altona, the commander of the police noted, "Happy is a city where one only worries about how much the quiet inhabitants and foreigners devote to the common good, and not what they believe."[58] The influx of new ideas and people and access to the outside world established the dynamic continuity that allowed both cities to prosper as their neighbors' economies stagnated and their governments fell prey to political unrest.

The founding documents of the Patriotic Society explained, "Our Republic is nothing more than a simple merchant city where . . . everyone derives his political life, his economy, and his very being from commerce."[59]

In 1794, the Patriotic Society proposed a prize competition to answer the question: "Based on experience from the distant past and near present, how does trade encouraged by cities such as Hamburg not only not harm neighboring states but also contribute to the prosperity of countries near and far to which they are connected? How does this experience apply to the current political and commercial relationships of the German ports?"[60] The judges were very disappointed to receive just one response and complained that it was poorly reasoned at that. Perhaps residents of Hamburg just assumed that free trade and open doors were essential for the prosperity of a republic. The answer seemed too obvious to warrant a response.

Free trade and neutrality complemented each other in the port cities open to the world, the Hanseatic minister stationed in Paris confirmed. Even in the midst of "the blasphemy of war, these neutral cities connect nations and offer the promise of peace."[61] That was in 1795, the same year that Immanuel Kant published his treatise on cosmopolitanism, *On Perpetual Peace*, affirming the right to hospitality as a moral claim and asserting the responsibility of republics to extend that welcome to foreigners. More merchants than aristocrats took up the offer of hospitality. While some, like the Barlows, assumed the right to visit and enjoy the resources of the land, others assimilated easily into what one referred to as the "merchant communalism" and stayed.[62] Engaged in commerce as were the governing circles of the cities, they readily fit into the neighboring cosmopolitan cities.

Sophie Reimarus translated Kant's treatise into French. She forwarded it to the French government at about the same time that Georg Heinrich Sieveking set off to represent his native city on a trade mission to Paris. Perhaps the philosophic treatise would serve to remind at least one set of Hamburg's and Altona's neighbors of the cities' neutrality and independence amid warring nations. Even if the majority of the refugees arriving in Hamburg and Altona were fleeing France, their reasons for leaving ranged widely, from those of counterrevolutionary aristocrats clinging to the monarchy to merchants seeking freer trade. Their neighbors had no reason to fear the open port cities guided by their adherence to free shipping and free trade.

CHAPTER THREE

French Connections

"For Commerce and Humanity"

In wartime, even more than in periods of peace, diplomacy and commerce were entangled. Altona and Hamburg adeptly navigated between their allegiance to the ideals of the French, on the one side, and the threats posed by their traditional commercial partners, the British, Prussians, and Austrians, on the other. While the port cities harbored French aristocratic émigrés, foreign-owned ships that trafficked in provisions for the French revolutionary armies.[1] At war with each other, their larger neighbors closed borders on land and hoisted blockades at sea, continually challenging the political and economic independence of the port cities. And yet, the two harbors were busier than ever in the last decade of the eighteenth century. The diplomatic relations of the cosmopolitan ports, though, were decidedly fraught.

Hamburg and Altona's powerful neighbors, eager for an alliance and exclusive trading privileges, claimed that they alone could promise the peaceful ports security—and hence prosperity—in the midst of the wars at the end of the eighteenth century. The Prussians persistently lobbied the Hamburg Senate to expel French revolutionaries sheltered in the city. Even though Hamburg was a free imperial city and part of the Holy Roman Empire, the Prussians worried about all of the immigrating merchants from France.[2] The French complained about the large contingents of royalist émigrés harbored in the ports. Both states were concerned about the

The busy port of Hamburg in 1814. "Hamburg, 1814," Robert Bowyer, *Hamburg—An Illustrated Record of Important Events in the Annals of Europe.* © image; Crown Copyright: UK Government Art Collection, United Kingdom. Courtesy of Government Art Collection.

political influence of the refugees on the supposedly neutral cities and furnished examples of recruitment posters for enemy armies as evidence.

It was more than theoretically possible to be an independent city-state or a small monarchy when neighboring powers were at peace, but during war, the Hamburg Senate and the Danish monarch struggled to keep diplomatic and commercial doors open. Merchants sitting in the Hamburg Senate who wanted to safeguard commerce by assuring their freedom to trade on the seas had to secure a course between their neighbors' fears. It was a constant balancing act made all the more difficult by their residents' sympathies with the French republic.

Free trade was key to the prosperity of the ports. The major highway leading in and out from Hamburg and Altona was the sea. At the end of the eighteenth century, more world commerce flowed over water than land. The problem in the 1790s was that Britain dominated the North Atlantic and the Baltic, and for much of the decade, it was at war with France. Hamburg and Altona were caught between the two. In response to the British seizure of neutral ships suspected of trading with France, Johanna Sieveking, whose husband was engaged in provisioning the French, compared the desperate Hamburg merchants to "a gathering of invalids in crisis."[3]

Illicit shipping posed daunting challenges at the diplomatic level, especially when neutral ships skirted embargoes and blockades. Illegal activity at sea intensified during the American Revolution. American shipping magnates pursing the burgeoning trade immigrated to Hamburg and Altona. Commercial ties linked them to revolutionary allies in France. Nervous Prussian and Austrian governments responded through every available diplomatic channel, vociferously protesting the revolutionary inclinations of their neutral neighbors. City officials did their best to placate these powers without disrupting shipping that was effectively evading British naval blockades and bound for France.

The success of the French Revolution not only fit the economic interests of the local merchants, but also often aligned with their politics, at least in the first half of the decade. In 1790, on behalf of Hamburg merchants, Georg Heinrich Sieveking approached officials in Paris to explore the possibilities of shipping substantial cargoes of grain from Hamburg to revolutionary France. He spoke, he said, as a free citizen of an independent republic, professing his admiration of the French constitution, which guaranteed the rights of man, all the while insisting on favorable trading terms. While in Paris, Sieveking also visited his friend the Marquis de Condorcet and ordered books in French by the carton to take home. Even though Hamburg was part of the German empire, Sieveking looked to Paris, not the much closer Prussian capital of Berlin, much less the emperor's capital of Vienna, as the hub not only of commerce, but also of free thought.[4]

On 14 July 1790, the Sievekings caught the attention of not only France, but also its enemies with their Bastille Day celebrations at their garden house in Harvestehude, just north of Hamburg. At half past twelve, they gathered their friends, including many members of the scholarly Reimarus family and the extended family of the economist Johann Georg Büsch. Joining this intermarried family circle were Caspar Voght, Sieveking's business partner; Adolph von Knigge, a fellow Freemason and widely read author; Karl Friedrich Cramer, a professor of Greek at the University of Kiel; and Friedrich Gottlieb Klopstock, the renowned poet who wrote and read two odes for the occasion. In addition to guests from Hamburg and Altona, acquaintances from Holstein, Hannover, America, Switzerland, and France joined in the festivities. A French aristocrat confided in a letter to her daughter that she was the only noble invited to the gathering.[5]

Women came attired in white, with hats and sashes trimmed in the French national colors of red and blue. Men bedecked themselves with revolutionary cockades. In the garden, young women formed a semicircle and sang revolutionary songs; the assembled guests made up the choir. Sophie Reimarus wrote that tears flowed freely, so moved were the guests.[6] Sieveking himself contributed a song, proclaiming, "Let us be joyful, free, free, free, free, and pure of heart." He heralded France as a sister nation to the independent German city-state and called on all good German burghers to join the French in driving sitting despots from their thrones. Voght described Klopstock's poem as the finest he had ever heard for its simplicity. Other poets contributed verses "praising freedom, equality, and brotherhood, and celebrating the French republic."[7]

In the Sievekings' garden the guests celebrated France for raising the banner of all the people "who have climbed the summit of freedom."[8] More than a victory for France alone, the French Revolution transcended national borders. "All are brothers," another guest proclaimed.[9] Sophie Reimarus noted that an American got so carried away, singing loudly and promising to broadcast news of the festivities far and wide, that he created quite a spectacle. Foreign newspapers reported that the evening ended with a toast to the demise of despotism in Germany.

Notably, the gathered guests toasted "freedom and virtue," not liberty and equality. That difference may have seemed subtle one year into the French Revolution, but it signaled difficulties ahead for the neutral ports. Most of the Hamburgers in attendance at the Bastille Day festivities even in 1790 would have said that they had no need to follow the revolutionary French because Hamburg citizens already enjoyed the rights for which the French were fighting. A few years into the French Revolution, these advocates of liberty would no longer support revolutions that overturned the existing order. In Hamburg and Altona, they represented that order and spoke out for what they defined as the public good of their independent city-state. The rifts in the port cities' politics, exacerbated by the intervention of their neighbors' enemies, widened, but somehow trade continued despite it all.

Neutral Diplomacy

The Hamburg Senate and presiding official of Altona, the Oberpräsident, and Altona councilors prided themselves on their ability to maintain neutrality and continue shipping in the midst of a warring continent.[10] Until the American War for Independence, commerce with England had constituted a significant portion of their trade. Over the course of the 1790s, treaty negotiations, shifting borders, naval blockades, and the movement of armies across the continent convinced entrepreneurial traders in Altona especially, but also in Hamburg, to diversify their commercial ties and shipping routes. Their diplomatic agility allowed them to continue to ship goods procured throughout Europe to ports around the shores of Europe and the Americas. They could also move imported goods from their ports inland, mostly to the German states.[11]

Many of the largest commercial houses in Hamburg and Altona turned increasingly to their connections in the French seaports of Nantes, Bordeaux, and Marseille. The French consul in Hamburg "[had never] seen so many expeditions for our ports as in the last four months."[12] Other than French colonies, Hamburg was the most important importer of French manufactured goods. Between 1787 and 1789, 40 percent of French exports passed through the port of Hamburg, including indigo, luxury goods, and wine from the colonies.[13] Wines and liquor transited by way of Hamburg to England. Although the revolution undermined France's economic position as the supplier of Germany and the rest of Europe with products from its colonies, the German states, especially the Hanseatic ports, including Hamburg, reinforced their position as providers of raw materials and of metals for nations at war. Grains, vegetables, and wood headed from Hamburg to France, making the small independent German republic the second largest source of French imports.[14]

Neutral countries negotiated the first years of continental war by nodding when neighboring powers warned them about shipping to "the enemy."[15] When embargoes limited shipping from Hamburg to France in 1792, many Hamburg merchants shifted their operations to the port of Altona, greatly expanding the number of ships calling at the Danish port.[16] In part, too, shipping increased so dramatically in those years as a direct result of the numerous French and Dutch emigrants in Altona who were able to found shipping companies and were willing to speculate.

In the summer of 1793 skirmishes at sea between Britain and revolutionary France seriously disrupted trade. French legislation forbade the depositing of funds in enemy banks, making international commercial transactions even more difficult. A Danish captain with a cargo of wheat embarked from Hamburg. The ship's registered destination was Livorno in Italy, but it landed instead in Dieppe. The captain could be paid only in assignats, the French paper currency deemed worthless by most foreign entrepreneurs.[17] Even for merchants who identified themselves as cosmopolitans and friends of the republic, the depreciation of French currency and unreliability of payment was problematic.[18] In addition, the French government limited potential profits by setting maximum prices on grain.

In the winter of 1793, British orders forbidding neutral countries to conduct commerce with French colonies made shipping from the ports even more difficult. Desperate for provisions, the city of Bordeaux sent an agent to Hamburg to buy grain directly, continuing the practice into 1794. Even that channel was not without problems—for example, when the French municipal agent negotiating with Jacques Chapeaurouge was arrested by the governing French Committee of General Security.[19]

Prussia reminded the Hamburg Senate that the city was part of the German imperial confederation and subject to certain obligations based on its ties with the empire. Austria, like Prussia, both resented and tried to expose the open secret that merchants sailing from Hamburg and Altona were provisioning revolutionary France. France, meanwhile, persistently reminded Hamburg merchants where their trade was most profitable—to France, no matter the obstacles.

The reality of republican trade amid war and revolution was messy. In trade negotiations in the summer of 1794 with the French, the Hamburg Senate had to respond to French accusations that the neutral ports were actively discriminating against France. Sieveking countered that the very existence of the port city depended on trade and on treating foreigners as the city did its own citizens.[20] Impartiality was integral not only to their neutral diplomacy, but also to their cosmopolitan patriotism. Clearly though, France expected preference, not impartiality. Pleading with the French not to take further hostile actions against Hamburg, in exasperation Sieveking asked: "Could the war of free men and philosophers be yet more destructive for commerce and humanity?"[21] Hamburg joined with emissaries of the other neutral states—the United States, Sweden, Genoa, Denmark, Bremen, and Lübeck—to protest the imposition of French embargoes.[22] Without neutrality, commerce would stagnate, they asserted.

Prohibitions from all sides threatened free trade as the eighteenth century neared to a close. Not only the British, but also the French interfered with shipping between neutral states and lucrative ports in Portugal and Spain. The British declared all raw materials to be war provisions and thus subject to seizure. At the same time, the Germans added pressure on Hamburg and the other Hanseatic ports to stop them from sending grains and military provisions, including food, leather, and fabrics, to France. The most daring Hamburg merchants skirted restrictions by continuing to ship from Altona and claiming Genoa instead of Dunkirk on the French coast as their destination.

Trade began to pick up on the French-Hamburg routes when the wars closed other northern ports. Hamburg took advantage of the occupation of the Netherlands to bolster its prominence as a port with access to the North Sea. Imports increased from 52.9 million pounds of sugar in 1791 to 86.8 million pounds in 1795, while coffee rose from 21.5 million pounds in 1791 to 42 million pounds in 1795, and pepper, from 864 sacks in 1791 to 5,723 sacks in 1795.[23] Trade also grew with the West Indies.

In 1796, the French severely restricted imports originating in enemy territory even if shipped by neutral powers, drawing Sieveking at the head of a Hamburg delegation back to Paris to negotiate on behalf of the city. The French Directory granted them an audience in the Luxembourg Palace, where the French government was meeting. The Hamburg merchants argued that any trade agreement in this revolutionary world should be based on the principles of liberty, equality, and reciprocity. The French countered that Hamburg should follow the lead of Denmark and recognize revolutionary France. "The French republic does not compromise when its national dignity is at stake," the president of the Directory told Sieveking before issuing orders for an embargo on all Hamburg ships.[24] Sieveking answered with a memorandum setting out Hamburg's shipping interests, and the Hamburg Senate voted to reaffirm its neutrality.

Countess Bentinck criticized what she perceived to be the French sympathies of her host city and its claims to diplomatic neutrality. She complained about the ships that "infest[ed] the seas" and that docked in the so-called neutral ports of Hamburg and Denmark.[25] From the aristocratic émigrés who gathered in her drawing room, she claimed to have organized a spy ring to count ships leaving port and to ascertain their destinations. The Scandinavians, in particular, were sending cows and pigs in immense quantities to the French, she alleged. The genteel spies passed along the names of the vessels and their Danish and Hamburg captains to neighboring enemies of the French Revolution. Spies also tracked false passports, guns, and traffic destined for America. That counterrevolutionary activity was corroborated by reports of a paid Senate informant who paid particular attention to the banks and to the purchase of materials that could be used for French war efforts.

The reports opened a debate in the Hamburg Senate on the vexing question of how to maintain neutrality and free commerce while allowing merchants, many of whom sat in the Senate, to provision revolutionary France. At issue, too, were the American merchants whose ships docked in their neutral harbors, contrary to British interests. The Senate worried about upsetting its traditional trading partner, Britain. Between 1789 and 1795, North American shipping to Hamburg tripled. At its peak in 1798–99, 192 out of the 1,960 ships arriving in Hamburg harbor were from the United States.[26] The British questioned the captains of ships from Hamburg and Altona that they routinely seized, asking them if they knew any of a list of merchants, including Georg Heinrich Sieveking, John Parish, and Jacques Chapeaurouge, or French agents known to be living in Altona. Pressure continued to mount on the Hamburg Senate to punish this illicit shipping as a threat to neutrality.[27] When the Austrians complained about increasing trade between France and Hamburg, the Senate responded by trying to placate its critics with a symbolic action. It summoned Jacques Chapeaurouge to defend his surreptitious provisioning of France. His retort was unapologetic. Why, he asked, should the Senate be surprised, given his family connections with the republic, that his ventures in banking and trade were primarily with France? The Senate was apparently satisfied, although the gesture did not alleviate the concerns of uneasy neighbors.

"Praising Freedom, Equality, and Brotherhood, and Celebrating the French Republic"

In May 1793, Sieveking published a widely read pamphlet defending his French friendships in what he argued was a free city. Noting the fears of many of his countrymen of "the anarchy, cabals, atheism, and murder" attributed to the French Revolution, he acknowledged that he was no Jacobin.[28] In conclusion, Sieveking appealed to the cosmopolitan spirit of Immanuel Kant: "Let the bond of the most faithful patriotism, the noblest friendship that has united us so far, also connect us with you and let us thus jointly justify the expectations of our fellow citizens."[29] This patriotism was outward-looking. The merchants extended their political and economic connections throughout Europe and across the Atlantic, wherever their ships traded and correspondence reached.

Not surprisingly, tensions flared between the two sets of immigrants, the aristocratic émigrés and the merchants, and were reflected in uneasiness among their hosts. One traveler observed: "I am certain that in no city in Germany has the French Revolution provoked such lively yet such diverse reactions as in Hamburg. One person exalts it as the triumph of human dignity and greatness while the other ridicules or condemns it as the maddest undertaking into which only [the] folly, wantonness and wickedness of short-sighted and malevolent individuals can always lead the sheepish race of men."[30] Any enthusiasm at the launching of the French Revolution in 1789 in the two ports faded as the decade wore on. For the most part, the governing circles of Hamburg after 1792 believed Hamburg had found a just middle as a republic. Although the French Revolution was not one to emulate, that did not preclude support. However, as news spread of the Parisian crowd's pursuit of the king and his guards into the Tuileries in August 1792 and of the storming of the prisons in September, straddling the middle became increasingly untenable.

Some prominent citizens, including members of Sieveking's circle and his fellow Freemasons, organized the Hamburger Lesegesellschaft (Hamburg Reading Society) and publicly threw in their lot with the French revolutionaries. The Hamburger Lesegesellschaft was at one and the same time a circle of friends and acquaintances, and a political club. One of its regulations banned all political discussion while the next allowed the society to discuss any matters of general interest.[31] Hamburgers who attended the Lesegesellschaft included Voght and other partners in shipping firms doing business with the French, Francophile writers, booksellers, and journalists.

Sieveking was elected as president of the society, with the French envoy François Lehoc as vice-president. Their regulations posted in French, they met at Lehoc's house. Although the officers of the society went to great lengths to clarify their intention to stay within the laws of their city and to honor its institutions, vowing they would not incite unrest, the secrecy of their meetings gave rise to suspicion. So too did the largely French membership. Some of them were merchants and others, officials of the government stationed in Hamburg. They were not shy in making their radical views known.

The assurances of legality were not enough for many of their fellow citizens, already set on edge by the wars surrounding them. Lehoc had not hesitated to get himself embroiled in Hamburg politics, whether among Sieveking's circle or in the Senate itself. He hired a German-speaking journalist with good local connections as his private secretary, striving to insinuate himself into society and to to gain intelligence to pass along to Paris. Anxious French émigrés in particular worried that the omnipresent Lehoc would exaggerate overheard conversations and turn their names over to officials in Hamburg and Altona as dangerous elements.

Stirring up fears was the new Prussian envoy stationed in Hamburg, Major Karl Siegmund von Göchhausen, who supplied Berlin with regular reports of Lehoc's especially provocative actions. The Austrian imperial envoy in Hamburg, for his part, warned Vienna about the sixty to seventy members who regularly attended the Hamburger Lesegesellschaft; Göchhausen alleged two hundred members frequented meetings of what he dubbed the Jacobin club. Foreign ministers' circles in Copenhagen, Hamburg, and Berlin buzzed with rumors of a threatened Jacobin uprising.

All attention in the fall of 1792 was focused on French military advances in Germany and rumors of an impending French invasion of the ports. The Hamburg Senate tried to tamp down stories of French revolutionaries inciting unrest in the city. The Lesegesellschaft was the obvious target of suspicions, stoked by its neighbors. Even though a number of senators openly attended the meetings, the Senate hired informers to report on it. The officers reassured Hamburgers that with so many gregarious young Frenchmen in attendance, nothing would remain secret anyway.

The timing of the organization of the Francophile reading society just ahead of the beheading of Louis XVI turned out not to be fortuitous. Sophie Reimarus, once sympathetic to the French, wrote her brother, despairing that liberty should have fallen into French hands rather than those of another state with a constitutional history.[32] Presumably, she meant Hamburg. At the end of December 1792, Sieveking resigned from the French-leaning group, affirming his continuing attachment to the cause of French republicans in a farewell letter.

The Austrians joined the Prussians in applying pressure on the Senate to expel the zealous Lehoc from their city-state in the spring of 1793. The Senate finally did. The Commercial Deputation of Hamburg expressed its gratitude to Lehoc for his service in promoting trade, and Sieveking made clear in his correspondence that this was not a Senate decision freely made.[33] Under the influence of the Austrian imperial ambassador in October 1793, the Hamburg Senate went further, banning all secret societies. Pushed by its neighbors to the east, the Senate also challenged Sieveking's and Voght's close commercial ties with the French that threatened to overrun the independent city-state's neutrality.

Diplomats on both sides hired agents to report on their enemies in the port cities, where they uncovered allegedly incendiary pamphlets.[34] The reports of the Austrians and Prussians of dangerous radical activity in Hamburg were grossly exaggerated. The French made their own unsubstantiated claims that French royalists who had been granted sanctuary in

Hamburg and Altona were implicated in counterrevolutionary plotting led by members of the French royal family in disguise. Perhaps, the monarchist émigrés who had fled France were not as innocent as their daily occupations as barbers and café owners might make it appear, they suggested. Tensions ran high.

The Senate apparently took the reports seriously. The evidence was too blatant to be ignored. What if the French refugees Hamburg sheltered were involved in counterrevolutionary plots? What if they were in league to undermine the republican liberty most senators celebrated, whether in France or Hamburg? After much discussion, the Senate responded by banning placards recruiting foreign armed forces but did little else.

The open borders that were integral to Hamburg's and Altona's economic and political liberty posed problems when exiles publicly staked out positions incompatible with the neutrality of the ports. The threat posed by political activity in the independent city-state and the Danish kingdom to their neighbors was obvious. The Prussians never missed an opportunity to remind their neighbors of the dangers lurking in the shadows of their harbors. But they were not the only fearful ones. French Jacobins also made no secret of their resentment of open borders. They resented neighboring governments, whether republics or monarchies, that allowed counterrevolutionaries to congregate. The two cities had to recalibrate their balance constantly and carefully to preserve the appearance of neutrality. They negotiated a precarious line.[35]

The Treaty of Basel in 1795 between Prussia and France, which ceded lands west of the Rhine to France, formally recognized Hamburg as a zone of neutrality. In effect, the peace agreement made Hamburg more dependent on Prussia, on the one side, but it also gave France new leverage to force Hamburg to accredit its new diplomatic envoy, on the other. Newly arrived, Charles Frédéric Reinhard moved quickly to establish himself, insinuating himself into Sieveking's circle. Actually, he moved into Sieveking's house in Neumühlen and married a Reimarus daughter with the provost of Altona presiding.

Everyone hoped that with the new treaty, peace would return to Europe, dissipating tensions in the neutral ports. That did not come to pass. Instead, the German empire redoubled its efforts to pressure the independent German city to rebuff French overtures while strengthening ties with the rest of the empire. At the same time, the French pushed for recognition of their revolutionary government.[36] The Danes did not blink, holding themselves out as the one truly neutral country in Europe besides Sweden.

There were arguments to be made on all sides. Büsch, the economist, reminded the Hamburg Senate of the commercial interests that fueled the city's prosperity. Hamburg could not afford to snub France. Without armies of its own, the independent city-state could not mount a defense if France attacked. From the other side, J. L. Hess, a proponent of free trade, countered with a moral defense of "the precarious liberty of weak states" and a stand in favor of solidifying Hamburg's position in the German empire.[37] Hamburg and Altona remained caught in the middle, a not uncommon posture of neutral governments, especially small ones.

Reinhard did solve one domestic diplomatic dilemma within Sieveking's circle. The daughter of Sophie and J. A. H. Reimarus, Christine, had recently been extracted from a relationship with a German physician, best known for his involvement in the concerted effort to free the Marquis de Lafayette from an Austrian Moravian prison. That attempt, although widely and well funded, failed when the prisoners rode the wrong way away from the prison on horseback. Christine's family was furious about the ill-advised affair. Shortly after, Reinhard, new to the scene and seven years older than Christine, courted her. She seemed to find him sufficiently inoffensive. The Reimarus and Sieveking circles were immensely relieved when Christine Reimarus and Charles Frédéric Reinhard married.

From the standpoint of the young bride and her diplomatic husband, their residence amid family and friends with frequent dinners at Neumühlen was ideal. Reinhard's secretary, Georg Kerner, a former Strasbourg medical student who joined them in residence, described the "festivity and generous hospitality."[38] The marriage did not turn out to be a happy one, but it gave Christine entrée into elite circles across Europe. She later reminisced in a nostalgic letter to her mother that her fondest memories were of singing verses on 14 July while raising a glass to "the whole earth."[39]

The Sievekings' Bastille Day celebration expanded from a private to a public festival under the guidance of French officials, with hundreds of people coming to plant a liberty tree in 1797. The crowd proceeded to the water's edge and boarded two ships, captained by French diplomats Charles Frédéric Reinhard and Philippe Lagau, to spend a pleasant day under tricolored flags. "The day was one of the most beautiful that could be wished for," Kerner commented. "The sun by its majestic brilliance contributed to the splendor of the festivities, and all of nature seemed to be smiling on this celebration of liberty."[40] Amid the cheering for the French republic, assembled guests listened to patriotic songs composed by French journalist Charles André Mercier. Chapeaurouge hosted the festivities in 1799.[41]

Christine Reimarus Reinhard, 720–11 215, R 741 [D]. Courtesy of the Staatsarchiv Hamburg.

Reinhard idealized the freedom of the city and the friendship of the Sieveking-Reimarus circle. He embraced Hamburg as his third homeland, next to France and his native Württenberg. A student of philosophy and theology and a convinced adherent of revolution, at least in theory, Reinhard was skeptical of the French Revolution as steered by the Jacobins. That said, he was no moderate Girondin, either. He had befriended the philosopher the Marquis de Condorcet, the philosopher, and conversed with the legendary diplomat Charles Talleyrand and the Abbé Sieyès, the revolutionary French author, in Condorcet's Paris salon. When Reinhard accepted a position as Talleyrand's aide in the French diplomatic corps, he realized that meant "renouncing my Fatherland and voting for France forever."[42] In many ways, his move out of Paris allowed his allegiance to shift to a less demanding and more outward-looking patriotism in Hamburg.

When Reinhard was away on travels, Christine wrote to remind him of the warmth that awaited him among friends, from Reinhold to Klopstock to Poel to Sieveking, all of whom rejoiced at news of French revolutionary victories.[43] Their biggest problem for the extended family, as it was for other French sympathizers in Hamburg, was the royalist émigrés. One evening Reinhard chased away a group of counterrevolutionaries who were breaking into the Reinhard house and drove them into the river. In 1798, the otherwise pleasant idyll in Hamburg came to an end as Reinhard was posted abroad. This time, it was the French, not the Hamburg Senate, that sent their envoy packing. Reinhard seemed to have gotten too close to the Hamburg circles. Members of the French Directory, like the Jacobins before them, did not trust what they saw as divided loyalties.

"Asylum to all Parties"

The Senate of Hamburg struggled to contain the exuberance of Hamburg republicans and to limit the impact of the merchants' connections to the French. New regulations required that foreigners staying in guest houses be registered.[44] A visiting Austrian businessman was surprised that sympathy for the French in Hamburg and Altona did not seem to have abated, even with the Terror.[45] What he missed was that while no strong reaction was provoked in Hamburg against the French Revolution, French violence had reinforced Hamburgers' loyalty to their own moderate republican institutions. The differences bolstered their sense of superiority and reinforced their civic cosmopolitanism.

French diplomatic envoys were emboldened to build liaisons with republicans in the port cities. They extended their influence, even at the risk of offending their hosts. In Altona, republicans organized an explicitly named "Jakobinerklub echter Republikaner zu Altona" (Jacobin Club of True Republicans of Altona). Altona's reputation drew radicals from across northern Germany to the Danish city. Baron Binder von Kriegelstein, an Austrian diplomat, reported that the membership grew daily, perhaps, he suggested snidely, as a result of the free lunch offered at the meetings convened in a hostel on the Altona town square. In pamphlets and handwritten notes posted throughout town, the Altona Jacobins called on fellow Danes "to exterminate their monarchy" by denying the unpopular king, Christian VII, his right to inheritance. They denounced aristocrats as "scum" and "court thieves."[46] Quoting from Thomas Paine's *The Rights of Man*, they cited the Americans as a model for ridding society of both kings and aristocrats. Usually, allusions to the Americans rather than the French signaled moderation, but not in this case.

The Oberpräsident of Altona, who was responsible for the public safety and order in the city, dutifully forwarded their leaflets to the Chancellery in Copenhagen. He was convinced that the Altona Jacobins were in contact with radicals in Hamburg and with Masonic lodges active in both cities.[47] The Prussians speculated that the French were at the bottom of it all.

It was not that simple, as shown by the widespread support in Hamburg among the strongest proponents of the French Revolution for one of the most notorious of all French revolutionary defectors, the Marquis de Lafayette. Efforts to spring the French aristocratic hero of the American Revolution from an Austrian prison after he defected from the French army were coordinated from Hamburg. Once freed and living in an estate in Holstein, just north of the city, Lafayette maintained his connections with émigrés and citizens alike in Hamburg and Altona. A spy reporting to the prefect in Hamburg alleged in April 1797 that on a certain Thursday evening thirty-six people, all constitutional monarchists, had been invited to a dinner celebrating Lafayette.[48] He did not show, but that seems to have had no effect on his allure. He remained a hero, a reputation bolstered by exile, first in Wittmoldt on his wife's aunt's estate in Danish Holstein, where he farmed, read, and entertained other refugees, and after February 1799 in Vianen, south of Utrecht. Neither France nor America would let him return to their shores.

Even Georg Kerner, personal secretary to Reinhard, realized the Terror had alienated moderates in the two ports. He appreciated that "the city of Hamburg is one of the points in Europe where foreigners from all countries come together," adding, "There are many interested, educated people in this city who need to be won over to our cause." That task was made much more difficult by the "thousands of emigrants, whose obsession is as great as their misery, and many of whom, far from improvement, still serve abroad to provoke turmoil in France."[49] Kerner's presence alarmed French émigrés, it turns out, with good reason.

In April 1797, Kerner organized the Philanthropic Society, naming himself president. Johan Heinrich de Chaufepié, a French doctor of Huguenot descent, served as secretary. Kerner felt much more at home here than in the circle frequented by Reinhard, which revolved around Sieveking and Reimarus. In the society, he was surrounded by French patriots and friends of liberty as he defined it.[50] Founded on the model of French "théophilanthropie," an esoteric Paris society whose followers subscribed to a rational religion, the Hamburg group carefully disavowed any religious unorthodoxy, a nonstarter in Lutheran Hamburg.

Members addressed each other as "citizen" and gathered every Thursday around an altar under the banner "Truth and Right."[51] Their regulations cited the need to "strengthen and solidify to win over all the Republicans in a common cause and to silence the opponents."[52] They publicly proclaimed their goal to be that of serving humanity by bringing together enlightened men in the cause of republican freedom. By the summer of 1797, there were twenty members—not a sizeable number—including the secretary of the French commercial delegation, a Dutch diplomat stationed in Hamburg, and the radical French journalist Charles André Mercier, brother of the more famous playwright, Sebastien Mercier. Local members included Jacques Chapeaurouge and Chaim Salomon Pappenheimer, a Jewish merchant who had accompanied Sieveking on his Paris mission. Beginning in French, by the end of the year they were keeping their records in German. Was there significance to the switch?

Although they did nothing in secret and sent tickets for admission to their detractors, this small group of men attracted attention from near and far. A Frenchman in attendance was reported to have denounced kings as crowned thieves and Hamburg senators as small tyrants. The Senate got worried, especially after an informant brought to its attention a long list of French Jacobins residing in Hamburg. It sent an agent to visit the Philanthropic Society to inquire into connections with revolutionary France. Kerner and the other officers reported that when they were questioned, it was with civility. But how ridiculous, he argued, that "in a free and republican state," they should not be allowed "to cultivate the principles and maxims of liberty?"[53] As in other societies in the free city, they read newspapers and discussed serious political questions. No well-constituted republic should have any reason to fear their law-abiding society, Kerner added.

Hamburg was widely known for its free press; the *Hamburgische Correspondent* had three times as many readers as the *London Times*. However, when Friedrich Wilhelm von Schütz, at the same time secretary to the French diplomat Lehoc and editor of the *Hamburger Merkur*, proclaimed the paper's support for the French Revolution, Hamburg banned the paper. The city government cited the need to preserve its neutrality. Following the shipping companies, the paper just moved to Altona. There, the *Altonaer Merkur*, published by the Sievekings' co-proprietor, Piter Poel, made openly hostile remarks about the aristocratic émigrés who enjoyed the hospitality of the open port cities.[54] Other newspapers including, *Minerva* and the *Niedersächsische Merkur*, sarcastically expressed their pity for the emigrants who had lost their titles and who "longed for the old despotism."[55]

It was difficult to ignore these political debates among the visiting French, especially in the theaters and at the opera. A twenty-five-person French theater company, forced to flee Brussels in 1794, made its way to Hamburg. Diplomats had their loges, and émigrés organized themed balls around the evening entertainment, all with local residents in attendance. During a production of *Richard the Lionhearted*, monarchists and revolutionaries in the audience reportedly came to blows.[56] Similarly, the opera, performing three times a week, drew nobles and prosperous merchants, refugees and citizens alike. Sophie Albrecht, a German poet and actress, started a democratic theater in Altona. Advocating republican equality and freedom, the point of the troupe's plays was to agitate. They did that, often setting émigrés against local residents or émigrés arguing with each other.[57] Journalists and actors who lived around Rainville's Garten café or hung out around the theater in Altona were said to be particularly dangerous because they were so well connected, so radical, and so adept at convincing others.

The Prussians and the Austrians both had their own spies with free run of the port cities. They served as the ever-watchful eyes of the Prussian ambassador, von Göchhausen, who was particularly interested in any gatherings of alleged Jacobin sympathizers, especially those festivities held on the French revolutionary anniversaries of 14 July and 10 August. These spies and foreign agents, Kerner charged, initiated lies and poisoned the atmosphere of Hamburg with its open borders. There were so many spies dispatched by all of the neighboring countries, including France, that the most notorious subjects of the reporting apparently came to recognize the spies because of their omnipresence.

One particularly active informant was paid by the prefect in Hamburg to watch "dangerous Frenchmen and women" whom he described as "the worst possible subjects." He classified some as Jacobins, others as ultra-Jacobins. The Philanthropic Society was of particular concern for him, though he lumped it together with the long-standing Patriotic Society and the Hamburger Lesegesellschaft. The informant positioned himself to overhear incendiary rhetoric and to intercept plots in all of these gatherings. In February 1798, he reported that French diplomats stationed in Hamburg had invited all the French republicans with the goal of establishing a "Patriotic Club." He heard they had decided not to recruit local residents. The Hamburg Senate responded to the reports by banning all assemblies that challenged governing authorities and admonishing foreigners in the city to avoid criticizing the governments of Hamburg and the empire.

Rainville's café on the Elbe River, 1795.511. Rainville Abbema Hansen, History and Art Collection/Alamy Stock Photo.

The spy was more concerned in his reports with outsiders than with the citizens of Hamburg. He gave their names and, when possible, their occupations and the address of their lodgings. Most of the ones he encountered and followed were staying at a small set of hotels, but others lodged with individuals. Some were just passing through, and others had come for the duration. A surprising number of French revolutionary sympathizers seemed always to be in motion. Hamburg and Altona offered temporary respite from the road. One woman who traveled incessantly, the prefect's spy reported, had just come back from Austria and France, where she dressed as a man. While in Hamburg, she visited the houses of both émigrés and republicans, always talking politics. When asked why she did not stay in France if she agreed with the revolutionary republic's politics, she answered that she traveled to understand other places. She had heard that "the city of Hamburg offers asylum to all parties who will submit to the wise laws of the land and who do not trouble the public order."[58] In this sense, the revolutionary refugees of all political stripes had been drawn to the ports by the same lure: tolerance and freedom of expression and trade, even if that brought them into conflict with one another.

Most of the spy's subjects of interest were French, a number having been expelled from asylum in England, but some had fought in other revolutions, including the Brabant Revolution in the Belgian provinces. A few had come via Jersey, one of the English Channel Islands. Their boats more often landed in Altona than Hamburg. To make it easier to enter Hamburg and blend in, they reportedly wore the typical round hats. Other émigrés had traveled to the Brabant, to Liège, to Cologne, to Munster, to Dusseldorf, and to Frankfurt. They moved among counterrevolutionaries in a diaspora that stretched across the Atlantic world.

In February 1797, a Hamburg Senate informant heard that there was to be an insurrection in the German city and that all the bourgeois and honest men should gather under the flags of the bourgeoisie. He got the details from a French émigré who played violin in the orchestra of the Comédie. Another musician had heard that a French émigré had been offered money to lead the uprising. That émigré apparently had refused.[59] Although the information led to a dead end, the informant continued to follow his subjects in and out of numerous cabarets. He also ventured into gardens and listened in on conversations. One Frenchman was overheard predicting that soon France would show Hamburg what it meant to be truly republican. Within five years none of the so-called free German cities would still be independent, this subject added.[60] The partisan declarations of another Frenchman would have revolted friends of good order, the informant, never one to hold back in his judgments, observed.[61] Some of the most dangerous suspects allegedly went nowhere without pistols. They were judged capable of starting an insurrection, even if they dressed, for the most part, as bourgeois. The informant reported on duels and brawls they provoked in the cafés he monitored, especially Rainville's café, which seemed to be infested with Frenchmen out of step with the politics of Hamburg and Altona.

The informant reported with alarm on potential plots, but he also lauded and recorded conversations about the wisdom with which Hamburg was governed. One new arrival from the Belgian provinces initiated what the informant thought was an intelligent discussion of the 1789 grievance petitions submitted to the French Estates General. The Hamburg Senate's informant also passed along reports that came to him from other spies, noting that he could not be everywhere at the same time, especially behind the closed doors of private houses. From time to time, he warned that he was not sure of the truth of what he had overheard.

In early December 1797, the informant learned that the Senate had compiled a list of dangerous individuals and groups to be prohibited. In January 1798, other countries, including Spain, suggested that given all this intelligence, the Senate "in all its wisdom" should set a date to expel foreigners.[62] The Senate did not. The two port cities assiduously held onto their reputation for open doors. The Oberpräsident of Altona and Senate of Hamburg had done their best through the last decade of the eighteenth century to placate their larger, warring neighbors while resisting the pressure to expel refugees perceived to endanger public order.

Cosmopolitanism, Luxury, and Revolution

In 1795, the enlightened philosopher Immanuel Kant of Königsberg, another city at another crossroads in northern Europe, defined cosmopolitanism as the welcome extended to strangers. Their doors wide open, Hamburg and Altona welcomed immigrants throughout the revolutionary turmoil that had convinced their larger neighbors to patrol and limit traffic across their borders. Many residents of the two cities traveled widely themselves and felt at home abroad. Travel broadened their perspective and confirmed their commitment to their own corner of the world. Like the French editor of the *Encyclopédie*, the Enlightenment philosopher Denis Diderot, they aspired to be "strangers nowhere in the world."[63] Cosmopolitanism was interwoven into the fabric of their civic culture. The cities followed the lead of the infamous Prussian baron-turned-French-revolutionary, Anacharsis Cloots, in rejecting the derisive category of "foreigners" as "a barbarous expression."[64]

As the decade of revolutionary wars dragged on, the onslaught of immigrants challenged the cosmopolitan convictions of the port cities. Residents steeped in what they celebrated as revolutionary civility worried about the corrosive influence of what they derided as "troublesome individualism." Introduced by the luxurious tastes of the émigrés, this preoccupation with material wealth had been exacerbated by the speculation of war. Consumerism had seeped in from the outside, essayists concluded, introduced by the aristocrats fleeing in France and then fed by the merchants drawn to the ports by the profits to be made through speculation.

The presence of what had become an overwhelming crowd of refugees, making up almost 10 percent of the population in both cities, added a new accent to the discussion of the nature of freedom, law, and duty in a republican polity. For the governing circles, the aristocratic values of the émigrés posed a serious threat. Two centuries later, societies offering asylum to refugees would worry instead about the influence of the religion and customs of the poorest migrants arriving at their borders from North Africa and Central America.

Prices rose in both cities through the last decade of the eighteenth century, especially in housing, because of the increased demand. Absorbing thousands of refugees, whether aristocrats without resources or merchants engaged in trading firms, placed enormous pressure on the supply of accommodation. Rents increased substantially in Hamburg but also in smaller Altona.

Manual laborers and artisans, firmly rooted in the port cities, were the most affected by the inflation, but they had no representation. In the summer of 1795, protests against the high prices making their lives so difficult escalated into riots. Three men lost their lives. The cause, as identified by the Hamburg Senate, was the influx of foreigners. The widely read journal *Der Totenrichter* blamed French immigrants for the high cost of food and rent, complaining that "the poorer burghers have become even poorer." The journal also observed that the benefits of the increase in trade flowed into just a "few coffers."[65] The target of blame was obvious to readers, as were the reasons for the intensifying criticism of the cities' open-door policy.

Although politically opposed to each other in the debate over the French Revolution, the two groups of immigrants to Hamburg and Altona together contributed to what was condemned by the local burghers as corrosive luxury. Their economic interests converged in consumption. Often settling on estates in Holstein, just outside of Hamburg, wealthy merchants, many newly arrived, encouraged a market for French table linens, English mahogany furniture, glassware and French porcelain, Wedgewood, antiques, and silk dresses. Shopkeepers in Hamburg lived off the handsome commissions. The influx of goods, especially from the colonies, contributed to the fortunes of merchants and the profusion of available goods. The preoccupation with obsessive consumption seemed to have local causes, but it was part of the consumption revolution that marked the end of the eighteenth century in general.

Hamburgers and Danes, in harmony with a pervasive late-eighteenth-century rhetoric, pointed to the corrosive effects of consumption on their civic values. From the arrival of the first émigrés, Georg Sieveking had criticized luxury as a threat to their civic republic in his brochure, *Fragmenten*. But he also recognized luxury as "a powerful force that drives useful activity." In Hamburg and Altona, cosmopolitanism and commerce went hand in hand. "It is valuable for the state and for individuals when they can fulfill their desires without neglecting their higher duties," he concluded.[66] Republican virtue coexisted with and was bolstered by commercial prosperity. In the port cities, commerce offered not only material possibilities, but also laid the groundwork for the exchange of ideas and understanding that promised a more peaceful world. Not everyone agreed. Discussions of materialism exposed a paradox at the core of the eighteenth-century definition of cosmopolitanism. Entrepreneurial merchants such as John Parish and Jacques Chapeaurouge assimilated into the mix that made up the trade-oriented cities. Little distinguished the economic possibilities of a citizen of long-standing from these newcomers. They resembled the residents. Not so in the case of the aristocratic émigrés, who wore out their welcome. Fortunately for the port cities, aristocrats seem to have taken Kant at his word that hospitality granted the right to visit but not settle. Most of them had left by 1798.

The aristocrats proved incapable of adapting to life in Hamburg. Senators charged with regulating immigration claimed to recognize the difference between stereotypical "fripons," the knaves caricatured in contemporary literature, and real-life émigrés sheltering in their city. These Hamburg burghers nevertheless deplored the aristocrats' inability to succeed in professional life in Hamburg and their unwillingness to socialize with the bourgeoisie. Sophie Reimarus condemned them in general, with the exception of the republican-leaning Madame de Genlis, as corrupt and stupid.[67] The Senate's spy corroborated that image when he investigated how aristocrats were scrounging a living. He reported with disdain his discovery that five distribution points to dispense charity to the displaced aristocrats had been set up in the city. The aristocrats did not adapt to port city politics, and instead they tried to convince their hosts of the superiority of the former French monarchy.

These aristocrats in exile revealed the limits of their own definition of cosmopolitanism. Most of them had traveled widely even before the French Revolution set them in perpetual motion. They continued to correspond incessantly, if the letters preserved over the decades are any indication, seemingly without regard to borders. With few exceptions, however, they refused to adapt to their new surroundings. They did not fit in comfortably either in Hamburg or Altona. By the end of the decade, although they were not denied entrance at the city gates, the doors to houses of citizens celebrating Bastille Day had definitely closed, excluding them.

Unlike the all-embracing and universal welcome extended for a short time by revolutionary France, the cosmopolitanism of Hamburg and Altona persevered, restricted only by the assumption that immigrants could contribute responsibly to the port cities. The hospitality on offer was therefore neither inclusive nor all-embracing. The cosmopolitanism of commercial connections negotiated in Hamburg and Altona fell short of the universalism that underpinned French revolutionary nationalism. And that may have been a positive thing. The proponents of civic republicanism in the port cities did not force others outside of their cities to embrace their values as universal. In many ways, theirs was a more modest proposal, locally rooted at a diplomatic and commercial crossroads.

Rather than setting out to alter history as did the French revolutionaries, Hamburg and Altona pursued the more limited goal of surviving the revolutionary era and prospering from the surrounding tumult. Openness to the outside world was key to that survival and their prosperity. They did both, at least until the French revolutionary armies invaded, extending Napoleon's empire in the first years of the nineteenth century, known to European historians as the century of nations.

CHAPTER FOUR

"The Right Papers" in a World of Nations

THE EVOLVING POLITICS OF new nations in the transitional era between revolutions had significant consequences on the far side of their borders and beyond their time. In the aftermath of the French Revolution and its wars, new nation-states attended to citizens within. They deliberately demarcated borders, separating their realms from those of their neighbors and avidly drawing boundaries between their own citizens and others. Yet men, women, and children, propelled by visions of a better life, continued in the nineteenth century, as they had during the American and French revolutions, to cross political borders separating one nation from the next.

The political unrest and agricultural failures of the first half of the nineteenth century produced tides of migration in numbers exceeding "the refugee crisis" of the late eighteenth century. Short-lived revolutions sent political refugees fleeing for safety across national borders while stunted crops and the halting pace of industrialization drove laborers and entrepreneurs abroad in search of improved economic opportunities. These refugees, mostly intellectuals and artisans, came from backgrounds markedly different from those of the aristocrats and merchants who had sought asylum in Hamburg and Altona. They carried with them ideas that did not reinforce the public spirit of the communities that offered them shelter from the storms in the rest of Europe, as the eighteenth-century immigrants had. Instead, refugees fleeing failed nineteenth-century revolutions introduced radical proposals that threatened to disrupt the political equilibrium of the neutral nations, such as the Swiss cantons, that took them in. The Swiss had every reason to send these refugees on their way but rarely did until the diplomatic pressure from their neighbors could not be ignored.

In these transitional decades, states introduced the paperwork and governmental bureaucracy to monitor and limit both emigration and immigration. Nations across Europe flexed their muscles, little limited by an outmoded and much disputed corpus of international law that agreed only on the sovereignty of nation-states. However, even if governments aspired to control migration in the decades following Napoleon's wars in Europe and the Caribbean, relatively porous borders and the acceleration of accessible transport hindered their ambition to restrict exits and entries for workers and artisans, as for merchants and scholars.

Arguments for asylum based on the Enlightenment-defined individual right of free movement ran headlong into the assertion of national sovereignty, also based on principles of revolutionary liberty. Throughout these decades of experimentation, authorities repeatedly recalibrated the balance between individual rights and national security. Their rebalancing was not always incremental. New restrictions were followed by periods of liberalization. Immigration debates were intense and acrimonious at all governmental levels. Very few political leaders advocated a world without borders guaranteeing free passage between nations. The question was more often posed, as it would be over the next centuries, about whom to admit and whom to exclude.

What, then, of foreigners caught abroad, whether driven from home by hunger, civil unrest, or a hostile political regime? These refugees in search of a safe place to settle after the American and French revolutions found offers of asylum fewer and farther between. They had become aliens, defined as non-nationals in a world increasingly populated and governed by nation-states.[1] Excluded from one community but not welcomed into another, refugees suffered what Hannah Arendt identified as "the loss of belonging."[2] As an ideal, natural rights were universal; in the nineteenth century, however, it became all too clear that this sense of belonging depended on the hospitality of nation-states.

The newly independent American and French republics went to substantial lengths to contrast their national citizenship as a consensual relationship with the allegiance subjects owed their monarch. Before the

American and French revolutions, nationality had not been all that important because subjects of a monarch or an emperor typically identified as residents of a locality. The municipality that doled out services functioned as the customary site of citizenship.

Although the term "citizens" has often been used more loosely to refer to the residents of a nation, regardless of their legal status, formally it continues to denote individuals who share in the rights and responsibilities of governance. President James Madison's secretary of the treasury defined American citizenship as "a political tie, . . . the effect of a compact," as opposed to the older allegiance to a monarch, which was "the offspring of power and necessity."[3] Patriotism also played a significant role in the French definition.[4]

Suspicions of foreigners coursed through these debates over citizenship on both sides of the Atlantic at the turn of the nineteenth century. A French deputy assured his compatriots that political rights would be extended to foreigners only when "the republic was entirely certain of their love for it."[5] As nations attempted to solidify their control over their territory within expanding borders, successive governments continued to institute measures to distinguish nationals from non-nationals using the growing collection of tools at hand.

Protective of their sovereignty, early nineteenth-century states guaranteed the political civil rights they defined for their own citizens—meaning independent white male heads of households. Most also specified religion. Excluded from this realm of rights were not only women, children, persons of color, and persons without property, but also aliens seeking refuge. *Patriotismus*, or patriotic pride in self-government and commercial prosperity, had been as inclusive as it was cosmopolitan in Altona and Hamburg. In the first decades of the nineteenth century, that patriotism would turn inward for most, but not all, nations confronting what seemed to them overwhelming waves of immigration.

"We Have No Inhabitants to Spare": Emigration and Immigration

Contrary to the expectations of many philosophers at the time, the nationalism that had reared up so aggressively to counter enemies during the wars of the French Revolution did not dissipate but remained a determining force in international relations. The quintessential nineteenth-century liberal, John Stuart Mill, questioned this inward-directed protectionism, asking rhetorically why anyone would prefer "to sulk on his own rocks, the half-savage relic of past times, revolving in his own little mental orbit, without participation or interest in the general movement of the world?"[6] Why would any reasonable individual choose to restrict their vision to the borders defining a nation? Even though philosophers and governments offered alternatives that reworked Enlightenment cosmopolitanism as it had existed in Hamburg and Altona, nationalism continued to strengthen, reinforced by other nineteenth-century movements, even including liberalism.

Movement across borders became suspect. National governments exerting sovereignty over their territories contested the mobility previously recognized as a universal natural right, at least by philosophers. During the American and French revolutions, to leave home and seek shelter across a border came to carry a political meaning. Loyalists, Black and white, escaping independent America and its slave-holding founders, headed not only north to Nova Scotia and south to the Caribbean, but east across the Atlantic. The Continental Congress claimed them as Americans despite their uncertain loyalty; the right to expatriate voluntarily remained under dispute into the nineteenth century.

Emigration rather than immigration was originally the most pressing problem for governments that did not want usefully employed people to leave. Chief Justice Oliver Ellsworth in 1799 described America as "but sparsely settled," arguing, "We have no inhabitants to spare."[7] The manpower demands of decades of war and revolution at the turn of the nineteenth century reinforced that understanding, causing many European states to continue to limit emigration.[8]

Émigrés deserting revolutionary France encapsulated governments' worst fears of the conspiratorial intentions of those who left. The French Constituent Assembly condemned fleeing aristocrats as counterrevolutionaries "who undermine the internal and external security of the State, and consequently the integrity of the nation."[9] French revolutionary legislation first authorized the seizure of the property of emigrants and then, in 1793, banned emigration altogether as a war crime under penalty of death.

German states levied taxes and fees on emigrants. They also routinely denied passports to their own subjects who were planning to leave unless they could give evidence that their destination country would admit them. New regulations passed in 1817 liberalized earlier restrictions, giving local, border, and port officials the authority to issue immigration documents.

The government of the Swiss canton of the Vaud disseminated a pamphlet aimed at potential emigrants, warning them that the economic crisis they were experiencing locally was global.[10] It could not be escaped by leaving the canton. Swiss liberals in particular considered emigration a loss. Other governments allowed only paupers and the marginally employed to leave for other shores.

"Refugees" at the time thus commonly referred to poverty-stricken workers and hapless political exiles, quite different from the exiles seeking asylum a few decades earlier in Hamburg and Altona. For impoverished or imperiled individuals and families who sought opportunities elsewhere, the search for asylum during this turbulent transitional period between revolutions was not often easy. Some nations demanded that migrants furnish statements of good conduct, as well as verification that the home municipality would take them back if they did not secure a position sufficient to support themselves abroad. What contemporaries called "pauperism" limited states' willingness to take in immigrants. Even states open to immigration were able to be selective when it came to newcomers.

One of the chief motivating factors in Britain limiting immigration was legislation stipulating that a "stranger" who settled in a local parish could be entitled to poor relief. Local officials in Britain were not alone in worrying that indigent travelers would become a public burden on municipalities during difficult times. Concerned about poor-relief burdens in their cities, the Belgians, otherwise known for their open borders, refused entry to Dutch citizens they doubted could support themselves. Few countries, however, turned away seasonal laborers with a workbook. Entrepreneurs were always welcome.

Almost no one made it possible for any of these immigrants to become citizens with full access to political as well as civil rights. Eligibility for citizenship in the first half of the nineteenth century by and large depended on descent within national borders. Very few nation-states carried on the tradition of Hamburg and Altona from the end of the eighteenth century by extending economic and social rights to newly arrived residents who might potentially contribute to their prosperous communities.

At the time, naturalization was the most obvious path followed by aliens seeking national citizenship. In 1790, the U.S. Congress passed the Naturalization Act, setting residency and character requirements for new citizens; these requirements and possibilities would ebb and flow over time depending on domestic politics. The tightening and loosening of terms for naturalization, however, made a difference only for white men. As long as political citizens were required to be independent property owners, most

Native Americans and African Americans were automatically disenfranchised. So, too, were women.

In the midst of their revolution, however, the French opened a wider path to citizenship, offering foreigners who had participated in the French Revolution a stake in the new nation. After five years of residence in France, aliens who swore a civic oath to France would enjoy all the rights of "active citizens," as long as they also established themselves in business or agriculture, purchased real estate, became burghers of a town, or married a French woman. These utility-based restrictions were liberalized in 1793, only to be tightened again in 1795. In the new French republic, as in the United States, citizenship requirements reflected the needs of manpower in forging a new nation.[11]

Until 1798 in Britain, immigrants could petition Parliament for a private act to become naturalized—obviously a very expensive option reserved for the elite. Thereafter, new citizens also required a certificate from the Home Office, though most applications were successful. Between 1811 and 1818, that changed. Under the guise of the preservation of law and order, few foreigners were naturalized because the incoming home secretary, Viscount Sidmouth, viewed most foreigners as potential revolutionaries. His restrictive policies ultimately came under attack in Parliament as arbitrary when wealthy merchants were turned down.[12] Two decades later, the Aliens Restriction Act of 1836 required non-nationals to present their passport at their port of entry and subjected travelers without a passport to interrogation and possible expulsion. Otherwise, Britain remained relatively open to all foreigners between 1826 and 1905, with some exceptions.

In the German states, variation was the rule. Each of the states had experienced the French revolutionary wars differently, with the only constant being the continual shifting of control and a redrawing of territorial borders. Naturalization was not an issue in Prussia as residents were subjects belonging to hierarchical orders, not equal citizens. In Bavaria, the 1808 constitution distinguished a category of active citizens, or *Staatsbürgers*. Permanent male residents born abroad who were twenty-one years old, economically independent, and Catholic, Lutheran, or Calvinist also qualified as long as they renounced allegiance to the country of their birth.

In France, not surprisingly, the Napoleonic regime centralized the process of naturalization and separated civil from political rights, including voting. The Civil Code of 1803 defined citizenship by blood rather than soil, limiting it to the descendants of male citizens. The path to citizenship opened again early in 1849, only to be replaced after suppression of the revolution by much more restrictive legislation.[13] Restrictions on immigration, like emigration, responded to economic needs and political anxieties.

The connections and contradictions between individual freedom of movement and the security of the state played out in the development of passports. In early modern Europe, passports were employed to control internal movement between cities or regions within a diffuse territory. Formerly a barrier to national integration, at the turn of the nineteenth century passports were repurposed to enable governments to demarcate national boundaries and differentiate citizens from foreigners. However, it was not until World War I that passports assumed their modern physical form. In the nineteenth century, they tended to be folio size, with a coat of arms at the head, followed by a physical description to introduce and identify the holder. For security, some had watermarks.

The instability of relations between warring nations and concern for national security in the 1790s contributed significantly to the evolution of the modern passport system.[14] Worried by all the foreigners arriving in revolutionary France, one Breton bishop pleaded for a passport system that would function as "the Argus of the patrie," referring to the monster with many eyes reputed to be a reliable watchman.[15] States that had worried more about internal migration and about emigration of useful laborers grew more concerned with immigration across their external borders.

Passports served to document the identity of new arrivals. The Swiss employed passports as official government identity documents, "conveying all the customary formalities" previously established by other residents living nearby.[16] Even without photos, as identity documents they functioned where an individual was not known, serving abroad as a kind of recommendation or witness to good character.

Modern passports helped the state to monitor the entry of aliens and the exit of citizens. They also allowed states to scrutinize individuals and to register and track them within their sovereign territories. For individuals, they established identity and gave permission to travel. Over time, passports lost their status as travel permits and were more likely to be considered as official state documents tied to formal citizenship. With significant variations from one country to another, the passport systems that differentiated strangers from residents developed as tools of exclusion rather than inclusion.[17]

While some states developed bureaucratic mechanisms to chart the movement of aliens across their borders, others—notably Great Britain and the United States—did not. Some states attempted to exert control at their frontiers, while others checked new arrivals at the point of settlement, both hoping to remove those who posed a security threat or required financial assistance. Driven by the same fears, in 1793 the British passed the Alien Act, authorizing the expulsion of undesirable aliens. A precautionary measure to limit the influence of French revolutionaries in Britain, it was also a reaction to émigrés from France who had sought shelter in London. In the United States, the Alien Acts of 1798, supported by John Adams as "war measures," allowed the American president to deport aliens considered dangerous or coming from enemy nations. Together with the Sedition Acts, which authorized the punishment of individuals defaming or otherwise attacking either the Congress or the president of the United States, they were signed into law on 14 July, the anniversary of the French storming of the Bastille.

In 1813, William III of Prussia demanded a new passport system, arguing that the survival of the crown depended on it. All immigrants were to be required to obtain a passport from Berlin; the Prussians did not trust the passports issued by travelers' home countries. Diplomats were exempted but not workers and artisans, who elsewhere relied on their work or journey books. Inside Prussia, foreigners were subjected to intense surveillance by security forces, innkeepers, and transport operators.

In France, under Napoleon, the Parisian police sent a daily report to the Interior Ministry, giving information on the identity of all arrivals in the capital, identifying their residence, their reasons for travel, and the expected length of their stay. The police also noted all travelers who left Paris with a visa. Marginal notes in the archived files indicate that the police reports were read closely by national authorities. In Marseille after a police raid of furnished apartments frequented by poorer immigrants, the police lamented that not one of the residents was carrying "the right papers."[18] The French government responded by intensifying instructions issued to local officials and regulating the paper and printing of passports so as to assure uniformity. Economic and political migration were closely intertwined in government regulation. Meanwhile, refugees arrived by the thousands from Portugal, Spain, and Italy in the first decades of the nineteenth century, later from Germany and Poland.

In 1831, the French put border guards in place to restrict the movement of travelers without independent means. Foreigners arriving at the French border had to leave their national passports at the city hall of the first town they entered. These documents were forwarded to the Interior Ministry, where they were stamped with a visa and returned to the travelers. French legislation in 1832 was the first to refer to "*étrangers réfugiés*," or "foreign refugees," who merited individual police dossiers. French law subsequently prohibited foreign political refugees from settling in Paris or other large French cities. Local police in the provinces watched new arrivals, especially political refugees, deserters from the military, and poorer laborers.[19] Surveilling lodging houses and cafés, hotel keepers considered themselves as auxiliaries of the police. To reinforce local police, spies and multilingual agents were hired to keep an eye on men that one prefect labeled as "amateur troublemakers . . . animated by fanaticism [and] hoping to demonstrate their ardor in a new revolution."[20] On their radar were exiles from the Polish revolutions who they feared would join with French republicans to sow discord. Even for a short stay, Poles had to receive permission to reside from the Interior Ministry.[21]

France was by no means alone in increasing border control over the course of the nineteenth century. French regulations directly influenced the Dutch introduction of passports, especially during the French occupation of the Netherlands between 1795 and 1813. A law in 1813 advised Dutch citizens to obtain a passport issued by the Ministry of Foreign Affairs before they traveled abroad.[22] Even with passport in hand, the Dutch were not allowed to leave if they had any outstanding obligations to the state. Foreigners visiting the Netherlands were required to have their passports initialed by the Dutch government, although aliens already residing in the Netherlands were exempted from passport regulations and enjoyed many of the same rights as citizens. Lodging house keepers were required to report all aliens staying with them. Actual enforcement varied from city to city. In the 1830s, newly independent Belgium also copied many of its immigration laws from France. Central authorities in the small kingdom reminded local police and magistrates that authority to regulate travel by passports resided at the federal level.[23] This contention over policing of foreigners was not uncommon during this transitional period.

After the French July Revolution of 1830, the Dutch turned laws developed by the French against potentially incendiary French travelers by requiring them to present not only a passport, but also a visa. The Dutch did not even require passports from English travelers. Bureaucratic change remained the rule as control of emigration and immigration proved a useful tool to states jockeying on an insecure continent. The variations from one place to another invited diplomatic pressure on the most lenient states with their open doors.

The Swiss Cantons: "Admitting and Harboring Whomever It Pleases"

In the last decades of the eighteenth century, the elite governing Altona and Hamburg had been firmly convinced that open borders and the immigrants who crossed them by carriage, cart, or boat, and even on foot, contributed to their cities' economic prosperity and political stability. In the first decades of the nineteenth century, as most nations tightened their borders, a few states shared these cosmopolitan convictions. They kept doors wide open to all comers. The Swiss Confederation, surrounded as it was by large states, was traversed by important north-south trading routes. With the reputation of open doors, the Swiss cantons received artisans, manual laborers, jurists, and poets, all seeking the freedom to work and some wanting to organize political movements.

In 1798, the Swiss constitution organized the cantons into a unified nation, the Helvetic Republic, modeled on the French revolutionary republic. Although the Swiss geographical territory has remained remarkably constant over the course of modern history, the government of the central institutions joining the thirteen cantons changed radically and often during these revolutionary decades. Swiss legislation governing immigration was transformed with each of the regime changes.

Republican citizenship conveyed rights and liberties, not limited to political participation, but extending to economic opportunities throughout the cantons. Only men with the financial means to render independent judgments qualified. Women were excluded not only from citizenship, but also from all public roles. Notably, the political status of Swiss citizenship explicitly excluded foreigners; they were the "others" left outside the regime of rights. In particular, revolutionary France was determined to rid the Helvetic Republic of enemies of liberty, including thousands of aristocratic émigrés who had taken up residence during the early years of the French Revolution. Foreigners were not only considered non-citizens, but, even worse, they were deemed enemies of the nation.[24] This differentiation was new to the Swiss.

The French commissioner stationed in the Helvetic Republic ordered a series of measures in May 1798 to control the movement of "foreigners, suspects, and vagabonds."[25] According to the regulations, every foreigner who intended to remain for more than one day had to present a passport, "because the foreigner is not known in this country, and there are no respectable citizens who can vouch for him."[26] Obtaining a passport involved the intervention of five authorities: delivery of documents to the residence

Between Lake Geneva and the Alps by Camille Corot, 1825.
Philadelphia Museum of Art, John G. Johnson Collection, cat. 925.
Courtesy of Philadelphia Museum of Art.

by local officials, approval by administrative authorities, verification by national prefects, legalization by an agent of the republic, and visitation from the commander of French troops stationed where the applicant resided.

The French-imposed nationalism, including immigration restrictions, proved a poor fit for the Swiss cantons accustomed to autonomy. These restrictive decrees met a storm of opposition, not only as an abrogation of cantonal independence, but also as an assault on individual liberties. In addition, the Swiss were accustomed to citizenship defined from below, at the communal and cantonal levels.[27] Although guilds had long limited access to trades to families in residence for generations, foreigners who could contribute to the Swiss republic were integrated into local communities. New legislation set naturalization procedures requiring immigrants to establish residency and prove their willingness to conform to Swiss values. The expectation that newcomers would integrate and assimilate by "cultivating the public spirit" echoed the civic republicanism of Hamburg and Altona, which welcomed enterprising merchants and shunned aristocrats and their luxury.[28]

In 1803, Napoleon restored sovereignty to the Swiss cantons, but as the Napoleonic era ended in Europe, the confederation dissolved its ties with France, establishing the Federal Pact of 1815 in conjunction with the Congress of Vienna. Political debates flourished within each of the cantons setting up new governments. Innovative incorporation of liberalism and radicalism merged with dreams still alive among revolutionaries from 1798. Central to the discussions of economic development were immigration and emigration policies. Some cantons tightened protectionist controls in the wake of crop failures in 1816 and 1817, while liberals in other cantons promoted the naturalization of foreigners to build up their industries.

The Federal Pact ended national citizenship, returning the definition of identity to the cantonal level.[29] After 1815, an individual born in an adjoining Swiss canton was considered foreign in the other cantons. The first census in 1850 indicated that 90 percent of the population had never moved in or out of the canton in which they had been born.[30] Foreigners made up 3 percent of the Swiss population at the time, a third from France, 27 percent from Sardinia, and 24 percent from Germany.[31] These percentages were much higher in border cantons: the population of Basel included 23 percent foreigners in 1846, and that of Geneva, 23.8 percent in 1850.[32]

German immigrants included large numbers of locksmiths, carpenters, joiners, shoemakers, tailors, coopers, and saddlers, while many of the French and Savoyards did public works for wages below what the Swiss would accept.[33] Many such laborers were itinerants, traveling from town to town in search of work and living for several weeks in crowded, dilapidated housing before moving on. The stereotypical image of a foreign laborer at the time, especially those from Germany, was of a single man, prone to alcoholism. To dispel the influence of taverns, welfare organizations organized clubs, giving immigrant workers another place to meet, read papers, eat, and pursue an education.

Innumerable political refugees also sought asylum in the Swiss cantons during the first decades of the nineteenth century. Each Swiss canton enacted slightly different rules regulating who could come and what political activities they were allowed. While some of the Swiss cantons were decidedly more liberal than others, this freedom of the press and a willingness to protect refugees from the societies they had fled encouraged a congregation of politically motivated immigrants.

In 1836, under substantial pressure from the Austrians and the French, the Federal Diet, the legislative and executive body of the Swiss Confederation, adopted restrictive language allowing it to expel "refugees . . . who have abused the asylum granted by the cantons."[34] Citizens mobilized with petitions and rallies to denounce this interference in Swiss immigration. Ten thousand people assembled in Flawil, in the canton of Saint-Gall, "to oppose the external pressure on our asylum policies."[35] The Diet then affirmed the necessity of immigration, protesting external pressure "that would deprive the Cantons of one of the first rights of a free state, that of admitting and harboring whomever it pleases on its territory."[36] It defined hospitality as a duty of the nation and a right of refugees.

Cantons tended to admit refugees who conformed to their political leanings or met their economic needs. The most liberal and industrial of the cantons were most open to political refugees and laborers. Organizers found a more receptive welcome in the Vaud and in Geneva than in Neuchâtel, where the Prussians exerted substantial influence, or the agricultural regions of Fribourg and le Valais. Sometimes, refugees expelled from one canton found asylum in another.

Bern cited its warm reception of Polish revolutionaries as in keeping with its traditional liberties. "You want to know why fugitives have a right to our sympathy? We answer: As our fathers in the time of William Tell, they wanted to be free and . . . after a heroic battle, they were defeated. Would not those with a free country be moved by compassion when they saw a brother who was equally worthy deprived of such a priceless asset?"[37] Swiss hospitality troubled France and Austria, members of the Holy Alliance, which assumed the right to interfere in neutral Swiss affairs to maintain what these neighbors defined as peace. To these monarchies, that meant suppressing democratic voices. They routinely sent agents to spy on political refugees reputed to be in league with insurgents within their own countries.

Immigration policies changed over time and from one canton to the next as labor needs varied and political alliances shifted. Occasionally, cantons capitulated to pressure from outsiders and suspended the press freedom of the refugees they were sheltering. A few cantons, though, obstinately did the opposite. They responded to foreign pressure by naturalizing refugees to protect them from extradition by foreign governments.

Refugees contributed substantially to the developing Swiss educational system, making up the bulk of the professorships at the universities in Zurich and Bern. For their part, manual laborers and artisans, not part of the traveling mix in Hamburg and Altona, helped to bolster the uneven Swiss economy. Some observers claimed, in a statement with contemporary resonance, that immigrants often did the work that the Swiss disdained. For Swiss authorities, as for their neighbors, the potential for trouble arrived when the political refugees and laborers came together.

Revolutionary Refugees and Journeymen in the Swiss Cantons: "Cosmopolitans despite Themselves"

The 1830 revolutions in France and Poland triggered waves of refugees. French liberals and republicans forced to flee after their revolution was crushed discovered a veritable international community of refugees in Geneva. Four to five hundred Polish revolutionaries also expelled from France and intending to head south settled instead in the Swiss cantons. The Great Emigration from Warsaw followed relentless repression by the Russian tsar, who executed and banished revolutionaries to Siberia while he slashed remaining freedoms throughout Poland. Germans who began arriving in larger numbers in 1834 shared their political interests and coalesced as republicans.[38] Some of the radicals expelled from Germany who intended to pass through the Swiss cantons put down roots.

Polish refugees adopted the slogan, "For our liberty and yours."[39] So many political refugees sheltered in the cantons in the 1830s that they attracted yet more visitors of like minds, some around the table of August Adolf Ludwig Follen. A theology and law student from Hesse-Darmstadt, Follen had fought in the Napoleonic wars and edited a newspaper before being arrested and imprisoned in Berlin. Ahead of the waves of refugees, Follen found refuge in Zurich, where he taught school, eventually becoming a citizen. Guests at his table included Friedrich Froebel, the founder of kindergartens, banned in his native Prussia, but allowed to flourish in Switzerland; the German poet Georg Herwegh, whose popular revolutionary verses earned him an audience with the Prussian king before he was banished; and the Russian anarchist Mikhail Bakunin.

Napoleonic supporters arrived from the Italian states and France after the emperor's defeat. The Tuscan-born French revolutionary Filippo Buonarotti preceded them. They were joined by defectors from the defeated revolutionary movements in Naples and Sardinia. Failed revolutionary movements not only sent refugees to Swiss doors, but also energized liberals and radicals in the cantons. Assemblies in many cantons in the 1830s called for reforms of cantonal constitutions. The ideas of Swiss liberals and radicals and revolutionary refugees entangled in clubs and publications. In Bern, the liberals in the government hoped the integration of the Polish heroes in the canton would inspire additional support for their own politics. The Poles were dispersed over three municipalities and provided with a daily subsidy.[40] Lausanne and Zurich were not as welcoming; the more conservative cantons raised objections to the Polish immigration.

Even notorious revolutionaries could prove their worth to the Swiss cantons as they sought to redefine the political structure of the federal state. As in Hamburg and Altona in the previous century, immigrants rose to assume significant roles in the governing of cantons and municipalities. For example, Ludwig Snell from the German state of Nassau wrote up the demands of Zurich's liberals in 1830, and once they came to power, he drafted legislation for them.

The jurist Pellegrino Rossi fled Bologna in 1816 after the fall of Napoleon's brother-in-law, whom he had supported. Rossi passed through France to settle in Geneva, where he became the first Catholic to teach at the Protestant university. Recognized as a professor for "his vast knowledge and his wise and moderate views," he earned "the esteem and confidence of the public" and was made a citizen.[41] That was not a common occurrence, but Rossi had adapted readily to Geneva. He married a Protestant, had two children, and bought a house in the countryside with a view of the lake and Mont Blanc.

Rossi still posed a potential threat to conservative forces in neighboring states, especially because of the circulation of his journal. When Metternich demanded that the Swiss expel "the Spanish and Italian revolutionary fugitives" who had found asylum in the cantons, Rossi disbanded the journal. He did not want to put his hosts in a difficult position. Rossi subsequently won election to the Conseil Représentatif. He was chosen as the spokesman to respond in 1823 to Austria's push for press censorship and the control of foreigners. He ascended to the Federal Diet in 1832 as part of the Genevan delegation and proposed a plan for stronger connections among the cantons. Devastated by the rejection of his revised constitution, Rossi left Geneva for France, where he would have more professional opportunities.[42]

In absolute numbers, political refugees were outnumbered by laborers. They were often indistinguishable. Then, as now, no firm line separated the two categories. German political refugees, in particular, took advantage of the conglomeration of laborers to propagate their ideas. The revolutionary aspirations of political refugees rarely abated. Instead, they tended to adopt causes from their new homeland to amalgamate with the old. They found an audience in their fellow refugees who had come seeking work.

One of the most successful was a German tailor, Wilhelm Weitling, who also availed himself of the press freedom in the Swiss cantons to publish his communist theories in newspapers and books. Weitling lodged in a room with two others in Zurich and lived on black coffee. Legend has it that he went without socks, underwear, or gloves.[43] Although he received minimal funding from the League of the Just to propagandize in Switzerland, he continued to earn his living as a tailor at a ladies' tailoring shop. He wrote articles and essays, balancing a board on his knees, and lectured in the evenings at taverns and the back room of the tailoring shop. Weitling mixed with the Swiss in singing societies wherever he landed.

Weitling joined the Arbeiterbildungsverein (Association for Workers' Education) when he arrived in Geneva. Austrian spies worried about the revolutionary tendencies of the association; Weitling was disturbed by the moderation of its members. Disappointed that even the most politicized workers adhered to the republican nationalism of the Young Germany, rather than a more cosmopolitan vision, Weitling attempted to propagate communism in their midst, enlisting the membership of German workers in his association.

Political refugees mixed with journeymen and other laborers in these clubs, imbibing their politics. The *Handwerkvereine* (craft associations) enlisted significant numbers of German laborers.[44] In Geneva, a Bildungs und Unterrichtsverein (Education and Teaching Association) served meals, lent books and maps, and offered instruction. Although ostensibly organized for nonpolitical purposes, its aims inconspicuously stretched.

Self-educated, Weitling did not shy away from making friends with the numerous Germans employed by the university in Zurich. He introduced them to workers' clubs. All the while, Weitling recruited followers, including journalist and teacher August Becker. The son of a minister, Becker became a fervent communist, striving to unify the different political factions to attack private property. The affable Simon Schmidt claimed to have been converted by his radical Swiss barber, Philippe Corsat, a wide-ranging traveler himself.[45] Schmidt, for his part, after touring the German-speaking cantons and meeting with the first Swiss communists in 1843, organized German workers in Lausanne. Unlike Weitling, Schmidt advocated a peaceful revolution. He focused on moral education "to root the idea of equality among the people."[46]

Weitling, supported by Becker and Schmidt, established clubs where, despite their innocuous sounding names—Harmonie (Harmony) and Eintracht (Unity)—new members were carefully vetted because these associations had a secret mission: spreading communism. Much of the meeting time was devoted to education through reading and lectures. The clubs subscribed to newspaper and journals, and in Lausanne, employed a teacher.

In the associations, Weitling promoted temperance, a comment on the role taverns played in the lives of most of the German artisans working in the Swiss cantons. He also instructed his fellow artisans in the responsibilities of citizenship, a role they would assume after the revolution. Some of the clubs met daily. The clubs spread to Lausanne, Aarau, Winterthur, St. Gallen, Kreuzlingen, Bern, and Zofingen, attracting a total membership estimated at somewhere between 530 and 1,100 members; Weitling claimed 1,300.[47]

In Bern in 1834, German refugees founded Jungen Deutschland (Young Germany) to organize German artisans. They were joined by a circle of German republicans in Zurich in advocating for improved conditions for laborers in a transnational movement.[48] One hundred twenty artisans and workers organized their own branch of Young Germany in Lausanne the next year under the leadership of Eduard Scriba. Scriba had emigrated after being expelled from theological studies in Germany for his participation in a student organization and in political banquets. He first secured a position as a tutor in the canton of Basel-Landschaft. After settling in Lausanne, he set off on a long walk through the canton, meeting other politically engaged refugees along the way. The next revolution, as opposed to those of the eighteenth century, Scriba was convinced, would extend to all of humanity.[49]

New associations and journals flourished, bringing together laborers and intellectuals, refugees and Swiss natives. One laborer noted that displaced refugees often became "cosmopolitans despite themselves."[50] They had no choice but to envision a future beyond the nation-state on their tortuous journeys. In larger cities, German workers' associations opened dining halls and taverns, even renting a house and garden in the town of Morsee. Weitling dreamed of profits enabling the establishment of a colony in America. He also expected that by 1844, the membership would be sufficient to start a revolution. In the end, these enterprises proved more threatening to police than actually successful. The Austrians told the Swiss that their agents had sixty-six dangerous men under surveillance.

Freedom of the press extended to visitors and immigrants as well as Swiss citizens and allowed communist and republican papers to flourish in several cantons. Swiss cities sheltered publications that would have been considered incendiary elsewhere, including poems and essays that propagated ideas for political change and the advancement of labor outlawed across the border. Some Swiss political leaders made their printing presses available to refugees while others lent financial support to the German workers' organizations. Men such as Louis-Henri Delarageaz, a mathematician and topographer by profession, were committed to the diffusion of communist and socialist tracts throughout the cantons.[51]

In Geneva, Weitling published a monthly paper, *Der Hülferuf der deutschen Jugend* (The Cry of German Youth for Help), which promoted the unity of workers over individualism. He exposed what he saw as the follies of nationalism, promoting universal brotherhood in religious terms. "The boundaries of the nations will crumble when the Son of Man comes to judge the quick and the dead," he prophesied.[52] In more secular terms, Weitling denounced passports and travel restrictions and translated excerpts from Socrates and Rousseau, and from utopian socialists such as Proudhon. Chased by the police out of Geneva, the paper moved operations to Bern, then to Lausanne, Vevey, and Langenthal. Its circulation extended to Berlin and northern Germany, Paris, and London.

In the end, diplomatic protests from abroad and complaints from within about the costs of assistance blunted the freedom of the refugees to organize politically. Many of the Poles continued their migration south. After the Swiss succumbed to pressure from Metternich to expel Scriba, he traveled with his brother to London and on to Liverpool in 1837. His influence on intellectuals and laborers in the cantons was longer lasting. In his order, the judge who banished Weitling from the canton of Vaud was clearly motivated by the desire to separate the intellectuals from the laborers. He was especially intent on shutting down the cafeteria where they mixed.[53] The *Handwerkvereine* so concerned neighboring governments that they successfully pressured the cantons to shut them down.

The arrest of Weitling in Zurich in 1843 incited political debate in the canton. Liberal groups championed Weitling and deplored the late-night raid of the police, while conservatives used the arrest to undermine the popularity of their political adversaries, including the German founder of kindergartens, Friedrich Froebel, who had shielded Weitling. Pamphlets flowed; the slogan "liberty and equality" was scrawled on walls. Weitling's conviction turned him into something of a martyr abroad. Released by Zurich authorities, instead of being greeted by a liberating band as he expected, Weitling was handed over, bound and gagged, to German authorities, who passed him from one jail to another until he reached Prussia and was allowed to return to his childhood home in Magdeburg. Not welcome there either, Weitling took a boat down the Elbe to Hamburg in August 1844, where he claimed to have been met at the dock by throngs of citizens. He stayed just five days before sailing to London. At least one of his associations survived the flight of its leaders and the defeat of the 1848 revolutions.

Weitling's arrest was enough to convince his friend, the anarchist Mikhail Bakunin, that the cantons were no longer safe for refugees who would be revolutionaries. Bakunin lived in one room overlooking the lake in Zurich. He is said to have spent his time reading the French writer George Sand and translating Schelling. Weitling and Bakunin moved in the same circles, each discussing the other in their voluminous correspondence with mutual friends. After Weitling's arrest, Bakunin left for Brussels.

Mazzini: In Search of "a Fatherland beyond the Everlasting Alps"

Among the coterie of men and women seeking asylum in the Swiss cantons, one of the most notorious was the Italian revolutionary Giuseppe Mazzini, who spent almost all of his life in exile under a death sentence. He had passed almost an entire year hiding in Marseille, reading French texts and writing letters. The French port city served as a gathering place for a coterie of exiles fomenting insurrection in Italy. From this base, Mazzini organized Giovine Italia (Young Italy), a group of refugees working for a united republican Italy.[54] After the Tuscans, the Pope, and the Austrians intercepted stacks of his incendiary letters, the French bowed to diplomatic pressure and expelled Mazzini.

In July 1833, Mazzini, recovering from injuries sustained in an attempted coup in Turin, set up new headquarters in Geneva. He remained in the Swiss cantons for the next three years, reading widely, corresponding, and working out his ideas of republican patriotism.[55] Mazzini obviously was not a good candidate for Swiss citizenship. Nevertheless, by all accounts, in neighborhoods including his final hiding spot in Grenchen, Mazzini as a refugee enjoyed the rights of a more informal social citizenship, including access to local public assistance and the kindness of neighbors.

Echoing Kant, Mazzini put his faith in an international federation of democratic republics allied in the interest of peace. Like many of the philosophers of the Enlightenment, Mazzini thought that cosmopolitanism and a national sentiment could be complementary.[56] He never lost his faith

Joseph Mazzini. Print Collection, Miriam and Ira D. Wallach Division of Art, Prints and Photographs, New York Public Library. Courtesy of New York Public Library.

that if one country led the way toward democracy, others would follow. The liberty of one nation was the best guarantee of the liberty of its neighbors, he believed. Although he struggled throughout his lifetime to emancipate nations, he was no nationalist.

Throughout his years in exile in the Swiss cantons, Mazzini knew his correspondence to his followers was being intercepted and read. He used that to his advantage, stoking fear among authorities. From his base in Geneva, Mazzini organized an armed expedition against Savoy that sent waves of fear throughout not only Italy, but the rest of Europe. Several hundred insurgents lined up to fight, including Poles, Italians, Frenchmen, a few Germans, and the Swiss themselves. Other Genevans lent their active support to Mazzini. When the insurgents were defeated almost before they began, Genevans hid them in their houses. The insurgents who made it to Savoy were not so fortunate; twelve, including Mazzini's closest friend, were executed. Mazzini was tried in absentia and sentenced to death.

Diplomats from neighboring states, fearing the contagion of that liberty, turned their attention to the Swiss cantons, exerting substantial pressure on the neutral Swiss to break up bands openly recruited by revolutionary refugees lodged in their midst. For the Federal Diet, the difficulties of harboring an insurrectionary who had drilled forces to attack another government mounted. Officials from Savoy, but also from Austria and France, demanded that the Genevans expel Mazzini. The Swiss capitulated to pressure from their fearful neighbors but not without years of soul-searching debate. Options offered to him of refuge in England and America were unappealing. They were too far away from potential revolutions, so he stayed in the Swiss cantons.

Mazzini went into hiding, moving from one clandestine address to another through the Swiss cantons of Vaud, Bern, and Solothurn. Rarely leaving the houses in which he found shelter, except at night, he complained in poetic terms of the monotony of an "existence mournful and dull as a stormy sky or the ashes of a dead fire; the suffering that has no name, that finds no vent in tears or words." Mired in debt and depressed, Mazzini later described these months as "a total desolation of the soul" that almost led him to suicide.[57] He preferred the company of a cat to the men bickering over the failure of the raid on Savoy. Short on funds, he yearned for home and his family. What buoyed him, he reminisced, were thoughts "of fatherland, beyond the everlasting Alps, those icy cherubim that guard the gate of the heart's Eden."[58]

From the deepest despair, Mazzini rallied to meet what he saw as his duty "to fight for liberty and country and humanity."[59] While in Bern, he had the grandiose design to expand Young Italy into Young Europe, one of the first transnational political associations. Building on the French revolutionary idea of individual liberty, he espoused liberty as a national principle. Polish émigrés were among the first members to join this movement for international brotherhood.

Mazzini did not refrain from mixing in Swiss politics while he was in hiding. In his newspaper, published in German and French for Swiss readers, he commented on the weakness of links among the Swiss cantons and denounced the oligarchic nature of some of the cantons. In contrast to other political exiles, who refrained from meddling in their host's affairs, he proposed Swiss reforms. In an earlier revolutionary decade, although French émigrés in Hamburg and Altona also used the press to propagate their arguments, they purposefully paid little attention to their immediate surroundings. During the 1840s, the Belgians received Karl Marx in their capital on the condition that he not try to overthrow their monarch; they may have learned from the Swiss example. Doors could be open for intellectual immigrants as long as philosophers read and even wrote treatises that were outward looking, directed toward their neighbors, but left their hosts to pursue their own policies.

Mazzini was able to settle into shelter offered by a family at Grenchen. His mother sent his favorite books, including those by Homer, Vico, and Lamartine. He learned German, reread Latin classics, and kept up with contemporary newspapers from Britain. Mazzini shared his asylum with two brothers of one of his closest revolutionary allies who had committed suicide in prison. They lived together for two more years, reading and writing about their vision of a continent of individual free nations and continuing from exile to organize groups across Europe and into South America.

The Austrians were so convinced of the threat posed by Mazzini that Chancellor of State Klemens von Metternich organized an Austrian agency with a staff of eighty to monitor dangerous refugees and deter revolutions. The Swiss bowed to Austrian demands and expelled the most radical Polish refugees as a threat to European security. Rome stepped up its surveillance of what it identified as "the immense designs of this extraordinary man."[60] Finally, in the summer of 1836, Swiss federal authorities yielded to the relentless diplomatic pressure and banned Mazzini from the cantons for life. Swiss federal authorities worried that the refugee's presence would tempt their neighbors to invade to set the Swiss house in order.

Mazzini tried to contest the Swiss expulsion. When he was blocked from appealing in court, the town council of Grenchen offered him honorary citizenship to protect him. Similarly, Louis Napoleon, the future Napoleon III who had plotted a coup in Strasbourg, relied on his own honorary citizenship in the canton of Thurgau for his protection. The Swiss refused to hand over a citizen, resulting in French troops amassing on the Swiss border. Graciously, Louis Napoleon thanked the Swiss for their hospitality and retreated to London. Mazzini stayed in hiding, moving from one safe house to another, blocking windows to conceal his location. Finally, he too left, traveling through Paris, where he was not wanted, to London, where he had friends and expected to be able to live openly again.

Mazzini felt bereft in Britain. "We have lost even the sky, which the veriest wretch on the Continent can look at," he lamented.[61] Initially, he found the Londoners suspicious of impoverished foreigners, a marked contrast to the Swiss cantons, where even though he was forced into hiding by police and Austrian agents, he enjoyed the hospitality of the people and a view of the Alps. "All of the lost spirits, adventurers, and those who have been caught up in social upheavals of Europe have found refuge in this unfortunate country," Metternich noted, citing the number of revolutionary refugees hiding out in the Swiss cantons.[62] Even if foreigners made up only 2.6 percent of the Swiss population in 1837, the cantons stood out, along with Britain and Belgium, as counterexamples to the borders closing around Europe. Their neighbors were solidifying their citizenship and sovereign control over their territory by excluding outsiders.

Open Borders, "Organizing Plots and Dreaming of a Republic"

Mazzini and Scriba spent the rest of their lives in Britain, while Weitling went to the United States. Mazzini continued to plan for an uprising in Italy, organized a union of Italian workmen, criticized the gradualism of the English reformers, including the Chartists, and wrote a *Manifest to the Peoples*.[63] Lord Palmerston complained about the plotting of foreign radicals on British soil. Especially worrisome were those political refugees openly advocating the overthrow of governments. The foreign minister forwarded incriminating correspondence from Mazzini to the Austrian government, setting off outrage on all sides.[64]

More urgently than at the height of the French revolutionary wars, in the nineteenth century, the presence of political refugees raised concerns, even in the neutral confederation of Swiss cantons. As the examples of Weitling and Mazzini, among others, made clear, many nineteenth-century revolutionaries abroad continued plotting. Their incendiary proposals for insurrection and the advocacy of internationalism often went hand in hand. Frightened by the influence of these refugees, critics of "this monster that is called radicalism," such as the state chancellor of the Swiss cantons, blamed foreigners for "nourishing an implacable hatred against their governments, for organizing plots, and dreaming of a republic or a universal communism."[65]

Would neighbors rooted to the status quo prevail, shutting doors, one nation-state after another? Not as long as hospitality to others was embraced as a national value. Reformers in Britain defiantly defined the offer of shelter to political refugees as constitutive of what it meant to be a liberal nation.[66] The underlying assumption in their argument was that these heroes had escaped repression and needed asylum. Liberal governments should open doors and extend assistance. In the midst of one flurry of debate, a group of escaped French political prisoners wrote a much-heralded collective letter to a radical British newspaper spurning public assistance but asking for the right to work. Within Britain, theirs and other stories of the struggles of individual refugees bolstered support for the government's humanitarian impulses. At times the British government even went so far as to petition the offending governments from which the refugees had fled. This proactive intervention foreshadowed modern initiatives to reform the abusive regimes of countries driving refugees from their homes.

Advocates of the rights of refugees in France, as in Britain, hailed the foreigners arriving on their shores as revolutionary heroes to be protected by the government. The reception of these arguments depended on the governmental regime. Against a celebrated revolutionary tradition of welcoming foreigners, monarchies enacted restrictive and inhospitable measures. Not surprisingly, more than three hundred texts were published between 1791 and 1824 in France debating immigration.

While banishing a few of its own citizens as well as some refugees for their politics, France received others with ideas more to the liking of the current regime. In 1839, France was home to 13,502 foreigners without passports or diplomatic protection. Three-quarters of them were Poles, newly arrived from the Warsaw uprising. The French government provided monetary assistance for them as fellow Catholics who had fought for the cause of liberty; it also directed the police to watch them.

One of the most persuasive arguments for allowing freedom of movement on both sides of the Atlantic was economic, not moral or political. Proponents of open borders cited the benefit of the relatively open transit of goods throughout the Atlantic world. They had statistics, such as they were, on their side. Equally convincing, if anyone had known where to look, were the historical examples of neutral ports such as Altona and Hamburg that had grown exponentially during the French revolutionary wars when economies around the Atlantic were constricting. The internationalism of free trade advocates, such as British radical Richard Cobden, melded these claims to those of global peace fostered through communications. Finally, there were arguments for the civilizing virtues of commerce.[67]

Still, in the first decades of the nineteenth century, cosmopolitan arguments for open doors were few and far between. A majority of national leaders during this period of political consolidation and centralization were looking inward. During these decades, the introduction of passports, immigration regimes, and the deployment of police agents in cities and national forces at borders hindered the search for sanctuary of many of the refugees fleeing economic hardship and political repression. Would individuals' rights to free movement across the globe succumb, the victim of neighboring nations' assertion of sovereign control over their hard-won territories?

The immediate answer was no. Brussels continued along the path infrequently taken, guaranteeing all on its territory "the right to have rights." Newly independent in 1830, the industrializing kingdom, with its railways extending beyond its borders in every direction, had every reason to worry. If revolutionary agents did not topple its still unstable monarchy, neighboring states not yet reconciled to the independence and neutrality of the Belgians might invade. Still, Belgium opened its doors. The welcome Belgium extended in the decade leading up to the Revolutions of 1848, even if with stipulations and surveillance, provided an important continuity with the hospitable asylum offered first by Hamburg and Altona and then by the Swiss cantons.

CHAPTER FIVE

Stateless in Brussels

Transforming the World

EXPELLED FROM PARIS IN February 1845, Karl Marx had twenty-four hours to find another country willing to offer his family asylum. He settled on Belgium, with its reputation for sheltering political refugees. The capital city of Brussels was nearby, located at a diplomatic crossroads among France, Britain, and his native Prussia. Surrounded in Brussels by refugees from states around the world, Marx found asylum not only to think, read, and write, but also to imagine a proletarian revolution in a world without borders. It was in the capital of the newly independent nation that this stateless political refugee—he had renounced his Prussian citizenship in 1846—called on the workers of all countries to unite.

Belgium consciously opened its borders in the middle of the nineteenth century, allowing the easy passage of individuals and goods. The contrast was stark between the immigration policies of a small industrializing nation and some of its larger, more protective neighbors, the same ones that had hemmed in the diplomacy and commerce of Hamburg and Altona half a century earlier. Belgium's 1831 constitution, the most liberal in Europe at the time, recognized the rights to freedom of speech, of the press, and of assembly to be enjoyed not just by its own citizens, but also by all individuals residing in its territory.

The Belgian capital's reputation in the middle of the nineteenth century as a hotbed of radical political activity was well deserved, but the nation's founders figured that was a small price to pay for the freedom guaranteed by its constitution. The Italian revolutionaries, Portuguese constitutionalists, German communists, and Polish freedom fighters who had gravitated to Brussels would discover three years later, in February 1848, whether these constitutionally guaranteed rights could withstand the threats to Belgian national security when the next round of revolutions embroiled the European continent.

At the end of the twentieth century, Palestinian-born writer Edward Said reminds us that the conditions driving refugees from their homes are "produced by human beings for other human beings." Over the centuries, the experience of exile, he laments, "has torn millions of people from the nourishment of tradition, family and geography." Philosophers and poets have chronicled this condition, designed to deny both dignity and identity. Beyond their essays and the biographies of such world-renowned individuals, the tragic fates of so many more refugees will never be told. "Paris may be a capital famous for cosmopolitan exiles," Said pointed out, "but it is also a city where unknown men and women have spent years of miserable loneliness."[1] Marx lived in Brussels amid hundreds of German, French, Polish, and Italian artisans in the years leading up to 1848. Their stories are more difficult to piece together from the archives left behind by refugees who have not yet captured a historian's imagination.[2]

Between 1846 and 1856, twenty thousand foreigners arrived in Brussels, more per capita than in any other European capital.[3] Unlike London and Philadelphia, two capital cities also attracting more than their share of political refugees in the early nineteenth century, travel to Brussels did not involve a channel crossing or—more demanding yet—an ocean journey. Most of the immigrants came to Brussels to work or to invest, attracted by the varied and vibrant labor market and the precocious industrial economy of the new Belgian nation.[4] Others fled political persecution at the hands of repressive governments. Whether they were immigrants seeking economic opportunity or escaping political retribution, these newcomers were welcomed by the thousands and asked to register in municipalities.

The early industrialization of the small nation, beginning in agrarian innovation in the eighteenth century, promised economic opportunities for laborers, artisans, and those with capital to invest. The first society to follow the model of the English industrial revolution in textiles and coal, Belgium relied on foreign as well as displaced agrarian laborers to fuel its manufacturing. In addition to the burgeoning labor market, the rapidly developing banking and insurance sectors attracted immigrants from neighboring countries to the capital. Some migrants settled and others commuted seasonally. Railways connected industrial basins, commercial centers, and harbors, stretching out to France, Prussia, and the English Channel on the state-engineered network.

Migration was a widely adopted adaptive strategy in an era of rapid and radical political change and economic transformation. Revolts across the European continent in the decades between the French Revolution and the myriad of revolutions of 1848 set refugees in motion by the thousands. Wherever insurrections were crushed or censorship laws tightened, political activists were forced to flee. The magnitude of migration had much to do with the founding of nation-states.[5]

Marx was but one of many refugees. He traveled from Paris to Brussels by mail coach with a young friend in tow and found lodging among other German travelers in the Grand Hôtel de Saxe in the center of the city. His wife, Jenny, pregnant with their second child, would follow him from Paris a week later. She had received dispensation from French authorities to stay behind to settle their financial affairs; she needed to get back their rent deposit and sell off their furniture. By the time Jenny arrived in Brussels, her husband had moved into a less expensive pension in front of the towering Saint Gudule cathedral. The Hôtel Bois Sauvage was not the cozy little house where she imagined she would find her husband writing. Not unlike other Germans seeking shelter in Brussels, the Marxes could not afford more than rooms in a lodging house.

This was not the first time Marx had been forced by his uncompromising ideas to flee ahead of government censors. In 1843, Karl and Jenny had left their home in Prussia when the government suppressed his newspaper, the *Rheinische Zeitung* (Rheinische Newspaper). At the beginning of what turned out to be a lifelong journey, with his ever-ready sarcasm, Marx thanked the Prussian government for giving him back his freedom to follow his convictions, just somewhere else. "I have become tired of hypocrisy, stupidity, gross arbitrariness, and of our bowing and scraping, dodging and hair-splitting over words," he wrote, reflecting on his last months of editing in Prussia.[6]

Looking forward to a fresh start, one of Marx's associates who accompanied the newlyweds to Paris in 1843 announced expectantly: "We are going to France, the threshold of a new world. May it live up to our dreams!"[7] It didn't. The French prime minister soon gave in to pressure from the Prussians to expel radical German journalists. Mixing with French republicans and socialists, the German refugees potentially posed a threat to the regime, the French government was convinced. The French king allegedly exclaimed: "We must purge Paris of German philosophers!"[8] Only sixteen months into his stay, Karl Marx was forced to search for asylum anew. He was not that different from a whole coterie of other republicans, socialists, and communists; however, while the French minister of the interior could locate most of the other dangerous journalists he sought, the police had to rely on Marx, whose address they did not know, to turn himself in.[9] Marx complied.

Marx arrived in Belgium just a decade and a half after the small country had secured its independence. For centuries, the Belgians had been governed by foreign powers, including, most recently, the French and the Dutch. After Dutch troops were driven out of the Belgian provinces by revolutionaries in September 1830, a provisional Belgian government, uniting rival Liberal and Catholic factions, devised a constitution for the new nation and selected a monarch to reign. The national anthem celebrated 1830, when after "century on century in slavery . . . the undaunted [Belgian] people . . . reconquered its name, its rights and its flag." One of the more progressive founding fathers, a republican, later wondered, "Was it worth shedding blood to achieve so little?"[10] Why, he asked, did the Belgians, who had just given themselves the most extensive guarantee of rights anywhere in Europe, need a monarch? Other than the invitation extended to Leopold of Saxe-Coburg to rule as king of the Belgians, the new nation succeeded in establishing, against all odds, a liberal constitutional regime with rights guaranteed to Belgians and non-Belgians alike.

The founding fathers of Belgium debated and worked out their differences, for the most part in public, over the next two decades. As before in Hamburg, Denmark, and the Swiss cantons, diplomats from neighboring states did not hesitate in the 1840s to interfere when an unlikely alliance brought together progressive Belgian Liberals and foreign communists, including Marx. These larger powers stopped just short of armed intervention. The grand experiment in cosmopolitan independence launched by a small state with porous borders surrounded by a sea of larger sovereignties would be put to the test in 1848.

"He's Just a Philosopher"

Marx's reputation as a dangerous radical preceded him to Brussels. The police in the industrial Belgian city of Liège, where he stopped overnight en route from Paris, alerted Brussels authorities that the radical journalist, expelled first from Prussia and then from France, was probably heading to the Belgian capital. The Brussels police should keep an eye out for him. Other dire warnings were conveyed through formal diplomatic channels to the Belgian Department of Public Security. The Belgian minister of foreign affairs answered his Prussia counterpart that there was little he could do. The Belgian government "found itself effectively deprived of all possibility of action in regard to the admission of foreigners in Belgium, and . . . there were no legal means of opposing anyone who wanted to settle in Belgium."[11] The constitution guaranteed the rights of foreigners within Belgium, even if the anxious national authorities charged with protecting public security did what they could to chip away at these guarantees with their decisions.

Belgian regulations implemented in 1840 required all new arrivals, whether from another Belgian municipality or another country, to register with the local police. Municipal authorities then passed along the information to the national government. So Marx filled out a bulletin on 8 February 1845, within a week of arriving in Brussels. But fearing that the Prussians, who expelled him from France, would try to convince the Belgians to follow suit, Marx went further than was required. Following the advice of a lawyer, Marx appealed directly to the king of the Belgians, Leopold I, for asylum. "Sire, the undersigned, Charles Marx, doctor of philosophy, aged 26, of Trier, Kingdom of Prussia, who has come to Brussels with the intention of settling with his wife and child in Your Majesty's State, respectfully takes the liberty of asking you for permission to establish his domicile in Belgium," he wrote, signing his formulaic letter, "With the deepest respect, Your Majesty, the most humble and obedient servant, Charles Marx."[12]

There is no evidence that the Belgian king ever directly responded to Marx. The director of public security, Baron Alexis de Hody, reporting to the Department of Justice, did. Hody, a lawyer who had risen rapidly through the ranks in Public Security, had recently launched a systematic campaign to surveil and expel foreigners who might disrupt the public order of the new nation. He directed the mayor of Brussels to have the municipal police probe further into Marx's intentions. After a month, the mayor begrudgingly transmitted the reassuring response received about Marx from professors at the Université libre de Bruxelles: "He's just a philosopher."[13] Marx, Brussels authorities affirmed, was writing a book on political economy. No cause for alarm.

Hody's surveillance, based on his suspicions, although reassuring to the Austrians and the Prussians, who trusted him as a conservative Catholic, ran counter to the open-door policies of a number of Belgian cities, especially Brussels.[14] Hody's attempts to curtail immigration into Brussels constituted just one salvo in a long-running battle in Belgium between the federal state and traditionally powerful municipalities. Liberal Brussels mayors often found themselves at odds with the Catholics governing the nation. In Marx's case in 1845, Brussels authorities apparently felt no particular urgency to comply with Hody's request. The struggle for power between the national director of public security and the mayors of Belgium would continue until 1852, when Hody's attempt to expel two refugees resulted in his dismissal.

At the same time, the chief of police in the German border town of Aachen, on the train line to Brussels, chided both Hody and the Belgian minister of foreign affairs for their laxity. He demanded to know why Marx, the Prussian editor of incendiary newspapers in Paris, for whom an arrest warrant was still outstanding, had been allowed to settle amid the growing coterie of German communists in the Belgian capital. These political refugees openly lodged in the seemingly ungovernable warren of small streets and dead-end alleyways between the grand avenues of Brussels, beyond the gaze of authorities. They posed a real threat, he alleged, not only to the new and still unstable nation, but also to its neighbors.

Hody summoned Marx for a personal interview. Marx promised the Belgian director of public security in writing that he would remain aloof from Belgian politics. He would not indulge in efforts to overthrow the still precarious Belgian throne.[15] For Marx, the vow to abstain from involvement in Belgian politics could have significantly limited his family's main source of income: political journalism. Or it might have if Marx had been interested in Belgian politics or in Belgium's intensifying economic crisis. But he wasn't. His promise not to write about the questions raised by his immediate surroundings meant that Marx could concentrate on the formulation of political and economic theory. He could do exactly what the Brussels professors claimed he would do: read, think, and, to a lesser extent perhaps, write.

After a series of international diplomatic exchanges that increased anxiety among ministers and officials in Public Security about the German communists' claim to their rights under the Belgian Constitution as Belgian residents, and of perfunctory inquiries at the municipal level instigated by the national government, Marx and his family were formally granted permission to stay in the Belgian capital.[16] Although he enjoyed freedom to speak and to write (just not about Belgium), like other refugees, Marx had no political rights. These were limited to Belgian citizens. Marx never expected to stay.

For other political refugees who, like Marx, had fled their homelands to escape arrest for their activism, the Belgian restriction on political involvement potentially placed unacceptable limits on their freedom. In contrast to all of the refugees who had taken professorships in the Swiss cantons in the 1830s, the Polish revolutionary leader Joachim Lelewel turned down a professorship at the newly established Université libre de Bruxelles because it required that he renounce political activities.[17] Such requirements echoed the censorship imposed by the regimes they had fled, landing them right back where they had been at home, except that now their families were typically poorly housed and inadequately fed, and they were deprived of their native language for communication. Lelewel informed the university president that he would have to decline because the Polish constitution of 1815 denied citizenship to anyone working for a foreign government. Political exile, even in a state with relatively strong protections built into the constitution, was not an easy road in the middle of the nineteenth century.

The French writer Victor Hugo, also a refugee, arrived in Belgium a few years later, after Louis Napoleon's 1851 coup drove him from France. Exile brought a "life of poverty, but freedom. . . . What does it matter if the body is constrained as long as the spirit sails free?"[18] That openness brought real advantages considering the plight of a political refugee. "To have nothing left to you, to have nothing on you, this is the best condition for combat," the author of *Les Misérables* commented.[19] That may have proved even truer for Marx than for Hugo. Brussels provided the future author of the *Communist Manifesto* with the conditions that prepared him for future combat, for the Revolutions of 1848 and beyond. The Belgian capital gave Marx, together with the other communists and radicals and democrats lodged in Brussels neighborhoods, the time to think and the space to imagine a new global community far beyond the Belgian borders.

These three years in residence in Brussels would prove to be among Marx's most productive in terms of his thinking and writing. Uprooted from his native Germany and displaced from the lively political scene in France, he now had time to work out his theories of political economy, grounding the emergence of the proletariat in a historical context. Although they moved house frequently while in Brussels, Marx and his fam-

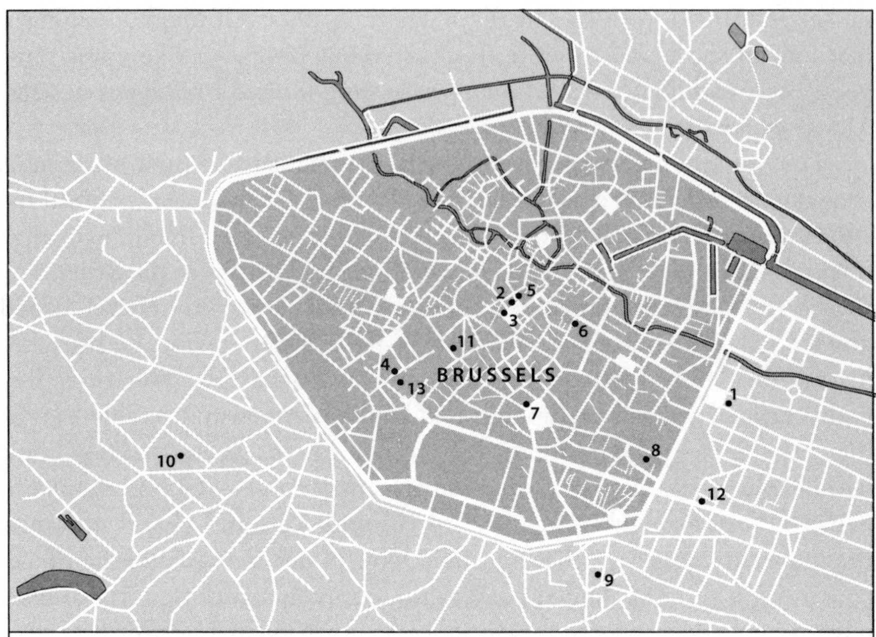

1 Gare du Nord/Noordstation
Arrival point for many refugees from Germany

2 Hotel de Ville/Stadhuis, Grand Place/Groot Markt
Seat of Brussels government

3 Café le Cygne, on Grand Place/Grote Markt next to Hotel de Ville/Stadshuis
Meeting place of Communist League/ Corresponding Society/ Workers' Education Association

4 Rue Bodenbroeck 8/Bodenbroekstraat, across from Kerk Onze Lieve Vrouw/Notre
Dame du Sablon ten Zavel/
Philippe Gigot's house,
Address for the Correspondence Committee

5 Maison des Meuniers, corner
Rue de la Tête d'Or/Guldenhoofdst and Rue des Pierres/Steenstraat
Association démocratique organized here

6 Café Mille Colonnes, Place de la Monnaie/Muntplace
Meeting place of Polish and other political refugees

7 Pension Le Bois Sauvage, Place Saint Gudule 19-21/Sint Goedelplein
lodging for Marx family, 2/9/1845-3/13/1845, 5/7/1846-10/19/1846, 2/26/1848-3/3/1848

8 Rue de Pachéco 35/Pachécostraat
Marx family lodging, 3/13/1845-5/3/1845

9 Rue de l'Alliance 5/Verbondsstraat Saint Josse/Sint Joost
lodging for Marx family, 5/3/1845-5/7/1846
Friedrich Engels and Mary Burns, Rue de l'Alliance 7
Moses Hess and Sibylle Pesch, Rue de l'Alliance 3

10 Rue d'Orléans 42/Orléansstraat Ixelles/ Elsene,
lodging for Marx family 10/19/1846-2/26/1848

11 Rue des Eperonniers 58/Spoormakersstraat
Home of Joachim Lelewel

12 Rue Royale 236/Koningstraat
Lucien Jottrand's residence

13 Bibliothèque Royal de Belgique, Palais de Charles de Loraine
Collection of books that Karl Marx read while living in Brussels

Brussels in 1843. Map by Bill Nelson, based on Map by Établissement géographique de Bruxelles. Norman B. Leventhal Map Collection, Boston Public Library.

ily resided in the Belgian capital longer than in any other place between his leaving the University of Berlin in 1842 and the family's securing residence in London in 1849.

Marx's Brussels years proved formative not only for him, but also, on the other side of the dialogue between sites of asylum and refugees, for Belgium. An anxious director of public security persistently reminded the Brussels mayor that the Belgians occupied a particularly delicate diplomatic position, squeezed between powerful nations who only reluctantly tolerated their independence. Troubled diplomatic relations with worried neighbors exposed the limits of state sovereignty for the small nation, even in times of peace. In particular, Belgium's ally, Prussia, needed to be placated. The Belgians, like Hamburg, Altona, and the Swiss cantons before them, did not want to provide an excuse for their neighbors to interfere in their domestic affairs. Nevertheless, they were determined to abide by the terms of their liberal constitution.

Together with France and Austria, Prussia made its vexation with Belgium's open borders known through diplomatic channels. Marx personally worried, as a Prussian citizen, that the Belgian authorities might bow to Prussian insistence that he be extradited. Preemptively, a few months into his asylum, Marx approached the Prussian government and asked for passports for his family to travel to the United States. It is unclear whether he actually intended to emigrate, but in any case, the Prussians refused. Marx responded by renouncing his Prussian citizenship. He would be stateless, without national obligations, but also without grounds to obtain a passport. Neighboring governments, out of respect for Belgium's sovereignty, however, made no attempt to cross borders to extricate the leader of a political movement that they deemed a threat.

In theory, national citizenship was becoming increasingly important in the decades after the French Revolution. In practice, few of the mobile individuals forced to forego a national identity found its absence problematic. Marx never considered applying for Belgian citizenship.[20] In the middle of the nineteenth century, the procedure for establishing nationality by naturalization was quite difficult, long, and expensive in Belgium, as elsewhere. And the rights citizenship conveyed at the national level were not as significant as they would become later. Marx would be stateless while in Brussels, a position not out of keeping with his developing philosophy of internationalism. Whether as a global citizen or a citizen of nowhere, Marx effectively put into practice what would become his theoretical position: looking beyond the nation-state for citizenship and the guarantee of human rights. Rights need not be tied to the nation-state, nor need citizenship be territorially bound. His family could secure what it needed for daily life in Brussels neighborhoods.

"Perfectly Legal, Perfectly Regular, and Perfectly Reassuring"

In the aftermath of the French Revolutionary wars, states throughout the Atlantic world fortified their national borders. National governments asserted control over the movement of individuals across their borders and over the right of individuals to settle within their territory. In the first decades of the nineteenth century, a full century before the adoption of the Universal Declaration of Human Rights, no guarantee of the right to asylum from persecution existed in international law. Instead, in this era of emerging nationalism, immigration tested the liberal principles of democracies at the national level. That makes Belgium, a new nation surrounded by larger neighbors, particularly intriguing.

Neutral in foreign affairs, small in size, and wedged amid larger nations, Belgium experimented with immigration policy, trying to find a balance between assuring national security and guaranteeing individual liberties. At one point, shortly after winning independence, the Belgian government tried setting up depots far from the capital to house all the Frenchmen and Poles streaming across the border. Parliament was caught between two impulses: attracting foreigners to propel its precocious industrialization and not undermining its still fragile constitutional monarchy. Open borders confirmed the progressive political vision of the nation's founders as they promised to stoke the industrial economy, lagging just behind that of England. Echoing the implicit assumption of Hamburg senators, a member of the Belgian constitutional convention stated clearly the prevailing argument for open borders and for asylum: "It makes sense to welcome all those who appear at our borders with capital for investing or with industrial knowledge, but no matter how much that man promises to contribute to our material prosperity, he should not be in a position to compromise our liberties or our political independence."[21] Like other nations, the Belgian government assumed the right to subordinate the rights of individuals to come to Belgian territory in the name of maintaining public order. Belgium also needed to reassure its neighbors who, on the one hand, did not want to lose their own best and brightest to emigration and, on the other, feared the proximity of rootless radicals from other states lodged on their borders.

The Belgian Constitution guaranteed the civil but not the political rights of all individuals within Belgium's territorial boundaries. Article 128, according full protection to all foreigners and their goods, was modeled after the Dutch constitution of 1815, which guaranteed these rights to all persons in the Netherlands; it also echoed the provisions in force in the independent city-state of Hamburg at the end of the eighteenth century. All individuals in Belgium, citizens and non-citizens alike, enjoyed the right to buy property, to start a business, to practice a profession, to marry, to practice a religion, to petition, and to profess their opinions freely in the press. These rights were delineated within the Belgian Constitution itself, differentiating it from American and French constitutional models with their separately passed enumerations of rights. German law, meanwhile, distinguished between citizens and non-citizens, limiting the rights to be enjoyed by foreigners. In the twentieth century, these same rights promised by the Belgian Constitution would be guaranteed by the Universal Declaration of Human Rights, including the right to life and security of person; the right to equal justice; the right to marry; the right to freedom of thought, opinion, conscience, and religion; the right to language and culture; the right to peaceful assembly; the right to own property; the right to free movement; and the right to work. In effect, Belgium as a nation was a century ahead of the international community.

The Belgian Constitution restricted the right of political participation to Belgian citizens, as had Hamburg's lawmakers. The framers of the Belgian Constitution assumed that only citizens would have a vested interest in preserving the independence and stability of the new monarchy. Foreigners, defined as non-Belgians, could neither vote nor stand for office. Nationality was defined by parentage, not place of birth. But if non-Belgians did not enjoy the exercise of political rights, neither did the majority of Belgians. Nationals without property who did not pay taxes above a certain threshold were not considered stakeholders capable of participating responsibly in political life in the middle of the nineteenth century. Economic status mattered in the definition of citizenship in Belgium, as it did in the United States and throughout most of Europe.

Even if Brussels was one of the Belgian cities with the highest number of university-educated citizens, only 3 percent of its residents met the qualifications for voting in the 1830s.[22] Forty years earlier in Hamburg, 4 percent of the residents qualified as citizens to vote or stand for office. In the middle of the nineteenth century, as at the end of the eighteenth century, voting remained the privilege of the elite. For context, the British

Reform Act of 1832, won through extensive struggle in the streets and in Parliament, extended the vote from 360,000 to 650,000 men, or to 2.7 percent of the population. Full universal manhood suffrage, a goal of only the most radical of the reformers, would have encompassed 25 percent of the population. Voting has continued in most nations to be limited to citizens, even if citizenship has shed its economic and property-owning qualifications.

In marked contrast to all of their larger neighbors, Belgians did not define their nationality on the basis of a common culture. Belgians spoke three major languages. Instead of a cultural affinity, they shared their history as a people whose forefathers had defended constitutional freedoms beginning in the Middle Ages. This sense of a new nation, amalgamating different cultures rather than protecting its homogeneity, made it easier for foreigners to blend into Belgian communities. By the middle of the nineteenth century, the previously Flemish city of Brussels was predominantly French-speaking; Marx spoke some Dutch and was fluent in French. Being Belgian in the middle of the nineteenth century meant belonging to an industrializing society with a prosperous agricultural heritage and living at the crossroads of Europe. Similar to the civic morality of Hamburg and Altona in the 1790s, it implied an openness to newcomers who promised to contribute to the flourishing economy, even if the definition of who could influence the national body politic was restricted.

Before fingerprints or photographic identification, it was practically impossible to control migration. That does not mean that governments did not try. If an immigrant is defined as "the person who moves from one nation-state to another," then immigrants constituted something of a relatively new phenomenon in the early nineteenth century, with the precedent of the 1790s.[23] When migrants, including political refugees, set forth on journeys in large numbers, some with the means to support themselves and others without, asylum offered a relatively untested promise of shelter.

Passports, so much taken for granted today, had been linked with nationality as state-issued identity papers for travelers only beginning with the French Revolution. Thereafter, they were retained in continental Europe as identity documents that allowed government authorities to distinguish nationals from foreigners. Workers were not required to have a passport but instead carried a work ledger that was checked by an employer. Marx's close friend and collaborator Friedrich Engels, for example, had to tell his favorite sister in May 1845 that he could not attend her wedding in Prussia because he had not been in Brussels long enough to secure a passport from Baron Hody. The Prussian passport that he had in hand gave him the right to leave Prussia, something he had already done, but not to reenter.

Open borders were complicated on the European continent by the railway, the new technology that in the 1830s revolutionized travel. Within a decade of adopting the quintessentially liberal constitution, the Belgians had mobilized their state resources to construct the densest railway network in the world. "Brussels is the crossroads of all the railways," an Austrian diplomat stationed in the Belgian capital noted. As a result, "It is the place of refuge, the receptacle for all the vagabonds," he complained.[24] Trains that traversed borders and covered distances at unaccustomed speeds lent new urgency to questions of immigration. How, without causing inordinate delays, could guards check every passenger on every train crossing the borders, especially in a small nation?

Over time, responsibility for policing Belgian borders passed from the municipalities that happened to be located at border crossings to the Department of Public Security. Organized at a national level, the department dispatched border guards to check documentation at specified border crossings. Political refugees accused of trying to overthrow their repressive governments risked being denied access to Belgium. But few were.

Beginning in 1846, a regulation unique to the statistics-obsessed central administration of Belgium required that new arrivals sign communal population registers, providing police and future historians with comprehensive data on who moved in and out of every house. The municipalities passed along the information to the director of public security, who initiated the process. There is no evidence that municipalities openly resisted the centralization and bureaucracy. There is little evidence that they complied efficiently either.

Belgium's neighbors, none of whom had developed quite such an elaborate registration system as Belgium or flaunted such open borders, were not convinced that the new nation had found a reasonable balance between rights and security. They feared the openness of a small country in their midst could have dangerous consequences, at least for them. The Belgians should immediately expel potential troublemakers, the French advised the Belgian foreign minister.[25] But where did these diplomats think the refugees would go next? Certainly not back across their own borders.

If the Belgians would not limit immigration, then their neighbors assumed the right and also the responsibility of tracking those individuals they had expelled within Belgian cities. The French kept an eye on their political refugees, including members of secret societies plotting coups against French King Louis Philippe. These troublemakers had found sanctuary next door and seemed determined to continue their politics, just from Brussels. Prussia and Austria, with their own informants, complained through diplomatic channels about the radical refugees they had thrown out of their countries who now lodged in Brussels, tolerated according to the terms of Belgium's "ultra-liberal" constitution.[26] Their spies were afoot in Brussels, and, as in Hamburg and Altona, they reported back to their governments. Refugees should be considered an international, not a national, issue, they insisted.[27] International cooperation at a governmental level, though, was even less likely then than it is now.

Necessarily attuned to pressure from larger countries, the Belgian government noted the concern of the French, the Prussians, and the Austrians. However, if they reacted too aggressively to curb the activities of the refugees, the Belgians told their neighbors, then they feared their own citizens would rise up to protest in support of the rights of refugees who lived in their midst.[28] Article 128 of the Constitution accorded all individuals on Belgian soil the right to free speech and assembly, so as long as refugees refrained from overt political activity, they were welcome to stay. At one juncture, the Belgian foreign office assured Austrian chancellor von Metternich that despite the appearances, "Nothing is happening that is not perfectly legal, perfectly regular, and perfectly reassuring."[29]

All the while, in reaction to the emergence of democratic movements in Belgium and in neighboring countries in the 1840s, Hody initiated his own contacts with foreign police forces. He saw the balance between rights and security differently than did his more liberal colleagues with their ties to Belgium's 1830 revolution. Spying was not out of the question, nor were communications shared through diplomatic circles with powerful neighbors. Hody and his Prussian and Austrian contacts were particularly concerned by newspapers edited by refugees, including Marx. They worried that Belgian republicans and foreign communists could be plotting insurrections while the Belgian government looked the other way, constrained as it claimed to be by Belgian law.

Immigration policy and practice not only strained Belgium's international relations, but also exacerbated the fraught relations between national and municipal authorities within the country. Mirroring discussions a decade earlier in the Swiss cantons, Belgian cities guarded the autonomy they had garnered in the Middle Ages. The right of immigrants to reside in Belgium was defined at the national level by Parliament, but for the most part, it was enforced locally in the neighborhoods by the municipal police. That was intentional, as diplomats stationed in Brussels noted, because the Belgian Parliament did not want to follow other nations' lead in relying on powerful and sometimes clandestine state police forces.[30] Moreover, municipal police could not and would not take marching orders from the minister of justice.

Although immigration policymaking had been formalized at the level of the nation-state, in the nineteenth century conditions on the ground in an open city had not changed dramatically from those of Hamburg and Altona in the 1790s. The contradictory impulses guiding the Belgian Parliament resulted in substantial flexibility in practice within the municipalities; the directives from above were anything but consistent. In cities controlled by the Liberals, that opening for local decisions was especially valuable. Delivering services at the neighborhood level benefitted from a problem-solving flexibility not necessarily found in the political debates at the level of national governments. A number of foreigners arriving without papers and wishing to stay below the radar neglected to appear before the municipality. If in theory the director of public security was notified of all registered aliens and had to consent to their stay, in reality, the national agency was woefully understaffed and totally dependent on local officials and police. Policymaking was much more ad hoc at the local level.

The innovation, openness, and flexibility that distinguished mid-nineteenth-century Brussels from formal Belgian policymaking continues to differentiate municipal and national governance into the twenty-first century. For that reason, in 2018, at a worldwide meeting of city leaders, the mayor of Bristol, England, called on cities, not nations, to take on "our shared challenges that come from global issues, from migration and global security to population inequalities and climate change."[31] The Global Parliament of Mayors accepted his challenge, pledging to tackle head on the crisis of migration caused by restrictive national immigration policies. In 2020, the United Nations recognized 105 cities for taking the lead in fighting climate change.[32] Even if nation-states had created the immigration problems, the solution, the mayors declared, lay within the purview of cities to resolve, often at the level of neighborhoods where refugees settled in sanctuary cities.

In the decades after the Belgian Revolution of 1830, the Liberal administration of Brussels did not share the Catholic faction's prioritization of state security in matters of immigration. The Catholics and Liberals had coalesced in 1831 to form a unionist government under the slogan "Union makes strength." Brussels Liberals pronounced the right of asylum integral to the history of Belgium. The administrative, political, and economic heart of Belgium in 1830, Brussels aspired to be a cosmopolitan capital at the center of an open nation. If anything, Brussels's tradition of municipal autonomy and its global aspirations have grown stronger over time, culminating in the 1993 revision of the constitution establishing a federal state. In addition, with the selection of Brussels as the seat of the European Union and of NATO, the city sees itself as truly cosmopolitan, as closely linked to cities outside the Belgian borders as to those within.

Brussels grew quickly in the nineteenth century, adding twenty-three thousand people between 1829 and 1842. This increase of 27 percent matched that of industrial metropolises like Birmingham and Manchester in England.[33] While some of the migrants were pushed from the rural regions of Flanders, which was suffering a downturn in the linen industry and failing potato and rye harvests, others were pulled from urban areas outside of Belgium. The capital of the second country in the world to industrialize, Brussels did not become home to large factories as did England. Instead, its economy continued to be dominated by small-scale workshops attracting artisans as well as manual workers from less affluent neighboring states. Although half of the people living in Brussels considered themselves laborers, only 4 percent worked in industry.[34]

Brussels also drew a sizeable number of immigrants with entrepreneurial and business skills, contributing to the launching of a dynamic banking and insurance sector. All of the administrative functions of a national capital and the affluence of this center of consumption appealed to the bourgeoisie, who in turn consumed more, driving production, so that as the French historian Louis Chevalier explained, "Immigration caused immigration."[35] At the same time, the presence of prominent political exiles attracted clusters of new refugees.[36]

At the time that Marx lived in Brussels, more than 50 percent of its 113,207 residents had been born elsewhere, and at least 8,503, or 7 percent, like him, were not Belgian. In comparison, the foreign population of the harbor city of Rotterdam at the time made up only 3 percent of the total population; it made up 2 percent in London and 5 percent in Paris.[37] The mayor of Brussels reported: "All the branches of human activity are prospering because illustrious foreigners have stimulated them."[38] Most of the foreign immigrants came from France (32 percent), Germany (19 percent), or the Netherlands (31 percent).[39] A substantial percentage settled in Brussels, seeking opportunities not found in the lands they left behind.

Just as the framers of the Belgian Constitution hoped, foreigners in the decades after independence played a disproportionate role in stimulating manufacture and finance. They were welcomed as entrepreneurs and scholars had been in the port cities on the Elbe River fifty years earlier because they would contribute to the dynamic growth of a prosperous economy. Other newcomers worked as artisans, especially tailors and cabinetmakers. Men dramatically outnumbered women among the immigrants in Brussels. Newly arrived Germans represented forty-seven different professions, but the majority were skilled artisans.[40] Theirs was a young group, with an average age of twenty-four. Immigration peaked during the years of economic crisis in the 1840s. Frenchmen—and they were predominantly men in 1847—were four years older on average than the Germans. In contrast to the Germans, who had traveled a circuitous route before finding work in Belgium, Frenchmen came directly.[41] In addition, French professionals were more likely to emigrate than workers. It should be noted that these figures represent only those foreigners who registered with the authorities and who did not live in a hotel or furnished rooms. Nevertheless, it is clear that the immigrants propelled Belgian industrialization, with new arrivals filling positions and adapting to life in their neighborhoods.

In an immigration provision that has reverberated through time and that went unquestioned when it was passed, immigrants to Belgium had to prove that they could support themselves. Legislation limited public assistance to those in residence in a municipality for at least eight years. In response to the agrarian crisis of the mid-1840s, the central government tried to close its borders to anyone who might compete with already underemployed agricultural laborers. Newcomers arriving for whatever reason were not expected to pose a burden at either a municipal or a national level. Immigration policies thereby favored professionals and skilled workers.[42]

Unrest in April 1834, blamed on newly arrived workers from abroad, sparked an intense debate in Parliament. Liberals subsequently attacked the government's expulsion of thirty refugees accused of espousing radical ideas on which they had yet to act. By a narrow margin, Parliament proceeded to pass legislation intended to protect the country against outsiders intent on overturning the Belgian monarchy. Based on French revolutionary law enacted in the 1790s, the Belgian government gave the Department of Public Security the power to surveil and to expel foreigners who were known to have committed crimes abroad or who threatened to disturb public order in Belgium.[43] The law marked a major turning point in Belgian immigration history. As a check on overreach, the law had to be renewed by Parliament every three years, as it was until 1897, when it became permanent. The minister of justice testified that between 1839 and 1849, of the 425 foreigners who were expelled from Belgium, none before February 1848 were for purely political reasons.

Thereafter, even with the constitutional guarantees of Article 128, only customary tolerance protected foreigners in Belgium. That had been strong enough for an independent city-state like Hamburg but not necessarily a small nation-state. In practice, the reception of refugees in Belgium was subject to political winds. The French poet Baudelaire, who found exile in Belgium in the 1860s less than hospitable, complained that it all came down to political economy; the impoverished and journalists were summarily deposited at the nearest border.[44] Even so, when the courts became involved, judges confirmed the founding principle that foreigners should be considered residents, not only if they managed an industry, but also if they had chosen to lodge within the country. Few, if any, were denied entrance before 1848. It would, however, become apparent in 1848, with revolutions breaking out all around them, that Belgian lawmakers could be convinced to adopt more restrictive measures. Nevertheless, in part because of the cosmopolitan convictions of the capital, the reputation for open borders lived on, even as the reality changed.[45]

Brussels was much more hospitable toward foreigners than the Belgian legislation passed in 1835 would suggest. French republicans publishing anti-clerical tracts, Polish revolutionaries in regular contact with their comrades in Warsaw, individual Italian anarchists, and circles of German communists gathering around Marx and Engels were infrequently troubled by local authorities. And that was only when they could not be ignored—for example, when Belgian workers and communist refugees began assembling together in cafés in the center of Brussels in the years leading up to 1848. All the while, the Belgian minister of justice continued to send the Brussels mayor lists of French refugees that the French considered too dangerous to be allowed to remain in the Belgian capital.[46] In a not atypical exchange, the commissioner of the Brussels police responded to Hody's inquiry about a worrisome political refugee that, as far as his agents had been able to observe, the individual in question had "an irreproachable conduct, in private and public, and had a good reputation."[47]

The nineteen Brussels agents and eight assistants who policed the capital understood the enforcement of immigration to be primarily checking hotels and lodging houses each morning and compiling a register of foreigners in residence. Under orders from Hody, they recorded the profession of all new arrivals, their place of birth, the place where they had received a passport, and the origin of their travel.[48] Municipalities, including Brussels, protested the cost of the required rounds and investigations of those without papers. Over a span of six weeks in 1847, the mayor of Brussels complained he had received 198 different investigations to be carried out with an "infinite number of questions."[49] Foreigners who arrived without papers or with "irregular papers," as was often the case, were supposed to get official authorization from local officials to stay. Lodging houses were threatened with a fine if their lodgers were discovered to be nonconforming. For a time, to encourage local diligence, the central government paid rewards to local police for every foreigner they apprehended without a passport, whether at a hotel or public gathering spot.[50]

Only when it was considered necessary to protect the public order in Brussels were meetings banned and agents dispatched to disperse crowds. The perennial celebrations of the anniversary of the Polish Revolution of 1830 and the participation of military officers in uniforms were deemed noteworthy.[51] However, whenever a police agent was spotted, groups dissolved to reform somewhere else. In response to brochures judged libelous by the central government, the Brussels police were asked to identify the authors and their printers. Here too, their efforts appear to have been remarkably cursory. Judging from the daily police reports, more often, the Brussels police spent their time gathering information on men who had fallen into canals or on the cause of fires.[52]

"The Pettiest and Meanest of Conditions"

Jenny Marx had sent Karl ahead to Brussels in February 1845 with a list of her expectations for their lodging in "our new fatherland."[53] She had experienced displacement once before, from her comfortable family home in Trier, when she married Karl and moved with him to France. Based on her two-year exile in Paris, she delineated her expectation to her husband that the children's room and his study in a Brussels house would be simply furnished; she would shop for equipment for the kitchen herself. Jenny arrived in Brussels ten days later with their one-year-old daughter, Jennychen. She complained of the bitter cold of the damp city. She was pregnant with their second child and ill.

Her husband, or Mohr, as he was known in the family circle, had not yet secured housing. So she joined him in the Hôtel Bois Sauvage, a lodging house favored by German travelers, located on the square in front of the

Jenny Marx with daughter Jenny, about 1850.
Pictorial Press Ltd./ Alamy Stock Photo.

cathedral of Saint Gudule, whose iconic spires towered above the central city. The Marx family moved six times during their three years of exile in Brussels, retreating back to the Bois Sauvage whenever their financial resources ran short. That peripatetic existence was not unusual for refugees.

Each time, it fell upon Jenny Marx to make a home in the midst of a new neighborhood. Es'kia Mphahlele, a South African who spent almost twenty years abroad, generalized the experience of exiles, whether in the nineteenth or twentieth century. "As soon as you find asylum in a country disposed to grant it," he noted, "you are an exile," with all that term implied.[54] Exiles had to learn to cope in unknown surroundings and to adapt to circumstances beyond their control. Conditions were uncomfortable at best and unbearable at worst. As Edward Said explained, for refugees through the centuries, "Exile is life led outside habitual order."[55] The challenge that Jenny Marx faced was to establish a new order. In contrast to Karl, who had the familiarity of his books, she attended to the family and neighborly relations. The trials of exile have often been gendered.

Living abroad for a refugee was linked almost inextricably to the loss of a regular income. Marx had a contract for a book that he never seemed to finish, but he was no longer contributing articles to newspapers, as he had in France, or being paid for his journalism. His new friend, Friedrich Engels, the son of a factory owner, raised a subscription for Marx when he arrived in Brussels "in order to spread [Marx's] extra expenses among us all communistically."[56] Engels secured some additional sources of funding for the Marx family throughout their stay in Belgium to complement the meager author's royalties Marx eventually received and the money sent periodically by Jenny's mother from Germany. The sums Engels provided would have easily sustained a worker's family at the time, but Marx spent freely, often on others, and the family always seemed in need of additional resources.

Although nations granted the right to reside, it was within a city, with neighbors, that exiles reestablished their lives. Within a month, Karl, Jenny, and their daughter moved to a house at 35 (now 95) rue Pachéco, across from Sint-Janshospitaal, where abandoned children were sheltered. The institution would have been their daily view when they left their house. From there, they moved to a small, terraced house owned by their friend and physician Albert Breyer at 5–7 rue de l'Alliance, a street lined with market stalls and small craftsmen in the nearby Flemish-speaking area of Sint-Joost-ten-Node.[57] Half of the residents of this neighborhood, just outside the old gates to the city, were working class, and half were middle class. Located near the North Railway Station, where passengers disembarked from trains arriving from Aachen, Germany, the neighborhood, not surprisingly, housed a substantial percentage of German immigrants.

In April 1845, Jenny's mother, the Baroness von Westphalen, helped the young household by sending them Helene Demuth, a baker's daughter who had worked for the Westphalen family in Trier since she was a child. Lenchen, as she was known, took over many of the day-to-day responsibilities, not only of childcare, but also of housekeeping. She essentially ran the house. That freed Jenny to help Karl with his writing, including deciphering his virtually illegible handwriting for his numerous collaborators. Jenny did whatever she could to make his work easier, retiring with the children to the upper floor to give him study and sleeping space in his office downstairs.

On the rue de l'Alliance, the Marxes lived in the middle of three houses, between Friedrich Engels, on one side, and Moses Hess, a communist and early German follower of the French utopian socialists, on the other. The

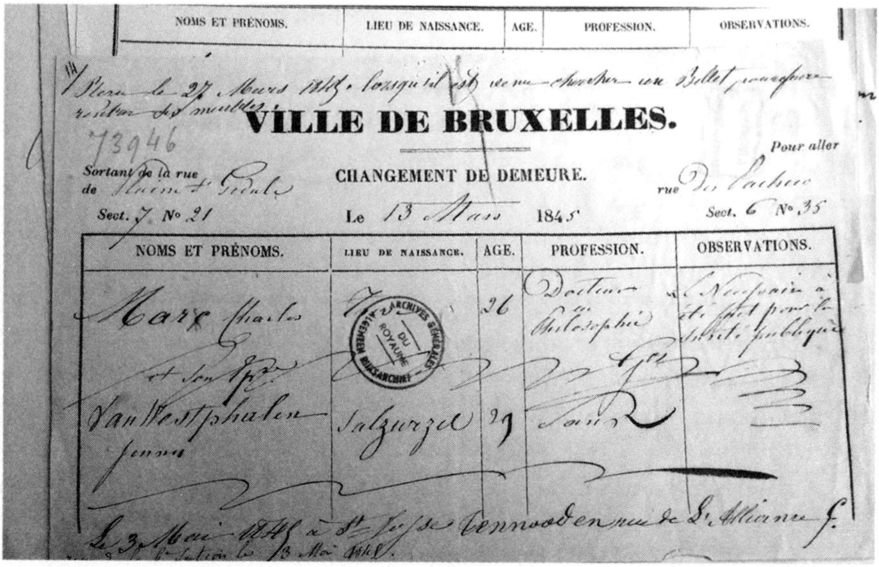

VILLE DE BRUXELLES.

CHANGEMENT DE DEMEURE.

Sortant de la rue de ... Sect. 7 N° 21

Le 13 Mars 1845

Pour aller rue de Pacheco Sect. 6 N° 35

NOMS ET PRÉNOMS.	LIEU DE NAISSANCE.	AGE.	PROFESSION.	OBSERVATIONS.
Marx Charles		26	Docteur en philosophie	
Van Westphalen Jenny	Salzwedel	27	Sans	

Change of residence form of Karl Marx and Jenny von Westphalen, 13 March 1845, from the Bois Sauvage Pension to the Rue de Pachéco/Pachecostraat. Ministère de la Justice, Police des Étrangers, Dossiers Individuels/Ministerie van Justitie, Vreemdelingen Politie, Individuele Dossiers, 073946. Archives générales du Royaume/Algemeen Rijksarchief/p. 68. Photo by author.

Marxes knew Hess from their time together in Cologne. Engels introduced his companion, Mary Burns, an outspoken daughter of Irish workers, to the group, while Hess brought Sibylle Pesch, a young seamstress he was rumored to have met in a brothel in Cologne. Apparently, Jenny disapproved of Mary Burns, whether for her background or her disposition. Marx commented to friends on the difficult relations between his wife, the daughter of an aristocrat, and the working-class woman who lived with his closest friend next door. Neighborly relations with the house on the other side were not much better, although Pesch helped the Marx family out with childcare. Within the year, Engels helped to smuggle Pesch, who had no passport, across the border to France. Marx eventually split from Hess because this former follower of the French utopian socialists could not be convinced that the next revolution would arise from class struggle.

Engels continued throughout their exile in Brussels to come and go freely from the Marx household, sharing meals and late evenings. Jenny's brother, Edgar, also spent the first winter with them, making their cramped space seem even smaller. Their door was always open to visitors seeking to meet the acerbic critic of both Prussian royalty and unsubstantiated socialist philosophy. German journalists, poets, writers, former soldiers, and Belgian professors and librarians joined the Marx family for meals. Jenny remembered the frequent additions to their circle of friends, many of them refugees, some planning to make their new home in Brussels and others just passing through. They often met at cafés in the evenings, traveling to nearby villages such as Vilvoorde for weekend outings.

All variety of communists, many in need of financial assistance, turned up on Marx's doorstep. Included among them was the German journeyman tailor Wilhelm Weitling, who had come from the Swiss cantons, where he had organized the forerunner of the Communist League, the League of the Just, and had been imprisoned. He was the author of *Mankind As It Is and As It Ought to Be* and *Guarantees of Harmony and Freedom*, "brilliant works," according to Marx.[58] In a common pattern, he collaborated enthusiastically with Marx and Engels until their ideological differences led to a dramatic break in March 1846. Marx complained that Weitling's appeals, tinged with religious mysticism, were not backed up by rigorous scientific ideas. Wilhelm Wolff, another German communist, came to Brussels after escaping four years imprisonment in Silesia on charges of violating press laws. Known to the Marx family as "Lupus," he loved to come to the house and play with their children.

During the summer of 1845, Marx and Engels left Brussels and traveled to London and Manchester to meet with other communists, read in the libraries, and observe factory conditions. They worked together in the Old Chatham Library, the oldest public library in England, sitting in a small alcove, with light from above diffused through stained glass windows. They surveyed all the available economic works of English writers, no matter their point of view.

Jenny took advantage of their absence to go home with her daughter to visit her mother in Trier. Not unlike other refugees, Jenny Marx compared life in exile to the very comfortable aristocratic home she remembered from her childhood. She acknowledged the "arch anti-German sentiment" shared by the circle of communist refugees who had been expelled from Prussia, including Karl himself, but commented that she was happy to return home. "I feel altogether too much at ease here in little Germany!" she reflected guiltily. Although France and Belgium each enjoyed "glorious" reputations as free and welcoming nations, she found herself in Brussels, living in "the pettiest and meanest of conditions." In her mother's house, she could "live quite happily in this old land of sinners." She acknowledged, "For men, it may be different, but for a woman, whose destiny it is to have children, to sew, to cook and to mend, I commend miserable Germany." There, unlike amid their colony of exiles in Brussels, "it still does one credit to have a child; the needle and the kitchen spoon still lend one a modicum of grace and, on top of that, as a reward for the days spent washing, sewing and child-minding, one has the comfort of knowing in one's heart of hearts that one has done one's duty."[59] She did not deny the ultimate higher communal calling of mankind as imagined by the communists, but for the moment, she was homesick for Trier. She did not question the life she and Karl had chosen, but back home, surrounded by the comforts of her childhood, she could not help but compare. She shared her husband's ideals, often pushing his thinking further, but gender necessarily influenced her lot as an exile.

Some biographers have taken Jenny Marx's comments about women's work to be ironic. They note that otherwise she seemed quite at home in the circle of German communists and French socialists in Paris and Brussels and that she did not hesitate to jump into the male-dominated discussions of political economy. It is clear that Karl relied on her not only to interpret his scrawled sentences, but also to critique philosophical concepts. Besides, in Brussels, Helene Demuth took up most of the housework and much of the child minding, making it possible for Jenny to join in discussions, whether in the Marx home or in cafés. That said, it is still entirely plausible that part of her never felt at home abroad. She had left her family in Germany and tried to make a life together with her husband among the fractious and uprooted political refugees in Paris and Brussels. But their finances were always desperate, and their accommodation was cramped, wet, and dark, quite different from the ennobled household where she had grown up.

The Marx's second daughter, Laura, was born in September 1845, two weeks after Jenny returned from her mother's house. In April 1846, after receiving an inheritance from Karl's uncle in the Netherlands, the family of four moved to the Brussels suburb of Ixelles, or Elsene, where they lived for sixteen months at 42 rue d'Orléans. The building, like much of Brussels, has since been destroyed, but a plaque remains at that spot commemorating their residence. Like Sint-Joost-ten-Node, Ixelles was a center of German refugees, if slightly more bourgeois than proletarian. Jenny's days were still spent in negotiations for credit with the baker, the butcher, and the greengrocer. A visitor described the house as "an extremely modest, one might almost say poorly furnished, little house in a suburb of Brussels."[60] In December 1846, their third child, Edgar, was born. Gifted and much doted upon, he died in 1855, perhaps of consumption. Family friends suggest he might have survived had he not been surrounded by such dire poverty.

All who visited the Marx family in Brussels describe Karl Marx's work during these three years as incredibly intense. One visitor wrote in November 1846 that although "Marx [was] regarded in a sense as the head of the communist party," activists would have been astonished if they had known that "he works like a madman on his history of political economy. For many years this man has not slept more than four hours a night."[61] An English friend suggested Jenny organize an "Anti 3 or 4 o'clock in the morning Association" to assure that the household was not disrupted by his revolutionary activity in the early morning hours.[62]

We actually know remarkably little about Marx's life, or that of Engels, during this first year in exile in Brussels. Of course, we know far less about the myriad of refugees who neither left their correspondence behind nor defined a philosophy for changing the world. Marx experienced these three years of exile in Brussels as a period of "freedom." His ideas ranged widely, stimulated by the company he kept, without significant interruptions. He considered the wider world, not Belgium, as his sphere of theory and action.

It is clear that more important to the Marx family than nationality was their de facto claim to residence. While Marx's reading and discussions extended far beyond national borders, his daily existence was locally rooted in a series of Brussels neighborhoods. The nation-state was young, and definitions of formal citizenship were still evolving, in particular the politics of who was a citizen, who enjoyed rights, and who wielded political influence. In this era of emerging nation-states, the municipal neighborhood was what mattered on a day-to-day level for refugees. They claimed their social rights at the local, not the national, level. Every day, they encountered neighbors in their cafés and shops or, in Marx's case, in the libraries. These ever-changing informal social spaces were defined by the groups that inhabited them, including numerous political refugees.

The lives of refugees were at the same time local and global. In exile, politics had no national center. Instead, it was multilayered. Foreigners, by definition, were excluded from state affairs, but they could hardly avoid being involved at the local level. The Brussels inhabited by Marx was what urban sociologist Warren Magnusson described as "not an order susceptible to sovereign authority."[63] In the central city and neighborhoods surrounding it, many workers' families crowded into single rooms in the warren of alleyways hidden between the grand boulevards.[64] Conditions in the neighborhoods of the capital of the most industrialized country on the European continent were so miserable that the Belgian government was compelled to launch an inquiry in 1846 into the low-lying regions of the city, where epidemics, unrest, and crime festered. The city of Brussels proved the perfect site for imagining a proletarian revolution and a fluid future without nation-states.

Historical Materialism

Walking up the hills of suburban Ixelles from his house on rue d'Orléans to the Royal Library in the center of Brussels, where he pored over economic statistics, Marx would have passed multitudes of out-of-work laborers and underemployed artisans newly arrived from the countryside. It mattered, more than most political theorists and economists have granted, that Marx was a refugee in the capital of a progressive, industrializing nation when he developed his economic understanding. Marx elaborated his theory of historic materialism in these fruitful years, between 1845 and 1847.

The numbers of the destitute increased over the three years the Marx family spent in exile in the Belgian capital. These were the years of a dramatic and worsening economic crisis with massive unemployment in the Flemish agricultural sector, beginning with flax, a product that had employed more than one-third of the population of the northern region of Belgium. Compounded by the failure of the potato crop in the summer of 1845, Belgian peasants in Flanders suffered what the progressive paper founded in 1844, *Le Débat social* (The Social Debate), described "as misery." Readers were led to believe unrest was imminent. When a pamphlet calling attention to the crisis and urging revolt elicited charges from more conservative media of foreign involvement, *Le Débat social* weighed in, trying to quell the scapegoating of outsiders; it was just the rumblings of hungry people, the editors suggested inclusively.[65]

The suffering of impoverished laborers was exacerbated by a typhus outbreak. By 1847 the situation in Belgium, as elsewhere in Europe, reached crisis proportions. Prices for basic goods continued to rise while wages fell, not only in Flanders, but also in the capital city. Three years of famine and unemployment boiled over, provoking the pillaging of bakeries in Bruges, for example, and riots in Kortrijk, Grammont, Ronse, and Ghent. Beggars by the hundreds were on the march, stopping at farms throughout the spring of 1847. Newspapers reported sightings of armies of the hungry and unemployed on the road, noting the readiness of troops. Nevertheless, Marx's eyes were in his books.

After his early experience with Prussian censorship, Marx had decided "to withdraw from the public stage to my study."[66] In Paris, during his first two years of exile, he had focused his attention on political economy, filling nine notebooks. Marx wrote an additional six notebooks during his first six months in Brussels, with notes from his reading and extracts from manuals of political economy and economic histories.[67] These notebooks contained 434 handwritten pages with notes on fifty-four different writers. Marx came to understand the worker and his labor through reading, including, no doubt, Engels's most recent publication, *The Condition of the Working Class in England from Personal Observation and Authentic Sources*, more than from his own observations of the increasing misery all around him in Belgium.

This period is distinguished by the most intimate collaboration between Marx and Engels, solidified by their study tour of England. Building on the ideas of other socialists, Engels and Marx turned their attention to political economy as the study of man's conscious life activity—that is, they looked to the working class as revolutionary actors and the factory as the stage on which the next revolution would begin. Engels focused on the expansion of trade, with an acknowledgment of Adam Smith's linkage of global commerce, liberty, and peace. Hamburg and Altona in the 1790s could be cited as the perfect examples of such a connection. For Engels, however, free trade, such as that envisioned at the end of the eighteenth century, led inevitably to competition among nations, the expansion of manufacturing, and increased misery. Marx would return to this critical question of freedom of commerce a year later.

From the beginning, his reading and discussions in Belgium and England led Marx to distinguish his socialism from all that surrounded him in terms of theory. He objected to philosophers and economists who accepted categories derived from their observations of existing structures. In publications and in person, he attacked Feuerbach for his abstractions, Proudhon for his failure to understand political economy, and Hegel for his idealism. His direct attack on Proudhon was published in July 1847 as the *Poverty of Philosophy*. The more general critique would not be compiled until after his death, when the pieces were published as the *German Ideology*.[68]

Marx was determined to understand the origin and meaning of capitalism so that he could contribute a critical analysis of the system. Man made himself through his labor, that much was clear for both Marx and Engels; changes in production propelled human history. For the next two years, the circle of socialists surrounding Marx in Brussels, including Jenny, "anxiously awaited" the publication of Marx's "book on political economy and politics." It would secure his reputation, establishing "for the whole of Germany what you already are for your friends," a supporter wrote. "With your brilliant prose style and the great clarity of your argumentation, you must and will assert yourself here and become a star of first rank."[69] Marx had signed a contract with a publisher for a two-volume work to be entitled *Critique of Politics and Political Economy.* But as he kept missing deadlines, even his publisher had become nervous that the promised book would never be finished. Nevertheless, he could explain: "From this moment on, the science of this historical movement will cease to be doctrinaire and will become revolutionary."[70] Marx could not avoid the pull of politics into the cafés and away from the libraries for long. Stateless, he felt at home among the refugees and their unsettled ideas.

CHAPTER SIX

Alliances

"Democrats from the World Over"

MARX'S IMAGINED COMMUNITY OF revolutionaries materialized in Brussels in the years leading up to the 1848 Revolution. Watchmakers, cabinetmakers, printers, cobblers, tailors, carpenters, and launderers, as well as a handful of journalists, professors, doctors, and lawyers, gathered in associations, some secret and others open to the public in the Belgian capital. Some of the politically engaged men and women had lived in Brussels their whole lives. Others were newly arrived, seeking refuge from struggling economies and repressive politics throughout Europe. Exiled at the crossroads between his native Prussia and revolutionary France, Marx mingled with them all, with republican lawyers, radical artisans and workers, and a few governing Liberals from Belgium, as well as French, German, Italian, and Polish socialists and communists. Their associations connected with similar organizations in London and across the continent, constituting the forerunners of socialist and communist internationals.

Brussels may not have offered the lively nightlife that political refugees had enjoyed in Paris, but it afforded space for a stimulating fraternity of intellectuals, artisans, and workers—Belgians and international refugees alike. The Belgian capital functioned as an example of what contemporary sociologists identify as the propensity within a city to tolerate divergent groups coexisting with their own rules while living side by side.[1] Newly arrived political refugees chased from less liberal states convened in conversation with lawyers who had founded the independent Belgian nation and workers and artisans who intended to extend the rights of the nation beyond propertied men of wealth. They intermingled in the city in international associations that were organized locally, crossing permeable boundaries of social class and nationality.

The freedom of movement guaranteed by the Belgian Constitution was a precondition for association and collaboration. Although rarely intervening, Brussels police monitored clandestine gatherings and public assemblies as well as they could with limited resources. Legend has it that police agents predictably made the rounds of Brussels cafés between nine and eleven o'clock in the morning and three and five in the afternoon.[2] In between, they could be counted on to retire to their own cafés for lunch and a beer. Even as the national government worried about agitators, it was reasonably safe for groups to assemble at midday or in the evening in the Belgian capital.

In Brussels, surrounded by refugees as well as local artisans, workers, and lawyers, Marx moved from theory to action, from writing to organizing. He could be found conversing in lecture halls and at conferences not only with utopian socialists from France, but also with the Belgian Liberals, who emerged as the dominant party in the national government in 1846. He openly collaborated with Belgian republicans. This give-and-take apparently escaped the gaze not only of the police doing their surveillance, but of many historians as well. Neither the police nor historians suspected that German communists would find common ground for collaboration with Belgian republicans and discussion with Belgian Liberals. The attention of the police turned to what they viewed as more incendiary alliances on the far left. And for their part, most political theorists and biographers read Marx's more rigid class analysis from works published in London in the last decade of his life back into his earlier experiences in Brussels.[3] The archives in Brussels tell a different story.

The picture that emerges of these years in the capital of the new industrial nation is one of experimentation and outreach. Nothing was yet set in stone. In struggles unfolding all around Marx and Engels and other refugees, the proletariat and the bourgeoisie, communists, republicans, and Liberals debated definitions of democracy. With its early industrialization and successful 1830 revolution for independence, Belgium provided Marx and Engels an ideal setting for understanding the historical dialectic leading from the French Revolution to the Revolutions of 1848.

Theories of class struggle that would determine the strategy of socialist and communist parties around the world into the twenty-first century evolved in the midst of discussions among communist refugees and Belgian democrats. Here, Marx and Engels recognized the development of capitalism as a precondition of communism. Over the course of these three years exiled in Brussels, Marx established himself as an astute analyst of economic development.

The newly independent Belgian nation was poised at the crossroads of French, British, and German movements for reform and revolution. The alliance forged among groups of exiles, from the Polish revolutionaries to the German artisans, with Flemish artisans and Brussels Liberals, propelled Marx and Engels onto an international stage. The groups' stories are usually told in isolation from each other, missing the dialectical relationship between refugees and the societies that offered them asylum.

Arrayed along a political spectrum, group memberships shifted, and alliances came apart and reformed. Categorization and differentiation of radicals, republicans, liberals, communists, and socialists is difficult, especially in terms recognized two centuries later. In the first half of the nineteenth century, "socialist" and "communist" were used interchangeably. Most of them identified as democrats who supported extending rights to the people. So, too, did the radicals, republicans, and liberals. Before they were sorted out by the barricades of 1848, members of the working and middle classes, revolutionaries and reformers, fit into this widely used, all-inclusive category. Some democrats were republicans who opposed the rule of monarchs and the consolidation of power. And yet "republican monarchy" was a term used by contemporaries to describe Belgium at its founding.[4] The relationships between them defined the possibilities and changing visions in this cosmopolitan capital in the center of Europe where disparate groups could collaborate. Their associations are testimony to the balance they forged, quietly and without great fanfare, in a city with relatively open doors.

Marx is known to his biographers for conflict, mainly from his many letters that have survived and been published. From his correspondence, it has been all too easy to conclude that this irascible founder of an embattled political economy was always feuding, at war with every thinker who questioned the tenets to which he ardently adhered. Even the chapters of his many biographies skim over the interactions with both the refugees and Belgian associations. These were critical in the formation of Marx as a political thinker and in the evolution of his theories.

Refugees played a significant role in a frenzy of burgeoning associations. The Correspondence Committee, which Marx and Engels founded in 1846 as a network linking French and English communists, not only bridged the distance, physical and ideological, between London and Paris, but also brought together refugees—primarily Poles, Germans, Italians, and Frenchmen—with Belgians within Brussels. At the meeting of the Association démocratique (Democratic Association), founded a year later, Belgian founding fathers shared center stage at large public meetings with German communists, French socialists, Polish radicals, and a Russian anarchist. These unlikely collaborations were reflected in reforms introduced in the Belgian Parliament by a Liberal prime minister who attended Marx's lectures and in the revolutionary strategies of secret communist societies. They would also fuel attempts by authorities to close the porous borders of an increasingly tumultuous industrializing society. Open doors were not a fait accompli in Brussels in the middle of the nineteenth century just as they had not been in the Swiss cantons in previous decades.

"The Masses Will Join Us"

For more than a decade before Marx arrived, radical coteries of Belgian workers and artisans gathered in cafés, bistros, cabarets, and dance halls scattered across the Belgian capital. Not without good reason, the novelist Honoré de Balzac identified "the café counter as the parliament of the people."[5] Here, secret groups strategized to expand the Belgian franchise, already the most liberal in Europe; to extend education, making it universal; to make taxation progressive; and to guarantee freedom of the press and assembly. Few of the men and women who assembled most evenings in these informal social spaces were eligible to vote. Like the political refugees with whom they would later coalesce, native-born Belgian workers and artisans had no stake in the government, which excluded them from the franchise. Rather than limiting their political engagement, however, this exclusion redirected their movement from the ballot box onto the streets.

In 1833, a decade before Marx, Engels, and most of the other German communists arrived in Brussels, Jacob Kats, a weaver by training and teacher and playwright by avocation, convened the first meeting of the Maatschappij der Verbroedering (Fraternal Association), to educate workers and propagate democratic principles. Subsequent meetings drew upward of three to four hundred men and women, mostly textile workers, tailors' assistants, shoemakers, joiners, and locksmiths.[6] The Catholic press anxiously warned its readers about the pillaging likely to follow from these unruly mass gatherings; the police obliged by dispatching provocateurs to stir up trouble.

The police arrested Kats and another ringleader one evening in 1836 at a meeting of five hundred workers in the center of Brussels. The crowd then "arrested" the police commissioner, who was not well disguised and easily recognized in the midst of the crowd. They forcibly escorted the commissioner to the police station, where Kats was being held. The commissioner was acquitted by an embarrassed magistrate, but Kats, the son of a Dutch military officer, was condemned to serve a term in prison. The incident in Brussels attracted international attention, inspiring the London Working Men's Association to send an "Address to the Working Classes of Belgium" in solidarity.[7]

One of Belgium's founding fathers, Lucien Jottrand, came to Kats's defense in an article entitled "Popular Meetings," praising the Belgian workers for emulating the famous meetings of English workers but warning Kats to be on guard against "the dangerous intrusion of foreigners barging into gatherings of those who wanted to discuss their rights as Belgians."[8] A widely respected lawyer, Jottrand continued to champion Kats and his "social doctrines," which accorded with Jottrand's own sympathy for the Flemish people and his view that work was the source of wealth. Other influential lawyers, such as Felix Gendebien, befriended and supported Kats financially. They regularly attended meetings and through their correspondence built bridges to English groups.

As soon as he was released, an unrepentant Kats rented a café near the newly built North Railway Station for meetings. Workers and artisans, men and women, gathered by the hundreds on Sunday mornings and Monday evenings for theater productions and meetings, which drew them into discussions of political affairs and economic questions, especially of universal suffrage and working conditions. Police informants reported on Kats's speeches denouncing the rich, who paid fewer taxes than the poor; demanding universal suffrage and women's emancipation; condemning the German-born Belgian king, who was never in residence in Belgium; and calling attention to the famine that was gripping the country and plunging workers into misery.[9] The Austrian ambassador complained in a letter to Klemens von Metternich about the revolutionary antics of Flemish workers that threatened the stability of the new nation.[10]

From her perspective fifty years later, Rosa Luxemburg, the Polish socialist in the leadership ranks of the German Social Democrats, described

Jacob Kats as "no doubt the most original of the international socialist pioneers, because he not only organized the first workers' movements, but also wrote the first democratic songs and directed the first popular theater in Flanders."[11] Through all these venues, Kats propagated his republican ideas about the equality and brotherhood of man, ideas that would lead him to share the speakers' platform with Marx in the 1840s. His 1835 play, *Het Aerdsch Paradys* (The Earthly Paradise), for example, featured a constitution for the "Colony of Liberty," set in a "republican community" living harmoniously in a remote corner of the United States.[12] Kats and his friends also organized a Flemish paper, *De Ware Volksvriend* (The True Friend of the People), to support their growing workers' movement.

In 1838 and 1839, workers and artisans took to the streets of Brussels to demand better working conditions, universal mandatory schooling, a republic, and universal manhood suffrage. The demonstrations began with a massive revolt in a Ghent cotton factory. Women and children joined the demonstrations, which spread to the Belgian capital. Speakers demanded to know why the Belgians who had revolted against foreign rule in 1830 were still starving. The target of their criticism was often the Belgian king, who seemed to take no interest in the suffering of his people. Kats, who led many of these meetings and demonstrations, not infrequently ended up behind bars.

Speakers denounced the spies dispatched by an increasingly alarmed national government. Workers and artisans pledged that they would not allow themselves to be deterred by the surveillance. "We may not be numerous, but we are informed of our rights, and when we parade with our flag, the masses will join us," one Belgian artisan proclaimed at a smaller than anticipated meeting on a summer Sunday evening in 1845.[13] Through the 1840s, the price of bread continued to rise and wages to fall, especially in the northern Belgian region of Flanders. All around Belgium, protests mounted.

In 1846, just before Easter, a pamphlet, printed in French and Flemish, claimed: "Our fertile homeland has never been so ravaged by famine." The blame fell not on crop failures but on the "harshness, egoism, greed, and inhuman conduct" of the rich and the aristocrats who lived well, while starving workers were forced to beg and steal food for their families.[14] To prevent a hunger march planned from Ghent to Brussels, Belgian authorities arrested the alleged authors and condemned them to six months in prison. Lucien Jottrand and Charles Spilthoorn, lawyers who would go on to play major roles in future democratic organizations, successfully defended the proletarian authors in court.

All of these struggles were covered by the Belgian press, most particularly *Le Débat social*. The weekly paper of eight pages was relatively affordable, read by workers and members of the middle class alike. Although its original editor resigned in 1846 because the paper had adhered too closely to the increasingly popular theories of the French utopian socialists when they toured Belgium, the paper continued consistently to advocate for the reform of governmental institutions, if not outright revolution. The editors of the paper, with its subtitle *Organe de la démocratie* (Organ of Democracy), consciously welcomed democrats of all persuasions—anyone who defined democracy as "the collective passion of the masses aspiring to transform political and social conditions, to remake the world, to establish justice and happiness for all."[15] Curiously, even as the paper moved further left, the classified advertisements at the back of the paper carried notices of "superb properties" and chateaux for sale. Apparently, King Leopold was a regular reader of *Le Débat social*.[16]

The editors appealed directly to the bourgeois with their argument that now was the time to extend rights they had won at the end of the eighteenth century to the workers.[17] All democratic forces—proletarian and bourgeois—needed to join together because there would be no individual happiness unless everyone was fed and sheltered. *Le Débat social* also carried extensive news of democratic movements outside of Brussels to define the context for reforms in their small country. The editors praised progressive causes in France and Germany, as well as the building revolutionary movement in the Swiss cantons.

The Brussels police kept Alexis de Hody and his national Department of Public Security apprised of anything they viewed as incendiary, especially if crowds involved laborers or foreigners. Police agents listened whenever speakers on the streets or in the cafés campaigned for workers' rights, and local Brussels authorities passed the intelligence on to the national government. As economic conditions deteriorated, workers claimed that the police paid café owners to deny them permission to assemble in their establishments.

What would happen if marginally employed laborers and foreign refugees, both groups restless and rootless, allied? Belgium's neighbors were worried about the new monarchy's ability to maintain order. Their fears were well founded. The active labor scene in industrializing Belgian cities, coupled with the deepening poverty in the Flemish countryside, formed the backdrop for Marx's first attempts at organizing workers. Marx would later refer to Belgium as the "paradise of continental capitalism" and the "hell of the proletariat."[18]

Communists from across the continent passed through Brussels and began gathering around Marx for informal discussions soon after he arrived in February 1845. They were drawn to his evolving critique of political economy and, as suggested by a Russian traveler, his "striking energy, will power and invincible conviction."[19] The largest number were German refugees. Although Jenny Marx would later reminisce that "the small German colony [of refugees] lived pleasantly together," fallings out frequently fractured the harmony.[20] Their conversations and heated debates reportedly stretched until two in the morning, as did their smoke-filled card games.

In addition to the Germans, hundreds of Polish émigrés had taken up residence in Brussels. The Polish Revolution for Independence ended when the Russians seized control of Warsaw in 1831, sending seven thousand revolutionaries fleeing. Most of them made their way to France. Some stopped in Belgium and ended up staying in Brussels, a substantially cheaper city than Paris. They were drawn to the circle of the Polish revolutionary leader Joachim Lelewel, who had been expelled from Paris in 1833 at the request of the Russian government. French police had threatened to arrest Lelewel at Lafayette's country estate for violating French asylum laws, but Lafayette rose to his defense. After the Austrians intervened to close most other doors, Lelewel was left with a choice of the United States, Britain, or Belgium. All had their drawbacks and risks. Lelewel chose Belgium because it already hosted many of his political allies and communication with other ports in the storm was easy. France tried to block his move to Belgium, and he later confided he was not altogether sure that "the honorable King Leopold would not deliver me to the Prussians or the Muscovites."[21] Lelewel would remain in Belgium for twenty-eight years at the center of a large Polish community.

On the road to Brussels, at the Belgian border, Lelewel was met by six Poles serving in the Belgian army, part of a sizeable contingent recruited by the king himself. Rather than arresting or interrogating him, they drove him to a champagne reception in the city of Tournai with leading Belgian radical democrats, including the social scientist and expert on public health Édouard Ducpétiaux. Crowds serenaded Lelewel under his hotel window his first evening in Belgium. Newly arrived Poles frequented a set of hotels where others had stayed before them. Lelewel and other leading intellectuals subsequently secured lodging in the center of Brussels, but other Polish refugees dispersed around Brussels, often ending up in the same neighborhoods as the German immigrants. Like Marx, they moved

Joachim Lelewel, 1832, by Nicolas Eustache Maurin. Lith. de Villain, 1832. Public domain. https://commons.wikimedia.org/wiki/File:Joachim_Lelewel_by_Maurin_with_signature_1832.jpg.

frequently.[22] Lelewel settled into two dingy rooms at the Estaminet de Varsovie.

Close ties developed between the Polish refugees and Belgian republicans who frequented the Mille Colonnes café in the center of Brussels. These alliances, spanning social classes and national borders, stand in contrast to the divisions that separated aristocratic French émigrés from local merchants in Hamburg and Altona in the 1790s.

Even if the Poles came from different backgrounds and spoke a different language, they seemed to share politics with Belgian democrats.[23] The Polish cause was especially poignant because the Polish revolution had miscarried when the Belgian had succeeded. A student leader at the Université libre de Bruxelles, speaking at a rally commemorating the Poles, bowed in tribute toward the generations of martyrs to the cause of progress and the emancipation of peoples.[24] Lelewel spoke at the funeral of the mayor of Brussels, just as Belgians attended and delivered eulogies at the funerals of Polish exiles.

Each year, republicans, both Belgians and refugees, got together to mark the anniversary of the 1830 Polish uprising on 29 November. Jottrand warned the Polish speakers, out of fear of reprisal from the Belgian government, to limit their remarks to the Polish situation and not venture into forbidden territory for outsiders by commenting on Belgian politics. Lelewel addressed the crowd, celebrating "the fraternity of peoples" and their causes that crossed national borders.[25] He pointed to Belgium's position as the hub of progressive movements, noting that humanity was interlocked, one struggle impinging on another. Finally, he acknowledged the liberties enshrined in the liberal Belgian constitution that gave him, a refugee, the freedom to speak.

Eking out an existence as a writer, indulging in politics when possible, the Polish revolutionary viewed "all peoples as part of one indestructible family. There are no foreigners, all fraternize as brothers." Poland came first for him, as Germany did for Marx, but Lelewel was convinced that there was no line dividing one nation's troubles from another's. In 1830, Polish revolutionaries fought under the banner "For your freedom and ours." "In envisioning the future of our own country, we also think about Belgium," Lelewel proclaimed in one of his many addresses to Belgian workers and artisans and to refugees from across Europe.[26] Not surprisingly, Lelewel befriended Marx in Brussels.

Communist circles in Brussels actively promoted the Polish cause, although skeptics questioned the rationale of supporting nationalism. To rally support for the Poles, especially in the midst of a nation that had successfully fought its own revolution in 1830, did not deny the ultimate international intentions of the communists, Engels answered.[27] The two went together. Lelewel, Marx, and Engels envisioned a future democracy defined in the cosmopolitan terms that mirrored their community in asylum in Brussels. Brussels proved an ideal place to organize a revolution—close to London, Paris, and Cologne and linked by political refugees and their correspondence.

For most of their time, Marx and Engels engaged in the solitary and painstaking work on their economic theory of historical materialism, but as they studied and wrote, it seemed more and more obvious to them that the next major revolution was close at hand. The time had come, they were convinced, to bring together the English Chartists, French socialists, and German communists, with all represented by refugees in Brussels. Unlike the last round of revolutions at the end of the eighteenth century, which had been centered in France, this workers' struggle, as they envisioned it, would be borderless. Who was better placed to lead the organizing than Marx and Engels, corresponding with other communists from the crossroads of Europe? Or so they figured.

"Proletarians of All Countries Unite": The Communist Correspondence Committee

To move from theory to action, a year into Marx's Belgian exile, in February 1846, Marx, Engels, and a Belgian, Philippe Gigot, organized the Kommunistisches Korrespondenz Komitee (Communist Correspondence Committee). They appealed to British, French, and German communists and socialists to coalesce under their leadership, rather than veering off on their own paths in separate directions. There was to be no doubt that the young German communist, Marx, would provide that leadership. Nonetheless, the aspiring communist leaders admitted there might be variations on the theme of revolution based in class struggle.[28] Only with an interchange of ideas, they explained, could the communists ultimately transcend borders imposed by nationality. Theirs was the first international socialist or communist movement with a central committee and international correspondents linked as far away as America.

Engels spelled out the organization of the Communist Correspondence Committee in October 1846, insisting on adherence to the foundational principle of class struggle. Rather than "All men are brothers," the slogan of London associations, the Brussels-based communists would look to the victory of the proletariat over the bourgeoisie. Workers would abolish private property and replace it with a common community of goods. Their democratic revolution would be violent.[29] The revolution would also be international, a key difference from the revolutions the bourgeoisie had organized within national borders, Engels repeated.[30]

Letters of affiliation arrived from London, Paris, Lyon, Cologne, Elberfeld, Kiel, and Zurich, among other centers of radical political activity. Correspondents used Philippe Gigot's house in the center of Brussels as their letter box. The twenty-six-year-old paleographer and archivist employed by the city of Brussels had first been inspired by Jacob Kats. Affectionately called "our good old Gigot" by Jenny Marx, this key organizer in the new movement had grown up in Vienna and was conversant in French, Dutch, German, and Spanish.[31] He handled correspondence with workers and intellectuals from France, Germany, England, Russia, and Italy, as well as Belgians, and remained close to the Marxes throughout their exile in the Belgian capital.

Marx and Engels formed alliances with radicals, socialists, and communists from across Europe, but they also scattered their opponents. They were especially biting in their attacks on utopian socialist followers, using all newspapers at their disposal to ridicule their ideas of free love and attractive work—that is, of revolution without class struggle.

Few communists or socialists escaped unscathed. In what Marx called a "sifting" of the party, communists who did not adhere to the founding principles of the Correspondence Committee were effectively marginalized.[32] Marx's attacks on the "True Socialist," Karl Grün, who had just published a history of the socialist and communist movements in France and Belgium for German readers, were typical. In his letter inviting Pierre-Joseph Proudhon, one of France's leading socialists, to join the Correspondence Committee, Marx denounced Grün as a "knight of the literary industry, a kind of charlatan who makes a business of dealing in modern ideas." Marx warned Proudhon to "watch out for this parasite."[33] When Proudhon rose in Grün's defense, Marx turned on Proudhon, a particularly fraught move given Proudhon's large following. Marx then took the trouble to rework Proudhon's *Philosophy of Poverty* as *Poverty of Philosophy*, attacking him for thinking he could introduce socialism without a revolution. As a result, Proudhon refused to join the committee as its Paris correspondent, accusing Marx and Engels of intolerance for insisting on a narrow orthodoxy. That was a blow to their movement but not a surprising one given their approach and the apparent urgency of the task at hand.

Many of the men Marx and Engels personally invited to join them in the inner circle also soon found themselves back on the outside, ostracized. Much of the correspondence has survived as testimony to Marx's irascibility. For example, Marx challenged his friend Wilhelm Weitling for daring to elaborate his dream of an egalitarian social order. Marx proclaimed that Weitling's "false hopes" would lead to the ruin "of the oppressed," not the salvation of the working class.[34] Weitling, who had shared midday meals with the Marx family, was subsequently subjected to a withering critique of his ignorance, complete with fist thumping. He left for America.

Marx and Engels eventually agreed to join forces with Weitling's League of the Just, renaming the international workers' association the Communist League. Although the league was headquartered in London, where it hosted an international congress attended by deputies from Paris, Brussels, and London, Marx and Engels did not relent in their intention to keep the center of gravity in Brussels. Wilhelm Wolff from Silesia represented the Brussels communists at the London meeting, while Engels spoke for the French. Marx cited his dwindling family finances as his reason for not traveling to London, but he agreed to become president of the Brussels "Congregation," with Gigot acting as secretary. The league formally adopted Marx's and Engels's goal of the overthrow of the bourgeoisie and all its members were sworn to secrecy. So effective were they that authorities in Brussels did not learn of its existence until after Marx had been expelled from the Belgian capital years later. The Communist League, meeting under the banner devised by Marx and Engels, "Proletarier aller Länder vereinigt Euch," or "Proletarians of all countries unite," marked a new stage in the organization of an international communist movement.[35]

Taking their cue from the London league, the Brussels Communist League founded a Deutsche Arbeiterverein (Workers' Educational Association) in the fall of 1847. English organizers in London who had initially despaired that "dismay, doubt, and apathy pervaded the broken ranks of the Germanic emigration" were heartened by the Communist League's organization of a reading room with subscriptions to ten newspapers; a library with five hundred volumes; and lectures and classes on history, drawing, and astronomy.[36] The Workers' Education Association met at Le Cygne, a café on the Grand Place in the center of Brussels. In the shadow of the Brussels town hall, the medieval symbol of Brussels's freedom, refugees discussed economic and political questions on Wednesdays. Frequently Marx lectured. Women attended on Sundays when they, like the men, read the newspapers of the week and were occasionally treated to a concert or a play.

The editors of *Le Débat social* noted that the Workers' Education Association gathered in the same café where Belgian founders had met in 1830.[37] Were the German refugees carrying forward the Belgian founders' struggle for rights and extending these rights to a larger sovereignty? Or did their organization mark a new phase in the history of revolutionary struggle? As if in answer, the Workers' Education Association, which had begun with just thirty-five members in Brussels, most of them friends of Marx and Engels, doubled within weeks, from one to two hundred active

The café Maison au Cygne, on the Grand Place/Grootmaarkt in Brussels. C-12101. Courtesy of the Archives de la Ville de Bruxelles/Stadsarchief Brussel.

members. The Brussels police took notice. They clearly did not see the laborers from across Europe as an extension of the founding fathers but as outsiders who warranted strict surveillance.

The circulation of newspapers grew along with the membership of the association. Marx and Engels, among a host of others, wrote for the *Deutsche Brüsseler Zeitung* (German Gazette of Brussels), founded in January 1847. Published twice a week, on Thursdays and Sundays, it was sold in bookstores and train stations in Brussels and the Belgian provinces, as well as abroad. Perhaps in keeping with Marx's pledge to the Belgian government—or because its attention was focused on the Germans and the British—the *Deutsche Brüsseler Zeitung* covered the larger neighboring countries of Europe but not Belgium itself. Given its language of publication, German, its influence among Belgian workers was probably small, but its articles were picked up by other papers.

The French and the Prussian governments, both tracking the movements of political refugees, warned the seemingly unconcerned Belgians that German communists had chosen their capital as "the center and hub of their operations."[38] Even if London was ostensibly the headquarters of the league, the settling of so many political refugees in Brussels made it the veritable command center of the communists. Their neighbors demanded to know why the Belgians did not immediately shut down the dangerous paper edited by refugees whom the French had already driven from their country. In a confidential memorandum, the French ambassador assured the Belgian foreign minister that the Belgians' decisive intervention would serve to demonstrate the country's regard for France.[39] Belgian ministers discussed the French directive, responding evasively that although they wanted to make themselves agreeable to their neighbor, they had to abide by Belgian law. The Prussians and the Austrians echoed the French, forwarding the most egregious issues of the paper to Belgian authorities, but to no avail.[40]

The new editor of the *Deutsche Brüsseler Zeitung*, Adelbert von Bornstedt, for whom Marx had written articles in Paris, had followed Marx to Brussels, drawn by the freedom of the press, at the time guaranteed only by governments in Switzerland, England, and Belgium. He established himself in the same neighborhood of Brussels as Marx. The Belgian minister of justice summoned Bornstedt for a meeting. A baron from an old Prussian family, Bornstedt indignantly answered that he was neither a refugee nor a democrat like Marx but instead, a Prussian citizen who was a supporter of Belgian independence and an admirer of the Prussian king. Bornstedt easily secured permission from the Belgian government to stay in Brussels. It appears that he agreed to spy on Marx and Engels for the Prussians, or so many of the other political refugees exiled from France and Prussia suspected. The Belgian minister was not above such clandestine surveillance, and it was easier to rely on less scrupulous neighbors to do their work.

Marx established himself as a formidable presence in the refugee community. A Russian exile who witnessed him in action described Marx as "a type of man formed all of energy, a force of will and unshakable conviction." He added, "[Marx] spoke only in the imperative, brooking no contradiction, and this was intensified by the tone, which to me was almost painfully jarring, in which he spoke."[41] Historians have emphasized the splits among the communists around Marx. They were a fractious group. The times made them more so. Marx and his sometime friends recognized the impending crisis; they all wanted to lead the transition to a new world beginning from the center of Europe.

Liberals Allied: "The Social Transformation towards Which the World Aspires"

Toward the end of 1846, Lucien Jottrand, the founding father who designed the Belgian flag in 1830, commented that everywhere in Europe the democratic spirit had begun to awaken. "The era of reaction has ended," the Belgian lawyer sighed with relief.[42] For him, that meant that at last, after almost two decades, the promise of the Belgian Revolution would be realized. Rights would finally be extended to all, even the propertyless workers.

All around them in the mid-1840s, democrats—liberals, republicans, radicals, socialists, and communists—saw signs of a dire economic crisis, as well as indications of broadening political engagement. Beyond Belgian borders, they were encouraged by the political banquets organized in France, by the momentum of a free trade campaign in England, and by the shifting power dynamics of diplomatic negotiations in central Europe. The Belgians were at the intersection of all these democratic movements, linked by the refugees who continued to arrive and to meet in the Belgian capital.

The expectation of change encouraged collaboration among different ideologies all along the left half of the political spectrum. Robust, if transitory, alliances marked the years of theoretical engagement in response to the economic and social crises of the 1840s. Discussions of capitalism and its crises brought men and women from different political circles into conversation, influencing evolving strategies for ameliorating the condition of labor and expanding the franchise.[43] At the edges, Belgian liberals and German communists found political ground for discussions in this rich period of ideological cross pollination.

Within Parliament, a coterie of Belgian liberals shared the expectation that the changing political landscape of the 1840s would offer new opportunities for organizing. Three hundred and fifty Freemasons founded a liberal alliance in 1841. When they admitted outsiders not belonging to their lodge, the membership mushroomed. The liberals agreed to a platform that included electoral reforms and the repeal of reactionary laws passed since the inauguration of the Belgian constitution, as well as improvements in the living and working conditions of the working class.

The Belgian Liberal Association formally convened in 1845 on the Grand Place in the Maison des Brasseurs. The next year, it convened a congress in the Hôtel de Ville/Stadhuis (City Hall). All around, the gilded guild houses, which now attract international tourists, were frequented by workers. Like today's tourists, these workers sought a beer, but then they proceeded to hold their political gatherings and to organize their demonstrations, now in the same neighborhood as the Liberals.

Inauspiciously, the Liberal Association had no sooner gathered for its first congress than it split between moderates and a more progressive wing over a proposition that would have limited participation in the group to Belgians with voting rights. On the left of the more orthodox Liberals, the Liberal and Constitutional Association avowed its faith in the 1830 Belgian Constitution. It would represent the bourgeoisie, its members declared openly, without neglecting the interests of the people, opening the door to cooperation with more radical forces, including the communists.

French King Louis Philippe advised his nephew, Leopold I, king of the Belgians to be on guard.[44] The French monarch considered the Liberal congress nothing short of a revolutionary national convention, an institution whose power to displace kings he knew all too well. Even if the Belgian Constitution notoriously allowed associations, surely it did not permit "an assembly of delegates elected without legal authority, deliberating and taking decisions."[45] Nevertheless, the French king acknowledged the limits of permissible French intervention. What would his nephew do, he asked. Leopold's response to his uncle has not survived.

Belgian reformers and revolutionaries alike worried about foreign interference from neighboring powers interested in maintaining the status quo. It was no secret that both the French and the Germans, who had expelled "dangerous democrats and communists" from their countries, were keeping track of suspicious men in Brussels and London—a closer eye, it appeared than the Belgians themselves.[46] What would they do with the intelligence they gathered and shared? Would Louis Philippe ally with the Germans to crush democratic movements in the smaller states in their midst, including Belgium and Switzerland? Would Leopold look for help abroad to prevent the Liberals from rising to power in his government?

In 1847, it happened. For the first time in Belgium's short national history, the Liberals won more seats than the reigning Catholics in national parliamentary elections. The Liberal leader, Charles Rogier, a hero of the Belgian Revolution of 1830, met with the king to discuss the formation of a government, as dictated by the constitution. Rogier's biographer called him "a democrat, but a governmental democrat."[47] Born in France and the son of a French army officer who died in the Russian campaign of 1812, Rogier had moved with his family to the Belgian city of Liège, where he studied law. He got Belgian citizenship under the constitutional provision that declared anyone residing on Belgian territory before 1814 a citizen. His passion was politics, beginning with a journalistic campaign against Dutch rule. He led a militia of citizens from Liège to Brussels to fight the Dutch, launching the Belgian Revolution. One of the most active of the patriots, he secured a place on the provisional government, subsequently serving as governor of Antwerp. Rogier encouraged the Liberals to separate from the more radical elements with whom they had coalesced.

Once formed, the new Liberal government got to work immediately in August 1847. Rogier toured the hardest hit regions of Flanders and established a bureau for Flemish affairs to implement assistance schemes. Although the harvests that summer had been bountiful, after several years of shortfalls, the reality of the deep-seated poverty in Flanders troubled the new Liberal ministry. Typhoid added to the crisis introduced by widespread unemployment. Rogier made clear that as a democrat, he intended to meet the needs of those who suffered. He explained, "The more I feel sympathy for their interests, the more I want to give legal power and authority to the government."[48] The Liberal government, he vowed, would do more than deploy limited Catholic charity. It would act. Government projects would get people working, a number of Liberals argued, against those advocating an approach of laissez-faire.

Rogier had extensive experience in public works, especially with the running of the Belgian railway, the first national rail system in Europe. He also had connections with Victor Considérant, an engineer and French utopian socialist Charles Fourier's most articulate follower. Influenced by utopian socialists, the Belgian engineers who organized the railway that would become the densest network in the world borrowed engineering designs from England, but in keeping with utopian socialist precepts to which they adhered, they turned to the state rather than private companies to serve the public interest.[49] Considérant celebrated Belgium as "that classical land of liberty and municipal sovereignty." The French utopian socialist expected that "independent and hospitable" Belgium would be "called upon to give the first example of the social transformation towards which the world aspires."[50]

Rogier had hosted Considérant on an 1838 tour that drew multitudes. Their tour through Belgium gave the French socialist and future Liberal interior minister of Belgium time to talk, reportedly for ten hours straight. In October 1845, when Considérant returned to Belgium for another speaking tour, in addition to Rogier, the future minister of war, the railway administrator, the inspector general of prisons, the director of finance, and several Liberal deputies, mayors, professors, journalists, artists, and industrialists listened attentively to Considérant's theories.

This unique collaboration between Belgian Liberals and utopian socialists only deepened when the Liberals took over the government. Placed throughout the government, Belgian disciples of the French utopian socialists rejected the "immoral" laissez-faire approach, advocating instead state planning in the public interest.[51] Free trade and the nationalizing of banks were up for discussion among the Liberals in the 1840s, as were a wide range of social reforms. Groups all along the political spectrum joined in the conversation.

The Democratic Association: "The Unity of Sentiments"

A range of democrats on both sides of the English Channel, including Giuseppe Mazzini, challenged the logic that assumed nation-states should constitute the foundation of democracy. Foreshadowing proposals that would gain traction again in the twenty-first century, they argued that democracy need not be contained within national borders. Instead, they recognized the worldwide unity of humanity and the universality of rights. They purposefully welcomed foreigners into the membership of their associations to demonstrate their shared opposition to tyranny across the globe. They were convinced, in accordance with Belgian terms of asylum, that these foreigners would not participate in discussions of Belgian politics but would instead take the common struggle home with them.

At the end of the summer of 1847, Marx and Engels collaborated with Lucien Jottrand and other Belgian democrats of all political variations in the organization of the Association démocratique (Democratic Association). They took their slogan, "All men are brothers," from the London Fraternal Democrats, with whom they were allied. The Democratic Association elected Lucien Jottrand as the first president. Karl Marx was away and missed the first meeting, but through Engels's maneuvering, he was chosen to serve as one of the two vice-presidents, alongside Jacob Kats's son-in-law, Jan Pellering. The treasurer was a Belgian art dealer who would be condemned to death in 1848 for his role in an armed uprising on the Franco-Belgian border, the Risquons-Tout affair.

Whereas the previous generation had fought to promote national movements, Jottrand explained, their successors would join together across borders. He was not only a Belgian patriot, but also a fervent internation-

Lucien Jottrand, from Louis Bertrand, *Histoire de la démocratie et du socialisme en Belgique depuis 1830* (Brussels: Dechenne, 1906), 1:145. Photo by Eleta Exline.

alist, stirred by what he saw as the universal republicanism of the French Revolution. He was also deeply committed to the revival of the independence movement in Poland. For him, freedom of speech, publication, thought, and conscience and religious, economic, and commercial liberty were human rights and the keys to individual happiness.

Sitting together, lawyers, philosophers, historians, politicians, artisans, and workers—Belgians and refugees—debated the organizational structure of the new association. The Poles, although theoretically committed to the goal of a democratic government, had been led by their own recent experience to distrust democracy within organizations. In the end, however, given the preponderance of input from the Belgians and the Germans, the association committed itself to working openly through committees. Its meetings were covered not only in *Le Débat social,* but also in the German communists' *Deutsche Brüsseler Zeitung* and in the left-leaning *L'Atlelier démocratique*, probably edited by a French refugee.[52] These newspapers were distributed in cafés but also in three German bookshops.

At a banquet held in September 1847 in a café in the neighborhood of the monumental Belgian Palace of Justice, 120 Belgians, Germans, Swiss, French, Poles, Italians, and a Russian assembled to listen to speeches in German, French, and Dutch celebrating international cooperation and commemorating the struggles of democrats across Europe. The orators looked to democratic unity to flourish and spread across borders as a result of the fraternity of peoples, not the diplomacy of nation-states. The shortcomings of the power diplomacy of nations and empires were clear to all, but so too was the promise of international cooperation among peoples.

Le Débat social praised the organizers of the Belgian banquet, modest though it was in contrast to those in neighboring France. It attracted not only intellectuals and other professionals, but also workers and artisans. Jottrand heralded the gathering as the coming together of oppressed peoples from across Europe on the free soil of Belgium. "The unity of sentiments was perfectly clear even if the speeches were delivered in different languages," he reported. Jottrand explicitly acknowledged the efforts of the German workers, who had done most of the organizational work that allowed "workers from a number of nations deprived of their political rights . . . to fraternize peacefully under the auspices of our national institutions."[53] The Democratic Association opened an opportunity for refugees to exercise political influence because Belgium's constitution guaranteed free speech for all residing within its borders.

The Fraternal Democrats reached out from London to congratulate the Democratic Association of Brussels. The London group had set the tone for international collaborations, vociferously repudiating "the term 'Foreigner,' no matter by, or to whom, applied" and condemning "the 'national' hatreds which have hitherto divided mankind." Nationalism, they charged, had been exploited "by the people's oppressors, to set them tearing the throats of each other." In the place of the nation-state with its wars, the Fraternal Democrats proposed an alliance of all "our fellow men, without regard to 'country,' as members of one family, the human race; and citizens of one commonwealth—the world."[54] The earth belonged to all, they asserted, echoing the cosmopolitans of the 1790s, who were themselves reacting to the earliest manifestations of nationalism. Their alliances across borders would show the way.

The officers of the Democratic Association accepted the invitation to affiliate not only with the Fraternal Democrats of London, but also with similar societies across the world. The Fraternal Democrats, for their part, were delighted to hear that "a society of Cosmopolites had been formed in Brussels."[55] Engels wrote Marx about his high expectations for this new association and its alliance, which would be "more grandiose and more universal" than any existing international organization.[56] Looking back from the end of their lives, Marx and Engels remembered the Democratic Association in Brussels as an "international and open society where delegates of the bourgeois radicals and socialist workers coalesced."[57]

Jottrand explained in his memoirs that cooperation was possible in 1847 between the Belgian republicans and the communists because Marx was not so well known publicly for his economic theories then. During this formative period leading up to the Revolution of 1848, Marx and Engels were still actively exploring, open to the influences of their surroundings, which included the Belgian Liberals and their Parliament. They were also reading voraciously. Marx read from a full range of economists from Pierre-Joseph Proudhon, the French socialist who identified as an anarchist, to the English utilitarian James Mill.

In September 1847, Marx was scheduled to speak at an international economic congress in Brussels. The congress presented an exceptional opportunity, according to Engels, because all leading European economists would be in attendance.[58] From the first day on, most of the speakers followed the lead of the delegates of the English Anti-Corn Law League, who had just succeeded in repealing tariffs on grain imported into Britain. They were echoed by European continental proponents of global free trade who argued that abolishing tariffs would lower the price of food for hard-pressed workers. It followed, they reasoned, that increasing consumption would result in more demand, expanding production and reducing unemployment. The end result, free traders argued, would be higher wages for all, including the workers. This free trade argument was more popular in England than on the continent, where protectionism drew more support.

In the end, Marx was not allowed to take the podium. Frustrated by the censorship of economists worried that as a communist, he would condemn trade, he gave his speech to a more restricted audience at a meeting of the Democratic Association in January 1848. Contrary to all expectations, Marx, too, argued for free trade. But he turned the free trade argument against itself. Capitalism was effectively preparing its own demise with unbridled competition.

Political theorists and economists often cite the speech on the question of free trade as the moment when Marx settled on his economic analysis. On the one hand, he argued, free trade would result in lower wages for workers, while on the other, it would encourage the accumulation of capital, accelerate industrialization to the benefit of the capitalists, and lead to the elimination of smaller manufacturers who could not compete. Free trade "is freedom of capital," Marx explained. "When you have overthrown the few national barriers which still restrict the progress of capital, you will merely have given it complete freedom of action." Then, free trade, Marx predicted, would reveal "the antagonism of these two classes," the bourgeoisie and the proletariat.[59] It would pose the question: "Whose freedom?," revealing the deleterious results of free competition.

In his speech, Marx confounded other socialists who supported protectionism instead of free trade as the most effective way to stall international capitalist development. Marx summed up his argument succinctly: "In general, the existing protective system is conservative, while the free-exchange system is destructive. It dissolves the old nationalities and pushes the antagonism between the bourgeoisie and the proletariat to the extreme. In a word, the system of free trade hastens social revolution. It is only in this revolutionary sense, gentlemen, that I vote in favor of free trade."[60]

Not only the other socialists, but also Liberals, including Jottrand, the president of the Democratic Association, objected to Marx's surprising turning of free trade on its head. He worried that it would be seen as committing the inclusive association to the path of communism. Marx circulated his speech proclaiming "We Are for Free Trade" to a number of newspapers, but almost all refused to carry it.[61] Over Jottrand's objections, the Democratic Association finally published Marx's speech as a pamphlet in both French and Dutch, at its expense.

Marx praised free trade, though not for its trickle-down benefits to the workers, as Liberals at the conference had done, but instead for its role in accelerating the demise of nationalism. The entrepreneurial merchants of Hamburg and Altona offered a compelling example of Marx's economic thesis. However, while celebrating the lowering of national barriers, this earlier generation of border-crossers, the immigrants who propelled shipping in Hamburg and Altona in the 1790s, would have stopped short of cheering on the social revolution that Marx predicted would follow the collapse of the national bourgeoisie. A diligent student of the French revolutionary era, Marx critiqued the cosmopolitanism espoused by these eighteenth-century speculators as "exploitation . . . that could only be engendered in the brain of the bourgeoisie."[62]

Marx developed the thesis of class struggle that would set him apart from the Liberals and radicals at the moment in time when he was most at ease collaborating with the bourgeoisie. In fact, he outlined his ideas on class antagonism on a platform that explicitly brought together a range of democrats, republicans, socialists, and communists. Their association would fracture under the strain of the Revolution of 1848, but in the years leading up to it, Marx found common ground for discussion with a range of democrats.

The lists of activists leading the Democratic Association constituted a veritable who's who of progressives residing in the Belgian capital in the year before the Revolution of 1848. It included five Belgians with backgrounds ranging from local workers and artisans, such as Kats and Jan Pellering, to influential lawyers, such as Jottrand and Charles Spilthoorn. There were seven German communists, four Poles, including the revolutionary leader Lelewel, and a Frenchman, Jacques Imbert. French militants were less numerous in the association and in Brussels at large because unlike the Poles, many of whom sought refuge for political reasons, more French men and women in Brussels had come to pursue professions foreclosed to them at home. They were not eager to join in a political cause, especially one that might threaten their legal standing in both Belgium and France. These French men and women tended also to be more settled than the German refugees, most of whom had arrived more recently and had come from more modest backgrounds. The political discontent of many of the German laborers had been exacerbated by their inability to eke out a living in Germany.[63]

The members of the Democratic Association could almost all agree on global democracy as their ultimate goal, but class struggle was problematic. However, the politically adept lawyer from Ghent, Charles Spilthoorn, who had been the commissioner in charge of the province of West Flanders during the Belgian Revolution of 1830, found a way to split the difference between the radicals and the communists. For the Democratic Association, he cast the class struggle in the innocuous terms of democrats versus aristocrats, terms borrowed from the French Revolution.[64] These labels would have been familiar half a century earlier among the governing circles in Hamburg and Altona, where Christine Reimarus had breathed a sigh of relief leaving the Comtesse de Bentinck's ball for what she called the "democratic" gathering in Sieveking's garden. In 1847, that compromise worked for a few minutes. Then, another speaker, possibly planted as a police agitator, riled up the audience by condemning the "egoist bourgeoisie" as the true enemy of the people.[65] Other speakers quickly piled on, telling the crowd of assembled workers and artisans—who were so numerous that they spilled out the doors of the meeting room, down the stairs, and out the door of the café—that it was kings who exploited the masses through Europe, even in constitutional monarchies.[66] The allusion to Belgium's King Leopold was obvious, especially to the many republicans in attendance. It was also incendiary.

A decade earlier, the Belgian minister of the interior, trying to reassure Catholics worried by the country's quintessentially liberal founding document, had confided: "Our constitution is good only because the people are willing not to demand we execute all of its provisions!"[67] As long as only the bourgeoisie could lay claim to full citizenship, there would be stability. That had worked for almost two decades. The leaders of the association were now calling Belgium's founders' bluff and demanding rights for anyone on Belgian soil.[68] Still, most of the Belgian leaders of the Democratic Association expected to work for reform, not revolution, and to remain within the bounds of the Belgian Constitution, which some of them had helped to draft.

Furthermore, with the Liberals in control of the national government for the first time, the possibilities for enacting reforms to extend full constitutional rights to all the people, not just those with property, were enticing. Marx was not far removed from these discussions among the governing Liberals. His lectures informed the Liberal parliamentary leaders who were now in a position to enact wide-ranging reforms. Writing to summon other political refugees to join him in Brussels, Marx observed the potential influence of their newspapers and associations. "There is more that can be accomplished in Little Belgium than in larger France," he wrote to a German poet in exile in Paris. He acknowledged that in the end Belgian Liberals, like their counterparts across Europe, would not stray from their self-interest, "for liberals always remain liberals."[69] But they could still open doors through which the communists could enter. The Belgian Constitution with its provisions welcoming refugees had done just that.

The mutual influence of the Belgian democrats and German communists over each other in this critical period may have been overlooked by most historians, but it was noticed by neighboring powers. Diplomats from France, Prussia, and Austria were not blind to these developments and conveyed their fears to the Belgian government. Austrian diplomats stationed in Brussels worried out loud about the influence communist refugees had over not only Belgian workers, but also Belgian Liberals in the government.[70] Without surveillance and with open borders, the Austrians warned, Brussels had become the veritable center of revolution in Europe.

Announcements of upcoming meetings of the Democratic Association billed them as gatherings of "Belgian democrats and foreigners" and cast their objective as "to deliberate on the establishment of a society for the propagation of democratic doctrines in Belgium and abroad by all the means authorized under the Belgian constitution."[71] The director of Belgian security, Baron de Hody, warned the minister of justice two weeks after the first meeting of the Democratic Association of his mounting fears because "the oppressed classes of all the nations had been invited to take part in the association."[72] He worried that these so-called reformers might act on their doctrines, and then the government would be blamed for having done so little to prevent disorder. Other than dispatch additional agents, there was little he could do legally.

In November 1847, at the second meeting of the Democratic Association, the honorary president, General Anne François Mellinet, joined Spilthoorn on the podium. Mellinet, a naturalized Belgian from France, had earned heroic stature leading a brigade in the Belgian Revolution. He continued to rally revolutionaries from 1830 to demand the establishment of an independent republic over the next decades. Fifteen Germans, four Poles, two Frenchmen, and a Dutchman, in addition to dozens of Belgians, all came forward to pay homage to Belgium's democratic institutions. Marx talked Russian anarchist Mikhail Bakunin, another refugee living in Brussels, into joining him at the meeting.

Marx seemed content to conform to the public platform of the Democratic Association. At each of the meetings, the presiding officers announced that theirs was an open association meeting within the terms defined by the Belgian Constitution. *Le Débat social* acknowledged that openness. Just as the seventeenth-century Dutch Republic, born of revolution, had offered "refuge to free thinkers, why should Belgium after its 1830 revolution not be the advanced sentinel of social progress and democratic principles?" the editors of the paper asked.[73] Afforded an asylum within Belgium that tolerated his public collaboration in the Democratic Association, Marx relied on the underground Communist League for clandestine and secret revolutionary activities.[74]

While political refugees, including Marx and Engels, were exploring the possibilities for democratic change in both public and secret organizations, the new Belgian nation that hosted them was figuring out its stance on constitutional liberties and security within its territory. This was a symbiotic relationship. Immigration was still a grand experiment in Belgium, first in the hands of the Catholics and then of the Liberals, some of them members of the Democratic Association now meeting with the German communists. That is not to say that the Brussels police or the Belgian security service tolerated unrest. Jan Pellering, one of the most active of the Belgian organizers of the working class, was arrested at least four times between 1846 and 1848, even while the Liberals controlled the government.[75]

Le Débat social repeatedly protested the recurring vote in the Belgian Parliament to extend the 1835 emergency legislation on immigration that permitted the expulsion of foreigners residing in Belgium without judicial intervention. The law, the editors charged, would allow the government to extradite the indigent without cause. It seemed a blatant violation of the constitution, which guaranteed full rights to all residing in Belgium. If innocent foreigners could be subject to such arbitrary authority, what would protect citizens?[76]

The dramatic influx of refugees to Brussels in the 1840s occasioned directives from the central government to exercise surveillance of foreigners at a local level. This suspicion had little effect on the daily lives of most of the refugees, who followed the rules of Belgian society studiously. From their close and frequent interactions and encounters, the political refugees, many of them communists, and their Belgian hosts, many sitting in the governing party, together envisioned a freer, more democratic society for the future.

"Eine Kleinere Kosmopolitisch-Demokratische Gesellschaft"

At the end of 1847, Marx and Engels traveled to London with the young Liègeois Victor Tedesco to celebrate the anniversary of the Polish revolution with Fraternal Democrats. A radical British paper, acknowledging the leadership of the German communists in the international body, welcomed Marx and Engels to London as "ambassadors, charged with the holy mission of organising the alliance of nations."[77] Marx had come as a delegate of the Democratic Association, which he described as "eine kleinere kosmopolitisch-demokratische Gesellschaft" (a small cosmopolitan-democratic community). He echoed the British call of international solidarity, appealing to "the veritable people, the Proletarians . . . for the establishment of universal brotherhood."[78] True fraternity among workers would open the path to liberty for the whole world.[79]

Engels joined Marx, conveying greetings from Paris. Marx invited all of the assembled democrats to the first international congress to be convened in September 1848 in Brussels. The correspondent for *Le Débat social* reported, "The deputy of the new Belgian democratic society, M. dr. Charles Marx," was received "with large applause."[80] The Fraternal Democrats conveyed the warmth of Marx's reception in their letter to the Democratic Association in Brussels. The Fraternal Democrats' meeting in London ended with the singing of the French revolutionary anthem, "The Marseillaise." Events in 1848 intervened.

CHAPTER SEVEN

"The Spectre of Communism" and a Revolution "on Our Doorstep"

THE WINTER OF 1847–48 was a particularly difficult time for the Marx family, as it was for many in Belgium and throughout Europe. Marx's personal misery, like the suffering of those around him, was subsumed in a deepening world trade crisis with rising prices and falling wages. Crops failed and unemployment rose across Europe. That winter in the company of Belgians and his fellow exiles, Marx wrote the *Communist Manifesto.* It would take the world some time fully to grasp the power of the manifesto, which opened with his unforgettable image of the "spectre of communism . . . haunting Europe."

Without a passport or other identity papers, Marx traveled from Brussels to London in December 1847, in part for the gathering of the Communist League, which would commission the *Manifesto.*[1] Marx's worries were financial, however, not bureaucratic. In a letter to a friend, he admitted his unease over his family's desperate situation, which almost kept him from traveling: "I left my family in the most difficult and hopeless situation. Not only are my wife and the children sick, but the current financial situation is so critical that my wife is literally harassed by creditors, and she finds herself in an utterly lamentable shortage of funds."[2] Victor Tedesco, a young Belgian lawyer, was at his side.[3] They joined Engels in

Ostend for a meal at the Hotel de la Couronne across from the railway station and continued together by boat across the channel. Engels had been in Paris writing his *Catechism for the League*, a pedantic first draft of the *Communist Manifesto.*

In London, over the next week, every evening after the adjournment of the public meetings hosted by the Fraternal Democrats, Marx retired in secret to a room above a pub for the clandestine meetings of the Communist League with German, French, Polish, and Italian communists. The league was so secret that Marx's friends and allies in the Democratic Association in Brussels knew nothing of its existence, nor where he went every evening.

The Communist League discussed, among other things, who would write a manifesto to call workers of the world to unite for "the abolition of the old bourgeois Society founded on class antagonism and the foundation of a new Society without class and without private property."[4] Although still in his twenties, Marx made a strong impression on all the members gathered at 20 Great Windmill Street, near Piccadilly. He was no dreamer, a delegate noted. Not known for his ability to work well with others, to his credit, Marx did not waste words. He got straight to the point, revealing his lucid logic and razor-sharp reasoning. The league's leaders handed the commission for the movement's founding document to Marx and Engels, urging haste. Little did they know how close they were to revolution.

The turn-around time to publication was short. Karl Marx wrote the *Communist Manifesto* in a month in the center of Brussels, possibly at a café, as the apocryphal story goes, but more likely downstairs in his house on the rue d'Orléans while Jenny and their three children slept upstairs or in the house just off the Sablon that served as the communication hub for the Communist League. The small pamphlet was transmitted to the publisher in London in February.

The rhetoric of the *Communist Manifesto* was international. It seemed a foregone conclusion at the dawn of the Revolutions of 1848 that the nationalism generated by the eighteenth-century French Revolution would give way to cooperation across national borders in this next round of revolutions. From their headquarters in Brussels, democrats and workers both collaborated across national lines in the middle of the nineteenth century. They were convinced that their vision of a new world would ultimately prevail. The Catholic newspaper the *Journal de Bruxelles* compared Marx, a German communist who had traveled to London to represent the Belgians, to the Prussian baron who had renounced his title and his nationality to become a French revolutionary fifty years earlier.[5] Anacharsis Cloots, calling himself the orator of humanity, had consciously rejected the nationalism that was sweeping France in the 1790s and defined himself as a cosmopolitan. Marx's cosmopolitanism was decidedly different. He had no use for the abstract promises of universal brotherhood. The *Communist Manifesto*, written amid refugees in Brussels, ended as forcefully as it began: "Let the ruling classes tremble at a communist revolution. Proletarians have nothing to lose in it but their chains. They have a world to win. Proletarians of all countries, unite."[6] A new revolutionary era had begun.

The *Communist Manifesto:* "The History of Class Struggles"

At the time, the publication of the *Communist Manifesto* went unnoticed. Like earlier drafts by Friedrich Engels and Moses Hess, Marx's *Communist Manifesto* is a document of its time and place but one with such a forceful legacy that those men and women summoned by it to the workers' revolution, and their historians, have forgotten its origins in a mid-nineteenth-century Brussels steeped in liberal reform. Marx foretold his vision of a new communist society based on his perceptions of the political and social realities around him.

Marx wrote his international call to revolution surrounded by German, Polish, French, and Russian refugees who had also found shelter in Brussels. Equally important were the Belgians with whom he worked. Notable among them was the Communist League's secretary, Philippe Gigot, in whose house Marx probably sought a reasonably quiet sanctuary for writing. "God, reason or human nature preserve us from becoming petits-bourgeois," Gigot pleaded of the small group that labored, wrote, and edited together.[7] Jenny Marx was also part of this intimate circle, serving not only as Marx's secretary because she was the only one who could read his illegible penmanship, but also as an editor and thinker in her own right. The one remaining manuscript page bears her writing.

After a few weeks, the Central Committee of the Communist League wrote to remind Marx that it was waiting for his draft of the commissioned pamphlet. Marx and Engels finished one week later, at the end of January 1848. The first run of five hundred copies of the *Communist Manifesto* was printed at a small shop in London on Liverpool Street in early

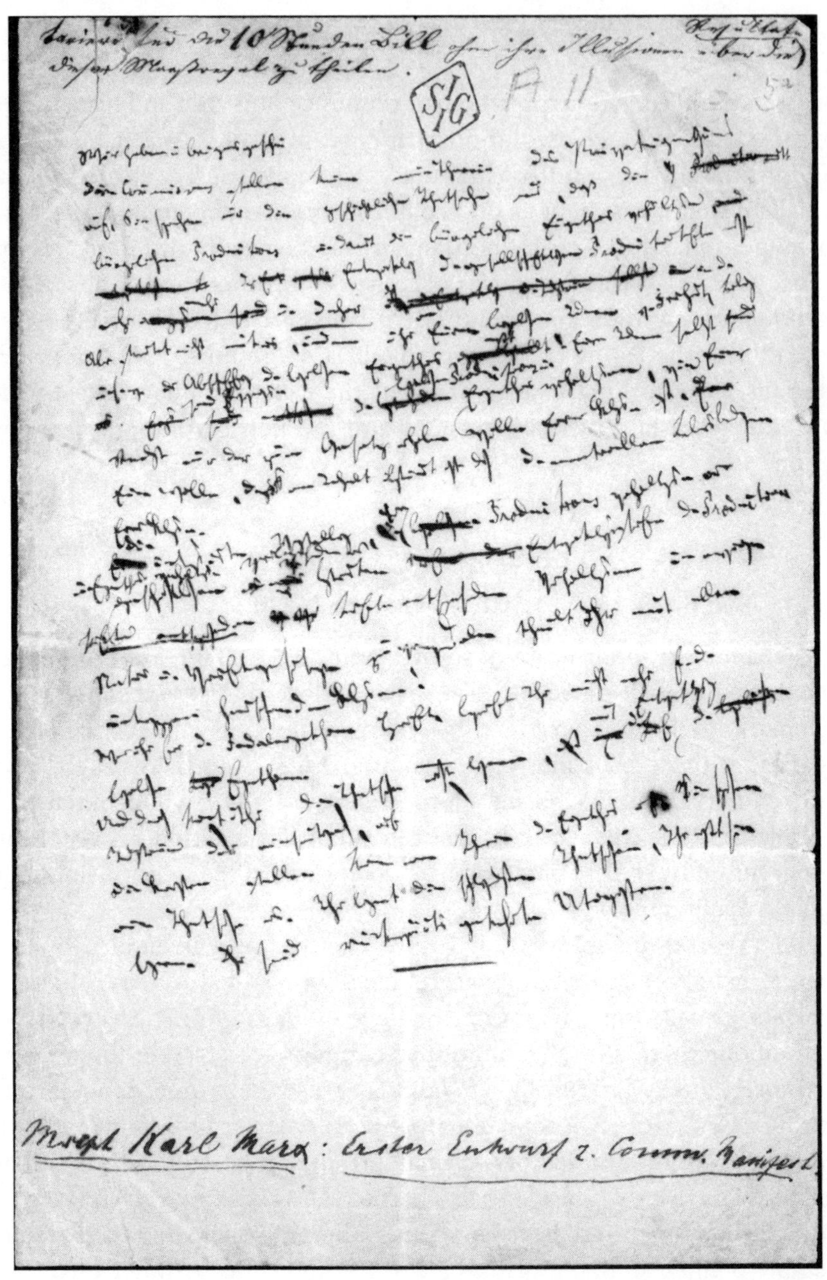

Mscpt Karl Marx: Erster Entwurf z. Comm. Manifest

The only remaining manuscript page of the *Communist Manifesto*, written by Karl Marx in 1847. The first two lines are written in Jenny Marx's handwriting. The text ends with the phrase: "Proletarians have nothing to lose in it but their chains. They have a world to win." Courtesy of the International Institute for Social History, Archive Karl Marx.

February, just as revolution broke out in Paris, and was delivered to the continent in early March.

Marx's *Communist Manifesto* got right to the point: "The history of all hitherto existing society is the history of class struggles."[8] Two hostile camps were facing off against each other. In Marx's riveting narration, the proletariat-exploiting, capital-accumulating bourgeoisie was forging the tools of its own destruction by industrializing and pulling workers onto the assembly lines in ever-larger numbers. All around him, Marx might have observed, but more often he discovered in his reading of French and English economists, the mechanization of industrial production and the division of labor. The bourgeoisie thereby created "its own grave diggers," as the proletariat worked cooperatively side by side. Reduced to mere appendages of the machines they manned, workers toiled in increasingly miserable conditions for meager wages. Their socialist revolution would be the first of the world's revolutions fought by the majority, not a minority.

In the later sections of *The Communist Manifesto*, which few readers now take seriously, Marx was more pragmatically attuned to the current crisis, especially in his native Germany. The *Manifesto* included a ten-point program applicable in "the most advanced countries" in which property would be expropriated, nationalized factories expanded, labor made universal, and free education extended to all children. In a statement that would have worked just as well in lectures to the Democratic Association, Marx concluded in the *Communist Manifesto*, "Finally, communists work everywhere for the unification and mutual understanding of democratic parties of all countries."[9]

Marx did not expect revolution to break out immediately. The *Communist Manifesto* foretold a future marked by the fall of the bourgeoisie and "the victory of the proletariat." Both were "equally inevitable" in Marx's extension of the historical dialectic into the future. Marx predicted a future when "national divisions and conflicts between peoples will increasingly disappear with the development of the bourgeoisie, with free trade and the world market, with the uniform character of industrial production and the corresponding circumstances of modern life."[10] Marx had expected an international congress of democrats called for the fall of 1848 in Brussels would precede the revolution.

Most of the pronouncements of the *Communist Manifesto* had been enunciated before by early historians of the French Revolution, by utopian socialists who critiqued industrialization, and by Marx and Engels themselves in their speeches and articles. What distinguished the *Communist*

Manifesto, and propelled it into a series of afterlives long after other calls to revolution had lost their audience, was its immediately accessible synthesis, told graphically as a story haunted by specters and stirred by capitalist sorcerers who had lost control of their spells. The *Communist Manifesto* found its purpose as a propaganda document. Its phrases have echoed through literature and political movements ever since. But the revolution it predicted had already begun in Paris without it, even if for historians, philosophers, and political theorists, the publication of what has become the world's best-known call to revolution and the eruption of the 1848 Revolutions must have been causally connected.

The *Communist Manifesto* captured the contradictions at the core of Marx's political practice during his Brussels exile. In the Democratic Association, Marx allied publicly with the most progressive of Belgium's governing Liberals. In public pronouncements, he heralded the liberal mission of the Belgian Constitution and paid homage to the country that hosted his family and that guaranteed his freedom of speech, association, and publication. At the same time, he explicated the exploitation of the proletariat inherent in the industrialization over which the liberal bourgeoisie presided. His critique of political economy not only appeared in works he published during his extremely productive exile, but it burst forth in his public lectures, attended by leading members of Belgium's Liberal government. Marx allied with the bourgeoisie at the same time as he called for its overthrow.

The rhetoric of class struggle posed a real problem for Engels's and Marx's democratic allies in Brussels. The communists introduced the language of antagonism and class struggle not only in the documents they were commissioned to write for the secret Communist League, but also in speeches they delivered to the Democratic Association presided over by Belgium's founding fathers. That language did not always square with the gradual reform agenda of the parliamentary Liberals with whom the communist refugees collaborated in the Democratic Association.

Democrats and Communists Allied: "The Benefits of a Liberal Constitution"

Political relations on the European continent were particularly fraught during the harsh winter of 1847–48, in Belgium as elsewhere. In Brussels, the new Liberal government was charting a carefully calibrated course—one that would become all too common over the decades to come—of reform negotiated between the Catholics, with whom they had collaborated in making the Belgian Revolution of 1830, and the radicals and communists supported by the yet disenfranchised workers and artisans.

The German Workers' Union celebrated the dawning of 1848 in Brussels with an international banquet. In a New Year's toast delivered in French, Marx voiced his appreciation of "the benefits of a liberal constitution, of a country where there is freedom of discussion, freedom of association, and where a humanitarian seed can flourish to the good of all Europe."[11] Other speakers included the Polish revolutionary leader Joachim Lelewel, the Germans Adelbert von Bornstedt and Wilhelm Wolff, and the Frenchman Jacques Imbert. They were joined at the podium by Belgians Philippe Gigot and Josse Meskens, president of one of the oldest workers' organizations in Brussels. Jenny Marx had done much of the organizing.

On the same day that the workers celebrated a new year of proletarian union, the Liberal president of the Belgian Chamber of Representatives paid his respects to King Leopold. "In the midst of the unrest in Europe, Belgium congratulates itself on already possessing the liberties other countries are still struggling to win," he assured his monarch. "Belgium is happy and proud to offer the world the glorious example of a people who reconciles the development of the most liberal institutions with the maintenance of order and peace."[12] Although Belgian Liberals acknowledged that working people were suffering, in parliamentary speeches they counseled all those suffering to take heart that at least 1847 had been less disastrous than the previous year. The Catholic leader presiding over the Senate praised the laboring classes for their courageous resignation in the face of the privations of the last two years. His paternalist rhetoric was far from that of either the Belgian republicans or the political refugees with whom they had allied in the Democratic Association.

That winter, the Democratic Association of Brussels attracted new members in droves. They ranged from parliamentary Liberals to workers and artisans to newly arrived political refugees. So many came, eager to join, that the association had to move its meetings from its regular café to larger quarters at the Vieille Cour de Bruxelles. Even if few leaders of the Liberal government actually attended the Democratic Association's meetings, other Liberals who had been present from the beginning of the organization of the Liberal Association participated in the banquets and meetings of the heterogeneous Democratic Association alongside workers and artisans, mostly Belgians, but also foreigners.[13]

Prospective branches of the Democratic Association throughout the country sought to affiliate with Brussels. A delegation from Brussels—including its president, lawyer Lucien Jottrand; labor leader Jacob Kats; and, filling in for an ailing Marx, the German refugee and editor Adelbert Bornstedt—traveled to Ghent. One hundred plates had been set at the Jardin de Flore for the democratic banquet to precede a public meeting that would draw more than two thousand men and women.

Charles Spilthoorn, a prominent Ghent lawyer who had served as a member of the provisional provincial government in 1831 and had been elected commander of the artillery of the civil guard in the Belgian Revolution, presided over the massive assembly. Looking beyond Belgian borders, he called on "democrats from the world over" to join the struggle for a democratic Poland.[14] Bornstedt, the editor who had followed Marx into exile, spoke at length, as he often did. He heralded European principles of democratic action that were bringing all the continent's peoples together. Carried away by his own eloquence, Bornstedt openly attacked the Prussian government as reactionary. This indiscretion would lead to his expulsion from Belgium. However, when agents arrived at his door, they found that he had already left for Paris.

Jacob Kats was equally incendiary, telling the assembled democrats that the time had come to rid Belgium of both its ministers and their king. He called on the Belgian people to unite and reclaim their rights in a new revolution.[15] At the same time, Kats assured middle-class listeners, who might have been getting nervous, that workers would not riot and pillage that evening. But, he added, they would not allow themselves to be pillaged day after day by the rich. He reminded the assembled workers of their right to petition. The meeting ended with the singing of the French call to revolution, "The Marseillaise," alternating with the national Belgian anthem, "The Brabançonne."

The provincial governor assured Rogier and his government that he found nothing alarming about these meetings. He did not think many members of the crowd were actually listening, and they all dispersed peacefully. If disorder did erupt, the forces of order in Ghent stood ready, he assured the national government. Three thousand people, mostly workers, attended a second meeting of the Ghent Democratic Association, another peaceful assembly with revolutionary rhetoric.

The notoriety and size of the meetings intensified the concerns of Belgian authorities, not only among Catholics, but also among some of the more moderate Liberals. The honorary president of the Democratic Association, General Mellinet, decried the escalating criticism of Belgian Liberals for associating with communist refugees. Writing in French in the *Deutsche Brüsseler Zeitung*, the German refugees' newspaper, Marx echoed General Mellinet in asserting that "the democrats from different nations in coming together under the name Association démocratique have no goal other than to exchange their ideas and to agree on the principles that will serve to achieve the union and fraternity of peoples."[16] Was not the free exchange of ideas a democratic ideal? he asked. Together with the editor of the *Deutsche Brüsseler Zeitung*, Marx paid a visit to the offices of the Catholic *Journal de Bruxelles* to protest personally its recent attacks on foreigners, in particular political exiles.

Compared to the unyielding terms of class struggle laid out in the opening pages of the *Communist Manifesto*, Marx's political relations in Brussels were surprisingly supple, his actions guided by pragmatism. Another German refugee with whom Marx had worked on newspapers in Paris, Karl Bernays, reminded Marx he had previously attacked all "those who do not strictly share our opinion," who "did not envision a new world order in its totality." Bernays urged his fellow communist "to critically contest these deviating tendencies," chiding Marx for being too pliable, too willing to accommodate the reformers around him.[17] Marx continued to cooperate with republicans and other radicals in Brussels as he wrangled with socialists and communists for control of the proletarian struggle.

This flexibility during this prerevolutionary period was also on display in Russian anarchist Mikhail Bakunin's willingness to join the Democratic Association. Like Marx, he had come to Brussels as a refugee from Paris. Bakunin had been thrown out of France after a particularly fiery speech at a Polish banquet. Although his oration was greeted by frantic applause from the Poles and Frenchmen in attendance, the indignant Russian ambassador had compelled the French to act. This pressure from anxious governments was becoming commonplace but also difficult to ignore. Dogged by rumors that he had been enlisted as a secret Russian agent, Bakunin traveled to Brussels in December 1847, his second stint in residence in the Belgian capital. He was enthusiastically welcomed by Lelewel, an old friend, and Marx, who vouched for him at the Democratic Association.

Bakunin wanted nothing to do with the Communist League, complaining that Marx was "ruining the workers by making theorists of them." Calling himself a man of action, Bakunin dismissed the German refugees clustered around Marx for their vacuous debate and verbal confrontation. In contrast, the Russian anarchist commended the Belgian president of the Democratic Association, Lucien Jottrand, as "active, strong, and really practical."[18] Marx would have agreed with Bakunin's assessment of the Democratic Association and of Jottrand.

Intensifying pressure from governments abroad and from Catholic politicians and journalists, as well as security forces within Belgium, strained the collaboration between the Belgian democrats and foreign communists. It faltered for months before finally breaking. In early February 1848, the tension between them was on full display after Jottrand published an article in *Le Débat social* that Marx subsequently condemned in the *Deutsche Brüsseler Zeitung*. Marx accused Jottrand of forgetting the cosmopolitan principles at the very core of the Democratic Association. Had not the association pledged to work for democracy everywhere, including within the "the country where it was headquartered?"[19] Did Jottrand shy away from criticizing Belgium just because it was the host of the Democratic Association?

Jottrand countered, pointing to liberal Belgium, where there was no need for utopians "to build castles in Spain" or spin elaborate revolutionary theories, because they had the ballot box. Unlike the refugees who had learned their politics abroad under authoritarian regimes, Belgians were pragmatists who availed themselves of the constitution to work within their system of government for equity. In conclusion, Jottrand pointed to the examples of America, Switzerland, and England, which had already made "a tolerable transition toward a more perfect system [of government]."[20]

Marx could not ignore Jottrand's blunt attack on the communists as outsiders. Communism was not a Prussian invention but had its roots in France and England, Marx reminded his friend. Germany might have a long way to go in its political development, but, Marx sneered, it would not bother to borrow its principles from "the radicalism of the small countries that were already free."[21] Would the association also strive to be acceptable to the security forces by banishing democrats holding ideas of political economy? "Foreigners take note!" Marx warned.[22]

Frank exchanges in dueling newspapers aside, the Democratic Association continued to meet and to correspond with its allies abroad. When Jottrand was unavailable, Marx chaired the meetings. They sat together on the committee planning the international democratic congress for Brussels in September 1848 with the Fraternal Democrats of London.[23]

The Belgian chief prosecutor, Hody, was unrelenting in his pursuit of incriminating evidence against the democrats, whether Belgians or refugees. He eagerly anticipated the occasion to unleash the security forces and to restore order. Little happened in cafés or the streets without the national government getting a report from municipal authorities. Belgium's neighbors were still nervous. They worried about the combustible potential of so many foreigners who had slipped through Belgium's open door into the kingdom, devastated as was the rest of Europe by agricultural displacement and also industrial discontent.

The Prussian and Austrian governments exerted pressure on their more liberal neighbors to expel the German refugees. Half a century earlier, these same powers had threatened the independence of the neutral city-state of Hamburg for offering asylum to political refugees. For Belgium in 1848, as for Hamburg and Altona in 1795, the recognition or repudiation of revolutionary France was the key question. How could nations coexist peacefully with an expansionist revolutionary power on one side and well-armed powers determined to protect the status quo on the other? How could they protect the diplomatic neutrality that allowed them to open their borders to the new arrivals and international trade on which their peaceful and prosperous societies depended? More particularly for the Belgians in the frigid winter of 1847–48, how could they offer hospitality to German communists aligned with their own incendiaries?

National borders posed no effective limit to agitation, either in terms of participation or the far-reaching revolutionary vision of the growing crowds. The Prussian minister of foreign affairs repeatedly pressed the Belgians to expel foreign instigators, especially German communists, including Marx, and the Polish refugees with whom democrats of all stripes sympathized. The Austrians and the Danes echoed the Prussians' call for tighter Belgian immigration controls, protesting their alarm at the dangerous combination of democratic agitation fomented by rootless workers and foreigners in the Belgian capital. Belgian republicans and exiled German and French journalists, editing a growing onslaught of newspapers, called out crowds that threatened not only the Belgian monarchy, but also the stability of its neighbors, foreign ministers warned through diplomatic channels.

If the Belgian government could not figure out how to stretch the terms of its constitution to restore order, neighboring powers suggested, it could follow the French, who, at least before their revolution, had no difficulty expelling foreigners. The French Chamber of Deputies had taken action against Bakunin shortly after his return to Paris from Brussels. Belgium's neighbors on all sides seriously misjudged the rapidly unfolding course of events, thinking Brussels would be a hub of disorder because of all the refugees it harbored. The coming weeks would demonstrate otherwise.

All attention centered on a large gathering in Brussels in the third week of February 1848. The Democratic Association convoked a massive public meeting at the Vieille Cour de Bruxelles to commemorate the ill-fated 1846 Kraków uprising in Poland. Members draped the hall with Polish and Belgian flags. Engels, speaking as a "German democrat," commemorated the revolutionary Poles and their struggle to secure the liberty of peasants, agrarian reform, and the emancipation of the Jews. "Nothing is clearer than that they are everywhere preparing the way for *us*, for the democrats and Communists," Engels declared.[24] Marx elaborated on that revolutionary history. He compared Polish insurrectionaries to eighteenth-century revolutionaries. "The Jacobin of 1793 has become the communist of the present day," he explained.[25] The same forces that had obliterated the liberal Polish constitution of 1791 had invaded and crushed the Polish revolution forty years later and were now pressuring Belgium, which had so recently won its independence. In his address, Marx drew upon his historic dialectic to predict the coming of the socialist revolution. Eighteenth-century revolutions enacted constitutional reforms granting rights to the middle class that were celebrated by Polish nationalists and Belgian Liberals. The communists in the next revolution, Marx explained, would go further to abolish class distinctions and property ownership.

Engels's and Marx's addresses brought class struggle to the fore, and Jottrand was quick with his retort. The divide between the two allies was becoming too obvious to bridge as rumblings of revolution could be heard in the distance. The quarrel within the Democratic Association in Brussels foreshadowed the struggles across Europe over the next year as the continent was engulfed in revolution.

Barricades in Paris: "An Irresistible Contagion"

Once again in February 1848, French revolutionaries erected barricades in Paris. Trigger-ready troops deployed in the French capital fired into the crowds. The next morning, the workers, standing firm on their side of the barricades, demanded a republic. King Louis Philippe abdicated and fled France. He was no stranger to exile. This time, older and more seasoned, instead of heading for Hamburg with Madame de Flahaut, the deposed king sought the help of his niece, Queen Victoria, in England. The French workers were showing the world the way forward to revolution, Engels proclaimed in the *Deutsche Brüsseler Zeitung*. Also in exile, Engels predicted the countries bordering France would be the first to follow the French example.

On the afternoon of 24 February, as revolution broke out in France, the Belgian Parliament was earnestly discussing reforms in the nomination process for mayors. With no consensus within reach, Rogier, the Liberal minister of the interior, silenced the contentious parliamentary debate. He called on his fellow Belgians for union "at the moment when France is tearing apart."[26] No one in the Chamber knew yet the full extent of the disruption unfolding in Paris.

The Belgian king sent his trusted loyal aide, Jules van Praet, to Paris the next morning to witness the unrest and report back. Van Praet, covered in dust and exhausted from his difficult journey, arrived in Paris at the Belgian ambassador's residence. He had been slowed down by the disruption of the rail lines.[27] Whether he conferred with Louis Philippe and helped him plan his route to exile in Britain is open to speculation.[28] In any case, his would not be the first report back to the Belgian king.

On the evening of 25 February, news first reached Brussels that the king of France had been overthrown and a republic declared. The messenger dispatched to Belgium by Louis Philippe to alert his son-in-law, King Leopold, of his precipitous fall was an unlikely one. The Comte de Hompesch, returning by train from Paris, dutifully informed the Belgian king first, as he had promised Louis Philippe he would do. Then, Hompesch communicated the news to his own lawyer, who happened to be Lucien Jottrand. Consequently, the president of the Democratic Association was one of the first Belgians to learn of the declaration of a republic next door. Rogier got information on the battles in Paris directly from his brother, a Belgian diplomat stationed in the French capital.

Jottrand immediately summoned his executive committee, including its vice-president, Karl Marx. Together they called a public meeting of the Democratic Association at their local café for the next day to discuss the impending spread of revolution across French borders. The association vowed, on Jottrand's suggestion, to meet every night to pressure the Belgian government, as was their right in a democratic society. They resolved their meetings would be open to the public.

The Democratic Association sent an address to alert the Fraternal Democrats in London of what was happening on the continent while dispatching another to congratulate the provisional government of France. The Belgian democrats reminded the triumphant French revolutionaries that they already enjoyed guarantees of freedom of speech for which the French were fighting. All the members of the association signed the address to the French; Jottrand as president and Marx as vice-president were the first. Their letters were published in the Belgian press.

On Marx's recommendation, the Democratic Association proposed that the Brussels City Council supplement the existing civic guard with armed workers to "maintain public peace and avoid all bloodshed."[29] The association urged the national government to act expeditiously, "exposed as we are to crises, by extending rights to all citizens and sharing out material resources before it is too late."[30] Only the Belgian members of the Democratic Association signed the address. The many refugees in attendance at the meeting abstained, wanting to avoid criticism of foreign involvement in domestic affairs.

While the Democratic Association was holding its emergency meetings, the Central Committee of the Communist League, unbeknownst to anyone but its members, who were sworn to secrecy, transferred its headquarters from London to Brussels to be nearer the center of revolution. Brussels emerged as the hub of the international communist movement. On 27 February 1848, the German political refugee lodged in Brussels, Karl Marx, became the de facto head of the first international communist movement. Apparently, none of the police agents in Brussels, on high alert given events in Paris, even suspected the existence of the Communist League.

The police did know about the gathering of fifty "notable democrats" at a lawyer's house to discuss an array of constitutional means of effecting a peaceful change in government such as that advocated by the Democratic Association. In an article published in *Le Débat social* entitled "The Crisis and the Way Out," they called for a new ministry composed primarily of progressive democrats. They also proposed a series of reforms to avoid the necessity of setting up a provisional government as the French had done. In the end, they urged their nation to maintain calm as discussions of a transition proceeded so that their neighbors on all sides would not be tempted to interfere in their affairs. The Prussians and the Austrians, if not also the British, needed only a minor excuse to intervene to restore order and the status quo in the young nation, while on the border, French revolutionaries might again launch their own revolutionary expansion as they had fifty years ago if they were given an opening. For their plan for a peaceful transition to succeed, the democrats counted on the good faith of the king.

Many members of the Democratic Association had openly voiced their expectation, one shared by several of Belgium's founding fathers, that it was time for Belgium to become a republic. They had settled for a king in 1830; now was the moment to go further. Word was that Leopold actually agreed. Rumors of the pending abdication of the Belgian king rippled through Brussels and beyond. They were heard in the streets of Paris and repeated by French ministers. Jottrand claimed the king had assured him in a private conversation that he had always been a republican. Leopold just wanted the change in government to be peaceful and expected a pension for himself.[31]

The Belgian king wrote Rogier, as head of the government, alerting him to "the grave circumstances" in France that made it necessary to "be prudent and attentive" in Belgium. Leopold called for increased surveillance, in case French revolutionary clubs sent agents to stir up trouble in Belgium. He suggested specifically that controls at the border be tightened and passports of foreigners checked.[32] The Liberal ministry seemed to be unified in its commitment to orderly change and on alert against trouble from the outside. Could the positions coexist?

Even if calm reigned in Belgium, the army stood ready. Hody augmented his national security forces. Local police were instructed to pass along reports of suspicious activities up through the chain of command to the minister of war. Informants slipped in amid the masses of disgruntled workers attending the meetings of the Democratic Association at branches around Belgium.[33] Hopes for a republic ran high as men and women packed the cafés around the Grand Place in Brussels, shouting "Long live the republic" and singing "The Marseillaise." Particularly alarming, a rewritten version of "The Marseillaise," intended for Belgium, was discovered by Hody's agents; it called Belgian workers to the struggle for their rights as promised in the Belgian Constitution. The mayor of Brussels banned meetings. He requisitioned artillery to defend the city hall and closed the gates to the city at nine every evening, to be reopened at five in the morning—an extraordinary measure, especially for a self-proclaimed bastion of liberalism.

Hody had meanwhile compiled a list of suspected republicans he had long wanted to arrest. As cover, he added the names of a number of refugees to his list. The arrest of foreign radicals would stir Belgian nationalism, he hoped, and deflect attention from the others. Agents tailed members of the Democratic Association following their meeting on 27 February and arrested stragglers who were heard shouting "Vive la République" as they made their way to neighboring cafés. In court, one of the arrested men testified that he had shouted only within the confines of a café, not on the streets, as was charged. He acknowledged that he was a member of the association, which had "for its goal to substitute a republican and democratic government by legal means for the constitutional government."[34] That admission was enough to land him in prison. A French woman living with a German communist was threatened with expulsion for not having a passport. As Engels noted in alarm, "Who ever before thought in Belgium of asking passports from a woman?"[35] An influential Belgian intervened on her behalf, preventing her expulsion. In general, Engels complained, Germans were chased from cafés throughout the Belgian capital.

Marx, for his part, seemed to be committed to honoring his pledge not to participate in Belgian politics. Even though ten years later Jenny would claim that her husband had helped to arm the insurgents in Brussels, in fact he seems to have stayed clear of all insurrectionary preparations. He did not take to the streets of Brussels even as packets of the *Communist Manifesto*, published fortuitously on 24 February, were being dropped throughout the continent from London. He refused to get involved in the politics of the country that had offered him asylum. His eyes were on Germany.

In an accident of unfortunate timing, in the second week of February, Marx happened to receive part of his inheritance. The Belgian police and prosecutor learned of the windfall and suspected that Marx must have solicited the funds in Germany to finance revolution in Belgium. His mother subsequently testified under questioning by suspicious Belgian authorities that the 6,000 francs—the equivalent of three years of his income—were an advance on her son's inheritance. Marx moved his family from Ixelles back to the hotel at the center of Brussels where he had started his exile. He dutifully notified the police of his change of residence. In hindsight, the move to a hotel may well have been the first geographical step away from Brussels toward revolution, whether in Paris or Prussia.

Some of Marx's closest associates, Belgians and refugees alike, were among those arrested. They included his children's preferred German playmate, the schoolmaster Wilhelm Wolff, and the Belgian secretary of the Communist League, Philippe Gigot. Under suspicion, too, was Marx's friend Victor Tedesco for wearing a worker's blue shirt, cap, and wooden shoes, clothes befitting a laborer, not a lawyer. He was allegedly overheard by a police agent predicting loudly, "If the people triumph, they will finally be able to enjoy their full rights. They will get a democratic organization that meets the needs of the proletarians."[36] The government could not turn up sufficient evidence to hold Tedesco on charges of trying to overturn the monarchy. So the general prosecutor of Brussels suggested to the Belgian minister of justice that they contest Tedesco's Belgian nationality, "which he had obtained by one means or another," and expel him from Belgium.[37] Tedesco had been born in Luxembourg.

After six days of incarceration, the foreigners were separated from the Belgians. One of the Belgians, a shoemaker, was condemned to four months in prison for having shouted "Vive la République." No charges were ever lodged against many of those arrested. There was no case to be made under Belgian law, at least not against Belgian nationals. The foreigners, however, were transported in police wagons to Quiévrain on the border. They were deposited in France with nothing in their pockets except their expulsion papers.

The Belgian government reinforced its borders with additional military detachments. Surveillance in train stations was also stepped up. Hody ordered all foreign workers expelled except for those who had an explicit invitation to labor for a Belgian industrialist. Any foreigners whose passports were out of order were also indiscriminately stopped and forced to leave the country, according to Engels.[38] Throughout the spring of 1848, Brussels police, under orders from national security officials, continued reporting on foreign workers living in their districts, with detailed observations of their employment and conduct. Fortunately, the police noted, the bad weather of late February limited the outdoor gatherings, restoring a modicum of peace to the Belgian capital.[39]

The xenophobia had its effect within progressive circles too. In the Democratic Association, alarmed members challenged the growing influence of the German refugees, including their own vice-president, Marx.[40] In the Masonic lodges, attended by many members of the Democratic Association, debates over Engels's and Marx's support for revolution put Jottrand on the defensive. The fear of German communism even stirred rumors among other refugee groups, notably the Poles. In moments of crisis, everyone seemed eager to deflect suspicion, to foreigners in general and to the German communists in particular. In ordering the surveillance of foreign members of the Democratic Association, the Belgian government reminded Belgian democrats of the promise of their liberal constitution and urged patience.

Engels chastised the Belgian government for playing to "the narrow sentiment of nationalism prevalent among a certain class of the population of a small country like Belgium." It was all too easy to spread rumors that the unrest in Belgian cities following the February revolution was all the fault of outside agitators. In Brussels, the police exploited fear of revolutionary foreigners to convince the owner of the café where the German Workers' Education Association met to deny the group entry. Without their own gatherings, more German refugees than ever attended meetings of the Democratic Association with "their Belgian brethren."[41]

Hody and his agents encountered the same dilemma that had bedeviled the Hamburg Senate half a century earlier. Liberals and other democrats in Brussels were openly collaborating with the very foreigners whom the police wanted to charge with disorder. These refugees had become friends and associates. The situation in Brussels in 1848 echoed that of the Sievekings' circle in Hamburg when outside events had given rise to calls for monitoring foreigners; in the 1790s, many foreigners had been guests in the Sievekings' gardens along the Elbe and were associates in their businesses. Integration into their open societies meant that the governing circles in both cities were entangled with the same immigrants who had come under suspicion.

Moreover, the inner circles of the government in Brussels in 1848, as in Hamburg in 1795, also included a substantial number of naturalized citizens. In both of these neutral cities, open to international trade, elite families often traced their roots across national lines. In Hamburg, it had typically taken families a generation to rise from the apprenticeships of new arrivals to share in major shipping firms and a political voice in the city. That rise took less time in nineteenth-century Belgium, another small place closely connected to its neighbors in times of peace.

Months later, Marx would taunt Belgian authorities by reminding them that the head of the Liberal government, Charles Rogier, a naturalized Frenchman, was in fact no more Belgian than the king, a German imported to rule the monarchy. Curiously, Marx continued, Belgian security was especially suspicious of those two neighboring nationalities, the French and the German. That struck Marx, the ultimate cosmopolitan critic of nationalism, as ironic.[42]

On the first of March, an exceptional issue of *Le Débat social* featured an article entitled simply "Royalty." It speculated on republicanism as a form of government for Belgium as well as France. The editor, suggesting once again that King Leopold saw things just as the paper did, commended the first Belgian king for his foresight. The king had apparently discretely dispatched agents to discuss abdication with leading Belgian republicans.

For his part, Jottrand was convinced that the moment had come to declare Belgium a republic. So, too, was Victor Considérant. The French utopian socialist who had been lecturing on Belgian tours for over a decade hurried to Brussels from Liège, where he had been invited to speak at a Masonic lodge. Considérant suggested that the Belgian king could show other monarchs in Europe how to make a dignified exit. Rogier listened to Considérant, his long-time close friend, but refused to rescind his public support of the Belgian monarch. Frustrated and unable to sleep, at four in the morning, Considérant addressed a second letter to his friend. At the head of the Belgian government, Rogier had power to wield, he wrote. It was time for Rogier to embrace a republic. "Think about it, my friend; there is in the great events, in the great acts of human life, a driving power, an irresistible contagion." Paris had shown that the future would be determined by the voice of the people. "The state of the world is changing, I remind you," Considérant pleaded.[43] To no avail. Faced with revolution, Rogier opted to restore order. That was also in his power, probably even more so, since he had allied with democrats in Belgium.

Instead of calling for a republic, then, Rogier sent a letter to the governors of the nine Belgian provinces, sharing news of the unrest next door. He confirmed his intention to stay the course and called on them to bolster their provincial and local security forces. "Neutral and independent, Belgium must keep a firm and vigilant watch over the free institutions it has set up," Rogier affirmed.[44] Otherwise, he warned, unrest threatened to disrupt the Belgian economy. He directed government officials and manufacturers to do their best to find work for the unemployed to forestall a crisis. Considérant predicted, as did Marx, that the world was dividing in two, polarizing on opposite sides of the barricades. Not, however, as it turned out, in Belgium.

"Legal and Constitutional Means"

At their session on 1 March, Liberal deputies in Parliament demanded that the Belgians take a stand on the revolution happening "on our doorstep."[45] But they were divided. Should they fortify their borders against the French revolutionaries, or should they instead recognize revolutionary France? Either way, they would anger powerful neighbors. As in the Hamburg Senate in 1794–95, there did not seem to be a middle ground. They were caught between France, with its goal of spreading revolution, and Prussia and Austria, both determined to preserve the existing order.

Addressing the Belgian Chamber of Representatives, the minister of foreign affairs conveyed assurance from the French government that its only interest as a republic was to live in peace. The vice-president of the Belgian Parliament and a close ally of Rogier responded forcefully, bringing the overflowing Belgian Chamber to its feet with his assertion: "The ideas of the French Revolution are making a world tour, but in order for liberty to triumph the world over, it does not need to stop here."[46] Three times, the Chamber broke out in applause with shouts of "Bravo." Finally, when order was restored, the spent deputy sank back onto his bench in tears, overcome with emotion. All of the neutral Belgian nation was united, the next speaker observed. He called on the French to remember their revolutionary principle: "Respect for nationalities."[47]

During the course of the parliamentary debate the next day, Liberal deputies argued that reforms now would safeguard Belgium against the violent agitation from abroad that threatened to destroy their national institutions and disrupt the economy. Bringing more people into the political process, they reasoned, would mitigate the fear of exploitation of the poor by the rich. A deputy who had proposed the expansion of the franchise a month earlier reminded his colleagues that then it had received only seventeen votes. Now that same proposition was heartily acclaimed as being in the national interest. Other speakers, many of whom had been present at Belgium's founding in 1830, reminded their fellow representatives that the Belgian Constitution had been intended for revision as times changed. The Chamber and the Senate both unanimously voted to expand the suffrage from 46,436 to 79,360 citizens. "We all must believe that in giving the vote to more citizens, we will attach them more strongly to our independence, to our nationality," a Liberal deputy concluded.[48] It was when people had no outlet to express their interests that violence erupted. France, as it had half a century earlier, offered a compelling example of angry, disenfranchised people forced to take to the streets to wrest change.[49] Belgium's Liberal regime had forestalled that.

They congratulated themselves on their success at avoiding revolution. Liberalism had come to the rescue of the small nation. After what they hailed as a historic parliamentary vote, the most consequential that they had taken in seventeen years, the deputy who proposed the extension of the franchise added, as a coda, that there were many other illiberal measures dating from 1831 also in need of reform. The Belgian Chamber of Representatives did not take them up. Instead, new parliamentary elections were scheduled. Quietly, the government also reorganized the civic guard, limiting participation to men on whom it knew it could count, and stepped up its surveillance of the cities and the borders. But what would the revolutionary principle, "the respect of nationalities," proclaimed to great acclaim in the Belgian Chamber in March 1848, mean for the political refugees and others residing outside the nation in which they had been born? With revolutions felling neighboring regimes, would Belgian doors remain open?

CHAPTER EIGHT

"Not Foreigners, but Democrats"

Refugees and a Revolution Averted

The revolutions of 1848 tested the young Belgian nation. Monarchies, both absolute and constitutional, were overturned and empires crumbled all around them. The distress of urban workers, artisans, and farmers—and in a typically Belgian mix, all those in between—was staggering. Hunger was rampant. A potato famine sent agricultural workers into cities seeking work just as the cotton industry bottomed out. The domestic linen industry could not meet the competition from mechanized industry across the channel; unemployment in Flanders reached 60 percent in 1844, and that was before the crisis years beginning in the winter of 1846. The conditions seemed ideal for a revolution. But revolution passed Belgium by.

Was it the supple response of the Liberal government of Charles Rogier that insulated the small country from revolutionary movements, some of which were planned in the center of its capital?[1] Was it the wisdom of a domestic agenda of Liberal reforms, conceived in concert with democrats in the capital, a group that included the liberal founding fathers of the constitutional monarchy and the political refugees who were emerging as the leaders of the communist international? After all, the Liberal government had partially alleviated unemployment with its vast program of public works, building canals and railroads, inspired by utopian socialists. Had the Liberal government convinced the Belgian people, both those with a voice and those yet without one, to rally around the constitution with all of its potential?

Or did Belgium skirt revolution because the Liberals had proven to be royalist in Belgian affairs while embracing republicanism in France?[2] Was it the pragmatic policy of diplomatic neutrality engineered to protect the small nation from the aggressions of its larger neighbors? Like the other small states that tried to weather the turbulence all around them, from Hamburg and Altona to the Swiss cantons, Belgium was situated between a foyer of revolution to its west and states bent on preserving the status quo to the east. The kingdom carefully adhered to the treaties of 1831 and 1839 that established its neutrality. They were its shield, protecting it from the politics of its neighbors.

Belgium was the first state to recognize the provisional government of revolutionary France, on the one side. On the other, it offered shelter to Klemens von Metternich in September 1849 when the deposed Austrian chancellor grew tired of the asylum offered by Britain. The pragmatic government overlooked rumors of French republican attempts to overthrow Belgium's monarch and ignored reiterated reminders of Austria's threats against the kingdom, which would not expel its refugees. With much debate and more compromise, Belgium kept its borders open.

If the political refugees and the Belgian government's practices of hospitality were mutually constitutive, why did that relationship unravel? When did "fellow democrats" become "foreigners"? What shifted in the midst of restive, protective nation-states to the immigration policy based on Kant's hospitality? Refugees have always been, as political scientist Leon Gordenker has observed, "unaccepted where they are, unable to return whence they came."[3] What would be their fate if the small states at diplomatic crossroads—Altona, Hamburg, the Swiss cantons, and Belgium—shut their doors?

The Expulsion of Karl Marx: "Perfectly lawful"

The police presence increased markedly in Brussels in the weeks after the February 1848 revolution in France. Agents kept Hody apprised of any outbursts overheard in cafés or, as seemed to happen with some frequency, the singing of "The Marseillaise" in theaters. They intercepted letters to Jacob Kats and reported on other Belgian workers and refugees who met him or even frequented the same notoriously "bad places." These agents reported that at least Kats was urging calm, in contrast to his son-in-law,

Jan Pellering, who had made a series of virulent speeches denouncing the monarch and calling for a republic. In addition to the artisans and workers and their known leaders, the police placed radical lawyers Lucien Jottrand and Charles Spilthoorn under surveillance. The police and prosecutors clearly did not know about the Communist League. If they had, they would have worried more. Jottrand responded to the governmental pressure by relinquishing his editorial position on *Le Débat social.* Neither he nor Spilthoorn wanted to be arrested.

Belgian authorities were particularly interested in Karl Marx, labeled "a warm supporter of the clubs and a republican orator."[4] Hody was determined to find grounds to deport the young German as he had other political refugees. Police agents making rounds in Marx's Ixelles neighborhood reported with frustration that contrary to expectations, there was little out of the ordinary happening. "The conduct of Charles Marx has been regular. He has received visits from a number of Germans," whose names the agent on duty had not been able to get.[5] Hody was nevertheless convinced that Marx was plotting to funnel his newfound wealth to buy weapons for an uprising.

On the grounds of his suspicions alone, without incriminating evidence, Hody asked the minister of justice to order Marx's expulsion. The German refugee was charged with violating the terms of his residence permit, an offense, according to the terms of 1835 legislation, that gave the king the right to expel foreigners who posed a threat to Belgium. The Council of Ministers obliged, approving the order on 1 March. The king confirmed it the next day. Marx was ordered to leave Belgium within twenty-four hours. How he had violated the terms of his residency was unclear.

Fortunately, Marx had just received a letter from the French Provisional Government voiding his 1845 expulsion order from France and inviting him to return to the revolutionary republic with his family. "The soil of the French Republic is a place of refuge for all friends of freedom," the new government promised. "If tyranny banished you [in 1845]," then, in 1848, "free France opens its doors to you."[6] Marx's move from his house in Ixelles to a hotel suggests that he had decided to take up the French on their offer to return to the center of revolution before he received notice of his expulsion from Belgium.

On 3 March, while the family was preparing to travel, Marx convened a meeting of the Communist League in his hotel. It went late, as the meetings often did. Members discussed a resolution, beginning with the customary: "Proletarians and all our brothers, unite." The leaders explained that with so many of the group's members, including many of the German refugees residing in Brussels, under arrest or threatened with orders of expulsion, the Central Committee of the Communist League had decided to move its headquarters yet again, this time to Paris, "which is now the center of the revolutionary movement."[7] Karl Marx would remain in charge of its activities. The members dispersed for the night, and Marx reentered his apartment on the third floor of the hotel to pack up his affairs.

As the police told the story, that evening, after an earlier meeting of the Democratic Association, several men, including a number of foreigners shouting their support for a republic, made their way through the streets of central Brussels to Marx's hotel. There, at eleven at night, they convened a meeting with a Russian, several Germans (including Dr. Breyer), and some Poles; the meeting went on until after midnight. The police assumed the men belonged to the German Workers' Educational Association. They still did not know about the Communist League. As the gathering dispersed, a police inspector entered and demanded that Marx turn over his papers. Unable to produce what was required, Marx was arrested.

The details of the justice minister's report diverged from the public statement of the Brussels police, agreeing just that Karl Marx had been served with a notice of expulsion the previous evening. But, the justice minister added, Marx had been discovered by the police in the midst of his preparations to depart. The justice minister concluded that the invasion by nine or ten armed agents and Marx's arrest happened despite the fact that "the position of Mr. Marx was perfectly lawful."[8] The national government, now in Liberal hands, charged the police of Brussels with responsibility for this rogue action.

The different stories diverged even more profoundly in the various recountings of the arrest of Jenny Marx, a much more sensitive and clearly bungled affair. The minister of justice elaborated in his account that Jenny Marx had been sleeping in the adjoining room when her husband was taken away. She dressed and was escorted by the son of the hotel owner to Jottrand's residence. En route, on the rue Royale, she met their friend Philippe Gigot, who started to accompany her. Gigot was then taken into custody, even though he was well known as a municipal employee. Jenny Marx was subsequently arrested and held overnight.

Marx added in his published account that his wife had gone herself to consult their friend Jottrand, a lawyer, about the necessary steps she could take to free her husband. When she returned to the hotel, she found a policeman, who advised her that if she wanted to speak to her husband, she should follow him. Instead, when she arrived at the station, she was interrogated about her reasons for visiting Jottrand and then charged with vagabondage for being out on the streets so late at night. She was imprisoned with "lost women." The next day, she was transferred under police escort to a cell at the magistrate's office. "At length she appeared before the magistrate who was astonished that the police had not carried their attentions to the extent of arresting the small children too," Marx wrote with a full measure of angry sarcasm. Their three children had been left behind in the hotel with a maid. Marx added: "The interrogation could only be a farce since the only crime of my wife consisted in the fact that, although she belonged to the Prussian aristocracy, she shared the democratic opinions of her husband."[9] Others' accounts further embellished on Jenny Marx's arrest and imprisonment. The arrest of a woman and her forced abandonment of her sleeping children had touched a nerve in Brussels.

Marx contacted three lawyers with connections to Rogier's government and to the court, including Jottrand, to negotiate a hold in his expulsion order because the Marxes had not been able to pack up their household while under arrest. No delay was granted, and the family was escorted to the border after hastily selling what it could. To reach France, the family had to skirt troop movements. Much of the French rail track had been torn up by men previously laid off by the French railway. The Marxes' belongings, packed in six crates, would not reach them for another eight months.

The day after the expulsion of the Marx family, Belgian newspapers demanded details. The Brussels police now claimed that they had played no part in the arrest ordered by the national government. Everyone was eager to shed responsibility. The king wrote Hody to express his surprise that no governmental newspaper had contradicted what he had interpreted as a false version of the events supplied by Jottrand to the press. In response, the justice minister anxiously consulted with Hody, who agreed to write what would pass as the definitive account, to be published in the official *Moniteur Belge*. The minister of justice cautioned Hody not to lay the blame wholly on the local police because that would scare them off involvement just when they were most needed to quell revolution. The minister also noted that the German communists had all left Brussels. The arrest had accomplished its aim, even if there was fallout to be cleaned up. Hody's account was published on 12 March. There was definitely fallout. More than Karl Marx's arrest, Jenny Marx's detention had shocked a nation proud of its liberal constitution that guaranteed rights to all residing within its borders.

In French and English newspapers, Marx and Engels subsequently published their own accounts of the events leading up to Marx's expulsion. "I was occupied in preparing my departure," Marx reported, "when a police commissioner, accompanied by ten civil guards, penetrated into my home, searched the whole house and finally arrested me on the pretext of my having no papers."[10] Marx claimed that he had handed over all the necessary documentation, his Belgian residence permit as well as the deportation pass that had just been issued. Engels embellished: while he was detained at the jail, "Marx had been put into a room with a *raving madman* whom he was obliged to fight every moment. The most brutal treatment on the part of the jailors was joined to the infamous conduct." Engels added that he was waiting for his own expulsion order from "this Belgio-Russian government." Was this the treatment a German democrat should expect "in this *free* country, which the [Belgian] papers allege, has no reason to envy the French Republic?" he asked.[11]

In a public letter to the *Northern Star*, a Chartist newspaper published in northern England, Engels commended Jottrand and the other Belgian democrats who had "shown themselves quite above all petty sentiments of nationality." Unlike the police and the security forces, "they saw in us not foreigners, but democrats."[12] Marx followed up, stressing the good will that existed between the Belgian democrats and the German refugees. He testified that "the Germans do not in the least deny that they openly associated with the Belgian democrats, and this without the slightest degree of hot-headedness." How ludicrous, then, that the king's prosecutor accused the Germans in Belgium of "arousing the workers against the bourgeois, making the Belgians suspicious of a *German* king they so dearly love, and opening the gates of Belgium to a French invasion." Marx accused the Belgian government "of aligning itself entirely with the policy of the Holy Alliance" by unleashing "reactionary fury on the German democrats with unprecedented brutality." He signed his letter, published in the French newspaper *La Réforme*, "Karl Marx, Vice-President of the Brussels Democratic Association."[13]

The Democratic Association, echoing these vivid accounts in the Belgian press, continued its criticism of the supposedly liberal government and its arbitrary arrests. Rogier, as minister of the interior, had clearly encouraged local authorities to rein in trouble and to maintain order as a national priority. The Brussels police were obviously acting on his orders. Responsibility for the events that violated Belgian practice rested with the national government.

Parliamentary deputies in their session of 11 March took up the expulsion of foreigners, especially Marx, contending that it violated the Belgian Constitution. Leading Liberals asked if the Germans' presence in the country had in any way constituted a threat to public tranquility as required by the law governing deportations. Could the refugees' actions be considered serious enough to warrant their exclusion under the 1835 legislation?

The justice minister tried to explain the actions of his officials. His justifications raised more questions than he answered, forcing Rogier to take the floor. Marx's expulsion was an isolated incident, the interior minister argued defensively, affirming, "Sirs, we will continue to respect legality and Belgian hospitality. I repeat what I said before: all foreigners who lead peaceful and tranquil lives and who honor and respect our institutions, all those who do not cause trouble or unrest in the country, all of those will continue to live as freely and peacefully as Belgians themselves are welcome to stay." He added that those foreigners guilty of inciting disturbances would be deported, or, in his words, "If there are foreigners who want to replace Belgian institutions with different ones, the door is open and they can return to their own countries to pursue their theories."[14] An "open door" clearly meant something quite different than it had to the Belgian government earlier in the decade.

Rogier's government then shrugged off all responsibility for the admittedly irregular incident involving Marx onto the Brussels police. Discussions continued in Parliament until the end of the month, when the debate was put to rest. Several additional expulsions followed, notably that of Engels. Baron Hody, to save face, requested that the police agent who led the raid be dismissed because, he reaffirmed, Belgium was a free country. The police had no right under Belgian law to seize papers. To answer the federal charges against the Brussels police, the city launched its own investigation into the expulsion. Investigators were embarrassed to learn that Jenny Marx, a sister of the governor of Pomerania, had been forced to share a cell with three prostitutes. The city of Brussels concluded that the raid on Marx's residence was unauthorized and acknowledged that police agents had found nothing suspicious in Marx's rooms.

In fact, Brussels officials had learned something—or so they thought. They discovered a copy of the proclamation of the Communist League. They concluded that the "society" over which Marx presided in Brussels had been dissolved and moved to Paris. They assumed that was the Democratic Association because they still knew nothing of the Communist League.

The chief prosecutor was relentless. Hody continued to try to trace the funds that he knew had come to Marx in February. Just before his departure, Marx had been observed withdrawing 2,100 francs from the bank, obvious proof to Hody that Marx was financing a revolution in Brussels. Driven by an intense distrust of the communists, Hody seized the opportunity to investigate Marx and his friends further. His agents interviewed restauranteurs, shopkeepers, and even a coachman who had once given Marx a ride. Everyone who had had any contact with Marx, either in Ixelles or in the center of Brussels, was questioned. They confirmed that a number of foreigners had visited him, and, they suspected, were trying to purchase holsters and sword belts. The chief prosecutor also wrote to authorities in Trier, Marx's birthplace, believed to be the source of Marx's windfall of 6,000 francs. Hody conflated two groups—the Democratic Association and the German Workers' Education Association—and so was convinced that Marx, the head of a democratic association of Germans, had moved operations to Paris, now the center of European revolution. Nothing came of the intense investigation.

The summary expulsion of the author of the *Communist Manifesto* from Belgium by the Liberal government with, if not the consent, then the acquiescence of Brussels authorities who had been so attentive to the safeguarding of rights, demonstrates the fate of the stateless in difficult times. Authorities, at the national and municipal levels, abandoned their conviction that free trade required free migration and that a liberal state opened rather than closed doors. Who was watching out for the human rights of refugees in an era of sovereign nation-states?

The Belgian government congratulated itself, in Marx's words, "as the best of all possible *republics*, proud that it possessed a model police force, directed by a man such as M. Hody, at one and the same time an old republican, a phalansterist, and a rejoined Leopolist." This was a "typically Belgian mix!" as Marx identified the agglomeration of seemingly opposed political identities, ranging from liberal to monarchist. Marx also lambasted the Liberal leader Rogier for rescuing the monarchy at a time when so many voices were raised against it. It seemed that even though "the Belgian people are republicans," Marx concluded, "Metternich has found a new ally in the frightened Belgian kingdom."[15] Threatened by revolution, the small nation had ultimately bowed to pressure from its reactionary neighbors, choosing stability over the rights guaranteed by its liberal constitution. From Paris, Marx sent a copy of his article complaining about the arbitrary policies of Rogier's government to Baron Hody with the friendly greeting "Salut" scrawled in the margins above his signature. Once again an exile, Marx had not lost his sense of humor.

Risquons-Tout: "Rise Up en Masse"

The Belgian prosecutor general blamed revolutionaries with foreign connections for stoking riots throughout the kingdom. His domestic surveillance unearthed informants who testified that "Kats or someone of his party" had addressed multitudes of workers gathered at the Vieille Cour de Bruxelles on 14 March 1848, asking everyone to sign a petition calling for bread and shelter. If the government took no action, they threatened to reverse the government and declare a Belgian republic. The French, who were so fortunate in their new republican government, allegedly promised they would cross the border to fight alongside the Belgians.[16]

On 15 March, a larger crowd of over two thousand unemployed workers demonstrated, demanding work. As unrest claimed the streets of Brussels, anxiety mounted in the palace and halls of Parliament. Engels reported: "It cannot yet be proclaimed out loud, but it is whispered everywhere in Brussels: 'Really, Leopold must go; really, only the republic can save us.'" Skeptically, though, he asked his readers, what was the point of "a good solid republic, without organization of labor, without universal suffrage, without the workers involved in running it!"[17] Even without a king, this Belgian republic would no doubt serve the interests of the bourgeoisie alone, not the workers. The workers needed to push for more radical change, he concluded.

Although most of the troublesome German political refugees had been expelled, the threat to the Belgian monarchy did not seem to have receded. In late March, the Belgian government worried not so much about what was happening in Brussels but about its connections to Paris. For years, many Belgian workers had sought employment across the border in northern France. Belgian republicans were reportedly coalescing in Paris. The Belgian ambassador, the Prince de Ligne, warned his government that in addition to Belgians, Germans and Frenchmen were being recruited for a revolutionary league organizing to march on Belgium. It was alleged that the commissioner of the Paris police had even offered to pay league volunteers to travel to the Belgian border, where local French police would open up arsenals for them.

The Belgian government enlisted customs agents as informants. "Placed at the border, your surveillance must be unceasing," a Belgian general told them. He instructed them to keep him "apprised of the smallest movements that might be part of an invasion of our territory by armed bands," adding, "I count on your energetic cooperation to repel and annihilate the miserable men who dare to bring trouble to our cherished Belgium."[18] King Leopold asked rulers in Berlin, Vienna, and London for assistance to help neutral Belgium fend off the threat of revolutionary France. He cast his nation at the European crossroads as the first line of defense. A sympathetic response arrived from Berlin because, as the Prussian put it, "A Belgian republic would essentially mean union with France; union with France would be general war; general war would bring with it the certain extermination of Belgium."[19] The country's neighbors saw the Belgian monarchy as a dike against the onslaught of war and revolution across Europe.

Whenever deputies from the Democratic Association traveled to Paris, they set off alarm bells. Charles Spilthoorn of Ghent and an aide did just that, carrying an address from the Democratic Association for the Provisional Government of France. Rumors swirled that Spilthoorn was planning to organize an invading force of unemployed Belgian workers amassing in the French capital. An informant, "la femme De Bie," alleged that she had heard that Spilthoorn hoped to chase Leopold from the throne.[20] Spilthoorn assured friends, in letters that were intercepted, that to the contrary, he had undertaken his mission to Paris to safeguard Belgian independence against French ambitions of annexation. He asserted with grandiloquence in his correspondence that "the independence of the country and even the peace of the world" depended on his effort to keep French armies from mobilizing along the Belgian border.[21]

Spilthoorn's nearly fatal error was that his trip to Paris coincided with rumors of the organization of the aptly named Risquons-Tout (Risk Everything) plot. The Belgian government had just received intelligence that more than two thousand men had signed up in Paris to fight for the republican cause and that thirty thousand guns were ready for them at the border.[22] Reports of the formation of this Belgian Legion made their way from the streets of Paris to the Belgian ministers in Brussels on 12 March. Spies supplied the details: recruits were flocking to Spilthoorn, enrolling in the Passage de Tivoli on the rue de Saint-Lazare between ten and two every day. The Parisian police prefect was said to be providing sustenance for the hungry recruits. As justification for intervening to topple the Belgian monarchy, some of the insurgents allegedly cited the fact that Leopold was the son-in-law of former French King Louis Philippe and that Brussels had long provided asylum to all the French aristocrats fleeing revolution.[23]

In an intercepted letter, it was reported that Jacques Imbert, a French member of the Democratic Association, had proposed that German refugees be armed too.[24] When he tried to return, Spilthoorn was arrested at the Belgian border.

The French Provisional Government had actually been encouraging unemployed Belgians to return home because there was no work in revolutionary France. Disregarding that counsel, calling themselves "Belgian patriots," the unemployed laborers went ahead to organize the Belgian League. One of their leaders, Louis Delestrée, traveled to Belgium on 22 March to coordinate plans. Delestrée was arrested in Brussels in the Grand Place and condemned to twenty days in prison for having letters from Bornstedt and Imbert in his pockets. That same day in Paris, 200–300 men carrying a red flag paraded in front of the house of the Prince de Ligne, the Belgian ambassador. When they returned to demonstrate a second day, the ambassador allegedly gave them the funds they demanded to get them to disperse. The ambassador's wife heard them proclaiming as they walked away satisfied: "Long live the Prince de Ligne, president of the Republic!"[25]

All the while the Belgian government continued to assure the Prince de Ligne that in contrast to Paris, all was peaceful in Belgium. Conferring with other leaders of the 1830 Belgian Revolution, Jottrand confided his expectation that without more competent leadership, the French provisional government would collapse. He had even less faith in the republican movement in Belgium.[26]

During the third week of March, recruits for the Belgian Legion, after parading through Paris shouting, "Long live the Belgian Republic," converged at the border. Informants confided that many of these Belgian workers were just seeking a free ride back home. They received arms and marching orders. Seventy-five Frenchmen encamped with them. A local government agent promised food and arms would be delivered by students from the polytechnical school at Saint-Cyr. The Belgian ambassador complained to the provisional government of France about what was happening on its territory. France could not control the movements of foreign democrats, the French minister of foreign affairs, Alphonse de Lamartine told the Prince de Ligne. Today, it was the Belgians; tomorrow it would be the Poles. To Lamartine's comment that for their part, the Belgians were welcome to meet any armed forces crossing their border with force, the Belgian ambassador assured him that that was what they intended to do. They had no need for French permission.[27]

On 26 March, the first armed band under the command of a retired cavalry officer crossed into Belgium at Quiévrain by rail. They carried a proclamation addressed to the people of Belgium, calling on them "to rise up en masse" to overthrow the corrupt monarchy.[28] By rallying to support the insurgent forces, the Belgians would thereby prove they were worthy of being called brothers of the French people. Their arrival was not a surprise. A French official had tipped off the Belgian government after being granted an audience with the Belgian king the previous day. Six companies of Belgian infantry and fifty men on horseback met the lightly armed band of men, women, and children at the Belgian border. Hody, convinced that everything in Brussels was under control, came to witness the battle.

Ever the strategist, Hody dispatched a Belgian locomotive to Valenciennes to hijack the aspiring revolutionaries' sixteen-car train. As soon as the French locomotive was detached from the cars carrying the insurgents, a Belgian locomotive gathered speed from behind and without stopping at the border, as had been promised, carried them into Belgium, where the band could be arrested. Two columns of Belgian troops met the train. Only the insurgents at the back escaped. When soldiers boarded the train, they discovered that it was still filled with weapons, proclamations, and a red flag. On 25 March, the Belgian foreign minister instructed his ambassador to inform the French provisional government that Belgium had crushed the "miserable affair."[29]

A second group of insurgents left Douai for Seclin on 25 March; there they were joined by the few men who escaped the first debacle. In total, about fifteen hundred men awaiting instructions and arms were lodged in the surrounding area with villagers. Two days later, the French minister of war ordered the artillery in Lille to give them fifteen hundred guns and to supply them with munitions. That evening, the arms were loaded onto five wagons. The band set off the night of 28 March. At three in the morning in the village of Bondues the insurgents received their weapons. Their paths leading to the Belgian border were so rough and narrow that they had to walk single file. The Belgians, attired in gray hats and shirts, were set apart from their French comrades, who sported red ties and belts. Leaders were distinguished by a paper attached to the band of their hats. "We left Paris to make a revolution in Brussels," an insurgent recounted. "We pledged to fight, death for death. . . . King Leopold had only to make his preparations for his voyage [into exile]."[30]

They crossed into Belgium at Tourcoing on 29 March. Their route was supposed to take them to Brussels via Mouscron. Instead, they met

Expédition de Risquons-Tout, 23 March 1848. From unknown author, *Histoire populaire contemporaine de la France* (Paris: Lahure, 1865) 2:72. Public domain. Photo Jessie Ball duPont Library.

two hundred Belgian soldiers and two canons in the small Belgian village of Risquons-Tout. The insurgents took shelter behind houses and walls as the battle began. Belgian government reinforcements arrived after an hour of continuous skirmishes that had nearly exhausted the munitions of the Belgian troops. At nine in the evening, the battle ended at the border. The Belgian army prevailed over the insurgents, but the soldiers dared not cross into France in pursuit of the remnants of the insurgents' forces. Many of the insurgents were arrested by customs officials when they fled the battle scene as they crossed back into Belgium. Against one death on the side of the Belgian soldiers, many of the insurgents perished.

Riots in Brussels on 29 March coincided with the invasion launched at Seclin. Tension had been building for weeks. Four hundred workers demonstrated in the streets of Brussels, calling for a republic. Eight hundred workers in the streets of Ghent set off panic when they started to construct barricades. Looting broke out in Bruges and Kortrijk. Arms were gathered and petitions circulated for joining France.[31] Workers dug up paving stones to use as weapons in Ghent in the Friday market, and coalitions of workers formed to the south in the Borinage and around Tournai. Their leaders believed that all it would take to launch a revolution in Belgium was an armed invasion from the French border. They appealed to their Belgian compatriots to join with republicans of all nations.

What the French government knew or whether it aided the insurgents is an open question. The French government as a whole was divided, hesitating between action and stalling, doubting the possible success of the Belgian mission. It is possible that while one minister, Alphonse de Lamartine, was disavowing territorial expansion as a revolutionary goal, another, Alexandre Ledru-Rollin, was providing arms. Moreover, after helping the Belgians foil the first invasion, other French officials may have intervened to feed Belgian volunteers and aid the organization of a second invasion at Seclin.

While rumors were circulating of French complicity in the Risquons-Tout affair, the Belgian minister of foreign affairs continued publicly to praise the foreign policy of the French Provisional Government. In many ways, the Belgians were following the same script that Hamburg and Denmark had used to navigate their renegotiation of trade with the revolutionary French government in the last decades of the eighteenth century. In the spring of 1848, the Belgian minister acknowledged that the French government had probably given the unemployed Belgians the means to return home by train and provided food to the insurgents as an act of humanity. Belgium needed to maintain good relations with all its neighbors. That good will was at the center of its economic prosperity and diplomatic self-preservation. Therefore, after a spirited parliamentary debate, Belgium was the first country to recognize the new French republic.

The combined threat posed by Risquons-Tout and the French Revolution of February 1848 was not enough to ignite a revolution in Belgium. Instead, the danger from at home and abroad galvanized the Belgians around their king. The success of his troops also gave Leopold I courage to persevere as monarch. He admitted to having been alarmed when the first news reached Brussels of the paltry force of only two hundred Belgian soldiers taking on the mass of insurgents in Risquons-Tout. By March, though, Louis Philippe's daughter, Belgian Queen Louise Marie, wrote to her mother that peace prevailed. The Belgian Parliament had even forgotten the divisions separating Liberals from Catholics. "All hearts are united, and it could be said that the country is forged as a single man around Leopold for the preservation of the monarchy and Belgian nationality."[32] For his part, the king, who had once called the Belgian constitution "absurd" and complained that he was bored, had warmed to his now much celebrated stature.[33] The troops returning from the border were met by crowds shouting, "Vive le Roi, Vive la Belgique" (Long Live the King, Long Live Belgium). Still, in June, after a calm spring, Belgian border agents continued anxiously to patrol the border, stopping Frenchmen coming in by fours and fives.

Other European governments congratulated the Belgians on the calm that prevailed as revolutions broke out all around them. Had the Belgian insurgents, supported by the revolutionary French, toppled the Belgian king, they feared general war would have ensued in Europe. The Netherlands, Bavaria, Britain, and Prussia pledged their support should the small, independent nation come under attack again. With the rest of Europe slipping into disorder, Queen Victoria singled out Belgium as "a bright star in the midst of dark clouds."[34] Belgian historians have adopted the same approach, seeing the nation that enjoyed extensive constitutional rights as a peaceful island in the midst of the chaos of 1848.[35] By downplaying the Risquons-Tout affair and Leopold's serious consideration of abdication, it seems that the Liberal government steered the nation through the revolutionary era in a way that a more conservative government could not have done. In communication with the socialists and communists who had found asylum in Brussels, the Liberals had enacted sufficient reforms to assure support for the fledgling government.

In the end, the Belgian government extinguished the revolution before it had time to start. The Liberal mayor of Brussels limited public gatherings of more than five people and excluded artisans and workers from the civil guard. The city proceeded to inspect the passports of all foreigners. The *Deutsche Brüsseler Zeitung* stopped publishing at the end of February 1848, and the Democratic Association disintegrated a few weeks later. Nevertheless, the German Workers' Educational Association, which Marx had founded in Brussels, survived until 1914. Belgians congratulated themselves that no barricades had been erected in Brussels.

Belgium may have enhanced its reputation for stability, at least for the immediate future, at the expense of offering asylum. The threat of revolution in 1848 convinced the Liberal government, the ministers, and parliamentary deputies, who had not only tolerated, but also exchanged ideas with the most radical of the political refugees, to close their doors as tightly as the constitution would allow.

"It Does Not Need to Stop Here"

Engels admitted that "in ordinary times," the small country of Belgium was of little interest.[36] These were not ordinary times. The Liberal government under Charles Rogier had secured the future of the newly independent Belgian nation with its open door and timely reforms amid a wave of revolutions in Europe. One of Belgium's founding fathers and the first justice minister, Alexandre Gendebien, chastised his compatriots at a meeting of the Democratic Association in 1848. Men who dared to start a revolution should know how to carry it through to a conclusion, he advised.[37] Did he mean that Belgium should finally extend the rights elaborated in the 1831 Belgian Constitution that had yet to be extended beyond property-owning men? Or was he referring to the general lack of support among Belgian democrats for the ill-fated Risquons-Tout uprising that was defeated at the border? The cause of his discontent was unclear. So too were his aspirations.

Belgium may have escaped the fate of its neighbors in 1848, but it could easily have gone the other way. In March 1848, the revolutionary French had offered Belgian democrats a clear path toward a republic. When France revolted, the Belgian capital was teeming with political refugees, past and future revolutionaries in correspondence with communists, socialists, and other radicals across the continent. At that tumultuous moment, the new nation was positioned at the crossroads of ideological possibilities. The Belgian Liberals' collaboration with political refugees might have contributed to radical experimentation or, as it happened, convinced them to cling more tightly to their constitutional monarchy.

Perhaps, in the end, it was the coexistence of a popular Liberal regime and radical refugees that saved the Belgian monarchy. The Belgian government could claim it had already written into law the principles for which the French were fighting. Liberal ministers did just that.

Neighboring regimes that had repeatedly urged the Belgians to expel their refugees ended up envying the liberal island where the monarch had strengthened his position as revolutions raged. The Revolutions of 1848 leapfrogged over Belgium, jumping from France to Prussia, in part at least because the Belgian Liberals had kept their doors open to all of the newly arrived political refugees, at least until the eruption of revolution.[38]

From its origins as a nation, when Belgium's founding father, Louis De Potter, had financed Polish revolutionaries and the French-born historian and liberal editor Adolphe Bartels had lent the political insurgents journalistic support, refugees had been extended hospitality in Belgium that was difficult to find elsewhere on the continent except in the Swiss cantons and France. The Belgian founders had welcomed Polish immigrants as fellow revolutionaries.

Two of the first German intellectuals to arrive in Brussels, the physician F. Albert Breyer and Professor K. Gustav Maynz, cultivated friendships in democratic circles in Brussels and in Liège with the Freemason Victor Tedesco. Together, these early immigrants welcomed the subsequent waves of German political refugees, communists, socialists, and radicals, as well as artisans, in the 1840s. All of these foreigners, especially the Germans and Poles, lent an international presence to the Democratic Association, linking the Belgian democrats to the international workers' movement.

Open doors worked both ways. Marx commended the hospitality in October 1847: "Here it is so different from Paris, where foreigners are isolated from the government."[39] In Belgium everyone, Belgians and foreigners alike, enjoyed rights under the constitution. Even if they could not vote or stand for office, they had a voice. At a meeting of the Democratic Association in January 1848, Marx, in French, toasted "the benefits of a free-minded constitution, a country where free discussion takes place, enabled by the right of association, and where a humanitarian seed can be sown for the benefit of the whole of Europe."[40] He added his acknowledgment that even under the Liberals, as in a Catholic government, it could all change suddenly. If threatened, he fully expected the bourgeoisie to call the police to enforce order. Or to close the borders. It did just that.

In the spring of 1848—since dubbed by historians "the springtime of the peoples"—the Liberal Belgian government strained the terms of its constitution to arrest forty-three people for their roles in the unrest. Among them were Ghent lawyer Charles Spilthoorn, eighty-year-old General Anne François Mellinet, Jan Pellering, Jacob Kats, and Victor Tedesco. The foreigners who had collaborated with the Belgians over the previous three years had already been deported.

For Belgians like Tedesco, their crime was associating with German refugees, carrying a copy of the *Communist Manifesto*, or simply being seen in a café with Frenchmen. One of the defendants was declared dangerous for having bought drinks for soldiers at a café to bribe them not to fire on the people. Papers seized at General Mellinet's residence showed that the hero of 1830 had been in communication with suspected insurgents in Paris in early March, and that was enough to incriminate him. It was further alleged that the general had organized a riot with Kats and Tedesco. In Kats's residence, agents found a text, *Project van eene nieuwe maatschap-*

pelijke Grondwet (Project for a New Constitution for Society), promoting egalitarian doctrines and a form of basic income.[41]

The accused were tried in August 1848 in Antwerp.[42] The jury found eight men guilty of leading a plot against the Belgian monarchy, including Spilthoorn, Mellinet, and Tedesco. Another ten men were found guilty of participating in the uprising. Fifteen were acquitted and freed. Spilthoorn was among those condemned to death. Mellinet's guilt had been decided by a simple majority of the jury, so he was spared. No one was actually executed because the British intervened to protest the severity of the sentences given the inconclusive nature of the evidence.[43]

Spilthoorn was finally released from prison in January 1855, on condition that he embark for the United States and establish residency abroad. He was amenable to emigration. The fifty-year-old Belgian started a new life; he was admitted to the New York bar in December 1856, continuing to practice law in both Canada and the United States. Admitted to try cases before the U.S. Supreme Court, the only limitation on the Belgian émigré's legal practice was that he had to turn down cases that required his presence in Belgium. Spilthoorn became an American citizen, as would many of the Forty-Eighters who had crossed the Atlantic before him. Even though, unlike Marx in Belgium, he gained citizenship, Spilthoorn still pledged not to get involved in the politics of his new homeland.

Spilthoorn wrote Jottrand to affirm that banishment to the United States posed no great personal hardship. He had always been a fan of the American republic. He reassured his friend that his American citizenship did not mean that he had turned his back on the country of his birth. Like Jottrand, he proudly had risked his life to secure Belgian independence in 1830 and again to fight for liberty in 1848. "If I meet supporters of foreign domination (and to my great sorrow there are many), then I tell them ardently to love their country, to unite with their compatriots, including the government," he wrote from America. His experience had taught him "not to raise irritating questions that would sow division or anger, and to stay firm, until death, while being moderate, to maintain the happiness and the glory of one's patrie."[44] He found good company in America with lawyers who conformed to the principles of what he called true cosmopolitanism. "With them, one can constitute a universal republic," he concluded wistfully, even if he feared he might stand as "the last exile in the world, because only Belgium never granted amnesty."[45]

Before his death, after twenty-three years of exile, Spilthoorn did return home to visit. He may well have met up with the other Belgians who had attended the Democratic Association and who had moved in Marx's circles. By then, Tedesco had risen in politics, chosen president of the provincial government of his native Luxembourg, so he would not have been in Brussels. Others suspected and arrested in 1848, though, had stayed and assumed responsible positions in the municipal council of Brussels. Six of the young Belgian lawyers associated with Marx during his three years in exile in Brussels, some of them communists, others progressive republicans, attained respectable positions either within the government or in the world of business.

Marx, though, never returned to the country that he had singled out as the paradise of the capitalists and hell for the proletariat. He probably would not have found the border open to him after the 1848 Revolutions. Doors of nation-states, including those of small neutral states dependent on free trade, closed, even if only intermittently, in times of turmoil. At the same time, fortunately for refugees, others opened.

CHAPTER NINE

The Forty-Eighters in America

The Promise of "an Asylum for Mankind"

IN 1848, REVOLUTION ENGULFED Europe. Students, workers, peasants, artisans, industrialists, lawyers, and others yearned for political rights and social justice to be guaranteed by constitutions yet to be written. Newspapers circulated stories of the uprisings erupting in one city after another. "One idea flashes through Europe," a participant in the transnational movement announced. "The old system shakes and falls into pieces."[1] In makeshift alliances, communists, radicals, and liberals coalesced behind barricades in insurrections spreading from Paris to Naples, Venice, and Palermo, to Vienna, Prague, Budapest, Krakow, and Berlin. Beyond demands for legislated rights, revolutionaries acknowledged the pressing urgency of the social right to eke out a living amid the grinding poverty of an industrializing continent. Together, these rights would be guaranteed as human rights but not for another century.[2]

Within the year, in another tide, this time of reaction, governments throughout Europe restored order. The uprisings that had ignited, one from the flames of another, beginning in Paris, ended similarly in a chain of suppression. Conservative forces crushed revolutionaries battling for national independence from empires and for the constitution of republican governments. "Whoever lived through 1848 must agree that 1849 was not an accident. . . . It may be that liberty is finished in Europe for a century," an 1854 editorial in the widely read German-language *New Yorker*

Staatszeitung (New York State Newspaper) reflected pessimistically. The writer suggested that democratic ideas "will have to be reintroduced some day from across the Atlantic."[3] The decades-long revolutionary era had begun in America, after all.

In unprecedented numbers, defeated revolutionaries fled their homelands, and through the ports of Le Havre, Antwerp, and Liverpool made their way to safety in America. They followed in the wake of Irish families who had fled famine caused by the potato blight a few years earlier. The Forty-Eighters—teachers, book dealers, shoemakers, doctors, and lawyers—many without passports, crossed national borders to escape persecution and to evade arrest at the hands of the regimes that had crushed their revolutionary movements. Uprooting their families in the immediate aftermath of 1848, refugees crossed borders in such large numbers that they swamped asylum systems, including that of the Swiss, who were accustomed to offering hospitality to individuals, one or ten at a time. Thus began our imagining of modern immigration: caravans of refugees at the border, full boats in the harbor.

Traditional sites of asylum were overwhelmed. Political refugees arriving in small numbers could be readily assimilated by the politically sympathetic, usually diplomatically neutral, states. The repression of the 1848 Revolutions sent whole armies of deserters into the Swiss cantons. From Baden, ten thousand men forded the Rhine. When the Austrian imperial forces established control of Lombardy and Venice, another wave of revolutionary soldiers flowed into Switzerland. Hungarians who had deserted the army in Italy joined them. Socialists and radicals fled France in equally large numbers after Louis Napoleon's victories.

In Switzerland, the new constitution specified the right of the federal state to expel foreigners who threatened public order.[4] With the Prussian army camped on their northern border and talk of military intervention, the Swiss reluctantly agreed to move along a number of the revolutionary leaders through France to England. Unlike the transit of refugees through Central America toward the southern border of the United States or from the southern rim of the European Union northward in the twenty-first century, the Swiss covered travel costs.

Setting out again, some refugees sailed in overcrowded small vessels down either the Rhine to Le Havre or the Elbe to Hamburg or Bremen. Others caravanned over land from Strasbourg in carts straining under the load of multiple families and their belongings. One observer described the sorry parade of Forty-Eighters as the "relics of some battlefield." In 1851 alone, more than thirty thousand emigrants embarked from Le Havre. Profiting from the influx of humanity, "immigrant runners" swarmed the streets along the harbor like "a horde of parasites" hawking assistance per head.[5] Families were often stuck in port for weeks at the mercy of these runners, unable to secure passage on ships to make the transoceanic voyage.

Under pressure from Paris, local authorities in Marseille tried to prevent a number of Hungarian refugees, including the former revolutionary regent-president Lajos Kossuth and his family, from disembarking from their ships arriving from the Ottoman Empire. The Hungarians, who had already been months en route, were expecting to continue their journey on foot toward the English Channel, eventually crossing to England. A crowd of fifteen hundred residents of Marseille protested against the government decisions, demanding that the Hungarian heroes and their families be free to land in France.

Only when it proved impossible to procure shelter, to earn a living, or to practice their beliefs, religious or political, nearby, did the first modern refugees travel farther afield, leaving their homelands far behind. England and the United States each promised basic freedoms that were now in short supply on the European continent. Many of the Forty-Eighters transferred their hopes from Europe to the new world of the American republic, even if it lay on the other side of an ocean still treacherous to cross.

The Forty-Eighters coming from the German states and Hungary arrived at the same time as half a million Irish refugees escaping a years-long agrarian crisis aggravated by government evictions. Many of them received free passage in exchange for leaving their homesteads. Almost one-tenth of the Irish perished on the passage.[6] Refugees crowding the ships crossing the Atlantic in the middle of the nineteenth century shared their discontent. The revolutionary exiles made up only a small minority of immigrants from Central Europe. Over 50 percent of the immigrants from Baden, for example, were farmers, while artisans made up 26 percent.[7] And the Germans and Hungarians were vastly outnumbered by the Irish refugees. Whether on board ship or once they landed, political refugees separated themselves from agrarian and industrial laborers.

The division of immigrants into two camps—those choosing to seek economic opportunities and those forced to flee political oppression—was anything but straightforward. The political and economic conditions creating the waves of refugees coming to the United States were intertwined. A German refugee stopping in the Swiss cantons in 1849 understood the connections: "Despotism drives the friends of liberty into foreign lands, and capital disposes of the proletariat by sending them across the ocean also."[8] Not all of the refugees did, even if their aspirations were actually quite similar.

By the thousands in the middle of the nineteenth century, Forty-Eighters, like millions of other European refugees, took up Thomas Paine on his 1776 invocation to the revolutionary republic to "receive the fugitive and prepare in time an asylum for mankind."[9] The United States beckoned as the protector of republicans. Crossing the ocean to start a new life, the refugees saw the promise of the United States, not its fractures in the decades leading to the Civil War.

What would happen when this unstable republic welcomed refugees arriving in ships by the thousands to escape political repression and agricultural failure? Would open doors close? Or would the need for laborers—especially white settlers to colonize lands to the west recently cleared of their indigenous occupants—eclipse fears of foreigners? How would their revolutionary dreams transform American politics?

"To Be Elsewhere": Settling in America

Drawing on his own experience, the literary scholar Edward Said described the journey into exile as "truly horrendous. . . . Like death but without death's ultimate mercy, it has torn millions of people from the nourishment of traditions, family and geography."[10] Said, who was born in Jerusalem in 1935, grew up in Cairo. As an adult, he settled in New York. So, too, did his fellow writer, André Aciman, an Italian American raised in Egypt. Aciman explains, "New York is my home precisely because it is a place from which I can begin to be elsewhere—an analogue city, a surrogate city, a shadow city that allows me to naturalize and neutralize this terrifying, devastating, unlivable megalopolis by letting me think it is something else, somewhere else."[11] New York is where most of the Forty-Eighters started their American journey too, though a century earlier.

Newspapers on the East Coast were filled with stories of the German beggars on the streets of New York and of the high mortality among sickly immigrants.[12] Debates on both sides of the ocean, from Le Havre to New York, smoldered about who should shoulder responsibility for the economic support of immigrants. In American port cities, aliens accounted for an outsized proportion of poor relief. For the most part, welfare was tied to local residence, not yet national citizenship. Immigration law was not settled.

From the eastern seaboard, many of the Forty-Eighters moved on. Those who left New York often traveled by steamboat up the Hudson, following the Erie Canal to Buffalo, where they booked passage on lake steamers to Detroit. They typically proceeded to Chicago or Milwaukee, where colonies of Germans had already settled. More rural areas, especially in Wisconsin, Iowa, and Illinois, also attracted communities of Germans and Hungarians.

The expectations of finding the fabled paradise of guaranteed liberties in this country of purportedly wide open lands could be as easily dashed as they had been raised. One of the first contingents of Hungarian exiles, hoping to build a "New Hungary" on the Midwestern prairies, established New Buda in southern Iowa, near the Missouri border. They did not recognize that the land had belonged to the Ioway or Báxoje people who had been expelled westward to the Kansas-Nebraska border by the government. Oblivious to the fate of the Indigenous peoples, the Hungarians were instead seeking to skirt the American cruelty they did know about: slavery.

The government policy of "Indian Removal" aimed to expel if not exterminate the impediments to white settlement. Congress considered a resolution to give this land free to Hungarians, encouraging the Forty-Eighters to farm lands that extended "as far as the eye could see, free and open."[13] Or so the European refugees were told and apparently believed. In effect, the involvement of the U.S. government in forcing Indigenous peoples to cede their lands and move beyond established borders of white cultivation created one set of refugees to settle another.[14]

Despite the fertile land, when former scholars, newly arrived from Europe, tried their hand at farming, as many did, few succeeded over the long term. Defeated by the land, they moved back to cities, taking up other pursuits. The New Buda refugees who remained cooperated and worked with their neighbors, including not only Hungarians, but also immigrants from Ireland and Germany. Their integration was not without challenges. The newcomers eagerly participated in American Fourth of July festivities that just happened to fall on a Sunday one year. German immigrants, thinking they were participating in a patriotic festival, planned a celebration, complete with cannon salutes in front of the local brewery. Former Hungarian revolutionaries paraded through town on horseback, ending up at the liberty pole, where they sang remembered songs of struggle. Local citizens were so alarmed that they appealed to the governor to call out the militia to stop the raucous violation of the Sabbath.[15] Although the refugees often overcame barriers separating them from other immigrants, full assimilation into Midwestern towns was more difficult.

Further south, in Texas, Friedrich Kapp, a Forty-Eighter who had come to the United States via Switzerland, stopped on his journey in the middle of the vast prairie at the hut of a man reputed to speak German. He was looking for company in the landscape that bore no resemblance to home. The German speaker was not home. Kapp decided to wait inside the small house, out of the sun, for him to return. There, in a photograph on the rough wall, Kapp was astonished to see himself pictured as a student. The hut owner turned out to be a friend from over ten years earlier.

In conversation, the settled German speaker elaborated on his view of living alone in the middle of Texas: "I am not exactly happy, but not unhappy either, for I live free and unfettered. I am independent of everyone except my oxen and the weather." This freedom struck him as quintessential American individualism. "No one hinders me in my plans and projects except the lack of money," he continued, adding, "No one prevents me from expressing my revolutionary sentiments except the absence of an audience."[16] He could dream, but the political change he had envisioned before leaving Europe no longer seemed within reach. The American life of the isolated farmer that refugees initially embraced as freedom was not for everyone. Like many other new immigrants, Kapp returned to the East Coast and joined a law firm in New York before taking over as editor of the *New Yorker Abendzeitung* (Evening Paper).

"A Republic of the Workers": Transatlantic Organizing

The Forty-Eighters' story is one of detachment from home, livelihood, family, language, and identity at the beginning of our modern era of mass migration. Many of these revolutionary refugees only gradually gave up their dreams of returning home when "*es wieder losgeht*" ([revolution] breaks out again).[17] The Polish exile Eva Hoffman observed over a century later, in 1989, that "Loss is a magical preservative."[18] For many of the refugees, as they settled into new neighborhoods, it was the dream of revolutionary change that survived their loss.

Some refugees who arrived in America before the Revolutions of 1848 returned to Europe to fight for what they envisioned as the eventual triumph of the cause of democracy worldwide. Notable among them was Wilhelm Weitling, the German tailor who had organized artisans in the Swiss cantons and against whom Marx launched a tirade in Brussels in 1846. Ostracized from the Communist League, Weitling had traveled to New York.

Revolution called Weitling back across the Atlantic. He did not really find his place among the revolutionaries of 1848, and after their defeat, he returned to America to work for reforms in social security and pensions, giving talks, organizing cooperatives, and editing a radical newspaper. Weitling's labor union, the Arbeiterbund, attracted five thousand members. Organizing was his calling, and this time he intended to build a "republic of the workers." After the union folded, he headed west, joining a community of German artisans, Communia, in Iowa. In 1855, that failed too. Weitling married another German immigrant, Dorothea Caroline Louise Toedt, and moved to New York. He supported his family of six children by returning to tailoring, while introducing improvements in the sewing machine. He abandoned neither his dreams nor his trade. The two were tied together.

Friedrich Hecker was another German revolutionary drawn back from his exile in Illinois to spearhead an uprising in Baden in 1848. Defeated and demoralized by the crushing of the revolution, he set sail for America for a second time. "With true longing," he wrote, he gazed "across the ocean to the far west and to my forest solitude [in America]. . . . I am so dreadfully tired of this [German] police state and shall praise the day when I can take my axe again and clear the woodland."[19] Hecker, whose role in the revolutions was more noteworthy than Weitling's, was received in New York with a torchlight procession. He was asked to speak at mass meetings and extended invitations across the United States—in Philadelphia, Cincinnati, and St. Louis, among other cities. His family finally resettled on a farm near Belleville, Illinois, where he prospered as an unlikely cattle raiser and viticulturalist.

A refugee from Vienna, Anton Füster, one of the key figures in the March revolution in Vienna in 1848, reminisced, "Only a year ago, we were reverently singing the German national anthem. Now it sounds different. What is the German Fatherland? Is it Austria? No, I was forced to flee from there. Is it Prussia? No. There I was arrested. Is it Saxony? No. Three warrants were issued against me. Is it the free city of Hamburg? No. There I was driven out by the police. Where is the German Fatherland? In England and America!"[20] Part of settling in America for Füster meant leaving an old world behind and severing those revolutionary connections.

Few of these German Forty-Eighters had much success starting new revolutionary movements in America. Joseph Weydemeyer, who had stayed in Germany after the defeat of the revolution in 1849 to raise money for refugees, sailed for New York in 1851 with his wife and two children. Karl

Marx gave him a letter of introduction to his American editor. Weydemeyer instead started his own newspaper. It lasted two issues. Bitter, Weydemeyer continued to try to get his articles placed in American newspapers while working as a labor organizer. For his part, Marx dismissed the rampant rumors of spirited feuds among different factions of German revolutionary émigrés in London and New York as mere "paper wars" between frogs and mice without real ideas.[21]

More or less subtly, Forty-Eighters often shed their communism in the United States. The architect Adolf Cluss, who had befriended the Marxes in Brussels, fought in the 1848 Revolutions and continued to correspond regularly with Karl Marx for years after joining other Forty-Eighters in exile in America. He quietly moved away from revolution other than continuing to favor red brick in his buildings—or so his critics commented. He would go on to become one of the most influential architects in the nation's capital. His Arts and Industries Building still stands on the National Mall in Washington, D.C.

Friedrich Engels warned Joseph Weydemeyer, his former ally in the Communist League, who had come to America to fight for socialism: "Your greatest handicap will be that the available Germans who are worth anything become easily Americanized."[22] One German Forty-Eighter eager to fit in among Americans, for example, advised his fellow refugees to give up their dreams for a revolutionary Germany and instead invest in American republican politics. He was booed off the stage for his bluntness. Even if they would not describe their adaptation to the United States in such stark terms, most of these refugees' politics changed as they integrated into new communities.

"An Even Greater Field of Activity than the Native": The Midwest

When Weitling, newly arrived, met a friend in New York who confided in him that he had started over in the soap business. Weitling is said to have replied, "I have no time for such material occupations. I must labor for principle."[23] Few immigrants had that luxury including Weitling. Like the émigrés from the French Revolution, but on a totally different scale, the Forty-Eighters had left behind their property. More to the point, they had left behind their work and the connections that allowed them to secure a livelihood.[24] The university training acquired by many did not equip them well for life abroad, where they lacked the language and the network to establish a professional career. That is not to say that a number, like Cluss, did not eventually achieve professional renown in the United States.

Not unlike the German communists in Brussels in the mid-1840s, the Forty-Eighters were mostly young; many clung to the hope of fashioning a new professional life. With the optimism of hindsight, one of the best known and most successful of the Forty-Eighters, Carl Schurz, characterized his fellow refugees as "inspired by fresh ideas which they had failed to realize in the old world, but hoped to realize here."[25] Schurz liked to retell the story of the reaction of a neighbor from southwestern Germany to the departure of a family for the United States. The man who stayed behind observed "how happy he would be if he could go with them to that great and free country, where a man could be himself." He had heard it said that in America "nobody need be poor, because everybody was free."[26] The abundant natural resources would guarantee them all a living. Schurz himself may have been more realistic.

Born near Bonn to a farming family, Schurz was a university student at the time that the revolution broke out in France in February 1848. When revolution spread to Germany, Schurz was eager to enlist and joined the staff of a democratic newspaper. For his participation in the armed uprising, Schurz's editor, Gottfried Kinkel, was sentenced to life in prison. Schurz then fled to Switzerland, where he hatched a successful plot with Kinkel's wife to spring the editor from prison. Karl Marx satirized the escape as "a re-enactment of the story of Richard Lionheart and Blondel with the difference that this time it was Blondel who was in prison while Lionheart played on the barrel-organ outside and that Blondel was an ordinary music-hall minstrel, and the lion was basically more like a rabbit."[27] Marx had even fewer kind things to say about "student Schurz."

Schurz achieved such notoriety in the successful prison break that he too had to go into exile. He sailed to England, where he met Margarethe Meyer, the daughter of a prominent Hamburg industrialist. Her sister had started one of the first kindergartens in London. One month after Schurz and Meyer married, they sailed for the United States. He was twenty-three, and she, nineteen. Their journey in 1852 to New York harbor took twenty-eight days. Both would build prominent careers in their new homeland.

In contrast to most of the émigrés in Hamburg and Altona and the communists and socialists in Brussels, Schurz and most of his fellow Forty-Eighters arrived on American shores planning to stay awhile. They were, in Schurz's recollections, "full of enthusiasm for the great American Republic which was to be their home and the home of their children." They "brought something like a wave of Spring sunshine" to America, Schurz

Carl Schurz and Margarethe Meyer Schurz, circa 1852.
Alpha Stock/Alamy Stock Photo.

commented.[28] He would look back after a successful career in American politics and reflect: "America is the country for ambitious capability, and the foreigner who studies its conditions thoroughly, and with full appreciation, can procure for himself an even greater field of activity than the native . . . and so I gained perhaps more rapidly than anybody in the land, a nation-wide reputation, a reputation which went far beyond my dreams."[29] Some of the merchants who ended up settling into successful entrepreneurial careers in Hamburg and Altona, like the industrialists and philosophers who remained in Brussels, might have shared this affectionate view of their new home and its possibilities.

The Schurzes moved first to Philadelphia and then to Wisconsin. Based on his scouting trip to the Midwest, Carl promised Margarethe, "The predominance of the German language would almost make you feel you were in the fatherland, if you did not hear the most varied German dialects, and here and there an American talking."[30] The land on which the Germans built their homes had formerly housed Ho-Chunks, Ojibwes, and Dakotas, viewed by the federal government "as temporary residents" and removed so that Wisconsin would attract more than sixty thousand white settlers, the threshold to become a state.[31]

The federal government compromised with Wisconsin when it was admitted to statehood in 1848 to allow "declarant aliens" to vote if they would swear to abide by the U.S. Constitution. Liberal citizenship laws already allowed immigrants in some states to attain their rights through naturalization after as little as five years in residence. Other states and territories followed suit in extending voting rights, a move to attract immigrants to northern states to counter the influence of the slave-holding South.[32] These same welcoming states excluded long-residing people of color from the franchise.

The small farming community of Watertown, Wisconsin, where Carl and Margarethe Schurz settled, had welcomed its first German immigrant in 1837. By 1853, half of the four thousand residents were Germans. That population had more than doubled by 1856, as Watertown developed rapidly as the center of a rapidly growing agricultural region.[33] New arrivals, mostly young and some with university educations, took whatever work they could find, often farming. Some took up cigar making because it required a relatively small initial investment. One opened a hotel, known after the revolution as the Kossuth House for the leader of the Hungarian Revolution; others opened taverns. Tavern keeping proved to be reasonably profitable as an enterprise in immigrant communities, and given the number of meetings it was a relatively political enterprise, in the New World as in the Old.

The daily lives of the refugees defined their impromptu citizenship, their sense of belonging. In a pattern not too different from that in Brussels, German refugees frequently congregated with other German speakers in public spaces, predominantly taverns, reading the same or competing German-language newspapers. Their German heritage remained a strong defining strand of their identity even as they moved into new communities and adapted to a new life.[34] Family members and friends who had preceded them received newcomers into their communities with their already established institutions and associations, as the Marxes had done for the roving communists arriving in Brussels.

At the same time, American citizens welcomed the Forty-Eighters as heroes of the European revolutions. News coverage of the 1848 Revolutions had been so extensive that the leaders had become household names throughout America. Defeated, the ill-fated European revolutions allowed Americans to gloat about their own revolutionary independence. Women across the country opened their homes to the political refugees. One onlooker marveled at the American women engaged in politics for championing "the world-wide cause of liberty" within their homes. By entertaining refugees, they thereby sweetened "the bitter cup of exile to a martyr of the principle." To extend this welcome hospitality, "a woman need not go out of the sphere of the home."[35] Some storied American households were as inclusive and welcoming as the Reimarus and Sieveking circles had been in Hamburg.

It did not take long for most of the new arrivals to commit to staying, displacing thoughts of a revolutionary future in Europe. One German who recrossed the ocean to settle his father's estate "quickly became heartily sick of Germany—a strange feeling."[36] In the end, before too much time had passed, many of the Central European refugees had assimilated into American society, as Engels had observed from afar. They also changed it.

Forty-Eighters were especially committed to extending the promise of public education in the United States. Whereas political refugees in the Swiss cantons just a few decades earlier had joined faculties of universities, in America they made remarkable contributions to the education of younger children. One historian has even called the kindergarten "one of the most successful and enduring achievements of the 1848 revolutions."[37] Kindergartens formed a part of a broader progressive platform. Consistent with ideals brought from Central Europe, early education also promoted the ideals of American citizenship, at least for European immigrants.

Margarethe Schurz opened her first kindergarten in Watertown in 1856, drawing on her training at the Hamburg College for Women in Germany. She had come to America prepared, bringing supplies with her from Europe, including shiny paper for weaving mats, colored yarn, and blue perforated cardboard. Her first pupils were friends of her daughter's. Some Americans greeted the new schools for young children as foreign, but kindergartens based on her model spread throughout the country.

Immigration, "The Mother of This Country"

Abraham Lincoln held up his friend Carl Schurz as "the foremost among the Republican orators of the nation."[38] In 1859 in Boston, Carl Schurz delivered a speech entitled "True Americanism," in which he celebrated the United States as "the *great colony of free humanity*, which has not old England alone, but the *world*, for its mother-country."[39] Elected to the Senate after the Civil War, Schurz claimed that the persistence of slavery drove him to continue his struggle as a Republican from Wisconsin to Washington. Schurz was not alone among Forty-Eighters to challenge the prevailing definition of political citizenship in the United States as that of propertied citizenship limited to white men.

Also settling in Wisconsin, Forty-Eighter Mathilde Franziska Anneke was one of the first women to edit a newspaper in America. Born into nobility in Westphalia, she was highly educated. Her experience divorcing her first husband and contending for custody of her infant daughter made her a lifelong advocate for rights for women. She wrote stories, a play, and poems to support herself before she married Fritz Anneke. Together they edited a daily newspaper for workers in Cologne, and after he was arrested, she carried on alone. When that paper was banned, in September 1848, she founded the first German feminist newspaper. A skilled horsewoman, she joined her husband, who happened to be Carl Schurz's commander, on the field of battle. After the fall of Rastatt, Fritz and Mathilde Anneke took refuge in France with their friend Moses Hess, Karl Marx's Brussels neighbor, before crossing the Atlantic.

In the United States, Anneke took up the cause of African Americans and of women, two American causes that would subsequently go their separate ways. Aligned with Susan B. Anthony and Elizabeth Cady Stanton, she addressed the National Women's Rights Convention, proclaiming: "The women of my country look to this country for encouragement."[40] The mother of seven children, Anneke established a school for girls in Milwaukee. In her wide-ranging public speaking, she challenged the devout obedience of American women to their husbands and the church at the same time that other Forty-Eighters looked to women to preserve "German spirit and nature" in the home in their new land.[41] When her husband was imprisoned in 1859 for defying the Fugitive Slave Act, Anneke organized a series of unsuccessful insurrections to free him. In 1860, together with the abolitionist Mary Booth and three of their children, Anneke moved to Zurich. They saw more promise there than in America.

What seemed to be contradictions were not unusual among the Forty-Eighters adapting to their new communities. Adolph Douai, a revolutionary who had served a prison sentence for high treason and rioting, got involved in reform movements as soon as he arrived in the German American community of New Braunfels, Texas. One of his visitors, the renowned landscape designer Frederick Law Olmsted, asked, "Where else could you hear teamsters with their cattle staked around them on the prairie, humming airs from 'Don Giovanni,' or repeating passages from Dante and Schiller."[42] Olmsted struck up a friendship with Douai, then the publisher of a German-language newspaper, the *San Antonio Zeitung*. Douai did not last long in Texas. After he advocated the founding of a free-labor state in west Texas, angering not only Texan slaveholders, but also many of the more conservative German Americans who had settled in the area, he chose to return to New York. There, he opened a kindergarten with instruction in German and English, hoping to educate children "to adapt to society and regard all comrades as equals."[43]

One movement, the Turnverein, which originated in Germany as gymnastics clubs and was closely associated with workers' organizations and democratic clubs, crossed the Atlantic with the refugees. A number of "Turner clubs" sprouted on American soil in Cincinnati in response to the visit of the German socialist Friedrich Hecker. In 1852, in a large rally, the Cincinnati club welcomed the Hungarian revolutionary hero Lajos Kossuth to the city. Turner clubs quickly began to spread across the country, drawing in liberals, radicals, clerks, artisans, and laborers by the hundreds. Unlike Marx in Brussels, the Forty-Eighters had signed no promise to abstain from American politics. To the contrary, these former revolutionaries saw political involvement as their civic responsibility. But, then, they intended to stay, as so many would after them.

A prominent group of German American reformers appealing to "All True Republicans in the Union" advocated "Liberty, prosperity, and education for all!" in the Louisville Platform. They castigated Americans for failing to live up to the founding principles of their constitution. Advocates of enfranchising women and freeing slaves, they also reminded their hosts that immigration "is the mother of this republic."[44] Citizenship and rights for immigrants were intricately bound up with the mobility and rights of free Black men. The two causes worked both for and against each other.

German Americans became some of the most outspoken of the abolitionists. August Willich, formerly a Prussian noble who had led a revolutionary unit that included Friedrich Engels in a struggle to unseat the monarchy of the Palatinate in 1848 and who had served for a short time on the Central Committee of the Communist League, worked as a carpenter upon arrival in the United States. Addressing a crowd described as "motley" for its inclusion of "bronzed Frenchman, the pale-faced American, and the rubicund Teuton" sharing benches with "the copper-colored African and the greasy-skinned and odorous Ethiopian," Willich exhorted listeners in Cincinnati "to whet their sabers and nerve their arms for the day of retribution," when those who continued to uphold the institution of slavery "would be crushed into a common grave."[45] The black, red, and gold flag of German republicanism was on display in the hall of the German Institute beside a banner in memory of John Brown and the flag of an African American delegation.

Unresolved for the United States, with its open doors and lingering slavery, was the thorny question of who belonged to the nation. Immigrants from Germany and Hungary could be absorbed into neighborhoods at the local level, but what about the freed Black men and women who had already labored for generations on American soil? Who would be included in the republic that had yet to forge a union? Who would be a citizen able to shape the course of the nation as well as the neighborhood?

The offer of asylum to immigrants eager to contribute and to make their own way did not continue uncontested in the United States, any more than in other societies that had opened their doors over the previous five decades. It was not long before the Forty-Eighters encountered political hostility—but not from neighboring nation-states. Instead, the challenge to the outspoken presence of the Forty-Eighters came from within the country. American citizens themselves questioned the cosmopolitan claims of refugees to asylum. In Hamburg, Altona, the Swiss cantons, and Belgium, it took a crisis to arouse opposition to the open doors on which their societies were based. Not in the United States.

Nativists along the eastern seaboard in the 1850s raised the alarm that the civic values on which their republic was founded were being corrupted by foreign influences. It was absolutely clear to the governor of Delaware that "American politics have been stained with vices foreign to the American character."[46] Similarly, a congressman complained about the revolutionary refugees who "clamor for 'universal suffrage,' for 'free farms,' and for 'intervention' in European affairs."[47] Only those born and educated in the United States should be citizens, they agreed. Paradoxically, these critics of immigration drew upon the same sense of American exceptionalism as Thomas Paine had held up in 1776 in his argument for the unique American promise to serve as an asylum for mankind. With no sense of the irony of their xenophobia, they used Paine's elegy to America to render immigrants outsiders to the American dream.

Organized first as a secret society exerting influence surreptitiously and then bursting forth on the political scene as a political party in its own right, the party of the Know-Nothings targeted the radical ideas of German immigrants. At its peak, the party counted the allegiance of more than one hundred congressmen, eight governors, and thousands of local politicians. It supported a twenty-one-year naturalization waiting period for citizenship, the deportation of beggars and criminals, the expulsion of Catholics from office, and mandatory Bible reading in schools, among other provisions. Abraham Lincoln, whose new Republican Party benefitted from the support of many of the Know-Nothings, countered their exclusive vision of the United States: "As a nation, we began by declaring that 'all men are created equal.' We now practically read it 'all men are created equal, except negroes.' When the Know Nothings get control, it will read 'all men are created equal, except negroes, and foreigners, and Catholics.'" Lincoln said at that point, "I should prefer emigrating to some country where they make no pretense of loving liberty."[48] The Know-Nothings did not stop at propagating their ideas through rallies and in print but instigated mob violence, climaxing in 1855. The party's power waned only when slavery eclipsed immigration as the most contentious question for Lincoln as for the rest of the nation.

Citizenship: A New Frontier

There is a continuity to the cosmopolitan interaction of open societies and refugees seeking asylum. While each society seems to confront immigrants as if for the first time in human history, it was as true in nineteenth-century America as it had been in Hamburg, Altona, the Swiss cantons, and Belgium in previous decades that the presence of refugees ultimately contributed to the political stability and economic prosperity of societies during turbulent times. The offer of asylum to Forty-Eighters bolstered America's image of itself as an open and progressive republic, even if the federal government deported Indigenous people to extend its sovereignty over lands then opened to European refugees. That promise had drawn refugees to its shores just as this open and progressive republic was so divided that it would soon break apart.

The refugees' imagined community of aspiring citizens transcended borders, while in practice, day to day, they became Americans and lived locally. They differed from earlier refugees in their aspiration to national citizenship. Nevertheless, they retained the values tested in revolution on the other side of the Atlantic. Their visions of more widespread liberty and social equality, so often frustrated in Europe, were given new life in America, with the obvious exception of the lines drawn by race and the defense of slavery. This vision may have derived from their status as outsiders.

The Forty-Eighters contributed to an American definition of their nation as at one and the same time a republic founded on the guarantee of rights and a land of immigrants.[49] Three-fifths of all of the world's immigrants from 1800 through the next half century made their way to the United States. Not until a century later, in the 1950s, would the responsibility of receiving displaced people be expected of all member nations in the United Nations. And yet, in the twenty-first century, the right of asylum is still vigorously contested, raising all too familiar questions across the globe.

Epilogue

"A Destabilized Citizenship" for Refugees

THE PROMISE OF IMMANUEL Kant's universal hospitality has been all but drowned out by national governments' insistence on repelling migrants unloosed by wars, political unrest, and a changing climate in the twenty-first century. The deportations of innumerable refugees through the nineteenth into the twentieth century, the so-called century of migration, only foreshadowed the dire crises of a globe devastated by droughts and threatened by rising seas. The late nineteenth-century poem at the base of the Statue of Liberty summoning the "huddled masses yearning to breathe free" to American shores rings hollow as the wealthiest and most powerful nations, including the United States, become more concerned with protecting themselves against refugees than with protecting refugees.[1] Kant's cosmopolitanism as a foundation of refugee rights has not fared well pitted against assertions of territorial sovereignty.[2]

If refugees at their doors challenged the security of newly independent nations and their neighbors in a world turned upside down at the end of the eighteenth and beginning of the nineteenth century, the globalization of ensuing centuries has only amplified that challenge. For so many individuals caught between nations, the shelter of asylum beckons but stays beyond reach. Just a small number of the families who fled Syria, the Democratic Republic of Congo, South Sudan, Afghanistan, Eritrea, and Somalia, among so many besieged places, have secured asylum in the first decades of the twenty-first century. One of every 122 people in the world was a refugee in 2014, the United Nations estimates.[3] In 2021, the United Nations High Commissioner for Refugees (UNHCR) identified 1,445,383 of the world's 26,000,000 refugees to be in need of resettlement.[4] That soaring numbers of refugees are forced to flee their homes while shrinking numbers of states consent to open their doors to welcome them is one of the most scathing indictments of international as well as national governance.

Climate change is causing a humanitarian disaster of unprecedented scope. The World Bank estimates that 216 million people will be forced to move by 2050. Droughts, floods, pandemics, and food and water insecurity have already devastated whole regions of the earth. The Climate and Environment Charter for Humanitarian Organizations opens with the stark warning: "Today's climate and environmental crises threaten the survival of humanity." It adds, "While the crises are impacting everyone, those who have contributed least to the problem are hit hardest—and it is only getting worse."[5] What are the responsibilities of those nations most responsible for the impending environmental crisis to the refugees forced to flee their homes? Or might the solution be sought at another level of governance?

With forced displacement at the highest levels in human history, even in a world of codified international laws, the question posed in the wake of the American and French revolutions remains: Who will grant asylum to the refugees? The UNHCR, Sadako Ogata, appealed with what should have been compelling urgency to the leaders of nation-states to remember their fundamental humanitarian obligations. "The refugee issue must be put to all governments and peoples as a test of their commitment to human rights," she concluded.[6] But is asylum possible in our modern world, divided between nation-states that control their borders and decide themselves who to admit and who to allow to remain on their sovereign territory? Has the dominance of the modern nation-state foreclosed a natural human right, that of mobility?[7] The desolate history of refugees caught between nation-states over the last two and a half centuries poses this fundamental question.

Italian political philosopher Giorgio Agamben set the question differently. He wondered if, at the turn of the twenty-first century, the refugee, "the figure that should have embodied human rights more than any other . . . marked instead the radical crisis of the concept [of national citizenship]?"[8] In an unstable world of nation-states jealously jostling against each other, who will willingly assure to each individual, in the words of the worldly philosopher Hannah Arendt, "the right to have rights"?[9] The crisis of "displaced persons," a term Arendt disparaged, renders refugees vulnerable, defined by what they do not have: a state. "Stateless," they are, American historian Linda Kerber explains, "the ultimate 'other' to the citizen."[10] In a world where states, people, and territory are assumed to be coterminous, Arendt asked: "Who will guarantee human rights to those who have lost their nationally guaranteed rights?"[11] It could only be humanity itself, Arendt answered, without great optimism.

International Law: "A Kafkaesque Legal Vacuum"

In 1948, one hundred years after the Revolutions of 1848 sent waves of refugees fleeing across the Atlantic to America, fifty-eight nations ratified the United Nations' Universal Declaration of Human Rights, which recognized "the inherent dignity and . . . equal and inalienable rights of all members of the human family" as "the foundation of freedom, justice and peace in the world."[12] A committee of philosophers organized by UNESCO and a commission chaired by Eleanor Roosevelt wrote the Declaration of Human Rights, defining, "for the first time, fundamental human rights to be universally protected" across the globe. This "milestone document in the history of human rights" included the right to asylum. Forty-eight of the fifty-eight countries in the United Nations signed. In 1993, the United Nations elaborated on provisions of the declaration, emphasizing that human rights might be "universal, indivisible and interdependent and interrelated."[13] Every nation in the United Nations has signed on to at least one of the several treaties affirming human rights.

International law in the twentieth century recognized the rights that had been defined as inalienable and universal in the eighteenth century, while acknowledging the role of the nation-states as guarantors of these rights. With its declaration, philosopher Seyla Benhabib ventured, the United Nations changed the landscape by effectively redefining the context in which nation-states made their laws and enacted them.[14] A testament to the shared conscience of the world, the United Nations declaration was dependent on national compliance. Nationality tied to territory, however, remained the foundational principle of these international agreements. Therein lay its potential and its limitation.[15] Would sovereign states consent to immigration and emigration laws that set porous borders? Would liberal democracies agree to treat all people who arrived on their shores equally?

Three articles of the Universal Declaration of Human Rights responded directly to the massive displacement of persons caused by two world wars. Article 13 acknowledged the right to freedom of movement; Article 14 declared: "Everyone has the right to seek and to enjoy in other countries asylum from persecution"; and Article 15 added: "Every person has a right to a nationality."[16] Signatory states agreed to respect and ensure the rights defined by the articles for all individuals within their territory, not just their national citizens. In this affirmation, the modern signatories to the UN declaration were following in the spirit of the communities that opened their doors in the revolutionary era at the turn of the nineteenth century. But there was a catch.

The 1951 Geneva Convention, ratified by 145 states, not including the United States, has stood as the key legal document defining refugees and setting international standards for their treatment. Additional conventions and covenants on stateless persons and further provisions laying out civil and political rights were signed in 1954 and 1961. The International Covenant on Civil and Political Rights, signed in 1966 and put into place in 1976, garnered the signatures of 172 state parties by 2018, including the United States and Canada.

The contemporary obligations of asylum are much more limited than the welcome advocated two centuries earlier by Immanuel Kant. The UN General Assembly's 1967 Declaration on Territorial Asylum affirmed the sovereign discretion of states in deciding whether to take in asylum seekers, a point several nations insisted be recognized before they would sign on. Asylum is defined "as a peaceful and humanitarian act," not an obligation. Although nations are required to allow people to leave, they are not obliged to admit those outside their borders unless the immigrants are their own citizens. Taken together, the regime of international laws established after World War II has created what Linda Kerber, citing the UNHCR, has referred to as "a Kafkaesque legal vacuum" for about 2.4 million people in the first decade of the twenty-first century.[17] The rights to emigrate and immigrate are asymmetrical, and in a world of territorially bound sovereign states, that is a problem.

Restating Kant's Enlightenment hospitality in contemporary terms, Seyla Benhabib reminds us that in a world of nations, "There is a fundamental human right to exit, only if there is also a fundamental human right to entry, to admittance, but not necessarily to membership."[18] All people have the right to leave their country, but then what? In the terms of the UN declarations, they do not necessarily have the right to enter another. Unless they are able to return safely to the country they have left, they are stateless. They are left in limbo, outside any community within which they could reclaim the rights that eighteenth-century philosophers and founders defined as natural and that Arendt affirmed as belonging to all of humanity.[19] Benhabib summed up the refugees' dilemma in 2002: "The old political structures may have waned, but the new political forms of globalization are not yet in sight."[20]

In 2006, the United Nations defined the rights owed non-citizens, the 3 percent of the world's population who "have not been recognized by a State as having an effective link with it." Broadly stated, non-citizens everywhere in the world deserve freedom from inhumane treatment, slavery, arbitrary arrest, etc., while enjoying rights to equality, marriage, labor, freedom of religion, and consular protection. International human rights law assumes "that all persons, by virtue of their essential humanity, should enjoy all human rights without discrimination." However, it allows for differences between citizens and non-citizens. For example, non-citizens are not guaranteed political rights that are left to the states. The report of the United Nations acknowledged "a large gap between the rights that international human rights law guarantees to them and the realities that they face in many countries."[21]

Are there international structures to respond to the urgent plight of refugees or non-citizens caught between nation-states? The United Nations General Assembly established the UN Refugee Agency and the UNHCR, giving the new agencies an international mandate to function as the spokespersons for the world's refugees. The UNHCR, however, distinguished among "the population of concern" separating refugees from asylum seekers, "internally displaced persons," and the stateless. Its mandate was limited to forcibly displaced people.

Regional agreements in Africa, Latin America, and Europe have expanded the United Nations' narrow definition of refugees. They recognize that war, civil unrest, and natural disaster, not just political persecution, often force people to flee their homes. The United States and Canada, for their part, extended refugee protection to cover gender-based crimes and practices. Several judicial rulings, including those in Germany and the United States, have also established that nation-states unable to guarantee a minimum standard of living to their citizens could be charged with the denial of human rights. The burden of proof, however, falls upon individual refugees, who must demonstrate that persecution—whether economic, political, social, or cultural—was what forced them to leave.[22] Even so, this broader definition of refugees as "persons whose basic needs are unprotected by their country of origin, who have no remaining recourse other than to seek international restitution of their needs," has finally come close to echoing the definition of refugees that prevailed in the revolutionary era. Notably, it breaks down the artificial division between economic and political immigrants and does not consider the cause of flight, whether regional warfare, domestic violence, or climate change.[23]

And yet there is still little agreement about who qualifies for protection. The U.S. State Department has acknowledged that "traditional distinctions between refugees from persecution and immigrants" continue to pose "hard questions concerning the scope and applicability of human rights."[24] Without a precise definition of "persecution," the United States and a number of European nations can continue to pick and choose among asylum seekers. For those few offered asylum, nation-states retain wide discretion to determine within their sovereign jurisdiction what rights they will grant them.

In the wake of the UN Declaration of Human Rights and the Geneva Convention, physical borders are still being fortified, reinforced by bureaucratic regimes of paper across the world, from India to South Africa to the United States. Malaysian-born London School of Economics political theorist Chandran Kukathas has stated the conundrum of the modern migrant in blunt terms: "Though some borders are easier to cross than others—or at least, easier for *some* people to cross—the presumption in the modern world is that 'thou shall not cross' without proper authorization."[25] There are multiple hurdles along the route to safety that deter all but the most desperate of refugees from attempting a transnational trek toward safety. States increasingly police at a distance, keeping migrants at arms length with what the British Home Office calls "off-shoring our border control."[26] More ubiquitous, refugee camps have been established en route, allowing regions to "manage" refugees by isolating, detaining, and surfeiting them. Caught between nations, families in flight are forced to subsist for years on end without access to education, health care, and work or even a legal identity to be registered at birth, marriage, and death.

John Stoessigner, a refugee serving on the International Refugee Organization, has observed that refugees have functioned throughout modern history as "the barometer of intolerance."[27] Arendt recalled that in the not too distant past, "The comity of European peoples went to pieces when, and because, it allowed its weakest member to be excluded and persecuted."[28] Despite the best intentions and unwavering dedication of human rights activists all over the globe, refugees still perish in ever greater numbers on the other sides of walls.

German philosopher Daniel Loick identifies the contemporary immigration challenges that beset our world with its minimalist international legal regime: "the illegalization and criminalization of migration, the militarization of borders, the internment of refugees, their subjection to administrative and police chicanery, as well as the struggle against the withholding of essential goods such as shelter and food, work and communication." How to respond? Loick replies boldly: "First is the recognition that nation states created and continue to create refugees."[29]

"Our Country Is Full": Nations

Nation-states in the twenty-first century are able to brush aside the declarations and protocols emanating from the United Nations that should guarantee refugees "the right to seek and to enjoy in other countries asylum from persecution." They can choose the categories of refugees they will consider admitting as they set up bureaucratic obstacles along the path to asylum. International proclamations have proven in the decades following their signing to be not only non-binding, but also dismissible.

Perhaps the most egregious example of the assertion of national sovereignty in defiance of international law was the inappropriately named U.S. "Commission on Unalienable Rights." In 2020, the U.S. State Department challenged the legitimacy of the Universal Declaration of Human Rights itself. Under a red, white, and blue banner depicting three founding fathers, the American report denied the very existence of universal human rights. Instead, it posited a "Distinctive American Rights Tradition" rooted in Protestant Christianity, Roman republicanism, and classical liberalism. Each nation should be able to define its own national traditions, the Americans argued, claiming "the ambitious human rights project of the past century is in crisis."[30] Without a global consensus, the protection of rights should be left to the nation-state, the authors of the claim to American sovereignty concluded.

Putting these assertions into practice, the administration of President Donald Trump threatened to "denaturalize" citizens, a policy with precedent in American history, and to deport the so-called "dreamers" who had been brought to the United States as children.[31] Through control of immigration, it attempted to define not only who is American, but also what it meant to be American. In stark contrast to the 1831 Belgian Constitution, which extended rights to all inhabitants of its sovereign territory, the United States in 2020 limited the right of permanent residence to its own citizens and excluded broad categories of non-citizens from receiving public assistance. The variations among contemporary states under the realm of clearly articulated international law is as great as the divergence in the reception of refugees two centuries earlier, when city-states, empires, and republics decided whether to open or close their gates with only the moral dictums of the Enlightenment as their guides. Then, as now, national security demands more often than not overrode the impulse toward a generous hospitality.

Between October 2019 and September 2020, the United States admitted only 11,814 refugees, the lowest annual admissions on record and an 86 percent drop from the nearly 85,000 refugees admitted in 2016.[32] Reversing decades of resettlement efforts, the American president not only declared, "Our country is full," but also urged other national leaders around the world to close their doors as well.[33] Faced with such national resistance, the refugee policies of the United Nations offer little recourse. Asylum seekers, refugees, and others without documentation suffer from what has been identified as a citizenship gap.[34]

A coterie of prominent refugees and their colleagues—including Albert Einstein, Aldous Huxley, François Mauriac, John Dos Passos, Bertrand Russell, and George Bernard Shaw—asked UN Secretary-General Trygvie Lie in 1948 why refugees were obliged to secure membership in a nation to enjoy their human rights. With foresight, they challenged the premise of the Universal Declaration of Human Rights that nation-states should be the building blocks of an international legal system.

The International Refugee Organization responded to the refugees' challenge, asking how without a nation-state they would access the work permits, passports, and hospitals required for everyday existence. The Inter-American Commission on Human Rights agreed, affirming the right to a nationality as "one of the most important rights of man, after the right to life itself, because all the prerogatives, guarantees, and benefits man derives from this membership in a political and social community, the State, stem from or are supported by the right."[35] International law, it asserted, is based on the premise that an individual's rights are guaranteed by the nation where the individual resides.

The illustrious refugees responded, countering the centrality of the nation-state as a source of human rights. The history that cast them out of nations at war had "made them citizens of the world," and they aspired to "be treated as such." Why, they asked, not "let the ideal of world citizenship subsist not exclusively in theories and programs, but also in courageous experimenting and in a genuine respect for the human person?"[36]

If this basic right cannot be realized in the form of membership of an existing nation-state, Daniel Loick writes, "then the challenge is to find or to invent a form of democracy that is not bound up with the principle of territoriality." Envisioning a global citizenship more universal than Kant's federation of nations or its modern incarnation in the United Nations, a number of contemporary philosophers have begun to define a citizenship disconnected from its restrictive ties to a delimited national territory. These contemporary cosmopolitan rights, like the inalienable natural rights that preceded them by two centuries, would apply "to humanity as a whole."[37]

If stateless refugees are an obvious indictment of the existing regime of international law, so, too, Linda Kerber explained with more than a glimmer of optimism, "statelessness can be made to sustain a cosmopolitan dream." In contrast to the exclusions implied by nation-bound citizenship, "a destabilized citizenship" might be "an enriched citizenship."[38] Refugees who are citizens of nowhere, as the philosophers of the Enlightenment aspired to be, might then become the first world citizens.[39] Theirs would be a multilayered citizenship, possibly building from the municipal neighborhoods where the merchants of Hamburg and Altona and Marx's family sensed they belonged in earlier times.

Cosmopolitanism and Neighborhoods: "A Destabilized Citizenship"

Eleanor Roosevelt, appointed convener of the first international commission on human rights for the United Nations in 1946, located the origins of human rights and their protection "in small places, close to home—so close and so small that they cannot be seen on any map of the world." The wife of the American wartime president expected "the displaced" to claim their "right to have rights" in neighborhoods at the heart of communities where they settled, however impermanently. If human rights have no meaning in the neighborhoods where individuals live, "they have little meaning anywhere," Roosevelt concluded.[40] Rather than looking globally, she set her sights locally.

At an international conference of writers half a century later, the Algerian-born French philosopher Jacques Derrida proposed an approach to sheltering refugees and guaranteeing their rights based in these small spaces. Rather than follow the United Nations and continue to appeal in vain to the largest, wealthiest nations to take in refugees, he proposed that "new cities" be enlisted to offer asylum freely to increasingly desperate refugees seeking asylum. "Could the City, equipped with new rights and greater sovereignty, open up new horizons of possibility previously undreamt of by international state law?" he asked. Why wait for some seemingly unattainable dream based on hopes for future international cooperation among increasingly belligerent nation-states?[41]

Urban governance by active citizens has a long history, stretching back centuries. In premodern cities, citizenship meant "the right to claim rights," Turkish-born Canadian political scientist Engin Isin elaborates.[42] It referred not to a legal definition but to mutual transactions between residents and governing authorities. Citizenship was a set of practices defined by active citizens themselves that changed over time. At its core was a shared civic vision. Isin's definition, based on urban citizenship of past centuries, is not that different from Hannah Arendt's "right to have rights."

At the dawning of the era of the nation-state, Kant had already proposed grounding the natural right to hospitality at the local level. Rather than waiting for some ever-more-distant future, Derrida suggested searching for a model of hospitable cities in history. "Perhaps—if it has already arrived," he suggested, "one has just not yet recognised it."[43] Open communities such as he envisioned for the future might be found in the past, in times of experimentation, when citizenship was not yet universally tied to the stability of the nation-state. Small spaces as sites of asylum were an idea with a "back to the future" quality.

The historical examples of commercial and intellectual crossroads illustrate the possibilities of a locally based cosmopolitanism. At the end of the eighteenth century, between the collapse of fragmenting empires and the rise of modern nations commanding the loyalty of geographically bound citizens, refugees enjoyed an informal citizenship at the local level. The independent city-state of Hamburg, like Altona in neighboring Denmark, or the small kingdom of Belgium half a century later, extended rights to non-citizens in residence. They were cosmopolitans before the introduction of global institutions or considerations of transnationalism.

The doors opened by Altona, Hamburg, the Swiss cantons, and Belgium at the beginning of the modern era enabled an interchange between refugees and citizens that transpired freely in homes, the marketplace, and public spaces. The refugees seeking asylum in small spaces between larger nations for two centuries found their natural and civil rights grounded locally. They staked a claim to what has been characterized by urban geographers as "destabilized citizenship" rights in the neighborhoods offering them asylum.

Not "an order susceptible to sovereign authority," in contrast to nation-states, urban neighborhoods such as those found in Hamburg, Altona, and Brussels could be described as "changeable, ungovernable, and unpredictable."[44] Canadian political theorist Warren Magnusson's description of the ideal urban governance as "self-regulation, mutual tolerance, and collective action for public benefit" characterizes not only a handful of sanctuary cities in our own time, but also Georg Heinrich Sieveking's and Jacques Chapeaurouge's Hamburg in 1795, Lucien Jottrand's and Karl Marx's Brussels in 1845, and in between, the Swiss cantons that welcomed Eduard Scriba, Giuseppe Mazzini, and scores of others.[45]

In the absence of national citizenship, local integration has often functioned as an ad hoc solution. Even where federal governments restricted political rights at the national level, refugees over the last two centuries have found new homes fostering their resettlement within local neighborhoods. Neighborhoods and their institutions have welcomed newcomers without the barrier of formal admission requirements. Neighbors can refuse to welcome someone, but only through appeal to outside authorities can they actually exclude a stranger.

That is not to characterize the lives of refugees residing in cities as without challenges, nor the proffered asylum as ideal. In the tumultuous era between revolutions, the lives of refugees were not often easy, nor were they always free from police interference. Potentially dangerous political exiles were not infrequently packed on their way, usually when national governments bowed to diplomatic pressure exerted by their more powerful neighbors, as Marx and Engels and their fellow German exiles discovered in Brussels.

From the founding of the revolutionary republics, Hamburg, Altona, the Swiss cantons, and Belgium hosted refugees in the bleakest of times, serving as counterexamples to the restrictions and fears of their neighbors. The United States, not unlike Britain and France, among other established nations, rose to meet the challenge of the Forty-Eighters. These revolutionaries were welcomed on much the same terms as earlier refugees in smaller spaces, although they ended up staying, setting down roots, and establishing national citizenship.

National citizenship was not an issue raised by many refugees before the Forty-Eighters came to the United States. Still, most of the Forty-

Eighters, even those who settled permanently, shared the transnational vision of the earlier political refugees seeking shelter at European crossroads. Margarethe and Carl Schurz, for example, carved out lives for themselves and their family in neighborhoods. For unlike the ever-shifting immigration and naturalization regulations legislated at the national level over the last two centuries, life negotiated daily at the local level proved amenable to the more immediate needs of refugees.

The president of the Eurocities network bluntly contrasted a national with a municipal reception of refugees in 2018: "Where member states talk, city states act."[46] New York political theorist Benjamin Barber, in his book *If Mayors Ruled the World*, added concrete detail to this comparison: "The politics of the city have a very different character to the ideological politics of the nation. [They] are about making things work—you've got to pick up the garbage, you've to keep the hospitals open, it doesn't matter if the immigrants are legal or illegal—they have children who get sick and who have to go to school, they ride buses, they drive cars. If you asked a mayor, 'Do you think immigrants should be allowed in or not?' they'd say: 'They are here.'"[47]

During the pandemic, rather than waiting for the U.S. Congress to debate, agree on an aid package, and distribute relief in the form of checks, mutual aid efforts in neighborhoods collected food and prevented evictions, no documentation required. Idealistic volunteers explained, "In these projects we see glimpses of a society where we meet one another's needs, not with shame but with the sense that contributing is an essential thing we do for one another."[48] Climate change is another global problem often approached most effectively at a local level. The Climate and Environment Charter for Humanitarian Organizations, an international organization, has committed to be guided by local communities, recognizing what slow-moving global and national policymakers have to learn from "local traditional and indigenous knowledge on mitigation and adaptation measures, including nature-based-solutions."[49] Locally led solutions, they conclude, are often the most durable.

In the first decades of the twenty-first century, cities of refuge allied in a network to open doors closed by nations. "Cities of refuge" and sanctuary cities have explicitly taken on the challenge of migration. More than four hundred cities signed the European Charter for the Safeguarding of Human Rights in the City. Where nation-states exclude, they pledge to facilitate inclusion. Their more flexible and adaptable municipal governments are simply better equipped to handle immigration, the Global Parliament of Mayors suggested in 2018.[50] Theirs is a working alliance of cities with open doors. They could take inspiration from the cities of the past.

Many mayors and activists for refugee rights have given up waiting for offers of asylum legislated at the national level. Some cities grant asylum to refugees despite closed national borders; others open municipal doors to education and work while providing access to medical care, legal assistance, and housing. Even in a world of sovereign nation-states, some cities have also granted newcomers the right to vote for municipal elections. Others, including New York City and Paris, have established a formal resident status with an identity card giving access to city services. Beginning in 2023, more than eight hundred thousand non-citizens will have the right to vote in municipal elections.[51] When pressed to justify their activism, significantly, mayors and urban activists have cited international human rights laws and norms and their own commitment to democracy. Similar laws are under consideration in several states that are also issuing drivers' licenses to immigrants.

The paradigm of national citizenship, while unchallenged, coexists in an increasing number of places with a vision of locally rooted citizenship.[52] Benhabib asked if the transition from civil to political citizenship might be encouraged at a level other than the nation-state.[53] Benjamin Barber, an advocate for strong municipalities, responded in the affirmative. Even if cities do not have ultimate sovereignty over the land on which they are built, Barber suggests confidently, "For all the contradictions and obstacles presented by cities, they remain a formidable alternative to the conventional nation-state paradigm in which our thinking has been imprisoned for the past three centuries."[54] Perhaps, cities might offer a feasible alternative to rights-granting nation-states for realizing the cosmopolitan promise of a borderless globe.

"A Formidable Alternative"

With increasing urgency, we are forced to wonder what happens when more and more people migrate. If exile is becoming the rule rather than the exception, what has become of notions of a home to be rediscovered or remembered or of citizenship as a settled state? Is there a way for people set in motion by climate and regime change not only to tolerate, but also to thrive in what Edward Said calls "a perpetual self-invention or a constant restlessness"?[55] Starting in the neighborhood, could the rights promised over the centuries by liberal democracies not be realized for all locally, including the still elusive rights to education, shelter, and work?

How can nation-states, overwhelmed by the sheer numbers of refugees at their borders, respond more humanely? The experiences of refugees during the tumultuous period of nation founding demonstrate other paths toward this end, ones not often taken amid fortifying nation-states. Marx and before him the merchants who settled in Hamburg and Altona offer a glimpse of what Benhabib calls "a new conceptualization of the relationship between international law and emancipatory politics."[56] Rather than looking to overarching international organizations to cajole recalcitrant nation-states into compliance with human rights globally defined, why not guarantee rights from the ground up, starting at the local level with its often informal authority?[57] As some cities, giving voice to the claims of refugees caught between nation-states, have begun to ask again, why must citizenship be coterminous with the nation-state?

A research associate in Uganda, Lucy Hovil, suggests that this local integration is not so much the "forgotten solution" as the "evaded" one.[58] The expectation of attaining unidimensional access to national citizenship "ignores local realities in which people create and maintain multiple forms of belonging, not least in order to ensure multiple forms of legitimacy and access to resources." Based on the research of the International Refugee Rights Initiative, Hovil explains, refugees in Uganda from Rwanda, and in Tanzania from Burundi, "have multiple identities, deploy multiple coping strategies, and often defy tidy categories."[59] Marginalized and disempowered by national and international attempts at solutions, the refugees from Rwanda and Burundi forge local connections that allow them to make a living, feed and shelter their families, and send their children to school. Of course, their existence remains precarious. The local situation is unstable, informal, and subject to disruption by national and international tensions that prioritize security.

If nation-states are fomenting wars and chaos on a global scale, might it not be the original site of democracy, the city, that offers an alternative? If more than half the world's population lives in cities today and if that population is rooted in neighborhoods, might the city not be a more welcoming and inclusive place than nations with their rigid borders?[60] Although cities were encircled by stone walls with gates closed at nightfall throughout much of their history, in the modern era, those walls have given way to boulevards carrying commuters and commerce in and out of the urban centers.

Cosmopolitan cities are discovering, as the smaller spaces realized in an earlier era of global turbulence, that newcomers can contribute significantly to the economic prosperity of the places that offer them refuge. Refugees also bring political stability to these spaces that welcome them. In what might seem paradoxical, especially in a world filled with the rhetoric of security-conscious, wall-building national leaders, the presence of foreigners contributed substantially to the political stability and economic prosperity of Hamburg and Altona at the end of the eighteenth century and the Swiss cantons and Belgium in the nineteenth century.

During the revolutionary era, unlikely alliances entangled refugees and governing citizens in fruitful conversations. In these decades of upheaval, theirs was an alchemy that worked. At its center, free-wheeling international trade allied refugees and citizens in support of civic republicanism and international peace at the end of the eighteenth century. The burgeoning capitalism of Hamburg and Altona in the 1790s sustained its most substantive critique from the next generation of refugees generating socialism, the refugees enjoying asylum in Belgium.

Half a century after the influential Hamburg senator Georg Heinrich Sieveking and his wife Johanna welcomed guests, citizens and immigrants alike, and assembled for dinner every Sunday at makeshift tables spread for a simple supper, Polish and German communists met Belgian republicans in cafés, and the Liberals governing the kingdom of Belgium listened attentively to Karl Marx's lectures on the consequences of free trade. Reforms legislated by the Belgian Parliament during this tumultuous decade may have staved off revolution. The Revolutions of 1848 skipped over the Belgian nation that had harbored Marx.

Whether in the salons of Altona or the cafés of Brussels fifty years later, the loyalties of refugees and citizens alike were not exclusively attached to territory. Their identity was multilayered. As transitory quasi-citizens, they were often drawn to an ideal global vision anchored by lives lived locally surrounded by the free trade of goods and ideas.[61] In their sanctuary cities, newcomers, like the self-conscious burghers, enjoyed constitutional protections and access to public space, even if they did not exercise full political rights as citizens at the national level. Their vision was global because they found the space to work and live locally. In small spaces, they secured the "right to have rights."

Notes

Introduction

1. Hannah Arendt, *The Origins of Totalitarianism* (New York: Meridian Books, 1958), 296. See also Alison Kesby, *The Right to Have Rights: Citizenship, Humanity, and International Law* (Oxford: Oxford University Press, 2012), 3.
2. Hannah Arendt, "We Refugees," *Menorah Journal* 31, no. 1 (1943); republished in *Altogether Elsewhere: Writers on Exile*, ed. Marc Robinson (New York: Harcourt, Brace, 1994), 110.
3. Charles Simic, "Refugees," in *Letters of Transit: Reflections on Exile, Identity, Language, and Loss*, ed. André Aciman (New York: New Press, 1990), 124.
4. Hannah Arendt, "Es gibt nur ein einziges Menschenrecht," *Die Wandlung* (1949); cited by Seyla Benhabib, *Exile, Statelessness, and Migration: Playing Chess with History from Hannah Arendt to Isaiah Berlin* (Princeton, NJ: Princeton University Press, 2008), 102.
5. Even histories of immigration, an obviously international story if ever there was one, tend to segregate arrivals, considering one nation at a time, usually France, Great Britain, or the United States. Before the mass movements of the last one hundred and seventy years, if not just of the two world wars, migration has been ignored and asylum dismissed as an insignificant issue in international relations. Diasporic history, most notably of Palestinian refugees, is a welcome addition to the literature.
6. Andrew Shacknove, cited in Matthew J. Gibney, "Political Theory, Ethics, and Forced Migration," in *The Oxford Handbook of Refugee and Forced Migration Studies*, ed. Elena Fiddian-Qasmiyeh, Gil Loescher, Katy Long, and Nando Sigona (Oxford: Oxford University Press, 2014), 50.
7. Sylvie Aprile and Delphine Diaz, "Europe and Its Political Refugees in the 19th Century," *Books and Ideas*, Collège de France, 18 April 2016.
8. Victor Hugo, cited in Sylvie Aprile, *Le siècle des exiles: Bannis et proscrits de 1789 à la Commune* (Paris: CNRS Editions, 2010), 7.

9. UN General Assembly, New York Declaration for Refugees and Migrants, 3 October 2016 (New York, 2016).
10. In 2015, the UN high commissioner for refugees suggested that "everybody use the term they want as long as they reflect on the meaning hidden behind the words." Cited by Aprile and Diaz, "Europe and Its Political Refugees in the 19th Century." The discussions of refugees as a category are many. See, for example, the following: Pamela Ballinger, "Entangled or 'Extruded' Histories? Displacement, National Refugees, and Repatriation after the Second World War," *Journal of Refugee Studies* 25, no. 3 (2012): 366–386; Jérôme Elie, "Histories of Refugee and Forced Migration Studies," in Fiddian-Qasmiyeh et al., *The Oxford Handbook of Refugee and Forced Migration Studies*, 23–35; and Katy Long, "When Refugees Stopped Being Migrants: Movement, Labour and Humanitarian Protections," *Migration Studies* 1, no. 1 (2013): 4–26.
11. André Aciman, "Prologue," in Aciman, *Letters of Transit*, 9.
12. Arendt, *The Origins of Totalitarianism*, 280.
13. Glossary, UNHCR, 2005; https://www.unhcr.org/449267670.pdf.
14. Edward Said, "Reflections on Exile," *Granata* 1, no. 3 (Autumn 1984): 148.
15. V. S. Naipaul, *The Enigma of Arrival* (New York: Vintage Books, 1988), 92.
16. Ibid., 103.
17. Immanuel Kant, "Toward Perpetual Peace," ed. Jonathan Bennett (Early Modern Texts, 2017), 11. https://www.earlymoderntexts.com/assets/pdfs/kant1795.pdf.; and Georg Cavallar, *Kant's Embedded Cosmopolitanism: History, Philosophy, and Education for World Citizens* (Berlin: De Gruyter, 2015).
18. See Martha Nussbaum, *The Cosmopolitan Tradition: A Noble but Flawed Ideal* (Cambridge, MA: Harvard University Press, 2019), ch. 1.
19. Hugo Grotius, cited by Greg Burgess, *Refuge in the Land of Liberty: France and Its Refugees, from the Revolution to the End of Asylum, 1787–1939* (New York: Palgrave Macmillan, 2008), 1.
20. Christian von Wolff, cited by Burgess, *Refuge in the Land of Liberty*, 1. It should be noted that Wolff gave states discretion over whom they admitted.
21. Denis Diderot, cited by Margaret C. Jacob, *Strangers Nowhere in the World: The Rise of Cosmopolitanism in Early Modern Europe* (Philadelphia: University of Pennsylvania Press, 2006), 1.
22. David Hume, cited by Thomas J. Schlereth, *The Cosmopolitan Ideal in Enlightenment Thought: Its Form and Function in the Ideas of Franklin, Hume, and Voltaire, 1694–1790* (Notre Dame, IN: University of Notre Dame Press, 1977), xiii.
23. Denis Diderot, cited by Peter Coulmas, *Les citoyens du monde: Histoire du cosmopolitisme*, trans. Jeanne Etoré (Paris: Albin Michel, 1995), 208.
24. Cavallar, *Kant's Embedded Cosmopolitanism*, 62.
25. Immanuel Kant, cited by Pauline Kleingeld, *Kant and Cosmopolitanism: The Philosophical Ideal of World Citizenship* (Cambridge: Cambridge University

Press, 2012), 78. See also Vincent Chetail, "Sovereignty and Migration in the Doctrine of the Law of Nations: An Intellectual History of Hospitality from Vitoria to Vattel," *European Journal of International Law* 27, no. 4 (2017): 922.

26. Hannah Arendt, cited by Seyla Benhabib, "Citizens, Residents, and Aliens in a Changing World: Political Membership in the Global Era," *Social Research* 66, no. 3 (Fall 1999): 711.
27. Nicolas de Condorcet, *Lettres d'un citoyen des États Unis à un Français sur les affaires présentes, par Mr. Le M** de C*** (Philadelphia, 1788), 1. Unless otherwise specified, all translations are mine.
28. Joel Barlow, cited by Yvon Bizardel, *The First Expatriates: Americans in Paris during the French Revolution*, trans. June P. Wilson and Cornelia Higginson (New York: Holt, Rinehart and Winston, 1975), 143.
29. Sujit Sivasundaram, *Waves across the South: A New History of Revolution and Empire* (Chicago: University of Chicago Press, 2020), 97–98. Sivasundaram reminds us that ideas traveled in both directions and insurrections reflected a multiplicity of influence from all directions, enacted within a local context.
30. Thomas Paine, cited by Coulmas, *Les citoyens du monde*, 208.
31. Anacharsis Cloots, cited by Sophie Wahnich, *L'impossible citoyen: L'étranger dans le discours de la Révolution française* (Paris: Albin Michel, 1997), 7.
32. Anacharsis Cloots, cited by Jeremy D. Popkin, *The History of the French Revolution: A New World Begins* (New York: Basic Books, 2019), 212.
33. Anacharsis Cloots, cited by Frank Ejby Poulsen, "Anacharsis Cloots and the Birth of Modern Cosmopolitanism," in *Critique of Cosmopolitan Reason: Timing and Spacing the Concept of World Citizenship*, ed. Kristian Petrov and Rebecca Letteval (New York: Peter Lang, 2014), 110.
34. Anacharsis Cloots, cited by Suzanne Desan, "Foreigners, Cosmopolitanism, and French Revolutionary Universalism," in *The French Revolution in Global Perspective*, ed. Suzanne Desan, Lynn Hunt, and William Max Nelson (Ithaca, NY: Cornell University Press, 2013), 94.
35. Marie-Joseph Chénier, cited by Desan, "Foreigners, Cosmopolitanism, and French Revolutionary Universalism," 86.
36. As stated by Marie-Jean Hérault de Séchelles and cited by Desan, "Foreigners, Cosmopolitanism and French Revolutionary Universalism," 91.
37. Marie-Joseph Chénier, cited by Desan, "Foreigners, Cosmopolitanism and French Revolutionary Universalism," 86.
38. Jean-Pierre Rabaut, cited by Janet Polasky, "Revolutionaries between Nations, 1776–1789," *Past and Present*, 232, no. 1 (August 2016): 197.
39. Maximilien Robespierre, cited by David Bell, *The Cult of the Nation in France: Inventing Nationalism, 1680–1800* (Cambridge, MA: Harvard University Press, 2003), 156.
40. Jean Lambert Tallien, cited by Peter Sahlins, "The Citizenship Revolution in Eighteenth-Century France," in *Migration Control in the North Atlantic World: The Evolution of State Practices in Europe and the United States from the*

French Revolution to the Interwar Period, ed. Andreas Fahrmeir, Olivier Faron, and Patrick Weil (New York: Berghahn Books, 2003), 21.

41. Thomas Paine, *Common Sense*, in Thomas Paine, *Collected Writings* (New York: Penguin, 1992), 36.
42. On the loyalists, see, among many, the following: Jan C. Jansen, "Flucht und Exil im Zeitalter der Revolutionen," *Geschichte und Gesellschaft* 44, no. 4 (October–December 2018): 495–525; Maya Jasanoff, *Liberty's Exiles: American Loyalists in the Revolutionary World* (New York: Vintage, 2012); and Cassandra Pybus, *Epic Journeys of Freedom: Runaway Slaves of the American Revolution and Their Global Quest for Liberty* (Boston: Beacon Press, 2006).
43. Ernest Renan, "What Is a Nation?" (1882).
44. Michael Walzer, "The Distribution of Membership," in *Boundaries: National Autonomy and Its Limits*, ed. Peter G. Brown and Henry Shue (Totowa, NJ: Rowman and Littlefield, 1981), 1.
45. Jean-Jacques Rousseau, "Considérations sur le gouvernement de Pologne et sur sa réformation projetée"; cited by Michael Rapport, *Nationality and Citizenship in Revolutionary France: The Treatment of Foreigners 1789–1799* (Oxford: Clarendon Press, 2000), 8.
46. Judith Lichtenberg, "National Boundaries and Moral Boundaries: A Cosmopolitan View," in Brown and Shue, *Boundaries*, 80.
47. Alexandre Gendebien, 7 February 1839; cited by Lucien Jottrand, *Charles-Louis Spilthoorn: Événements de 1848 en Belgique.* (Brussels: Imprimérie de Charles Vanderauwera, 1872), 26.
48. Benhabib, "Citizens, Residents, and Aliens in a Changing World," 730. See also Seyla Benhabib, *The Rights of Others: Aliens, Residents and Citizens* (Cambridge: Cambridge University Press, 2004), and Peter Gatrell, *The Making of the Modern Refugee* (Oxford: Oxford University Press, 2013), 13.
49. Ferdinand Beneke, 14 February 1796 and 21 March 1796, in *Die Tagebücher, 1, 2, 1796 bis 1798*, ed. Frank Hatje and Ariane Smith et al. (Hamburg: Wallstein Verlag, n.d.), 21 and 43. I have adopted some of the translations from Steven Daniel Uhalde, "Citizen and World Citizen: Civic Patriotism and Cosmopolitanism in Eighteenth Century Hamburg" (PhD dissertation, University of California, Berkeley, 1984), 22–23.
50. Eric Min interviewed by Thijs Kleinpaste, "Niemand houdt van deze onbegrijpelijke stade," *De Groene Amsterdammer* (9 December 2015). Although historians, journalists, and tour guides alike situate the location as the Café Le Cygne (The Swan) and visitors pose for their pictures in front by the droves, it is probably a myth. Although Marx gathered listeners in clubs and associations in cafés, including, notably Le Cygne, often in the back rooms, he probably wrote the *Communist Manifesto* at home, in space his wife Jenny had cleared for him at their house on the rue d'Orléans in the hills of Ixelles, just to the south of central Brussels.
51. Friedrich Engels, cited by Bert Andréas, *Marx Verhaftung und Ausweisung aus Brüssel* (Trier: Karl-Marx-Haus, 1978), 49.

52. Sarah Knott, "Narrating the Age of Revolution," *William and Mary Quarterly* 73, no. 1 (January 2016): 3.
53. Arendt, *The Origins of Totalitarianism*, 297.

1. Aristocratic Émigrés and Luxurious Temptations

1. The numbers range from ten to forty thousand in Hamburg. For the range based on contemporary sources, see Maike Manske, *Möglichkeiten und Grenzen des Kulturtransfers. Emigranten der Französischen Revolution in Hamburg, Bremen und Lübeck* (Saarbrücken: VDM Verlag Dr. Müller Aktiengesellschaft & Co. KG, 2008), 27.
2. "Die Doktorinn," Sophie Reimarus, cited in Philipp Rudolph, "Frankreich im Urteil der Hamburger Zeitschriften in den Jahren 1789–1810." In *Seminar fur romanische Sprachen und Kultur* (Hamburg, 1933), 4.
3. Cited in "Emigrés français en Allemagne et émigrés allemands en France," *Annales historiques de la Révolution française* 56 (January 1, 1984): 279.
4. Friedemann Pestel, "French Revolution and Migration after 1789," EGO, European History online, 2017, 4–5. Pestel suggests that even though the percentage is small in comparison with the 65 percent of commoners who emigrated, a number of them were domestic servants who followed their nobles into exile and others were employed in luxury trades. See also Jan C. Jansen, "Flucht und Exil im Zeitalter der Revolutionen (1770er—1820er Jahre): Perspektiven einer atlantischen Flüchtlingsgeschichte," *Geschichte und Gesellschaft* 44 (2018): 495–525.
5. Recent histories of these aristocratic emigrants in Britain include the following: Kirsty Carpenter, *Refugees of the French Revolution* (New York: St. Martin's Press, 1999); Donald Greer, *The Incidence of the Emigration during the French Revolution* (Cambridge, MA: Harvard University Press, 1951); Caroline Shaw, *Britannia's Embrace: Modern Humanitarianism and the Origins of Refugee Relief* (New York: Oxford University Press, 2015); and Sidney Watts, "The Jersey Émigrés: Community Coherence amidst Diaspora," in *French Emigrants in Revolutionised Europe: Connected Histories and Memories*, ed. Laure Philip and Juliette Reboul (Cham, Switzerland: Palgrave Macmillan, 2019), 71.
6. Félix Magnette, *Les émigrés français aux Pays-Bas (1789–1794)* (Brussels: Académie Royale de Belgique, 1907), 12; and Matthias Winkler, "Interaction and Interrelation in Exile: French Émigrés, Legislation, and Everyday Life in the Habsburg Monarchy," in Philip and Reboul, *French Emigrants in Revolutionised Europe*, 49.
7. Franklin Kopitzsch, "Altona-ein Zentrum der Auflärung am Rande des dänischen Gesamtstaats," in *Der dänische Gesamstaat, Kopenhagen, Kiel, Altona*, ed. Klaus Bohnen and Sven Aage Jorgensen (Tubingen: Niemeyer, 1992), 92.
8. *From the Souvenirs of Jean-Étienne-Maris Portalis, Member of the Council of Ancients, Forced to Flee after the Coup of 18 Fructidor (4 September 1797);* cited

by Paul S. Spalding, "Unwanted Refugee: Lafayette in Holstein, 1797–1799," *Gazette of the American Friends of Lafayette* 92, no. 1 (June 2020): 24. I am grateful to Professor Spalding for sharing his paper with me before publication. See also Burghart Schmidt, "'Französisches Emigranten Volck in Hamburg nach dem Leben gemahlt,' Regionalgeschichtliche Überlegungen zum Wirtschafts-und Kulturtransfer im Zeitalter der Französischen Revolution," in *Hamburg und sein norddeutsches Umland. Aspekte des Wandels seit der Frühen Neuzeit. Festschrift für Franklin Kopitzsch*, ed. Dirk Brietzke, Norbert Fischer, and Arno Herzig (Hamburg: DOBU, 2007), 97–122.

9. Charlotte Sophie Bentinck to her granddaughter, 10 February 1792; cited in Aubrey LeBlond, *Charlotte Sophie Countess Bentinck: Her Life and Times, 1715–1800. By Her Descendant* (London: Hutchinson, 1912), 1:199.

10. Christine Randig, "'Eine glühende Aristokratin': Charlotte Sophie Reichsgräfin von Bentinck, geb. von Aldenburg, in den Hamburger Jahren (1767–1800)," *Zeitschrift des Vereins für Hamburgische Geschichte Hamburg* 102 (2016): 36.

11. Immanuel Kant, *Perpetual Peace: A Philosophical Sketch* (1795); https://www.mtholyoke.edu/acad/intrel/kant/kant1.htm. This principle of hospitality for visitors would be reaffirmed in the Universal Declaration of Human Rights.

12. Estimates of the exact number of refugees vary from ten to forty thousand. See G. Arvengas, "L'émigration française à Hambourg, 1795–1799," *Deutsch Frazosische Monatschafte* 6 (1939): 17; Berit Christine Ruth Royer, *Sophie Albrecht (1757–1840) im Kreis der Schriftstellerinnen um 1800. Eine literatur-und kulturwissenschaftliche Werk-Monographie* (PhD dissertation, University of California, Davis, 1999). They are listed in Pieter Schmidt-Eppendorf, *Priester-Emigranten in Hamburg und Schleswig-Holstein in der Zeit der Französischen Revolution* (Husem: Matthiesen, 1990).

13. Madame de Ménerville, *La fille d'une victime de la Révolution française: Madame de Ménerville, née Fougeret. Souvenirs d'émigration* (Paris: Roger, 1934), 78–79; cited by Britt Petersen, *Aristocracy Redeemed, Narratives of Redemption and Regeneration in Noblewomen's Memoirs of the French Revolution and Emigration* (PhD dissertation, Northwestern University, 2011), 194. See https://www.mtholyoke.edu/acad/intrel/kant/kant1.htm.

14. Trophime Gérard de Lally Tollendal, *Défense des émigrés français adressée au peuple français* (Paris: Cocheris, 1797), 52.

15. See, for example, Émile Bégin, *Villers. Madame de Rodde et Madame de Stael* (Metz: Verronnais, 1839).

16. Mme. de Neuilly, cited by Ghislain de Diesbach, *Histoire de l'émigration 1789–1814* (Paris: Bernard Grasset, 1975), 321.

17. Jules Bertaut, *Les belles émigrées: La comtesse de Polastron, Madame de Flahaut, la comtesse de Balbi, la marquise de la Tour du Pin, la princesse Louise de Bourbon Conde* (Paris: Flammarion, 1948), 119–121.

18. William Howard Adams, *Gouverneur Morris: An Independent Life* (New Haven: Yale University Press, 2003), 254.

19. *Deux célébrités feminines aux XVIIIe et XIX siècles: Madame de Genlis et Madame Vigée Le Brun. Souvenirs personnels* (Paris: Librairie Saint Paul, n.d.), 130.
20. Countess de Neuilly, cited by Arvengas, "L'Émigration française à Hambourg," 20.
21. J. de Norvins, *Souvenirs d'un historien de Napoléon: Mémorial de J. de Norvins* (Paris: E. Plon, 1896), 1:327.
22. Georg Heinrich Sieveking, cited by Mary Lindemann, *Liaisons Dangereuses: Sex, Law, and Diplomacy in the Age of Frederick the Great* (Baltimore: Johns Hopkins University Press, 2006), 62.
23. Charlotte Sophie Bentinck to Charlotte Milnes, 3 September 1793; in *Une femme des Lumières: Écrits et lettres de la Comtesse de Bentinck 1715–1800*, ed. Anne Soprani and André Magnan (Paris: CNRS Editions, 1997), 163.
24. Countess Bentinck, 10 February 1792 and 30 May 1795; cited in LeBlond, *Charlotte Sophie Countess Bentinck*, 1:241 and 2:89.
25. Norvins, *Souvenirs d'un historien de Napoléon*, 1:325.
26. Jean Pierre Blanchard, *Relation de la vingtième voyage ascension de M. Blanchard, qui a eu lieu à Hambourg le 23 août 1786* (Aix la Chapelle: n.p., 1986), 8.
27. Cited in Arvengas, "L'Émigration française à Hambourg," 21.
28. Gouverneur Morris, 25 December 1794; in Gouverneur Morris, *The Diaries of Gouverneur Morris, European Travels 1794–1798*, ed. Melanie Randolph Miller (Charlottesville: University of Virginia Press, 2011), 55.
29. Mary Wollstonecraft, *Letters Written during a Short Residence in Sweden, Norway, and Denmark* (London, Cassell, 1889), Letter 23.
30. Paul S. Spalding, "Hamburg als weltweites Kommunikationszentrum wahrend Lafayettes Gefangenschaft und Exil (1792–1799)," in *Hamburg. Eine Metropolregion zwischen Früher Neuzeit und Aufklärung*, ed. Johann Anselm Steiger and Sandra Richter (Berlin: Akademie Verlag, 2012), 349–360. For a fuller treatment, see Paul S. Spalding, *Lafayette: Prisoner of State* (Columbia, SC: University of South Carolina Press, 2010).
31. Marquis de Lafayette to Germaine de Staël, 23 July 1798; cited by P. Spalding, "Unwanted Refugee," 24.
32. Marquis de Lafayette to Adrienne de Lafayette, 2 August 1798; cited by P. Spalding, "Unwanted Refugee," 30
33. Marquis de Lafayette to Princesse d' Hénin, 27 March 1798; cited by P. Spalding, "Unwanted Refugee," 28.
34. Charlotte Sophie Bentinck to Sophie Hawkings, 14 November 1794; cited by Randig, "'Eine glühende Aristokratin,'" 35.
35. Countess de Flahaut to Mr. Morris, Bremgarten, 24 February 1795; in Jared Sparks, ed., *The Life of Gouverneur Morris, with Selections from His Correspondence and Miscellaneous Papers* (Boston: Gray and Bowen, 1832), 3:467.
36. Charlotte Sophie Bentinck, 12 October 1792; in LeBlond, *Charlotte Sophie Countess Bentinck*, 1:282.

37. Charlotte Sophie Bentinck, 29 July 1792; in LeBlond, *Charlotte Sophie Countess Bentinck*, 1:241.
38. Charlotte Sophie Bentinck to Sophie Hawkins, 16 January 1794 and 6 October 1797; cited by Randig, "'Eine glühende Aristokratin,'" 39–40.
39. Charlotte Sophie Bentinck to Général Nicolai, Hamburg, 31 October 1793; in Soprani and Magnan, *Une femme des lumières*, 162.
40. "Lettre d'un habitant de Paris," *Le Spectateur du Nord*, 17 May 1797, 291.
41. Antoine de Rivarol, cited by Gabriel de Broglie, *Madame de Genlis* (Paris: Perrin: 1985), 278.
42. Antoine de Rivarol, cited by Michel Cointat, *Rivarol: Un écrivain controversé* (Paris: L'Harmattan, 2001), 65.
43. Antoine de Rivarol, cited by Diesbach, *Histoire de l'émigration*, 315.
44. Katherine Aaslestadt, *Place and Politics: Local Identity, Civic Culture, and German Nationality in North German during the Revolutionary Era* (London: Brill, 2005), 146. See Georg Heinrich Sieveking, "Fragmente über Luxus, Bürger-Tugend und Bürger-Wohl für Hamburgische Bürger, die das Gute wollen und können." Handscriften, Staat-und Universitätsbibliothek Hamburg, Hamburg.
45. Friedrich Johann Lorenz Meyer, "Skizzen zu einem Sittengemälde von Hamburg"; in Aaslestadt, *Place and Politics*, 153–154.
46. *Hamburg und Altona* 2 (1804): 278; cited by Aaslestadt, *Place and Politics*, 155.
47. Joseph Scholz, *Hamburg oder vollständige Geschichte und Beschreibung dieser Stadt* (Hamburg, 1810), 9–11; cited by Aaslestadt, *Place and Politics*, 133. See more examples in Manske, *Möglichkeiten und Grenzen des Kulturtransfer*, 47–54.
48. Norvins, *Souvenirs d'un historien de Napoléon*, 1:320.
49. Charlotte Sophie Bentinck, 12 October 1792; in LeBlond, *Charlotte Sophie Countess Bentinck*, 1:282.
50. Charlotte Sophie Bentinck to Wilhelmine Marie von Aldenburg, 10 August 1770; cited by Randig, "'Eine glühende Aristokratin,'" 28–29.
51. Charlotte Sophie Bentinck, 30 May 1795; in LeBlond, *Charlotte Sophie Countess Bentinck*, 2:90. See also Hella S. Haasse, *Charlotte Sophie Bentinck* (Amsterdam: Querido, 1996)
52. Marquis de Messey, 1792; cited by Manske, *Möglichkeiten und Grenzen des Kulturtransfers*, 94.
53. Madame de Neuilly in Comte de Neuilly, *Souvenirs et correspondance*, 326; cited by Diesbach, *Histoire de l'émigration*, 333.

2. "A Temple Always Open to Peace"

1. Johanna Sieveking, Hamburg, 22 July 1794; s. 452, 622–1/86, 1/D2, Staatsarchiv, Hamburg. The title of this chapter comes from Friedrich Jachim Schlüter, cited in Steven Daniel Uhalde, "Citizen and World Citizen: Civic Patriotism and Cosmopolitanism in Eighteenth Century Hamburg" (PhD dissertation, University of California, Berkeley, 1984), 409.

2. Ferdinand Beneke, 14 February 1796, and 21 March 1796, *Die Tagebücher, 1, 2, 1796 bis 1798*, ed. Frank Hatje and Ariane Smith et al. (Hamburg: Wallstein Verlag), 21 and 43. I have adopted some of the translations from Uhalde, "Citizen and World Citizen."
3. Beneke, 21 March 1796, *Die Tagebücher*, 43.
4. Christine Reimarus to Magdalena Pauli, Hamburg, 4 February 1791; 622 1/421, Staatsarchiv, Hamburg.
5. Historian Sidney Watts applies this term, from Mary Louise Pratt, to the Channel Islands to explain the results of the islands' open-immigration policies.
6. Beneke, 14 February 1796, *Die Tagebücher.*
7. Franklin Kopitzsch, *Grundzüge einer Sozialgeschichte der Aufklärung in Hamburg und Altona* (Hamburg: Verlag Verein für Hamburgische Geschichte, 1990), 139–143.
8. Fred-Konrad Huhn, "Die Handelbeziehungen zwischen Frankreich und Hamburg im 18 Jahrhundert unter besonder Berucksichtigung der Handelsvertrage von 1716 und 1769," 2 vols. (Phil. diss., Hamburg, 1952), 219.
9. Kersten Krüger and Stefan Kroll, *Die Sozialstruktur der Städte Kiel und Altona um 1800. Demographie, Erwerbsstrukture und wirtschaftliche Leistungsfähigkeit* (Neumünster: Wachholtz Verlag, 1998), 186.
10. In contrast, the contract dating back to 1612 with the Jews did not allow for assimilation.
11. Almut Spalding and Paul S. Spalding, *The Account Books of the Reimarus Family of Hamburg, 1728–1780: Turf and Tailors, Books and Beer* (Leiden: Brill, 2015), 1:6 and 2:808. The Hamburg Senate debated and decided internal security and foreign policy, while the larger Citizen Board exercised legislative power, dealing primarily with financial administration. The librarian of the Patriotic Society, Friedrich Johann Lorenz Meyer, solidified the ties between the government and the Patriotic Society.
12. L. S. Rede, "A Sketch of Hamburg"; cited by Katherine Aaslestadt, *Place and Politics: Local Identity, Civic Culture, and German Nationality in North Germany during the Revolutionary Era* (London: Brill, 2005), 50. For a discussion of what historian István Hont called "commercial society," see Paul Cheney, "István Hont, the Cosmopolitan Theory of Commercial Globalization, and Twenty-First Century Capitalism," *Modern Intellectual History* (2021): 1–29.
13. A. Spalding and P. Spalding, *The Account Books of the Reimarus Family of Hamburg*, 11. On the requirements and responsibilities of citizenship in cities before 1800, see Maarten Prak, *Citizens without Nations: Urban Citizenship in Europe and the World c. 1000–1789* (Cambridge: Cambridge University Press, 2018), ch. 1.
14. Piter Poel, cited by Almut Spalding, *Elise Reimarus (1735–1805), the Muse of Hamburg: A Woman of the German Enlightenment* (Würzburg: Königshausen and Neumann, 2008), 192.

15. Sophie Reimarus to Adolph Knigge, 13 October 1795; cited by Karin Strater, *Frauen briefe als Medium bürgerlicher Öffentlichkeit. Eine Untersuchung anhand von Quellen aus dem Hamburger Raum in der zweiten Hälfte des 18. Jahrhunderts* (Frankfurt: M. Peter Lang, 1991), 77.
16. See a typical letter from Sophie to Adolph Knigge, 19 December 1794, in Günter Jung and Michael Rüppel, *"Verehrungswürdiger, braver Vertheidiger der Menschenrechte!" Der Briefwechsel zwischen Adolph Knigge und Sophie und Johann Albert Heinrich Reimarus, 1791–1796* (Göttingen: Wallstein Verlag, 2019), 76–78.
17. Elise Reimarus, cited by A. Spalding, *Elise Reimarus*, 163.
18. Monique Bernard, *Charles de Villers: de Boulay à Göttingen: Itinéraire d'un médiateur franco-allemand* (Metz: Éditions des Paraiges, 2016), 98. See also Heinrich Sieveking, *Lebensbild eines Hamburgischen Kaufmanns aus dem Zeitalter der französischen Revolution* (Berlin: Verlag Karl Curtius, 1913).
19. Karl August Böttinger, cited by Inge Stephan and Hans-Gerd Winter Stephen, *Hamburg in Zeitalter der Aufklärung* (Hamburg: Reimer, 1989), 292–293.
20. Kopitzsch, *Grundzüge einer Sozialgeschichte der Aufklärung in Hamburg und Altona*, 540.
21. Karl August Böttinger, cited by Uhalde, "Citizen and World Citizen," 73.
22. See letters in 622–1/107, VIII 22, and 622–1/421, 1–3, Staatsarchiv, Hamburg.
23. On these ornamental gardens inspired by British examples, see *Gärten, Landhäuser und Villen des hamburgischen Bürgertums. Kunst, Kultur und gesellschaftliches Leben in vier Jahrhunderten* (Hamburg: Museum für Hamburgische Geschichte, 1975).
24. Jean de Chapeaurouge to Elisabeth Dorothea Glashoff, 27 January 1793, and 28 January 1793; 622–1/20, D1, Staatsarchiv, Hamburg.
25. Gesellschaftsverträge mit Ignace de Urquillu, 1791–92; 622–1/20, C2, Staatsarchiv, Hamburg.
26. *Die Entwicklung der Gesellschaft 'Harmonie" von 1789. Ein dokumentarischer Beitrage ur Geschichte burgerlicher Kultur und Geselligkeit in Hamburg* (Hamburg: n.p., 1979), 18.
27. Franklin Kopitzsch, "Miglied der Patriotischen Gesellschaft," in *Patriotische Gesellschaft 1990. Ein Jubilaumsjahr Hamburg* (Hamburg: Patriotische Gesellschaft, 1991), 18. See list of members in 622–1/90, C8, and 622–1/86, C1, Staatsarchiv, Hamburg. Bericht des Senators Hudtwalcker, 622–1/90, C3, Staatsarchiv, Hamburg.
28. "Das Lesezimmer der Gesellschaft, Harmonie, in Hamburg," *Hanseatisches Magazin;* cited by Aaslestadt, *Place and Politics*, 111.
29. "Rapport fait par un commissaire de la société projetée sous la dénomination de salle de lecture et projet du règlement," 6 December 1792; 111 Senat 1756, C11, Lit Pb vol. 8c fasc. 2, Staatsarchiv, Hamburg.
30. See, for example, Tamar Herzog, "Merchants and Citizens: On the Making

and Unmaking of Merchants in Early Modern Spain and Spanish America," *Journal of European Economic History* 52 (2013): 137–163.

31. J. L. von Hess, *Topographisch-politisch-historisch Beschreibung* (Hamburg, 1790); cited by Aaslestadt, *Place and Politics*, 51.
32. Caspar Voght, cited by E. Baasch, "Die Führenden Kaufleute und ihre Stellung in der Hamburgischen Handelgeschichte," in *Hamburger Übersee-Jahrbuch 1922* (Hamburg: Alster-Verlag, 1922), 48.
33. John Parish, Journal, 1793, p. 84; Parish Family Papers, John Parish, 622–1/138, B, Staatsarchiv, Hamburg.
34. John Parish, Journal, 1793, p. 29; 622–1/138, B, Staatsarchiv, Hamburg.
35. Claudia Schnurmann, "His Father's Favored Son: David Parish," in *Immigrant Entrepreneurship: German-American Business Biographies, 1720 to the Present*, vol. 1, ed. Marianne S. Wokeck (Washington, D.C.: German Historical Institute, 2015).
36. On the practice of naming foreigners consuls during this period, see Margrit Schulte Beerbühl, "Hard Times: The Economic Activities of American Consuls on the North Sea Coast under the Continental System," *German Historical Institute London: Bulletin* 40, no. 2 (November 2018): 3–31.
37. Jean Sylvain Bailly, mayor of Paris, to G. H. Sieveking, 622–1/90, C7, Georg Heinrich Sieveking Briefwechsel 1775–1798, Staatsarchiv, Hamburg.
38. John Parish, Journal, 1777, p. 36; 622–1/138, B, Staatsarchiv, Hamburg.
39. Claudia Schnurmann, "A Scotsman in Hamburg: John Parish and His Commercial Contribution to the American War of Independence, 1776–1783," in *Small Is Beautiful? Interlopers and Smaller Trading Nations in the Pre-Industrial Period*, ed. Markus A. Denzel, Jan de Vries, and Philipp Robinson Rössner (Suttgart: Franz Steiner Verlag, 2011), 159.
40. Gouverneur Morris, cited in John Parish, *Domestick Economy*, p. 176; 622–1/138, B, Staatsarchiv, Hamburg; and Hamburgische Geschlechterbuch, p. 158; cited by Schnurmann, "A Scotsman in Hamburg," 159.
41. John Parish, Journal, 1793, p. 29; 622–1/138, B, Staatsarchiv, Hamburg.
42. John Parish, Journal, 1793, p. 84; 622–1/138, B, Staatsarchiv, Hamburg.
43. Jo Gerard, "Edouard de Walckiers, le La Fayette belge," in *La Revue generale*, Éditions Duculot (June–July 1989): 87–94; and Jean Bouchary, "Les manieurs d'argent sous la Révolution française: Le banquier Edouard de Walckiers," *Annales historiques de la Révolution française* 15, no. 86 (March–April 1938): 133–155.
44. John Parish, Journal, 1795, p. 99; 622–1/138, B, Staatsarchiv, Hamburg.
45. John Parish, Journal, 1795, p. 98; 622–1/138, B, Staatsarchiv, Hamburg.
46. Hannah Arendt, "We Refugees," *Menorah Journal* 31, no. 1 (1943); republished in *Altogether Elsewhere: Writers on Exile*, ed. Marc Robinson (New York: Harcourt, Brace, 1994), 116.
47. John Parish, cited by Claudia Schnurmann, "A Scotsman in Hamburg," 159. Parish calculated that once he moved to Bath, he entertained twenty-four

thousand people at his table over twelve years and that seventy-two thousand French dinners had been served in his dining room and the servants' hall.

48. Ruth to Joel Barlow, 9 January 1793; S 39, Ms Am 1448, Houghton Library, Harvard University, Cambridge, MA.
49. On the practice of dodging neutrality, see Beerbühl, "Hard Times," 22.
50. Joel Barlow, cited by Richard Buell Jr., *Joel Barlow: American Citizen in a Revolutionary World* (Baltimore: Johns Hopkins University Press, 2011), 191.
51. Joseph Gales in William S. Powell, "The Diary of Joseph Gales, 1794–95," *North Carolina Historical Review* 26 (1949): 338.
52. Winifred Gales to Jared Sparks, 16 October 1821, North Carolina Department of Archives and History; cited in Powell, "The Diary of Joseph Gales," 338.
53. Lyndall Gordon and Gunnar Molden, "The Treasure Seeker," *The Guardian*, 7 January 2005. See also Per Nystrom, "Mary Wollstonecraft's Scandinavian Journey," trans G. R. Otter, in *Acta Regiae Societatis Scientiarum et Litterarum Gothoburgetensis, Humaniora* 17 (Gothenburg: Royal Society of Arts and Sciences, 1980), 19.
54. Mary Wollstonecraft, *Letters Written during a Short Residence in Sweden, Norway, and Denmark* (London: Cassell, 1889), Letter 34.
55. Wollstonecraft, *Letters Written during a Short Residence in Sweden, Norway, and Denmark*, Letter 14.
56. John Quincy Adams, 29 October 1797; in *Memoirs of John Quincy Adams Comprising Portions of His Diary from 1795 to 1848*, ed. Charles Frances Adams (New York: AMS Press, 1970), 1:201.
57. Wollstonecraft, *Letters Written during a Short Residence in Sweden, Norway, and Denmark*, Letter 12; and Mary Wollstonecraft, Copenhagen, 6 September 1795; in Janet Todd, *The Collected Letters of Mary Wollstonecraft* (New York: Columbia University Press, 2003), 320.
58. Johann Peter Willebrand, *Grundriss einer schönen Stadt;* cited by Franklin Kopitzsch, "Altona—ein Zentrum der Aufklärung am Rande des dänischen Gesamtstaats," in *Der Dänische Gesamtstaat. Kopenhagen, Kiel, Altona*, ed. Klaus Bohnen and Sven-Aage Jorgensen (Tübingen: Max Niemeyer Verlag, 1992), 94.
59. Cited by Mary Lindemann, "The Anxious Merchant, the Bold Speculator, and the Malicious Bankrupt: Doing Business in Eighteenth-Century Hamburg," in *The Self-Perception of Early Modern Capitalists*, ed. Margaret C. Jacob and Catherine Secretan (New York: Palgrave, 2008), 62.
60. *Verhandlungen und Schriften der Hamburgischen Gesellschaft zur Beförderung der Künste und nuütliche Gewerbe* (Hamburg 1792–1807), vol. 5; cited in Uhalde, "Citizen and World Citizen," 231–232.
61. Friedrich Jachim Schlüter, cited in Uhalde, "Citizen and World Citizen," 409.
62. Aaslestadt, *Place and Politics*, 35. See also Seyla Benhabib, *The Rights of Others:*

Aliens, Residents and Citizens (Cambridge: Cambridge University Press, 2004), especially ch. 1, "On Hospitality."

3. French Connections

1. English shipping increased from 71 vessels per year in 1793 to 165 in 1794. Erwin Wiskemann, *Hamburg und die Welthandelspolitik. Von den Anfängen bis zur Gegenwart* (Hamburg: Friedrichson, De Gruyter, 1929), 129; and Hamburg, 27 March 1793; 111–1 Senat 1756, Cl1 Lit Pb vol 8c fasc. 2, no. 2, Staatsarchiv, Hamburg. Quote in chapter title is from Georg Heinrich Sieveking, "Mémoire for Charles François Lebrun 1793," 622 1/90, C7, Georg Heinrich Sieveking Briefwechsel 1775–1798, Staatsarchiv, Hamburg.
2. 1740, 1794–95, 302 Preussen: Depecher 1771–1848, Departement for de Udenlandske Anliggender, Rigsarkivet, Copenhagen.
3. Johanna Sieveking, S. 288, Hamburg, 26 February 1793; 622–1/86, D2, Sophie Louise Reimarus an ihren Bruder August Hennings 1785–87; and Correspondence of Sieveking, 111–1, Senat 1917, Staatsarchiv, Hamburg. See also Sam Ali Mustafa, *Merchants and Migrations: Germans and Americans in Connection, 1776–1835* (Burlington, VT: Ashgate, 2001), 68.
4. Georg Heinrich Sieveking, 31 December 1790; 622–1/90, C13, Schreiben an das Comité du Commerce in Paris 1790, Staatsarchiv, Hamburg; and Nicolas de Caritat, Marquis de Condorcet, to Georg Heinrich Sieveking; 622–1/90, C7, Georg Heinrich Sieveking Briefwechsel 1775–1798, Staatsarchiv, Hamburg; and 622–1/90, C19, Georg Heinrich Sieveking Abrechtung mit Schlüter 1796–1800, Staatsarchiv, Hamburg.
5. Hans-Werner Engels, "Alles war so möglich! Auftakt für ein neues Europa; Hamburgs Bürger feiern die Französische Revolution," in *Der Französischen Revolution verpflichtet. Ausgewählte Beiträge eines Hamburg-Historikers*, ed. Michael Mahn and Rainer Hering (Nordhausen: Bautz, 2015), 152.
6. Sophie Reimarus to August Hennings, in Heinrich Sieveking, *Lebensbild eines Hamburgischen Kaufmanns aus dem Zeitalter der französischen Revolution* (Berlin: Verlag Karl Curtius, 1913), 47–49.
7. Cited by Engels, "Alles war so möglich!" 153.
8. Hermann Tiemann, "Hanseaten im revolutionären Paris (1789–1803). Skizzen zu einem Kapitel deutsch-französischer Beziehungen," *Zeitschrift des Vereins für Hamburgische Geschichte Hamburg* 49/50 (1964): 115.
9. J. L. Hess, *Verbreit;* cited in David Weber, *Jonas Ludwig von Hess (1756–1823) et Hambourg: Un engagement politique des Lumières tardives à l'occupation napoléonienne* (Bern: Peter Lang, 2014), 295.
10. 1794 Protokoll Deputation Commerz, Commerz Bibliothek, Hamburg.
11. Rainer Ramcke, "Die Beziehungen zwischen Hamburg und Österreich im 18. Jahrhundert. Kaiserlich-reichsstädtisches Verhältnis im Zeichen von Handels-und Finanzinteressen" (dissertation, Universität Hamburg, 1969).

12. Cited by Roger Dufraisse, "Les relations économiques entre la France révolutionnaire et l'Allemagne," in *Deutschland und die Franzöisische Revolution*, ed. Jürgen Voss (Munich: Artemis Verlag 1983), 232.
13. Georg Heinrich Sieveking; 622–1/90, C13, Schreiben an das Comité du Commerce in Paris 1790, Staatsarchiv, Hamburg.
14. Burghart Schmidt, "Les relations consulaires entre les villes hanséatiques et la France (XVIe–XVIIIe siècles)," in *La fonction consulaire à l'epoque moderne: L'affirmation d'une institution économique et politique (1500–1800)*, ed. Jorg Ulbert and Gerard Le Bouëdec (Rennes: Presses Universitaires de Rennes, 2006), 211–258; and Erwin Wiskemann, *Hamburg und die Welthandelspolitik. Von den Anfängen bis zur Gegenwart* (Hamburg: Friedrichson, De Gruyter, 1929), 120.
15. In 1792, Sieveking interceded in delicate negotiations to convince the French to establish commercial regulations consistent with Hamburg practices so that disputes could be resolved and delays at sea minimized. S-599 52 rot Wechselrecht I, Materialien zum Wechselrecht von GH Sieveking mit Anmerkungen 1792 Exchange. Monita zu Sievekings Estwurf, Commerzbibliothek, Hamburg.
16. Kersten Krüger and Stefan Kroll, *Die Sozialstruktur der Städte Kiel und Altona um 1800. Demographie, Erwerbsstrukture und wirtschaftliche Leistungsfähigkeit* (Neumünster: Wachholtz Verlag, 1998), 186.
17. 15 Ventôse l'An II, La Commission des Subsistances de l'An II, in *Procès-Verbaux et Actes*, ed. Pierre Caron (Paris: Librairie Ernest Leroux, 1925), 2:448.
18. "Moyens de relever la valeur des assignats et de les retirer successivement de la circulation, proposés aux législateurs de la République Française" (Hamburg: P. F. Fauche, 1795), 622–1/90, C10, Staatsarchiv, Hamburg.
19. 30 Germinal l'An II, La Commission des Subsistances de l'An II, in Caron, *Procès-Verbaux et Actes*, 2:643.
20. Senat, 30 July 1794; 622–1/90, C17, Sieveking Handakten und Instruktion 1795–1799, Staatsarchiv, Hamburg.
21. Sieveking to Lebrun (1793); 622 1/90, C7, Georg Heinrich Sieveking Briefwechsel 1775–1798, Staatsarchiv, Hamburg.
22. Johann Valentin Meyer, 1794–95, Protokoll Deputation Commerz, Commerzbibliothek, Hamburg.
23. Wiskemann, *Hamburg und die Welthandelspolitik*, 129.
24. Cited in Sieveking, *Levensbild einer Hamburgischen Kaufmanns*, 203.
25. Charlotte Sophie von Bentinck to James Hawkins, Whitshed, 27 February 1794; in *Une femme des Lumières: Écrits et lettres de la Comtesse de Bentinck 1715–1800*, ed. Anne Soprani et André Magnan (Paris: CNRS Editions, 1997), 163.
26. Fred-Conrad Huhn, "Die Handelbeziehungen zwischen Frankreich und Hamburg im 18 Jahrhundert unter besonder Berucksichtigung der Handels-

vertrage von 1716 und 1769" (Hamburg: Phil. diss Hamburg, 1952), 221; and Wiskemann, *Hamburg und die Welthandelspolitik*, 132.

27. 24/3 1794–11/7 1795, Protokoll Deputation Commerz, Commerzbibliothek, Hamburg.
28. Georg Heinrich Sieveking, *An meine Mitburger;* 622 1/90, C15, Georg Heinrich Sieveking. Verteidigung gegen Angriffe tegen seine sympathien fur Frankreich 1793, Staatsarchiv, Hamburg.
29. Georg Heinrich Sieveking, cited in Sieveking, *Lebensbild eines Hamburgischen Kaufmanns*, 85.
30. Friedrich Wilhelm Basilius von Ramdohr, *Studien zur Kenntnis der schönen Natur. Der schönen Kunste. Der Sitten und der Staatsverfassung. Auf einer Reise nach Danemark* (Hanover, 1792), 44; cited by Steven Uhalde, "Citizen and World Citizen: Civic Patriotism and Cosmopolitanism in Eighteenth Century Hamburg," (PhD dissertation, University of California, Berkeley, 1984), 381.
31. Walther Grab, *Demokratische Stromungen in Hamburg und Schleswig-Holstein zur Zeit der ersten franzosicschen Republik* (Hamburg: H. Christians, 1966), 89.
32. Sophie Reimarus to August Hennings, 17 December 1792; in Grab, *Demokratische Strömungen in Hamburg und Schleswig-Holstein*, 93.
33. 15/4 to 20/3, 1794, Protokoll Deputation Commerz, Commerzbibliothek, Hamburg.
34. "Découverte d'un espion françois dans la Ville de Hambourg" (Cologne: Pierre Marteau, 1791).
35. Georg Heinrich Sieveking, Mémoire; 622–1/90, C7, Georg Heinrich Sieveking, Briefwechsel 1775–1798, Staatsarchiv, Hamburg.
36. 22 December 1795; Box 1741, 302, Dept. for de Udenlandske Anligg. 1771–1848. Preussen: Depecher. July–December 1795, Rigsarkivet, Copenhagen.
37. J. L. Hess, *Muss Hamburg den französischen Minister anerkennen?*, in Weber, *Jonas Ludwig von Hess*, 325.
38. Georg Kerner, *Jakobiner und Armenarzt. Reisebriefe, Berichte, Lebenszeugnisse* (Berlin: Rütten and Loening, 1978), 47.
39. Christine Reimarus Reinhard, cited in Engels, "Alles war so möglich!" 153.
40. Georg Kerner, cited in Andreas Fritz, "Georg Kerner (1770–1812). Fürstenfeind und Menschenfreund; eine politische Biographie" (dissertation, University of Stuttgart, 1998–99), 385.
41. 20 July 1799, 1–111, 1789, Berichte Emigranten, Staatsarchiv, Hamburg.
42. Charles Reinhard, cited in Inge Grolle, *Eine Diplomatenehe im Bann von Napoleon und Goethe. Karl Friedrich Reinhard (1761–1837), Christine Reinhard geb. Reimarus (1771–1815)* (Hamburg: Edition Temmen, 2007), 17.
43. Hans-Werner Engels, "Republikaner ohne Republik: Georg Kerners 'Reisen' 1796–1801," in *Europäisches Reisen im Zeitalter der Aufklärung. Konferenz zum Thema "Reise und Reisebeschreibung in Europa (1700–1800)* (Heidelberg: Carl Winter, 1992).

44. Maike Manske, *Möglichkeiten und Grenzen des Kulturtransfers. Emigranten der Französischen Revolution in Hamburg, Bremen und Lübeck* (Saarbrücken: VDM Verlag Dr. Müller Aktiengesellschaft & Co. KG, 2008), 33. "Asylum to all parties" comes from Hermann Tiemann, "Hanseaten im revolutionären Paris (1789–1803): Skizzen zu einem Kapitel deutsch-französischer Beziehungen," *Zeitschrift des Vereins für Hamburgische Geschichte Hamburg: Verl. Verein für Hamburgische Geschichte* 49/50 (1964): 118.
45. Grab, *Demokratische Strömungen in Hamburg und Schlewig-Holstein*, 156.
46. Ibid., 103.
47. Hans-Werner Engels, "Georg Kerner und die Philanthropische Gesellschaft in Hamburg, Ein Beitrag zum Thema Hamburg zur Zeit der Französischen Revolution," in *Quatuor Coronati. Jahrbuch für Freimaurerforschung Bayreuth. Freimauerische Forschungsgeschichte* 25 (1988), 193–207.
48. 21 April 1797, 32, 111–1, 1789, Dem Prätorestalte Berichte Emigranten, Staatsarchiv, Hamburg.
49. Kerner, *Jakobiner und Armenarzt*, 49.
50. Fritz, "Georg Kerner," 367.
51. Tiemann, "Hanseaten im revolutionären Paris," 118.
52. Fritz, "Georg Kerner," 369.
53. "Rapport fait par le Citoyen Kerner à la Société philanthropique"; Société philanthropique, 111–1, 1787. Clubs 1797–98, Staatsarchiv, Hamburg.
54. 27 April 1797, 111–1, 1789e, Dem Prätorestalle Berichte: Emigranten, Staatsarchiv, Hamburg.
55. *Minerva*, 1793, cited in Philipp Rudolf, *Frankreich im Urteil der Hamburger Zeitschriften in den Jahren 1789–1810* (Hamburg: Seminar für romanische Sprachen und Kultur, 1933), 25.
56. G. Arvengas, "L'Émigration française à Hambourg, 1795–1799," *Deutsch Frazosische Monatschafte* 6 (1939): 17–25; Manske, *Möglichkeiten und Grenzen des Kulturtransfers*, 77.
57. December 1797, 111–1, 1789g, Dem Prätorestalle Berichte: Emigranten, Staatsarchiv, Hamburg.
58. 10 March 1797, 26; 111–1, 1789d, Dem Prätorestalle Berichte: Emigranten, Staatsarchiv, Hamburg.
59. 3 February 1797, 21; 111–1, 1789d, Dem Prätorestalle Berichte: Emigranten, Staatsarchiv, Hamburg.
60. 15 December 1796; 1–111, 1789c, Dem Prätorestalle Berichte: Emigranten, Staatsarchiv, Hamburg.
61. 19 February 1797, 24a; 111–1, 1789d, Dem Prätorestalle Berichte: Emigranten, Staatsarchiv, Hamburg.
62. 12 January 1798, 65; 111–1, 1789h, Dem Prätorestalle Berichte: Emigranten, Staatsarchiv, Hamburg.
63. Denis Diderot, "Cosmopolite, ou Cosmopolitan," in Denis Diderot, *Encyclopëdie*, 19:600; cited by Thomas J. Schlereth, *The Cosmopolitan Ideal in En-*

lightenment Thought: Its Form and Function in the Ideas of Franklin, Hume, and Voltaire, 1694–1790 (Notre Dame, IN: University of Notre Dame Press, 1977), 47.

64. Anacharsis Cloots, cited in Sophie Wahnich, *L'impossible citoyen: L'étranger dans le discours de la Révolution française* (Paris: Albin Michel, 1997), 7.
65. *Der Totenrichter*; cited in Walther Grab, *Zwei Seiten einer Medaille. Demokratische Revolution und Judenemanzipation* (Cologne: Papy Rossa Verlags GmbH, 2000), 58.
66. Georg Heinrich Sieveking, "Fragmente über Luxus, Bürger-Tugend und Bürger-Wohl"; cited by Mary Lindemann, *The Merchant Republics: Amsterdam, Antwerp, and Hamburg, 1648–1790* (Cambridge: Cambridge University Press, 2015), 85. Hamburg and Altona were not the rustic agrarian societies idealized by philosopher Jean-Jacques Rousseau or by the mercantilist economists. Nor did they want to become the urban spaces corrupted by luxury that the philosophers and economists condemned for their contrast to the virtuous countryside.
67. Sophie Reimarus to Adolph Knigge, 16 August 1795; cited by Weber, *Jonas Ludwig von Hess*, 315.

4. "The Right Papers" in a World of Nations

1. Carmen Tiburcio, *The Human Rights of Aliens under International and Comparative Law* (The Hague: Martinus Nijhoff, 2001), 1. See also Nathan Perl-Rosenthal, *Citizen Sailors: Becoming American in the Age of Revolution* (Cambridge, MA: Harvard University Press, 2015), for an argument that sailors between nations fought to establish their national identity.
2. Hannah Arendt, *The Origins of Totalitarianism* (New York: Meridian Books, 1958), 296.
3. Alexander Dallas, cited by Kunal M. Parker, *Making Foreigners: Immigration and Citizenship Law in America, 1600–2000* (New York: Cambridge University Press, 2015), 51.
4. Peter Sahlins, "The Citizenship Revolution in Eighteenth-Century France," in *Migration Control in the North Atlantic World: The Evolution of State Practices in Europe and the United States from the French Revolution to the Interwar Period*, ed. Andreas Fahrmeir, Olivier Faron, and Patrick Weil (New York: Berghahn Books, 2003), 21.
5. Joseph Lakanal, cited by Michael Rapport, *Nationality and Citizenship in Revolutionary France: The Treatment of Foreigners 1789–1799* (Oxford: Clarendon Press, 2000), 265.
6. John Stuart Mill, cited by Will Kymlicka, *Politics in the Vernacular: Nationalism, Multiculturalism and Citizenship* (Oxford: Oxford University Press, 2001), 206.
7. Oliver Ellsworth, cited by Lucy E. Salyer, *Under the Starry Flag: How a Band*

of Irish Americans Joined the Fenian Revolt and Sparked a Crisis over Citizenship (Cambridge, MA: Harvard University Press, 2018), 66.

8. Aristide Zolberg, "The Exit Revolution," in *Citizenship and Those Who Leave: The Politics of Emigration and Expatiation*, ed. Nancy L. Green and François Weil (Urbana: University of Illinois Press, 2007), 34.
9. Cited by Sylvie Aprile, *Le siècle des exiles: Bannis et proscrits de 1789 à la Commune* (Paris: CNRS Editions, 2010), 21.
10. Gérald Arlettaz, *Libéralisme et société dans le canton de Vaud, 1814–1845* (Lausanne: Bibliothèque historique vaudoise, 1980), 32.
11. See Andreas Fahrmeir, *Citizenship: The Rise and Fall of a Modern Concept* (New Haven: Yale University Press, 2007), 39–42, for a more detailed discussion.
12. Margrit Schulte Beerbühl, "British Nationality Policy during the Napoleonic Wars," in Fahrmeir, Faron, and Weil, *Migration Control in the North Atlantic World*, 63.
13. Jacques Grandjonc, *Exils et migrations d'allemands 1789–1945: Textes et études rassemblés par Jacques Grandjonc e.a.* (Aix-en-Provence: Université de Provence, 1987).
14. Perl-Rosenthal, *Citizen Sailors*, 257–265.
15. Bishop Claude Le Coz, January 1792; cited by John Torpey, *The Invention of the Passport: Surveillance, Citizenship and the State* (Cambridge: Cambridge University Press, 2000), 32.
16. Silvia Arlettaz, *Citoyens et étrangers sous la République helvétique (1798–1803)* (Geneva: Georg, 2002), 330. See also Tiburcio, *The Human Rights of Aliens under International and Comparative Law* (The Hague: Martinus Nijhoff Publishers, 2001).
17. Fahrmeir, *Citizenship*, 46 and 75.
18. Letter from the police commissioner of the neighborhood of the Castellane to the mayor of Marseille, 6 May 1850; cited by Delphine Diaz, "Receiving, Selecting and Rejecting Foreign Migrants and Refugees in Port Cities: A Comparison of Bordeaux and Marseille during the Early Nineteenth Century," in *Migration Policies and Materialities of Identification in European Cities: Papers and Gates, 1500–1930s*, ed. Hilde Greefs and Anne Winter (New York: Routledge, 2019), 159.
19. Vincent Denis, "Le contrôle de la mobilité à travers les passeports sous l'empire," in *Police et Migrants*, ed. Marie-Claude Blanc-Chaléard, Caroline Douki, Nicole Dryonet et al. (Rennes: Presses universitaires de Rennes, 2001); and Delphine Diaz, *En exil: Les réfugiés en Europe de la fin du XVIIIe siècle à nos jours* (Paris: Gallimard, 2021), 101.
20. H. Gisquet, cited by Lloyd Kramer, "The Rights of Man: Lafayette and the Polish National Revolution, 1830–1834," *French Historical Studies* 14, no. 4 (Autumn 1986): 528.
21. Diaz, "Receiving, Selecting and Rejecting Foreign Migrants and Refugees in Port Cities," 156.

22. Leo Lucassen, "Passport System in the Netherlands," in *Documenting Individual Identity: The Development of State Practices in the Modern World*, ed. Jane Caplan and John Torpey (Princeton, NJ: Princeton University Press, 2001), 244.
23. Ellen Debackere, "The Use of Travel and Identity Documents in Antwerp during the Second Half of the Nineteenth Century," in Greefs and Winter, *Migration Policies and Materialities of Identification in European Cities*, 177.
24. S. Arlettaz, *Citoyens et étrangers*, 313.
25. Ibid., 321.
26. Ibid., 330.
27. Marc Vuilleumier, "Switzerland," in *The Encyclopedia of Migration and Minorities in Europe: From the Seventeenth Century to the Present*, ed. Klaus J. Bade and Corrie von Eijl (Cambridge: Cambridge University Press, 2011), 94. The medieval institution of the *Bürgergemeinde*, or civic community, conveying political and economic rights through inheritance, endured and encompassed all residents.
28. Hans Mahnig and Andreas Wimmer, "Integration without Immigrant Policy: The Case of Switzerland," in *the Integration of Immigrants in European Societies: National Differences and Trends of Convergence*, ed. Friedrich Heckmann and Dominique Schnapper (Berlin: De Gruyter Oldenbourg, 2016), 135–164. This evocation of a Swiss community and the expectation of integration and assimilation persisted through the series of regime changes into the twenty-first century.
29. Radicals argued that a Swiss nationality recognized all citizens as equal and free to enjoy their full political rights. See Wilhelm Marr, *Das junge Deutschland in der Schweiz. Ein Beitrag zur Geschichte der geheimen Berbindungen unserer Tage* (Leipzig: Verlag von Wilhelm Jurcany, 1846), 15–30.
30. G. Arlettaz, *Libéralisme et société dans le canton de Vaud*, 33.
31. Ibid., 32.
32. Vuilleumier, "Switzerland," 96.
33. G. Arlettaz, *Libéralisme et société dans le canton de Vaud*, 32–33.
34. Arrêté de la Diète fédéral sur les réfugiés, 11 August 1836; Archives de l'État de Genève, G 133/2; cited by Diaz, *En exil*, 102.
35. Cédric Humair, *1848: Naissance de la Suisse moderne*, 55; cited by Diaz, *En exil*, 102.
36. M. Rojoux, Adresse de l'Association nationale suisse au Comité genevois; Bibliothèque de Genève, 436/5 (10); cited by Diaz, *En exil*, 103.
37. Cited by Markus Somm, "Zinnsoldaten der Innenpolitik. Die Asylpraxis der Schweiz gegenüber revolutionären polnischen Flüchtlingen im 19. Jahrhundert," in *Asyl und Aufenthalt. Die Schweiz als Zuflucht und Wirkungestätte von Slaven im 19. und 20. Jahrhundert*, ed. Monika Bankowski, Peter Brang, Carsten Goehrke, and Werner G. Zimmermann (Basel: Helbing and Lichtenhahn, 1994), 51.

38. Wolfgang Schieder, *Anfänge der deutschen Arbeiterbewegung. Die Auslandsverein im Jahrzeht nachder Julierevolution von 1830* (Stuttgart: Ernst Klett Verlag, 1963), 203.
39. Cited by Aprile, *Le siècle des exiles*, 86.
40. Somm, "Zinnsoldaten der Innenpolitik." 51–53.
41. Jean Graven, *Pellegrino Rossi: Grand Européen* (Geneva: Librairie de l'université, 1949), 16.
42. Luc Marco, "Un journaliste écléctic Pelegrino Rossi," *Revue d'histoire de la pensée économique* 98, no. 2 (1988): 293–302.
43. Carl Wittke, *The Utopian Communist: A Biography of Wilhelm Weitling, Nineteenth-Century Reformer* (Baton Rouge: Louisiana State University Press, 1950), 35.
44. Wolfgang Frühwalk, Georg Jäger et al., eds., *Bildung und Organisation in den deutschen Handwerksgesellen-und Arbeitervereinen in der Schweiz* (Tübingen: Max Niemeyer Verlag, 1983), 4:3–8 and 38–198.
45. Marc Vuilleumier, "Weitling, Les communistes allemands et leurs adeptes en Suisse: Quelques Documents (1843–1847)," *Revue européenne des sciences sociales* 11, no. 29 (1973): 44. Philippe Corsat, born in the canton of Vaud, after traveling in France, participated in the republican insurrection in Neuchâtel. He spent time in Lausanne, settling in Geneva, where his barbershop served as a library. He founded an association of Swiss workers that echoed the principles of the German Arbeiterverein.
46. Simon Schmidt, cited by Vuilleumier, "Weitling," 47.
47. Wittke, *The Utopian Communist*, 41.
48. Antje Gerlach, *Deutsche Literatur im schwizer Exil. Die politische Propaganda der Vereine deutscher Flüchtlinge und Handwerksgesellschaften in der Schweiz von 1833 bis 1845* (Frankfurt am Main: V. Klostermann, 1975), 67; and Schieder, *Anfänge der deutschen Arbeiterbewegung*, 203.
49. Schieder, *Anfänge der deutschen Arbeiterbewegung*, 205. See also Gerlach, *Deutsche Literatur im schweizer Exil*, 93.
50. Jacques Mallet du Pan, 6 December 1797; cited by Aprile, *Le siècle des exiles*, 42.
51. Vuilleumier, "Weitling," 38.
52. Wittke, *The Utopian Communist*, 46.
53. Vuilleumier, "Weitling," 49.
54. Denis Mack Smith, *Mazzini* (New Haven: Yale University Press, 1992), 6.
55. Giuseppe Mazzini, *A Cosmopolitanism of Nations: Giuseppe Mazzini's Writings on Democracy, Nation Building, and International Relations*, ed. Nadia Urbinati (Princeton, NJ: Princeton University Press, 2009).
56. See Mark Mazower, *Governing the World: The History of an Idea, 1815 to the Present* (New York: Penguin, 2012), 49; and Nadia Urbinati, "The Legacy of Kant: Giuseppe Mazzini's Cosmopolitanism of Nations," in *Giuseppe Mazzini and the Globalisation of Democratic Nationalism, 1830–1920*, ed. C. A. Bayly and Eugenio F. Biagini (Oxford: Oxford University Press, 2008), 19.

57. Giuseppe Mazzini, cited by Mack Smith, *Mazzini*, 17.
58. Giuseppe Mazzini, cited by Bolton King, *The Life of Mazzini* (London: J. M. Dent and Sons, 1912), 53.
59. Giuseppe Mazzini, cited by King, *The Life of Mazzini*, 58.
60. Mack Smith, *Mazzini*, 12.
61. Giuseppe Mazzini, cited by King, *The Life of Mazzini*, 74.
62. Klemens von Metternich, cited by Marc Vuilleumier, *Immigrés et réfugiés en Suisse: Aperçu historique* (Zurich: Pro Helvetia, 1989), 22.
63. See Salvo Mastellone, "Mazzini's International League and the Politics of the London Democratic Manifestos, 1837–50," in Bayly and Biagini, *Giuseppe Mazzini and the Globalisation of Democratic Nationalism*, 104.
64. Caroline Shaw, *Britannia's Embrace: Modern Humanitarianism and the Imperial Origins of Refugee Relief* (New York and Oxford: Oxford University Press, 2015), 65–67.
65. Georges Boisot, *Mémoires inédits*, ch. 55, 3; as cited by G. Arlettaz, *Libéralisme et société dans le canton de Vaud*, 568.
66. Shaw, *Britannia's Embrace*, 3. Shaw argues that "the forgotten history of the British nineteenth century invention of modern refugees demonstrates the power of moral storytelling to kindle popular enthusiasm for a broad-based humanitarian commitment" (214).
67. Mazower, *Governing the World*, ch. 2.

5. Stateless in Brussels

1. Edward Said, "Reflections on Exile," *Granata* 1, no. 3 (Autumn 1984): 138 and 139.
2. On this neglect, see, among others, Jérome Elie, "Histories of Refugee and Forced Migration Studies," in *The Oxford Handbook of Refugee and Forced Migration Studies*, ed. Elena Fiddian-Qasmiyeh, Gil Loescher, Katy Long, and Nanco Sigona (Oxford: Oxford University Press, 2014), 30–31.
3. Sophie de Schaepdrijver, *Elites for the Capital? Foreign Migration to Mid-Nineteenth-Century Brussels* (Amsterdam: Thesis Publishers, 1990), 16.
4. Of the 340,000 refugees over the nineteenth century, only 1,190 came for political reasons. L. Vandersteene, cited by Idesbald Goddeeris, "Van Favoritisme naar Legaliteit: De Belgische Tolerantiedrempel voor politieke Activiteiten van Ballingen, 1830–1914," *Revue belge d'histoire contemporaine/Belgische Tijdschrift voor nieuwste Geschiedenis* 40, no. 3 (2010): 314.
5. Philip Marfleet, "Displacements of Memory," *Refuge* 32, no. 1 (2016): 7–17.
6. Karl Marx to Arnold Ruge, Cologne, 25 January 1843; in *Karl Marx and Frederick Engels, Collected Works* (New York: International Publishers, 1975), 1:397.
7. Arnold Ruge, *Zwei Jahre in Paris;* cited by David McLellan, *Karl Marx: His Life and His Thought* (New York: Harper and Row, 1973), 62.

8. Louis Philippe, cited by McLellan, *Karl Marx*, 135.
9. Jonathan Sperber, *Karl Marx: A Nineteenth-Century Life* (New York: W. W. Norton, 2013), 150–152.
10. Louis De Potter, cited by Louis Bertrand, *Histoire de la démocratie et du socialisme en Belgique depuis 1830* (Brussels: Dechenne, 1906), 1:39.
11. Albert Goblet d'Aviella to Prussian ambassador, in Guido Ros, "De Pers van de Duitse radicale en communistische Emigranten te Parijs en te Brussel 1844–1848: Van Deutsch-Französisische Jahrbücher tot Deutsche-Brüsseler-Zeitung" (dissertation, Universiteit Gent, 1980), 494.
12. That letter is preserved in a slender folio documenting Marx's residence in the Belgian capital. Dossier Karl Marx, Ministère de la Justice, Police des Étrangers, Dossiers Individuels/Ministerie van Justitie, Vreemdelingen Politie, Individuele Dossiers, 73946, Archives Générales du Royaume/Algemeen Rijksarchief, Brussels. The reorganization of the file and potential disappearance of documents have been the subject of some discussion. Guido Ross, "Het Dossier Karl Marx in Het Algemeen Rijksarchief, Brussel," *De Brug* 15 (1971): 31–42.
13. Dossier Karl Marx, Ministère de la Justice, Police des Étrangers, Dossiers Individuels, 73946, Archives Générales du Royaume/Algemeen Rijksarchief, Brussels. On the interchange among authorities, see also Ros, "De Pers van de Duitse radicale en communistische Emigranten."
14. Count Felix Woyna to Prince Klemens von Metternich, 4 December 1845; Correspondance politique, Vienne, 1845, Archives des Affaires Étrangères/ Archief Buitenlandse Zaken, Brussels.
15. Karl Marx to Heinrich Heine, Brussels, 24 March 1845; in *Karl Marx and Friedrich Engels, La Belgique: État constitutionnel modèle* (Paris: Éditions Fil du Temps, 1977), 125.
16. Baron Alexis Hody, Piece 13, 22 March 1845; Dossier Karl Marx, Ministère de la Justice, Police des Étrangers, Dossiers Individuels, 073946, Archives Générales du Royaume/Algemeen Rijksarchief, Brussels.
17. Idesbald Goddeeris, *La grande émigration polonaise en Belgique (1831–1870): Élites et masses en exil à l'époque romantique* (Frankfurt: Peter Lang, 2013), 78.
18. Victor Hugo, cited by René Maurice, *La fugue à Bruxelles: Proscrits, exilés, refugiés, et autres voyageurs* (Paris: Éditions du Félin, 2003), 8.
19. Victor Hugo, "What Exile Is," in *Altogether Elsewhere: Writers on Exile*, ed. Marc Robinson (New York: Harcourt, Brace, 1994), 80.
20. Marx would later try unsuccessfully to reclaim his Prussian citizenship.
21. Baron de Stassart, cited by Frank Caestecker, Bernadette Renauld, Nicolas Perrin, and Thierry Eggerickx, *Devenir Belge: Histoire de l'acquisition de la nationalité belge depuis 1830* (Mechelen: Wolters Kluwer, 2016), 11.
22. See Els Witte, "Politiek Leven—1830–1914," in *Brussel, Groei van een Hoofdstad*, ed. J. Stengers et al. (Antwerp: Mercatorfonds, 1979), 188.
23. Carl Strikwerda, "Tides of Migration, Currents of History—The State, Econ-

omy and the National Transatlantic Movement of Labor in the Nineteenth and Twentieth Centuries," *International Review of Social History* 44, no. 3 (1999): 372.

24. Count Woyna to Prince Metternich, 18 August 1845; Correspondance politique, Vienne, 1845, Archives des Affaires Étrangères/Archief Buitenlandse Zaken, Brussels.
25. French agent to Constant Hoffschmidt, Correspondance politique, Réfugiés 1, p. 92, Archives des Affaires Étrangères/Archief Buitenlandse Zaken, Brussels.
26. Count Dietrichstein, 6 January 1844, Correspondance politique, Vienne, Legations, 10.945, 1843–46, Archives des Affaires Étrangères/Archief Buitenlandse Zaken, Brussels; and Count Woyna to Prince Metternich, 19 January 1846; Correspondance politique, Vienne, 1845, Archives des Affaires Étrangères/Archief Buitenlandse Zaken, Buitenlandse Handel en Ontwikkelingsamewerking, Brussels.
27. French agent to Constant d'Hoffschmidt, Correspondance politique, Réfugiés 1, p. 97, Archives des Affaires Étrangères/Archief Buitenlandse Zaken, Brussels.
28. Brussels, 6 April, Correspondance politique, Réfugiés 1, p. 95, Archives des Affaires Étrangères/Archief Buitenlandse Zaken, Brussels.
29. Constant d'Hoffschmidt, 9 February 1848, Indicateur A N2278, Politique Intérieure, classement B, Archives des Affaires Étrangères/Archief Buitenlandse Zaken, Brussels.
30. Count Woyna to Prince Metternich, 23 March 1846; Correspondance politique, Vienne, 1845, Archives des Affaires Étrangères/Archief Buitenlandse Zaken, Brussels.
31. Marvin Rees, City Metric; https://www.citymetric.com/politics/marvin-rees-case-global-parliament-mayors-4243.
32. United Nations, "Number of Global Cities Recognized for Climate Change Doubles," 18 February 2020; https://unfccc.int/news/number-of-global-cities-recognized-for-climate-leadership-doubles.
33. Schaepdrijver, *Elites for the Capital?*, 14.
34. Edward de Maesschalck, *Marx in Brussels: 1845–1848* (Louvain: Davidsfonds, 2005), 30.
35. Louis Chevalier, cited by Schaepdrijver, *Elites for the Capital?*, 46.
36. Goddeeris, *La grande émigration polonaise en Belgique.*
37. Alexander Coppens, "Tussen Beleid en administratieve Praktijk: De Implementatie van het Belgisch Migratie Beleid in negentiende-eeuws Brussel" (PhD dissertation, Vrije Universiteit Brussel, Letteren und Wijsbegeerte, 2016–2017), 69–70; and Schaepdrijver, *Elites for the Capital?*, 49.
38. Municipal bulletin 1856, 227; cited by Schaepdrijver, *Elites for the Capital?*, 81.
39. Nicolas Coupain, "L'expulsion des étrangers en Belgique (1830–1914)," *Bel-*

gisch Tijdschrift voor Nieuwste Geschiedenis/Revue belge d'histoire contemporaine 33, nos. 1–2 (2003): 7; Coppens, "Tussen Beleid en Administratieve Praktijk," 72; and Schaepdrijver, *Elites for the Capital?*, 49.

40. Coppens, "Tussen Beleid en administratieve Praktijk," 71–72. For information on the Germans in residence, see Francis Sartorius, "Activités politiques, économiques et sociales des allemands à Bruxelles 1842–1850: Première approche," *Revue belge d'histoire contemporaine/Belgisch Tijdschrift voor Nieuwste Geschiedenis* 1 (1974): 167–180; and Francis Sartorius, "L'importance, composition et évolution du mouvement migratoire des artisans et ouvriers allemands vers Bruxelles durant les années 1840: L'exemple de 1847," *Cahiers de CLIO* 71 (1982): 91–93.
41. Francis Sartorius, "Les Français en Belgique," in *Histoire des étrangers et de l'immigration en Belgique de la préhistoire à nos jours*, ed. Anne Morelli (Brussels: Vie Ouvrière, 1992), 144.
42. Schaepdrijver, *Elites for the Capital?*, 65; and Sartorius, "L'importance, composition et évolution du mouvement migratoire des artisans et ouvriers allemands," 91–92.
43. Coupain, "L'expulsion des étrangers en Belgique (1830–1914)," 7; F. Cuvelier, *Technique de l'arbitaire ou le "Statut" des étrangers en Belgique* (Brussels: Maison Ferdinand Larcier, 1939); and Maurice, *La Fugue à Bruxelles*, 7.
44. Goddeeris, *La grande émigration polonaise en Belgique*, 79.
45. See Goddeeris, "Van favoritisme naar legaliteit," 313–344.
46. Correspondance politique, Réfugiés 1, Piece 93, Archives des Affaires Étrangères/Archief Buitenlandse Zaken, Brussels.
47. Le Commissaire de Police to M. le Bourgmestre, 25 June 1849, MM 150, Archives de la Ville de Bruxelles/Stadsarchief Brussel, Brussels.
48. Archives de la Ville de Bruxelles, Police des étrangers, 1840–48, Stadsarchief Brussel/Archives de la Ville de Bruxelles. On policing regulations coming down from the central government, see Luc Keunings, "Geheime Politie en politieke Politie in België van 1830 tot 1914," *Panopticon* 9, no. 2 (1988): 136.
49. Le Commissaire de Police, 12 August 1847, MM 150, Stadsarchief Brussel/Archives de la Ville de Bruxelles. By the end of the nineteenth century, Brussels would have the largest per capita police force of any European city.
50. Alexander Coppens and Ellen Debackere, "De Toepassing van het Belgische Imigratiebeleid in de negentiende Eeuw: Omzendbrieven als Schkels tussen het centrale en lokale Beleidsniveau (1830–1914)," *Journal of Belgian History* 14, nos. 2/3, (2015): 30.
51. Commander of the Belgian Army to Commissioner of Police, 29 December 1846, MM 16, Archives de la Ville de Bruxelles/Stadsarchief Brussel, Brussels.
52. Police, 26 December 1846, MM 16, Archives de la Ville de Bruxelles/Stadsarchief Brussel, Brussels.
53. Jenny Marx to Karl Marx, Paris, 10 February 1845; in *Karl Marx and Frederick Engels, Collected Works* (New York: International Publishers, 1982), 38:527.

54. Es'kia Mphahlele, "Africa in Exile," in Robinson, *Altogether Elsewhere*, 120.
55. Edward Said, "Reflections on Exile," in Robinson, *Altogether Elsewhere*, 149.
56. Friedrich Engels to Karl Marx; cited by McLellan, *Karl Marx*, 138; and Friedrich Engels to Karl Marx, Bremen, 22 February–7 March 1845; in *Der Bund der Kommunisten. Dokumente und Materialien*, ed. Herwig Förder, Martin Hundt, Jefim Kandel, and Sofia Lewiowa, vol. 1: *1836–1849* (Berlin: Dietz Verlag, 1970), 210.
57. F. Albert Breyer arrived in Belgium in 1837 from Germany. He pursued his medical studies at the university in Brussels while attending democratic meetings organized by Jacob Kats, along with Philippe Gigot. He befriended Belgians and foreigners alike, including Marx, Engels, Victor Tedesco, and Lucien Jottrand. In Sint-Joost-ten-Node, he opened a free medical practice for workers. Francis Sartorius, "Breyer, Frédéric, Albert, Martin," *Le maitron. Dictionnaire biographique: Mouvement ouvrier, mouvement social*; https://maitron.fr/spip.php?article158598.
58. Karl Marx, cited by Michael Löwy, *The Theory of Revolution in the Young Marx* (Leiden: Brill, 2003), 74.
59. Jenny Marx to Karl Marx, 24 August 1845; in *Karl Marx and Frederick Engels, Collected Works*, 38:527.
60. Stefan Born, cited by Gareth Stedman Jones, *Karl Marx: Greatness and Illusion* (Cambridge, MA: Harvard University Press, 2016), 223.
61. Georg Weerth, November 1846; cited by Marcello Musto, "The Formation of Marx's Critique of Political Economy: From the Studies of 1843 to the Grundrisse," *Socialism and Democracy*, 24, no. 2 (July 2010): 74.
62. Cited by Mary Gabriel, *Love and Capital: Karl and Jenny Marx and the Birth of a Revolution* (New York: Back Bay Books, 2011), 98.
63. Warren Magnusson, *Politics of Urbanism: Seeing Like a City* (New York: Routledge, 2011), 4 and 5.
64. Janet Polasky, *Reforming Urban Labor: Routes to the City, Roots in the Country* (Ithaca, NY: Cornell University Press, 2010).
65. *Le Débat social*, cited by A. Vermeersch, "De pers en het paupérisme in Vlaanderen: 1845–1848," *Bijdragen voor de Geschiedenis der Nederlanden* 13, no. 2 (1958): 86 and 89.
66. Karl Marx, "A Contribution to the Critique of Political Economy. Part One," in *Karl Marx and Frederick Engels, Collected Works*, 29:263; as cited by Musto, "The Formation of Marx's Critique of Political Economy," 69.
67. Marx read Sismonde de Sismondi, Henri Storch, and Pellegrino Rossi on the basic concepts of political economy and Charles Babbage on large-scale manufacturing. Add his pledge to refrain from involvement in Belgian politics to the widespread interest in English, not Belgian, industrialization, and it is not surprising that Marx and Engels read seventeenth-century English economists, including William Petty and Charles Davenant, as well as contemporary British economists, such as David Ricardo, James Mill, Thomas

Hodgskin, John Ramsay McCulloch, and British socialists, such as John Francis Bray and Robert Owen.

68. Terrell Carver, "Whose Hand Is the Last Hand? The New MEGA Edition of 'The German Ideology,'" *New Political Science* 41, no. 1 (March 2019). With appreciation to Jonathan Sperber for calling the issue to my attention.
69. Hermann Ewerbeck to Karl Marx, 31 October 1845; and Georg Jung to Karl Marx, 18 March 1845; as cited by Jones, *Karl* Marx, 229.
70. Karl Marx, *Le misère de la philosophie;* cited in Bertrand, *Histoire de la démocratie et du socialisme*, 1:203.

6. Alliances

1. Warren Magnusson, *Politics of Urbanism: Seeing like a City* (New York: Routledge, 2011), 23.
2. Eric Min, cited by Thijs Kleinpaste, "Niemand houdt van deze onbegrijpelijke stade," *De Groene Amsterdammer*, 9 December 2015.
3. A similar propensity for collaboration can be found in Marx's earlier editorial work before he left Germany.
4. Brecht Deseure, "Republican Monarchy in the 1830 Revolutions: From Lafayette to the Belgian Constitution," *History of European Ideas* 45, no. 7 (2019): 992–1010.
5. Honoré de Balzac, cited by Anne-Marie Pirlot, "Bruxelles et ses cafés" (Brussels: Ministère de la Région de Bruxelles-Capitale, n.d.), 14.
6. Louis Bertrand, *Histoire de la démocratie et du socialisme en Belgique depuis 1830* (Brussels: Dechenne, 1906), 1:146–158.
7. Cited by Widukind De Ridder, "On the 'Absence of Spirit': The Legacy of the Abstinence from Revolution in Belgium," in *The 1848 Revolutions and European Political Thought*, ed. Douglas Moggach and Gareth Stedman Jones (Cambridge: Cambridge University Press, 2018), 199.
8. Lucien Jottrand, "Les réunions populaires," *Courrier belge*, 8 September 1836; cited by Bertrand, *Histoire de la démocratie et du socialisme*, 151. For a brief biographical note on Jottrand, see Julien Kuypers, *Lucien Jottrand (1804–1877)* (Ghent: Drukkerij Erasmus, 1956).
9. For more on police actions against Kats, including spying, see Luc Keunings, "Geheime Politie en politieke Politie in België van 1830 tot 1914," *Panopticon* 9, no. 2 (1988): 135.
10. Count Dietrichstein to Klemens von Metternich, Brussels, 16 September 1836; cited by A. Vermeersch, "De pers en het paupérisme in Vlaanderen: 1845–1848," *Bijdragen voor de Geschiedenis der Nederlanden*" 13, no. 2 (1958): 105. Dietrichstein called such gatherings "une singerie révolutionnaire."
11. Rosa Luxemburg, cited by Julien Kuypers, "Les liens d'amitié de Karl Marx en Belgique," *Socialisme* 58 (July 1963): 412.
12. Jacob Kats, *Het aerdsch Paradys*, as cited by De Ridder, "On the 'Absence of Spirit,'" 197.

13. Meeting of 18 May 1845; cited in Guillaume Des Marez, "L'Agitation démocratique révolutionnaire de 1841–56," in *Études inédites: Publiés par un groupe de ses anciens élèves*, ed. Henri Pirenne, B. Delanne, and Georges van Campenhout (Brussels: Falk, 1936), 152 and 154.
14. Cited by by Bertrand, *Histoire de la démocratie et du socialisme*, 1:253–256.
15. *Le Débat social*, 30 May 1847.
16. Vermeersch, "De pers en het paupérisme in Vlaanderen," 108.
17. "Comment le peuple s'affrancira," *Le Débat social*, 2 November 1845, 155.
18. Karl Marx in *Karl Marx and Friedrich Engels, La Belgique: État constitutionnel modèle* (Paris: Éditions Fil du Temps, 1977), 253.
19. Pavel Annenkov, *Extraordinary Decade*, 167–168; cited by Gareth Stedman Jones, *Karl Marx: Greatness and Illusion* (Cambridge, MA: Harvard University Press, 2016), 224.
20. Jenny Marx, "Short Sketch"; cited by Jones, *Karl Marx*, 223.
21. Joachim Lelewel, cited by Idesbald Goddeeris, *La grande émigration polonaise en Belgique (1831–1870): Élites et masses en exil à l'époque romantique* (Frankfurt: Peter Lang, 2013), 88.
22. Idesbald Goddeeris, "Des révolutionnaires polonais à Bruxelles (1830–1870)," in *Le Bruxelles des révolutionnaires de 1830 à nos jours*, ed. Anne Morelli (Brussels: CFC Editions, 2016), 35.
23. Faith Hillis, *Utopia's Discontents: Russian Emigrés and the Quest for Freedom, 1830s–1930s* (New York: Oxford University Press, 2021), 19–20.
24. Felix Gendebien, "Le Belge," 1 December 1840; in John Bartier, "Le Mouvement démocratique à l'ULB," *Socialisme*, January 1960, 21.
25. Joachim Lelewel, "La Commémoration polonaise de 1845," *Le Débat social*, 11 January 1846, 242.
26. Joachim Lelewel, cited by Goddeeris, *La grande émigration polonaise en Belgique*, 81.
27. Friedrich Engels, in *Karl Marx and Friedrich Engels, La Belgique: État constitutionnel modèle* (Paris: Éditions Fil du Temps, 1977), 102; see also Karl Marx, Brussels, 22 February 1848; in ibid., 115–119.
28. Charles Marx to Pierre Joseph Proudhon, 3 May 1846; in *Der Bund der Kommunisten. Dokumente und Materialien*, ed. Herwig Förder, Martin Hundt, Jefim Kandel, and Sofia Lewiowa, vol. 1: *1836–1849* (Berlin: Dietz Verlag, 1970), 318.
29. Friedrich Engels to Comité de Bruxelles, Paris; 23 October 1846; cited by Bert Andréas, *La Ligue des Communistes* (Paris: Aubier, 1972), 24.
30. Friedrich Engels, "La Fête des Nations," in *Karl Marx and Friedrich Engels, La Belgique: État constitutionnel modèle*, 153–156.
31. Jenny Marx, cited by Bartier, "Le mouvement démocratique à l'ULB," 15.
32. Karl Marx, cited by Jones, *Karl Marx*, 215.
33. Karl Marx to Pierre-Joseph Proudhon, MEGA 3/2, 8; cited by Jonathan Sperber, *Karl Marx: A Nineteenth-Century Life* (New York: W. W. Norton, 2013), 182.

34. Karl Marx, cited by Jones, *Karl Marx*, 215. For Weitling's stand on revolutionary strategy, see "Diskussionen im kommunistischen Arbeiter-Bildungsverein in London," 18 February 1845–14 January 1846, in Hundt, Kandel, and Lewiowa, *Der Bund der Kommunisten*, 1:227.
35. Karl Marx, *Manifesto of the German Communist Party*, tr. Helen Macfarlane, in the *Cambridge Companion to the Communist Manifesto*, ed. Terrell Carver and James Farr (New York: Cambridge University Press, 2015), 282.
36. "Annual Banquet of the German Democratic Society for the Education of the Working Classes, 9 February 1846," *Northern Star*, 14 February 1846; in Hundt, Kandel, and Lewiowa, *Der Bund der Kommunisten*, 1:274–279.
37. *Le Débat social*, 14 November 1847.
38. Helmut Elsner, Jacques Grandjonc, Elisabeth Neu, and Hans Pelger, eds., *Fragmente zu internationalen demokratischen Aktivitäten um 1848* (Trier: Schriften aus dem Karl-Marx-Haus, 2000), 23.
39. H. de Rumigny to Adolphe Dechamp, as cited by Elsner, Grandjonc, Neu, and Pelger, eds., *Fragmente zu internationalen demokratischen Aktivitäten um 1848*, 28.
40. Guido Ros, "De pers van de Duitse radicale en communistische emigranten te Parijs en te Brussel 1844–1848: Van Deutsch-Französische Jahrbücher tot Deutsche-Brüsseler-Zeitung" (dissertation, Universiteit Gent, 1980), 520.
41. Pavel Annenkov, cited by Boris Nicolaievsky and Otto Maenchen-Heffen, *Karl Marx: Man and Fighter* (New York: Routledge, 2015), 118.
42. Lucien Jottrand, *Des quinze années précédentes et de la situation nouvelle* (Brussels: Wouters, 1846), 5.
43. See Els Witte, *Belgische Republikeinen: Radicalen tussen twee Revoluties (1830–1850)* (Antwerp: Polis, 2020), 263.
44. Lucien Jottrand, "D'Anvers à Genes"; in *Association démocratique ayant pour but l'union et la fraternité de tous les peuples: Eine frühe demokratische Vereingung in Brussel 1847–1848*, ed. Bert Andréas et al. (Trier: Schriften aus dem Karl-Marx-Haus, 2004), 30.
45. Louis Philippe to Leopold I; cited by Bertrand, *Histoire de la démocratie et du socialisme*, 1:230.
46. Elsner, Grandjonc, Neu, and Pelger, *Fragmente zu internationalen demokratischen Aktivitäten um 1848*, 17.
47. Ernest Discailles, *Charles Rogier (1800–1885), d'après des documents inédits* (Brussels: J. Lebègue, 1894), 3:94.
48. Charles Rogier, cited by Discailles, *Charles Rogier*, 3:94.
49. Greet de Block, *Engineering the Territory: Technology, Space and Society in 19th and 20th Century Belgium* (Heverlee: Katholieke Universiteit Leuven, 2011).
50. Victor Considérant, cited by Bertrand, *Histoire de la démocratie et du socialisme*, 194.
51. Emile Claperon et al., *Vues politiques et pratiques sur les travaux publics de France;* cited by Block, *Engineering the Territory*, 139.

52. Jacques Grandjonc, "Deutsche Emigrationspresse in Europa wahrend des Vormarz 1830–1848," in *Heinrich Heine und die Zeitgenossen. Geschichtliche und literarische Befunde*, ed. Akademie der Wissenschaften der DDR, Zentralinstitut für Literaturgeschichte (Berlin, Weimar, 1979); Jacques Grandjonc, "L'Atelier Démocratique, Bruxelles (1846–1848): À la recherche d'un journal introuvable," in *Mega Studien. Hrsg. Von der internationalen Marx-Engels-Stiftung* 1 (1997): 96; and Ros, "De Pers van de Duitse radicale en communistische Emigranten," 517.
53. Lucien Jottrand, "Banquet des travailleurs à Bruxelles," in Andréas et al., *Association démocratique*, 287 and 315; *Le Débat social*, 3 October 1847, 163; cited by Luc Somerhausen, *L'humanisme agissant de Karl Marx* (Paris: Richard-Masse, 1946), 168; and Lucien Jottrand, in *Le Débat social*, cited in Andréas et al., *Association démocratique*, 286.
54. Julian Harney, London, 21 September 1846; cited in Andréas et al., *Association démocratique*, 232.
55. The Fraternal Democrats, 22 November 1847; in Andréas et al., *Association démocratique*, 345.
56. Cited by Francis Sartorius, "L'Association démocratique (1847–1848)," *Socialisme* 136 (August 1976): 6.
57. Paul Lafargue, preface to Friedrich Engels, *Socialisme utopique et socialisme scientifique;* in Andréas et al., *Association démocratique*, 10.
58. Friedrich Engels, "Der ökonomische Kongress," *Deutsche-Brüsseler-Zeitung*, 23 September 1847; in Institut für Marxismus-Lenismus, *Karl Marx. Friedrich Engels. Werke* (Berlin: Dietz, 1959), 4:291.
59. Karl Marx, "On the Question of Free Trade: Public Speech Delivered by Karl Marx before the Democratic Association of Brussels, January 9, 1848"; https://www.panarchy.org/engels/freetrade.html.
60. Karl Marx, cited by Somerhausen, *L'humanisme agissant de Karl Marx*, 205–206.
61. Karl Marx, cited by Mark Mazower, *Governing the World: The History of an Idea, 1815 to the Present* (New York: Penguin Books, 2012), 55.
62. Karl Marx, "On the Question of Free Trade."
63. Sartorius, "L'Association démocratique," 2 and 3.
64. Charles Spilthoorn, Association démocratique, Brussels, 29 November 1847; in Andréas et al., *Association démocratique*, 376.
65. A. de Bornstedt, in Andréas et al., *Association démocratique*, 379.
66. Stephen Born, in Andréas et al., *Association démocratique*, 381.
67. M. Nothomb, cited by Bertrand, *Histoire de la démocratie et du socialisme*, 1:139.
68. Sartorius, "L'Association démocratique," 1.
69. Karl Marx to Georg Herwegh, 26 October 1847; in *Karl Marx and Friedrich Engels, La Belgique: État constitutionnel modèle*, 164; and *Karl Marx and Frederick Engels, Collected Works* (New York: International Publishers, 1982), 38:141.
70. Count Woyna to Prince de Metternich, Brussels, 13 May 1847; Correspon-

dance politique, Vienne, Archives des Affaires Étrangères/Archief Buitenlandse Zaken, 1847, Brussels; and Count Woyna to Prince de Metternich, Brussels, 14 May 1847; Correspondance politique, Vienne, Archives des Affaires Étrangères/Archief Buitenlandse Zaken, Brussels. The Austrian diplomats were very aware of the gatherings and at least considered mounting their own surveillance. Count Woyna to Prince de Metternich, 23 March 1846, Brussels; Correspondance politique, Vienne, 1845, Archives des Affaires Étrangères/Archief Buitenlandse Zaken, Brussels.

71. *Le Débat social*, 31 October 1847; in Andréas et al., *Association démocratique*, 322.
72. Baron Alexis de Hody to the minister of justice, 7 October 1847; in Andréas et al., *Association démocratique*, 307–308.
73. "De la mission de la Belgique en Europe," *Le Débat social*, 12 July 1846, 14.
74. For a very different interpretation of this period of "democratic" political collaboration, the editor of one of the few volumes focused on Marx in Brussels comments, "Marx-Engels descended into the hell of bourgeois democratic relations . . . gaining a foothold in their adversaries' metaphysical system to dissolve it with their corrosive criticism, effected on the very ground of their enemy." *Karl Marx and Friedrich Engels, La Belgique: État constitutionnel modèle*, 135.
75. Kuypers, "Les liens d'amitié de Karl Marx en Belgique," 413.
76. "Une Nouvelle Tauride," *Le Débat social*, 8 February 1846, 277.
77. J. Harney, *Northern Star*; in Andréas et al., *Association démocratique*, 396.
78. "Adresse der Fraternal Democrats an die Association Démocratique," London, 6 December, 1847; in Andréas et al., *Association démocratique*, 422.
79. Karl Marx to Georg Herwegh, Brussels, 26 October 1847; in Andréas et al., *Association démocratique*, 287.
80. *Le Débat social*, 12 December 1847, 282–283; cited by Somerhausen, *L'humanisme agissant de Karl Marx*, 187.

7. "The Spectre of Communism" and a Revolution "At Our Very Door"

1. Beginning in 1848, all inhabitants in Belgium were required to register. Those coming or going from abroad had to present their passports to municipal authorities. On Belgian immigration, see Frank Caestecker, Bernadette Renauld, Nicolas Perrin, and Thierry Eggerickx, *Devenir Belge: Histoire de l'acquisition de la nationalité belge depuis 1830* (Mechelen: Wolters Kluwer, 2016), 7; and Frank Caestecker, *Alien Policy in Belgium, 1840–1940* (New York: Berghahn Books, 2000).
2. Karl Marx to Pavel Annenkov, 9 December 1847; cited by Jean Stengers, "Ixelles dans la vie et l'oeuvre de Karl Marx," *Revue belge de philologie et d'histoire* 82, nos. 1–2 (2004): 350.
3. On Victor Tedesco, see Rudolf Kern, *Victor Tedesco—ein früher Gefährte von*

Karl Marx in Belgien. Sein Leben, Denken und Wirken in der ersten Hälfte des 19. Jahrhunderts (Münster: Waxmann, 2014); and Julien Kuypers, "La contribution de Victor Tedesco à l'élaboration du Manifeste communiste de 1848," *Socialisme* 11 (1964).

4. Report of the Communist League; cited by Luc Somerhausen, *L'humanisme agissant de Karl Marx* (Paris: Richard-Masse, 1946), 185.
5. *Journal de Bruxelles;* cited by Somerhausen, *L'humanisme agissant de Karl Marx*, 190.
6. Karl Marx, *Manifesto of the Communist Party*, trans. Terrell Carver; in *The Cambridge Companion to The Communist Manifesto*, ed. Terrell Carver and James Farr (New York: Cambridge University Press, 2015), 250.
7. Philippe Gigot to Friedrich Engels; cited by Stengers, "Ixelles dans la vie et l'oeuvre de Karl Marx," 355.
8. Marx, *Manifesto of the Communist Party*, 237.
9. Ibid., 259.
10. Ibid., 250.
11. Karl Marx, New Year's Eve Celebration, *Deutsche Brüsseler Zeitung*, 31 December 1847; in *Marx & Engels Collected Works. Marx and Engels 1845–48* (London: Lawrence and Wishart Electric Book, 2010), 6:639.
12. Charles Liedts, cited by Louis Bertrand, *Histoire de la démocratie et du socialisme en Belgique depuis 1830* (Brussels: Dechenne, 1907), 1:273.
13. Bert Andréas et al., eds., *Association démocratique ayant pour but l'union et la fraternité de tous les peuples: Eine frühe demokratische Vereingung in Brussel 1847–1848* (Trier: Schriften aus dem Karl-Marx-Haus, 2004), 140–187. Among the Liberals participating in the association whose names figure on the list are Jean Funck, Gustave Guiolmot, and Carl Maynz.
14. Charles Spilthoorn, cited by Somerhausen, L'*humanisme agissant de Karl Marx*, 210.
15. Jacob Kats, "Uit verschillende Inlightingsbladen, 6 February 1848"; in Hubert Wouters, *Documenten betreffende de Geschiedenis der Arbeidersbeweging (1831–53)*, 3 vols. (Louvain and Paris, 1963), 1:422.
16. Karl Marx, *Deutsche Brüsseler Zeitung*, 19 December 1847; cited by Somerhausen, *L'humanisme agissant de Karl Marx*, 191.
17. Karl Bernays to Karl Marx, August 1846; cited by Edward de Maesschalck, *Marx in Brussel: 1845–1848* (Louvain: Davidsfonds, 2005), 127.
18. Mikhail Bakunin, cited by E. H. Carr, *Michael Bakunin* (London: Macmillan, 1975), 246.
19. Karl Marx, *Deutsche Brüsseler Zeitung*, 11 February 1848; cited by Somerhausen, *L'humanisme agissant de Karl Marx*, 219.
20. Jottrand, *Le Débat social*, 6 February 1848; cited by Somerhausen, *L'humanisme agissant de Karl Marx*, 218.
21. Karl Marx, *Deutsche Brüsseler Zeitung*, 11 February 1848; cited by Somerhausen, *L'humanisme agissant de Karl Marx*, 220.

22. Karl Marx, *Deutsche Brüsseler Zeitung*, 11 February 1848; cited by Somerhausen, *L'humanisme agissant de Karl Marx*, 219.
23. "The Association Démocratique of Brussels to the Fraternal Democrats Assembling in London"; in *Marx & Engels Collected Works*, 6:640.
24. Friedrich Engels, "Speech on Poland," 29 November 1847; in *Marx & Engels Collected Works*, 6:388–389.
25. Karl Marx, "On the Polish Question," 22 February 1848; in *Marx & Engels Collected Works*, 6:545.
26. Charles Rogier, cited by Ernest Discailles, *Charles Rogier (1800–1885), d'après des documents inédits* (Brussels: J. Lebègue, 1894), 229.
27. Carlo Bronne, *Jules van Praet* (Brussels: La Belgothèque, 1943).
28. Brison D. Gooch, *Belgium and the February Revolution* (The Hague: Martinus Nijhoff, 1963), 34.
29. Hal Draper, *The Marx-Engels Chronicle: A Day by Day Chronology of Marx and Engels; Life and Activity* (New York: Schocken Books, 1985), 30.
30. Association démocratique, cited by Somerhausen, *L'humanisme agissant de Karl Marx*, 231.
31. Maesschalck, *Marx in Brussel*, 165.
32. King Leopold to Charles Rogier, 26 February 1848; in Bronne, *Jules van Praet*, 230.
33. Léonard Ganser to François-Philippe De Haussy, 26 February 1847; in Wouters, *Documenten betreffende de Geschiedenis der Arbeidersbeweging*, 1:411.
34. Th. Dassy, in Wouters, *Documenten betreffende de Geschiedenis der Arbeidersbeweging*, 1:429.
35. Friedrich Engels, "To the Editor of the *Northern Star*"; in *Marx & Engels Collected Works*, 6:561.
36. Victor Tedesco, cited by Widukind De Ridder, "On the 'Absence of Spirit': The Legacy of the Abstinence from Revolution in Belgium," in *The 1848 Revolutions and European Political Thought*, ed. Douglas Moggach and Gareth Stedman Jones (Cambridge: Cambridge University Press, 2018), 211.
37. Procureur-generaal te Brussel to François-Philippe De Haussy, minister van justitie, 11 March 1848; in Wouters, *Documenten betreffende de Geschiedenis der Arbeidersbeweging*, 1:446.
38. Friedrich Engels, "To the Editor of the *Northern Star*"; in *Marx & Engels Collected Works*, 6:561.
39. Léonard Ganser, procureur-generaal te Gent, to François-Philippe De Haussy, minister van justitie, 26 February 1848; in Wouters, *Documenten betreffende de Geschiedenis der Arbeidersbeweging*, 1:424.
40. Els Witte, *Belgische Republikeinen: Radicalen tussen twee Revoluties (1830–1850)* (Brussels: Polis, 2020), 275.
41. Friedrich Engels, "To the Editor of the *Northern Star*"; in *Marx & Engels Collected Works*, 6:558–561.
42. Karl Marx, "Persecution of Foreigners in Brussels," *La Réforme*, 12 March 1848; in *Marx & Engels Collected Works*, 6:567.

43. Victor Considérant to Charles Rogier; cited by Bertrand, *Histoire de la démocratie et du socialisme*, 1:281.
44. Charles Rogier, 26 February 1846; cited by Bertrand, *Histoire de la démocratie et du socialisme*, 1:288.
45. Adelson Castiau, cited by Bertrand, *Histoire de la démocratie et du socialisme*, 1:292.
46. Noël Delfosse, cited by Léon Maes, *L'Affaire de Risquons-Tout* (Mouscron: Éditions du terroir, 1935), 66.
47. *L'Observateur*, cited by Bertrand, *Histoire de la démocratie et du socialisme*, 1:295.
48. M. Moreau, 2 March 1848; cited by Bertrand, *Histoire de la démocratie et du socialisme*, 1:296.
49. On this advocacy of the franchise as a decision against revolution, see Witte, *Belgische Republikeinen*, 288.

8. "Not Foreigners, but Democrats"

1. For this argument, see Georges-Henri Dumont, *Le miracle belge de 1848* (Brussels: Le Cri, 2005).
2. Brison D. Gooch, *Belgium and the February Revolution* (The Hague: Martinus Nijhoff, 1963), 107.
3. Leon Gordenker, cited by Emma Haddad, *The Refugee in International Society between Sovereigns* (Cambridge: Cambridge University Press, 2008), 1.
4. "Uit verschillende Inlichtingsbladen," 3 Maart 1848; in Hubert Wouters, *Documenten betreffende de Geschiedenis der Arbeidersbeweging (1831–53)*, 3 vols. (Louvain and Paris 1963), 1:436.
5. Police commissioner, Ixelles; cited by Luc Somerhausen, *L'humanisme agissant de Karl Marx* (Paris: Richard-Masse, 1946), 236.
6. Cited by Hal Draper, *The Marx-Engels Chronicle: A Day by Day Chronology of Marx and Engels; Life and Activity* (New York: Schocken Books, 1985), 30.
7. Comité central de la Ligue des communistes à Bruxelles, 3 March 1848; cited by Somerhausen, *L'humanisme agissant de Karl Marx*, 238.
8. Minister of justice, cited by Louis Bertrand, *Histoire de la démocratie et du socialisme en Belgique depuis 1830* (Brussels: Dechenne, 1907), 1:302.
9. Karl Marx, "To the Editor of *La Réforme*," 6 March 1848; *in Marx & Engels Collected Works. Marx and Engels 1845–48* (London: Lawrence and Wishart Electric Book, 2010), 6:565.
10. Karl Marx, "To the Editor of *La Réforme*," 6 March 1848; *in Marx & Engels Collected Works*, 6:566.
11. Friedrich Engels, "To the Editor of the *Northern Star*," 5 March 1848; in *Marx & Engels Collected Works*, 6:562; emphasis in original.
12. Friedrich Engels, "To the Editor of the *Northern Star*," March 5, 1848; in *Marx & Engels Collected Works*, 6:563. See also Friedrich Engels, in Bert Andréas, *Marx Verhaftung und Ausweisung aus Brüssel* (Trier: Karl-Marx-Haus, 1978), 49.

13. Karl Marx, "To the Editor of *La Réforme*," 8 March 1848; in *Marx & Engels Collected Works*, 6:564–565; emphasis in original.
14. Rogier in *Annales parlementaires*, 1847–48, 11 March 1848, pp. 1029–1039; cited by Somerhausen, *L'humanisme agissant de Karl Marx*, 246.
15. Karl Marx, "Persecution of Foreigners in Brussels," *La Réforme*, 12 March 1848; in *Marx & Engels Collected Works*, 6:567–568.
16. Jean Bueren, 16 March 1848; in Wouters, *Documenten betreffende de Geschiedenis der Arbeidersbeweging*, 1:462.
17. Friedrich Engels, 18 March 1848; in *Marx & Engels Collected Works*, 6:569.
18. Cited by Léon Maes, *L'Affaire de Risquons-Tout* (Mouscron: Éditions du terroir, 1935), 69.
19. Pierre Nothomb, cited in ibid., 14.
20. Charles De Bavay, *Attaque à main armée de Risquons-Tout. 29 Mars 1848. Acte d'accusation* (Brussels: Em. Devroye, 1848), 8.
21. Charles Louis Spilthoorn to Eeman, Paris 6 March 1848; in Wouters, *Documenten betreffende de Geschiedenis der Arbeidersbeweging*, 1:440.
22. De Bavay, *Attaque à main armée de Risquons-Tout*, 6.
23. M. Dessal, "Les incidents franco-belges en 1848," in *Actes du congrès historique du centenaire de la révolution de 1848, Paris 1948* (Paris: Presses Universitaires de la France, 1948), 113.
24. Louis Delestrée to Jacques Imbert; cited in *Attaque à main armée de Risquons-Tout*, 7.
25. Princesse de Ligne, cited by Dumont, *Le miracle belge de 1848*, 92.
26. Lucien Jottrand to Louis De Potter, Brussels, 18 March 1848; cited by Wouters, *Documenten betreffende de Geschiedenis der Arbeidersbeweging*, 1:472.
27. Maes, *L'Affaire de Risquons-Tout*, 80–82.
28. Proclamation cited in ibid., 79.
29. François Hoffschmidt to Prince de Ligne; cited in Maes, *L'Affaire de Risquons-Tout*, 80–81.
30. Lille, 2 April 1848; cited by Maes, *L'Affaire de Risquons-Tout*, 91.
31. Els Witte, *Belgische Republikeinen: Radicalen tussen twee Revoluties (1830–1850)* (Brussels: Polis, 2020), 297–298.
32. Queen Louise Marie, cited by Maes, *L'Affaire de Risquons-Tout*, 65.
33. Leopold I, cited by Gooch, *Belgium and the February Revolution*, 2.
34. Queen Victoria, cited by Gooch, *Belgium and the February Revolution*, 84.
35. For an alternative view, see Witte, *Belgische Republikeinen*, 283, 294–295.
36. Friedrich Engels, "To the Editor of the *Northern Star*," 5 March 1848; in *Marx & Engels Collected Works*, 6:559.
37. Alexandre Gendebien, in Wouters, *Documenten betreffende de Geschiedenis der Arbeidersbeweging*, 1:416.
38. Els Witte, "De Belgische Radikalen," *Tijdschrift voor Geschiedenis* 90 (1977): 40.
39. Karl Marx to Georg Herwegh; cited by Jean Stengers, "Ixelles dans la vie et l'oeuvre de Karl Marx," *Revue belge de philologie et d'histoire* 82, nos. 1–2 (2004): 353–354.

40. "Bericht Über dans Neujahrsfest des Deutschen Arbeiterbildungsvereins in Brüssel, 31 Dezember 1847," *Deutsche Brüsseler Zeitung*, 6 January 1848; in *Bund der Kommunisten, Dokumente und Materialien*, ed. Herwig Förder, Martin Hundt, Jefim Kandel, and Sofia Lewiowa (Berlin: Dietz Verlag, 1970), 1:642.
41. Widukind De Ridder, "On the 'Absence of Spirit': The Legacy of the Abstinence from Revolution in Belgium," in *The 1848 Revolutions and European Political Thought*, ed. Douglas Moggach and Gareth Stedman Jones (Cambridge: Cambridge University Press, 2018), 212–213.
42. *Neue Rheinische Zeitung* 74 (13 August 1848); in *Fragmente zu internationalen demokratischen Aktivitäten um 1848*, ed. Halmut Elsner, Jacques Grandjonc, Elisabeth Neu, and Hans Pelger, eds. (Trier: Schriften aus dem Karl-Marx-Haus, 2000), 338.
43. Howard de Walden to Lord John Henry Palmerston, Brussels, 31 August 1848; in Elsner, Grandjonc, Neu, and Pelger, *Fragmente zu internationalen demokratischen Aktivitäten um 1848*, 386.
44. Cited in Lucien Jottrand, *Charles-Louis Spilthoorn: Événements de 1848 en Belgique* (Bruxelles : Imprimérie Charles Vanderauwera, 1872), 103.
45. Ibid., 133 and 125.

9. The Forty-Eighters in America

1. Mannheim Assembly, February 1848; cited in Axel Körner, "The European Dimension in the Ideas of 1848 and the Nationalization of Its Memories," in *1848—A European Revolution? International Ideas and National Memories*, ed. Axel Körner (New York: St. Martin's Press, 2000), 15. "An asylum for mankind" comes from Thomas Paine, *Common Sense*, in Thomas Paine, *Collected Writings* (New York: Penguin, 1992), 36.
2. Office of the High Commissioner, United Nations Human Rights, "Key Concepts on ESCRs—Are Economic, Social and Cultural Rights Fundamentally Different from Civil and Political Rights?" https://www.ohchr.org/en/issues/escr/pages/areescrfundamentallydifferentfromcivilandpoliticalrights.aspx.
3. Cited by Carl Wittke, *Refugees of Revolution: The German Forty-Eighters in America* (Philadelphia: University of Pennsylvania Press, 1952), 50.
4. Each of the Swiss cantons set its own immigration policies but was required to register the refugees, verify their identity, and provide surveillance of their activities. The federal government forbade cantons from expelling refugees into neighboring cantons and subsidized support for the refugees. If cantons harbored refugees deemed dangerous by the federal government, it could intervene, demanding their expulsion. More often, neighboring states exerted diplomatic pressure, compelling intervention.
5. Wittke, *Refugees of Revolution*, 51.
6. Kerby A. Miller, "Emigration to North America in the Era of the Great

Famine, 1845–55," in *Atlas of the Great Irish Famine*, ed. John Crowley, William J. Smyth, and Mike Murphy (New York: New York University Press, 2012), 214.

7. Wittke, *Refugees of Revolution*, 44.
8. German refugee in *New Yorker Staaszeitung*, 16 July 1852; cited by Wittke, *Refugees of Revolution*, 50.
9. Thomas Paine, *Common Sense*, in Thomas Paine, *Collected Writings* (New York: Penguin, 1992), 36. See also Caroline B. Brettell and James F. Hollifield, "Introduction," in *Migration Theory: Talking across Disciplines*, ed. Caroline B. Brettell and James F. Hollifield, 2nd. ed. (New York: Routledge, 2008), 1.
10. Edward Said, "Reflections on Exile," *Granata* 1, no. 3 (Autumn 1984): 138.
11. André Aciman, "Shadow Cities," in *Letters of Transit: Reflections on Exile, Identity, Language, and Loss*, ed. André Aciman (New York: New Press, 1990), 30.
12. Marilyn Hoskin, *Understanding Immigration: Issues and Challenges in an Era of Mass Population Movement* (Albany: State University of New York Press, 2017), 6.
13. Béla Vassady, "New Buda: A Colony of Hungarian Forty-Eighters in Iowa, *Annals of Iowa* 51, no. 1 (Summer 1991). See Claudio Saunt, *Unworthy Republic: The Dispossession of Native Americans and the Road to Indian Territory* (New York: W. W. Norton, 2020), for a history of the battle over the expulsion of Indigenous peoples and its effects on the American republic.
14. Similarly, Isabel Wilkerson used the term "refugees" to describe those who undertook the great migration north in America. See Isabel Wilkerson, *The Warmth of Other Suns: The Epic Story of America's Great Migration* (New York: Vintage Books, 2010), 179.
15. Charles J. Wallman, *The German-Speaking Forty-Eighters: Builders of Watertown, Wisconsin* (Madison, WI: Max Kade Institute for German-American Studies, 1992), 19.
16. Cited by Hildegard Binder Johnson, "Adjustment to the United States," in *The Forty-Eighters: Political Refugees of the German Revolution of 1848*, ed. A. E. Zucker (New York: Columbia University Press, 1950), 46.
17. Cited by Ernest Bruncken, *German American Forty-Eighters, 1848–1998*, ed. Don-Heinrich Tolzmann (Indianapolis, IN: Max Kade German-American Center, 1998), 35.
18. Eva Hoffman, *Lost in Translation: A Life in a New Language;* cited in Aciman, *Letters of Transit*, 37.
19. Friedrich Hecker, cited by Binder Johnson, "Adjustment to the United States," 48.
20. Anton Füster, cited in Heléna Tóth, *An Exiled Generation: German and Hungarian Refugees of Revolution 1848–1871* (Cambridge: Cambridge University Press, 2014), 202.
21. Karl Marx, *Heroes of the Exile;* in Works of Karl Marx and Frederick Engels 1852, trans. Rodney Livingston. https://www.marxists.org/archive/marx/works

/1852/heroes-exile/index.htm, XIII, "The Great War between the Frogs and the Mice."

22. Friedrich Engels to Joseph Weydemeyer; cited by Carl Wittke, *The Utopian Communist: A Biography of Wilhelm Weitling, Nineteenth-Century Reformer* (Baton Rouge: Louisiana State University Press, 1950), 142.
23. Cited in Tolzmann, ed., *The German-American Forty-Eighters*, 34.
24. In one study of three hundred newly arrived Forty-Eighters for whom biographies were available, seventy-four became journalists in the United States; thirty-seven, physicians; twenty-five, teachers; twenty-two, lawyers; twenty-one, businessmen; twelve, farmers; and eleven, diplomats. A. E. Zucker, cited by Wittke, *Refugees of Revolution*, 61–62.
25. Carl Schurz, *Reminiscences*, iii; cited in Tolzmann, *The German-American Forty-Eighters*, 11.
26. Cited in Bruce Levine, *The Spirit of 1848* (Urbana: University of Illinois Press, 1992), 54.
27. Karl Marx, *Heroes of the Exile;* in *Works of Karl Marx and Frederick Engels 1852*, trans. Rodney Livingston. https://www.marxists.org/archive/marx/works/1852/heroes-exile/index.htm, III, Kinkel's Trial and Escape.
28. Carl Schurz, *Reminiscences*, iii; cited in Tolzmann, *The German-American Forty-Eighters*, 11.
29. Carl Schurz, cited by Bayard Quincy Morgan, "Carl Schurz," in Zucker, *The Forty-Eighters*, 228.
30. Carl Schurz, cited by Ann Taylor Allen, *The Transatlantic Kindergarten: Education and Women's Movements in Germany and the United States* (New York: Oxford University Press, 2017), 49.
31. Lewis Cass, cited by Bethel Saler, *The Settlers' Empire: Colonialism and State Formation in America's Old Northwest* (Philadelphia: University of Pennsylvania Press, 2015), 252.
32. Andreas Fahrmeir, *Citizenship: The Rise and Fall of a Modern Concept* (New Haven: Yale University Press, 2007), 68.
33. Wallman, *The German-Speaking Forty-Eighters*, 4.
34. Allison Clark Efford, *German Immigrants, Race, and Citizenship in the Civil War Era* (Cambridge: Cambridge University Press, 2013).
35. Cited by Tőth, *An Exiled Generation*, 208.
36. Wallman, *The German-Speaking Forty-Eighters*, 44.
37. Allen, *The Transatlantic Kindergarten*, 58.
38. Abraham Lincoln, cited by Wittke, *Refugees of Revolution*, 215.
39. Carl Schurz, cited by Efford, *German Immigrants*, 53. Emphasis in original.
40. Mathilde Franziska Anneke, cited by Allen, *The Transatlantic Kindergarten*, 46.
41. Jacob Müller, cited by Efford, *German Immigrants*, 38.
42. Frederick Law Olmsted, cited by Mischa Honeck, *We Are the Revolutionists: German-Speaking Immigrants and American Abolitionists after 1848* (Athens: University of Georgia Press, 2011), 40.
43. Adolph Douai, cited in Allen, *The Transatlantic Kindergarten*, 48.

44. German American Position Statement: The Louisville Platform; in Tolzmann, *The German-American Forty-Eighters*, 99.
45. August Willich, cited by Honeck, *We Are the Revolutionists*, 73.
46. Cited by Levine, *The Spirit of 1848*, 107.
47. Thomas R. Whitney, cited by Levine, *The Spirit of 1848*, 108.
48. Abraham Lincoln to Joshua Speed, Springfield, Illinois, 24 August 1855; http://www.abrahamlincolnonline.org/lincoln/speeches/speed.htm.
49. Kunal M. Parker, *Making Foreigners: Immigration and Citizenship Law in America, 1600–2000* (New York: Cambridge University Press, 2015), 2.

Epilogue

1. Olivier Barsalou and Alain-Guy Sipowo, "Les crises migratoires globales à l'aune de la raison souveraine," *Études internationales: Le droit international des réfugiés face à une gouvernance mondiale en crises*, 49, no. 2 (2018): 236.
2. Pauline Kleingeld, "Kant's Cosmopolitan Law: World Citizenship for a Global Order," *Kantian Review* 2 (1998): 77.
3. UNHCR, "Facts and Figures about Refugees"; cited by Maria Cristina Garcia, *The Refugee Challenge in Post-Cold War America* (New York: Oxford University Press, 2020), 206.
4. UNHCR, "Projected Global Resettlement Needs 2021," 13; https://www.unhcr.org/protection/resettlement/5ef34bfb7/projected-global-resettlement-needs-2021-pdf.html. See also Marilyn Hoskin, *Understanding Immigration: Issues and Challenges in an Era of Mass Population Movement* (Albany: State University of New York Press, 2017), 2.
5. "The Climate and Environment Charter for Humanitarian Organizations"; https://www.climate-charter.org/; and Center for Strategic and International Studies, "The Global Humanitarian Overview 2022: Climate, Gender, and Humanitarian Response," 27 January 2022; https://www.csis.org/analysis/global-humanitarian-overview-2022-climate-gender-and-humanitarian-response.
6. Sadako Ogata, cited in Fact Sheet No. 20, "Human Rights and Refugees," UN Office of the High Commissioner for Human Rights, July 1993; https://www.refworld.org/docid/4794773f0.html.
7. David Miller, "Is There a Human Right to Immigrate?" Centre for the Study of Social Justice, Department of Politics and International Relations, University of Oxford Working Papers Series, SJ033, April 2015; and Magali Bessone, "Le vocabulaire de l'hospitalité est-il républicain?" *Éthique publique* 17, no. 1 (2015).
8. Giorgio Agamben, "Beyond Human Rights," in Giorgio Agamben, *Means without Ends: Notes on Politics* (Minneapolis: University of Minnesota Press 2000), 92.
9. Hannah Arendt, *The Origins of Totalitarianism* (Cleveland: Meridian Books,

1958), 296. See also Alison Kesby, *The Right to Have Rights: Citizenship, Humanity, and International Law* (Oxford: Oxford University Press, 2012), 3.

10. Linda Kerber, "Presidential Address. The Stateless as the Citizen's Other: A View from the United States," *American Historical Review* 112, no. 1 (February 2007): 9.
11. Hannah Arendt, cited by Kerber, "Presidential Address," 30. See also Seyla Benhabib, *Exile, Statelessness, and Migration. Playing Chess with History from Hannah Arendt to Isaiah Berlin* (Princeton, NJ: Princeton University Press, 2018), 109.
12. Universal Declaration of Human Rights; https://www.un.org/en/universal-declaration-human-rights/.
13. Vienna Declaration and Programme of Action Adopted by the World Conference on Human Rights in Vienna on 25 June 1993; https://www.ohchr.org/en/professionalinterest/pages/vienna.aspx.
14. Benhabib, *Exile, Statelessness, and Migration,* 111.
15. The political scientist Daniele Archibugi writes with obvious understatement: "Ever since the UN's foundation, its profile has remained much lower than originally expected." Daniele Archibugi, *The Global Commonwealth of Citizens: Toward Cosmopolitan Democracy* (Princeton, NJ: Princeton University Press, 2008), 153. Ayten Gündoğdu goes further to ask, "To what extent do the ordering principles of the current international system, including existing human rights norms, contribute to the precarious conditions of various categories of migrants?" Ayten Gündoğdu, *Rightlessness in an Age of Rights: Hannah Arendt and the Contemporary Struggles of Migrants* (Oxford: Oxford University Press, 2015), 3.
16. Universal Declaration of Human Rights. See also Gordon Brown, *The Universal Declaration of Human Rights in the 21st Century: A Living Document in a Changing World* (Cambridge, England: Open Book Publishers, 2016), 106; https://www.jstor.org/stable/j.ctt1bpmb7v.
17. Kerber, "Presidential Address," 13.
18. Seyla Benhabib, "Citizens, Residents, and Aliens in a Changing World: Political Membership in the Global Era," *Social Research* 66, no. 3 (Fall 1999): 732.
19. Arendt, *The Origins of Totalitarianism,* 297.
20. Seyla Benhabib, "Transformations of Citizenship: The Case of Contemporary Europe," *Government and Opposition,* 37, no. 4, (2002): 441.
21. Office of the UN High Commissioner for Human Rights, "The Rights of Non-Citizens" (New York and Geneva: United Nations, 2006); https://www.ohchr.org/documents/publications/noncitizensen.pdf.
22. Geoff Gilbert, "Tackling the Causes of Refugee Flows," in *Strangers and Citizens: A Positive Approach to Migrants and Refugees,* ed. Sarah Spencer (London: IPPR/Rivers Oram Press, 1994), 20–21.
23. Matthew J. Gibney, "Political Theory, Ethics, and Forced Migration"; cited

by Guy S. Goodwin-Gill, "The International Law of Refugee Protection," in *The Oxford Handbook of Refugee and Forced Migration Studies*, ed. Elena Fiddian-Qasmiyeh, Gil Loescher, Katy Long, and Nando Sigona (Oxford: Oxford University Press, 2014), 51.

24. U.S. State Department, *Report of the Commission on Unalienable Rights*, 2020, 52; https://www.state.gov/wp-content/uploads/2020/08/Report-of-the-Commission-on-Unalienable-Rights.pdf.
25. Chandran Kukathas, "Are Refugees Special?" in *Migration in Political Theory: The Ethics of Movement and Membership*, ed. Sarah Fine and Lea Ypi (Oxford: Oxford University Press, 2016), 252.
26. Cited by David Scott FitzGerald, *Refuge beyond Reach: How Rich Democracies Repel Asylum Seekers* (Oxford: Oxford University Press, 2019), 5.
27. John Stoessigner, cited by Matthew Frank and Jessica Reinisch, "Refugees and the Nation-State in Europe, 1919–1959," *Journal of Contemporary History* 49, no. 3 (July 2014): 477.
28. Hannah Arendt, "We Refugees," *Menorah Journal* 31, no. 1 (1943); republished in *Altogether Elsewhere: Writers on Exile*, ed. Marc Robinson (New York: Harcourt, Brace, 1994), 119.
29. Daniel Loick, "We Refugees," Public Seminar, New School for Social Research, 2016; https://publicseminar.org/2016/05/we-refugees/.
30. U.S. State Department, *Report of the Commission on Unalienable Rights* (2020), 5 and 8; https://www.state.gov/wp-content/uploads/2020/08/Report-of-the-Commission-on-Unalienable-Rights.pdf.
31. Dara Lind, "Denaturalization, Explained: How Trump Can Strip Immigrants of Their Citizenship," 18 July 2018; https://www.vox.com/2018/7/18/17561538/denaturalization-citizenship-task-force-janus.
32. Bill Frelick, "US, Australia Hit New Lows on Refugee Resettlement: Declining Numbers Leave Most Vulnerable at Risk," 21 October 2020, Human Rights Watch; https://www.hrw.org/news/2020/10/21/us-australia-hit-new-lows-refugee-resettlement.
33. Cited in Editorial Board, "In a New Term, Trump Would Further Seal the Gates of a Fortress America," *Washington Post*, 11 September 2020.
34. Alison Brysk and Gershon Shafir, cited by Gündoğdu, *Rightlessness in an Age of Rights*, 3.
35. "Report on Chile," 1985, as cited by Carmen Tiburcio, *The Human Rights of Aliens under International and Comparative Law* (The Hague: Martinus Nijhoff, 2001), 5.
36. IRO Records 43 AJ-232, as cited by Eric Fripp, *Nationality and Statelessness in the International Law of Refugee Status* (Oxford: Hart Publishing, 2016), xvi.
37. Loick, "We Refugees."
38. Kerber, "Presidential Address," 7.
39. Pierre Hassner, "Refugees: A Special Case for Cosmopolitan Citizenship," in *Re-imagining Political Community: Studies in Cosmopolitan Democracy*, ed. Dan-

iele Archibugi, David Held, and Martin Köhler (Stanford, CA: Stanford University Press, 1998), 274. Refugees for Giorgio Agamben are "nothing less than a border concept that radically calls into question the principles of the nation state and, at the same time, helps clear the field for a no longer delayable renewal of categories." Giorgio Agamben, cited by Gibney, "Political Theory, Ethics, and Forced Migration," 54.

40. Eleanor Roosevelt, "Where Do Human Rights Begin?" in *Courage in a Dangerous World*, ed. Allida M. Black (New York: Columbia University Press, 1999), 190.
41. Jacques Derrida, *Cosmopolites de tous les pays, encore un effort!* (Paris: Éditions Galilée, 1997), 22. For a translation see Jacques Derrida, *On Cosmopolitanism and Forgiveness: Thinking in Action* (New York: Routledge, 2001), 11–12.
42. Engin Isin, cited by Maarten Prak, *Citizens without Nations: Urban Citizenship in Europe and the World c. 1000–1789* (Cambridge: Cambridge University Press, 2018), 6. See Prak for an extended discussion of urban citizenship as a more democratic alternative to the modern nation-state.
43. Derrida, *Cosmopolites de tous les pays*, 58.
44. Warren Magnusson, *Politics of Urbanism: Seeing Like a City* (New York: Routledge, 2011), 5.
45. Magnusson, *Politics of Urbanism*, 32.
46. Cited by Barbara Oomen, "Cities of Refuge: Rights, Culture and the Creation of Cosmopolitan Cityzenship," in *Cultures, Citizenship and Human Rights*, ed. R. Buikema, A. Buyse, and A. Robben (London: Routledge, 2019).
47. Benjamin Barber, cited by Phil Wood, "Urban Citizenship: Making Places Where Even the Undocumented Can Belong," Intercultural Cities, Exploratory Workshop, 28–29 November 2018, Botkyrka, Sweden.
48. Maira Khwaja, Trina Reynolds-Tyler, Dominique James, and Hannah Nyhart, "We Built Community as Neighbors," Sunday Review, *New York Times*, 14 March 2020, 5.
49. The Climate and Environment Charter for Humanitarian Organizations; https://www.climate-charter.org/.
50. Marvin Rees, "City Metric"; https://www.citymetric.com/politics/marvin-rees-case-global-parliament-mayors-4243.
51. Grace Ashford, "Noncitizens' Right to Vote Becomes Law in New York City," *New York Times*, 9 January 2022; https://www.nytimes.com/2022/01/09/nyregion/noncitizens-nyc-voting-rights.html.
52. This is not to argue, as Michael Walzer infamously did in the 1980s, that "Neighborhoods can be open only if countries are at least potentially closed." Michael Walzer, *Spheres of Justice: A Defense of Pluralism and Equality*, 38; as cited by Kunal M. Parker, *Making Foreigners: Immigration and Citizenship Law in America, 1600–2000* (New York: Cambridge University Press, 2015), 15.
53. Benhabib, "Citizens, Residents, and Aliens in a Changing World," 729.

54. Benjamin Barber, *If Mayors Ruled the World: Dysfunctional Nations, Rising Cities* (New Haven: Yale University Press, 2013), 18.
55. Edward Said, "No Reconciliations Allowed," in *Letters of Transit: Reflections on Exile, Identity, Language, and Loss*, ed. André Aciman (New York: New Press, 1990), 111.
56. Benhabib, *Exile, Statelessness, and Migration*, 103.
57. Daniel Halberstam, "Local, Global and Plural Constitutionalism: Europe Meets the World," in *The Worlds of European Constitutionalism*, ed. Grainme De Burca and J. H. H. Weiler (Cambridge: Cambridge University Press, 2012), 170.
58. Lucy Hovil, "Local Integration," in Fiddian-Qasmiyeh et al., *The Oxford Handbook of Refugee and Forced Migration Studies*, 488.
59. Lucy Hovil, "When Refugees Are Cast as Outsiders, They Create New Ways to Belong," *New Humanitarian;* https://deeply.thenewhumanitarian.org/refugees/articles/2017/01/16/when-refugees-are-cast-as-outsiders-they-create-new-ways-to-belong.
60. The United Nations expects that more than 68 percent of the world population will live in urban areas by 2050. United Nations, Department of Economic and Social Affairs, 16 May 2018; https://www.un.org/development/desa/en/news/population/2018-revision-of-world-urbanization-prospects.html.
61. Sarah Song, "The Significance of Territorial Presence and the Rights of Immigrants," in Fine and Ypi, *Migration in Political Theory*, 225–248.

Further Reading

AT THE VERY BEGINNING, when this book was still just an idea, a wise editor suggested I look at histories of exile during other periods of the past. He recommended E. H. Carr, *The Romantic Exiles* (New York: Penguin Books, 1968), and Jean-Michel Palmier, *Weimar in Exile: The Antifascist Emigration in Europe and America* (New York: Verso, 2006), the first centering on Alexander Herzen and other mid-nineteenth-century Russian exiles and the second on the emigration and continuing fight of intellectuals from Nazi Germany. I also reread François Furstenberg, *When the United States Spoke French: Five Refugees Who Shaped a Nation* (New York: Penguin, 2014), about the refugees from the French Revolution who came to America, and Faith Hillis, *Utopia's Discontents: Russian Emigrés and the Quest for Freedom, 1830s–1930s* (New York: Oxford University Press, 2021), about the Russian colonies and their networks abroad. These four histories are notable because each relates gripping stories while engaging readers in compelling questions about the forces that set the refugees in motion, the institutions and regulations that constrained their travel, and societal transformations caused by their odysseys. I was drawn to the descriptions of those open spaces that welcomed refugees in the midst of worlds torn apart.

Asylum between Nations is framed by this cosmopolitanism, experienced in the present as well as studied from the past. Students in my Global Citizenship class at the University of New Hampshire begin their journey through a world motivated by universal concern and respect for differences in Kwame Anthony Appiah, *Cosmopolitanism: Ethics in a World of Strangers* (New York: W. W. Norton, 2006). Among the other eminent contemporary philosophers and political theorists whose works occupy a bookshelf readily at hand are the following: Daniele Archibugi, *The Global Commonwealth of Citizens: Toward Cosmopolitan Democracy* (Princeton, NJ: Princeton University Press, 2008); Ulrich Beck, *The Cosmopolitan Vision*, trans. Ciaran Cronin, (Cambridge: Polity Press, 2006); Jacques Derrida, *Cosmopolites de tous les pays, encore un effort!* (Paris: Éditions Galilée, 1997); David Held, *Cosmopolitanism: Ideals and Realities* (Cambridge: Polity Press, 2010); Martha C. Nussbaum,

The Cosmopolitan Tradition: A Noble but Flawed Ideal (Cambridge, MA: Harvard University Press, 2019); and Kok-Chor Tan, *Justice without Borders: Cosmopolitanism, Nationalism, and Patriotism* (Cambridge: Cambridge University Press, 2004). Their responses to the fundamental question posed by Appiah—What do we owe a stranger?—have guided the writing of this book.

The foundation of contemporary asylum policies was defined by a notable set of Enlightenment philosophers in the eighteenth-century: Nicolas de Condorcet, Denis Diderot, and David Hume, and their predecessors, including Hugo Grotius and Christian von Wolff. Immanuel Kant's text, "Toward Perpetual Peace," written in 1795 in the midst of a continent at war, has launched debates over immigration policies into the present. Thomas J. Schlereth's *The Cosmopolitan Ideal in Enlightenment Thought: Its Form and Function in the Ideas of Franklin, Hume, and Voltaire, 1694–1790* (Notre Dame, IN: University of Notre Dame Press, 1977) is broader than its title implies and is a useful guide to these thinkers, as is the concise but suggestive article by Sophia Rosenfeld, "Citizens of Nowhere in Particular: Cosmopolitanism, Writing, and Political Engagement in Eighteenth-Century Europe," *National Identities* 4, no. 1 (2002): 25–45. Margaret C. Jacob, *Strangers Nowhere in the World: The Rise of Cosmopolitanism in Early Modern Europe* (Philadelphia: University of Pennsylvania Press, 2006), focuses on those who comfortably lived amid and traded with others who were different from themselves.

Some philosophers have suggested that refugees make the best cosmopolitans. The essays of refugees reflecting on their experiences are collected in two pithy compilations. The first is short: André Aciman, ed. *Letters of Transit: Reflections on Exile, Identity, Language, and Loss* (New York: New Press, 1990); and the second, more extensive: Marc Robinson, ed. *Altogether Elsewhere: Writers on Exile* (New York: Harcourt, Brace, 1994). See also the insightful essay by Edward Said, "Reflections on Exile," *Granata* 1, no. 3 (Autumn 1984), about an experience that has torn "hopelessly large numbers" from all they have known with no prospects of ever returning home.

My thinking about refugees has been shaped by Hannah Arendt's meditations on "the right to have rights." Especially relevant are the ninth chapter in *The Origins of Totalitarianism* (Cleveland: Meridian Books, 1958) and her essay "We Refugees," published first in the small Jewish journal *Menorah* in 1943 and subsequently widely republished. Arendt wrote about loss, focusing on a time when "the comity of European peoples went to pieces . . . because it allowed its weakest member to be excluded and persecuted" ("We Refugees," 77). Explications of Arendt's philosophy in the context of modern mass migrations can be found in several works by Seyla Benhabib, including *Exile, Statelessness, and Migration: Playing Chess with History from Hannah Arendt to Isaiah Berlin* (Princeton, NJ: Princeton University Press, 2008) and *The Rights of Others: Aliens, Residents and Citizens* (Cambridge: Cambridge University Press, 2004); Ayten Gündoğdu, *Rightlessness in an Age of Rights: Hannah Arendt and the Contemporary Struggles of Migrants* (Oxford: Oxford University Press, 2015); and Alison Kesby, *The Right to Have Rights: Citizenship, Humanity, and International Law* (Oxford: Oxford University Press, 2012).

There are many histories of refugees and exiles, but the ones that I find both comprehensive and generally insightful are the following: Sylvie Aprile, *Le siècle des exilés: Bannis et proscrits de 1789 à la Commune* (Paris: CNRS Editions, 2010); Greg Burgess, *Refuge in the Land of Liberty: France and Its Refugees, from the Revolution to the End of Asylum, 1787–1939* (New York: Palgrave Macmillan, 2008); Delphine Diaz, *En exil: Les réfugiés en Europe de la fin du XVIIIe siècle à nos jours* (Paris: Gallimard, 2021); and Gérard Noiriel, *La tyrannie du national: Le droit d'asile en Europe (1793–1993)* (Paris: Calmann-Lévy, 1991). Two indispensable collections of articles cover all facets of exile: *The Oxford Handbook of Refugee and Forced Migration Studies*, ed. Elena Fiddian-Qasmiyeh, Gil Loescher, Katy Long, and Nando Sigona (Oxford: Oxford University Press, 2014); and *Migration in Political Theory: The Ethics of Movement and Membership*, ed. Sarah Fine and Lea Ypi (Oxford: Oxford University Press, 2016). The most useful distillation of the changing vocabulary of exile is a short piece by Delphine Diaz and Sylvie Aprile, "Europe and Its Political Refugees in the 19th Century," *Books and Ideas*, Collège de France, 18 April 2016.

Seen from this perspective, the reverse side of statelessness is citizenship. Linda Kerber frames that discussion in her invaluable article "Presidential Address. The Stateless as the Citizen's Other: A View from the United States," *American Historical Review* 112, no. 1 (February 2007): 1–34. For the foundations on which citizenship is constructed, see Andreas Fahrmeir, *Citizenship: The Rise and Fall of a Modern Concept* (New Haven: Yale University Press, 2007); Nathan Perl-Rosenthal, *Citizen Sailors: Becoming American in the Age of Revolution* (Cambridge, MA: Harvard University Press, 2015); and John Torpey, *The Invention of the Passport: Surveillance, Citizenship and the State* (Cambridge: Cambridge University Press, 2000). Especially attuned to the intertwining development of citizenship, emigration, and immigration law are Ernst Hirsch Ballin, *Citizens' Rights and the Right to Be a Citizen* (Leiden: Brill, 2014), and Kunal M. Parker, *Making Foreigners: Immigration and Citizenship Law in America, 1600–2000* (New York: Cambridge University Press, 2015), as well as a number of recently published edited volumes: *Migration Control in the North Atlantic World. The Evolution of State Practices in Europe and the United States from the French Revolution to the Interwar Period*, ed. Andreas Fahrmeir, Olivier Faron, and Patrick Weil (New York: Berghahn Books, 2003); Nancy L. Green and François Weil, eds., *Citizenship and Those Who Leave: The Politics of Emigration and Expatriation*, ed. Nancy L. Green and François Weil (Urbana: University of Illinois Press, 2007); *Documenting Individual Identity: The Development of State Practices in the Modern World*, ed. Jane Caplan and John Torpey (Princeton, NJ: Princeton University Press, 2001); *Migration Policies and Materialities of Identification in European Cities: Papers and Gates, 1500–1930s*, ed. Hilde Greefs and Anne Winter (New York: Routledge, 2019); and *Strangers and Citizens: A Positive Approach to Migrants and Refugees*, ed. Sarah Spencer (London: IPPR/Rivers Oram Press, 1994).

Urban as opposed to national citizenship has recently generated a rich and growing paper trail. Among others see the following: Benjamin Barber, *If Mayors*

Ruled the World: Dysfunctional Nations, Rising Cities (New Haven: Yale University Press, 2013); Barbara Oomen, "Cities of Refuge: Rights, Culture and the Creation of Cosmopolitan Cityzenship," in *Cultures, Citizenship and Human Rights*, ed. R. Buikema, A. Buyse, and A. Robben, (London: Routledge, 2019); Maarten Prak, *Citizens without Nations: Urban Citizenship in Europe and the World c. 1000–1789* (Cambridge: Cambridge University Press, 2018); and the quintessential guide to a localized approach: Warren Magnusson, *Politics of Urbanism: Seeing Like a City* (New York: Routledge, 2011).

The era of the French Revolution generated provocative debates over the definition of citizenship that in turn have given rise to thoughtful, far-reaching historical studies including the following: Suzanne Desan, "Foreigners, Cosmopolitanism, and French Revolutionary Universalism," in *The French National Revolution in Global Perspective*, ed. Suzanne Desan, Lynn Hunt, and William Max Nelson, (Ithaca, NY: Cornell University Press, 2013), 86–100; Edward James Kolla, *Sovereignty, International Law, and the French Revolution* (Cambridge: Cambridge University Press, 2017); Michael Rapport, *Nationality and Citizenship in Revolutionary France: The Treatment of Foreigners 1789–1799* (Oxford: Clarendon Press, 2000); Peter Sahlins, *Unnaturally French: Foreign Citizens in the Old Regime and After* (Ithaca, NY: Cornell University Press, 2004); and Sophie Wahnich, *L'impossible citoyen: L'étranger dans le discours de la Révolution française* (Paris: Albin Michel, 1997).

The best guides to individual refugees and their hosts in Altona, Hamburg, the Swiss cantons, and Brussels are the endnotes above, which lead to memoirs, collections of correspondence, and archives. What follows is a very selective set of suggestions.

Aristocratic émigrés fleeing the French Revolution have attracted the attention of generations of historians and their readers. Most scholarship has focused on French nobles and other counterrevolutionaries seeking asylum in England. Kirsty Carpenter has captured the details of the lives and writings of many of the émigrés, especially those who made their ways across the English Channel. In addition to her numerous articles and book chapters, see her monograph *Refugees of the French Revolution* (New York: St. Martin's Press, 1999), and a collection of essays covering Europe: *The French Émigrés in Europe and the Struggle against Revolution 1789–1914*, ed. Kirsty Carpenter and Philip Mansel (London: MacMillan, 1998).

On the émigrés who arrived in Hamburg and Altona, see Paul Piper, *Altona und die Fremde, insbesondere die Emigranten vor hundert Jahren* (Altona: J. Harder Verlag, 1914); Friedemann Pestel, *Kosmopoliten wider Willen. Die "monarchiens" als Revolutionsemigranten* (Berlin: De Gruyter, 2015); and Burghart Schmidt, "'Französisches Emigranten Volck in Hamburg nach dem Leben gemahlt,' Regionalgeschichtliche Überlegungen zum Wirtschafts-und Kulturtransfer im Zeitalter der Französischen Revolution," in *Hamburg und sein norddeutsches Umland. Aspekte des Wandels seit der Frühen Neuzeit. Festschrift für Franklin Kopitzsch*, ed. Dirk Brietzke, Norbert Fischer, and Arno Herzig (Hamburg: DOBU, 2007), 97–122.

The central set of works on the neighboring cities of Hamburg and Altona at the end of the eighteenth century has been written by the historian Franklin Kopitzsch, who knows the region and era better than anyone. In addition to important articles and chapters too numerous to cite, see his magisterial two-volume work, *Grundzuge einer Sozialgeschichte der Aufklarung in Hamburg und Altona* (Hamburg: Verlag Verein fur Hamburgische Geschichte, 1990). In English, there are several insightful histories of eighteenth-century Hamburg and Altona as centers of trade and civic patriotism, including the following: Katherine Aaslestadt, *Place and Politics: Local Identity, Civic Culture, and German Nationality in North German during the Revolutionary Era* (London: Brill, 2005); Mary Lindemann, *Patriots and Paupers: Hamburg 1712–1830* (New York: Oxford University Press, 1990); and Steven Uhalde, "Citizen and World Citizen: Civic Patriotism and Cosmopolitanism in Eighteenth Century Hamburg," (PhD diss., University of California, Berkeley, 1984). Together these works paint a consistent picture of the civic patriotism that encompassed longtime residents and newcomers alike, engaged in the commercial life of the thriving cosmopolitan center.

The correspondence and publications of the elite circle of senators and entrepreneurial merchants and their families are preserved, for the most part, in the Staatsarchiv of Hamburg and the manuscripts collection in the Staats-und Universitätsbibliothek, Carl von Ossietzky, Hamburg.

For histories of the Sieveking and Reimarus families that reveal much about life in the adjoining cities, see especially the articles and books by Almut and Paul Spaulding, including the following: Almut Spalding and Paul S. Spalding, *The Account Books of the Reimarus Family of Hamburg, 1728–1780: Turf and Tailors, Books and Beer,* 2 vols. (Leiden: Brill, 2015); Almut Spalding, "Aufklärung am Teetisch. Die Frauen des Hauses Reimarus und ihr Salon," in *Formen der Geselligkeit in Nordwestdeutschland 1750–1820*, ed. Pieter Albrecht, Hans Erich Bodeker, and Ernst Hinrichs (Tübingen: Niemeyer, 2003), 261–270; Almut Spalding, *Elise Reimarus (1735–1805), the Muse of Hamburg: A Woman of the German Enlightenment* (Wurzburg: Köningshausen and Neumann, 2005); and Paul S. Spalding, "Hamburg als weltweites Kommunikationszentrum wahrend Lafayettes Gefangenschaft und Exil (1792–1799)," in *Hamburg. Eine Metropolregion zwischen Früher Neuzeit und Aufklärung*, ed. Johann Anselm Steiger and Sandra Richter (Berlin: Akademie Verlag, 2012), 349–360; as well as works by a Sieveking heir, Georg Herman Sieveking, "Aus der Familiengeschichte de Chapeaurouge und Sieveking 1794–1806," in *Zeitschrift des Vereins für Hamburgische Geschichte Hamburg. Verl. Verein für Hamburgische Geschichte* (1908), 12:207–234; and the indispensable guide to the circles: Georg Heinrich Sieveking, *Lebensbild eines Hamburgischen Kaufmanns aus dem Zeitalter der französischen Revolution* (Berlin: Verlag Karl Curtius, 1913).

On the connections between commerce and patriotism, in addition to Lindemann and Aaslestadt, see the following: Peter Uwe Hohendahl, *Patriotism, Cosmopolitanism, and National Culture: Public Culture in Hamburg, 1700–1933* (Amsterdam and New York : Rodopi, 2003); and Claudia Schnurmann,"A Scotsman in Hamburg: John Parish and His Commercial Contribution to the American War of Independence, 1776–1783," in *Small Is Beautiful? Interlopers and Smaller Trading Nations in the Pre-Industrial Period*, ed. Markus A. Denzel, Jan de Vries, and Philipp Robinson Rössner (Stuttgart: Franz Steiner Verlag, 2011), 157–176.

Although some of the most radical Frenchmen who passed through Hamburg and Altona have found historians, the best guides to the groups that gathered in coffee houses and clubs are Hans-Werner Engels, "Alles war so möglich! Auftakt für ein neues Europa; Hamburgs Bürger feiern die Französische Revolution," in *Der Französischen Revolution verpflichtet. Ausgewählte Beiträge eines Hamburg-Historikers*, ed. Michael Mahn and Rainer Hering (Nordhausen: Bautz, 2015), 148–157, and the many comprehensive articles and books by Walther Grab, especially *Demokratische Stromungen in Hamburg und Schlewsig-Holstein zur Zeit der Ersten Granzosicschen Republik* (Hamburg: H. Christians, 1966).

On the asylum offered by the Swiss cantons and their changing immigration policies, see the following: Gérald Arlettaz, *Libéralisme et société dans le canton de Vaud, 1814–1845* (Lausanne: Bibliothèque historique vaudoise, 1980); Gérald and Silvia Arlettaz, *La Suisse et les étrangers: Immigration et formation nationale (1848–1933)* (Lausanne: Éditions Antipodes et Société d'histoire de la Suisse romande, 2004); and Silvia Arlettaz, *Citoyens et étrangers sous la République helvétique (1798–1803)* (Geneva: Georg, 2002). On the many immigrants who sheltered in the Swiss cantons in the first half of the nineteenth century, see the individual biographies and the following: Antje Gerlach, *Deutsche Literatur im schweizer Exil. Die politische Propaganda der Vereine deutscher Flüchtlinge und Handwerksgesellschaften in der Schweiz von 1833 bis 1845* (Frankfurt am Main: V. Klostermann, 1975); Wilhelm Marr, *Das junge Deutschland in der Schweiz. Ein Beitrag zur Geschichte der geheimen Berbindungen unserer Tage* (Leipzig: Verlag von Wilhelm Jurcany, 1846); Beatrix Mesmer, "Die politischen Flüchtlinge im 19. Jahrhundert," in *Der Flüchtling in der Weltgeschichte. Ein ungelöstes Problem der Menschheit*, ed. André Mercier (Bern: Peter Lang, 1974), 209–240; Markus Somm, "Zinnsoldaten der Innenpolitik. Die Asylpraxis der Schweiz gegenüber revolutionären polnischen Flüchtlingen im 19. Jahrhundert," in *Asyl und Aufenthalt. Die Schweiz als Zuflucht und Wirkungstätte von Slaven im 19. und 20. Jahrhundert*, ed. Monika Bankowski, Peter Brang, Carsten Goehrke, and Werner G. Zimmermann (Basel: Helbing and Lichtenhahn, 1994); and Marc Vuilleumier, *Immigrés et réfugiés en Suisse: Aperçu historique* (Zurich: Pro Helvetia, 1989).

The history of immigration policy in Belgium has stirred a lively debate over the actual implementation of the policies of the new nation. A good place to begin is the informative work by Frank Caestecker, *Alien Policy in Belgium, 1840–1940* (New York: Berghahn Books, 2000), and a more recent collection of essays: Frank Caestecker, Bernadette Renauld, Nicolas Perrin, and Thierry Eggerickx, *Devenir Belge: Histoire de l'acquisition de la nationalité belge depuis 1830* (Mechelen: Wolters Kluwer, 2016). Belgian historian Sophie de Schaepdrijver sets these questions in their socio-economic context in *Elites for the Capital? Foreign Migration to Mid-*

Nineteenth-Century Brussels (Amsterdam: Thesis Publishers, 1990). The strongest argument for skepticism about the intentions of the government can be found in Idesbald Goddeeris, *La grande émigration polonaise en Belgique (1831–1870): Élites et masses en exil à l'époque romantique* (Frankfurt: Peter Lang, 2013); and Anne Morelli, ed., *Histoire des étrangers et de l'immigration en Belgique de la préhistoire à nos jours* (Brussels: Vie Ouvrière, 1992). There are many older collections of essays on individual political refugees and the freedom they enjoyed in Belgium at the crossroads of ideological currents.

For the socialists and communists gathering in Brussels, most of them refugees, in addition to the sizeable biographical tomes, the best sources are the edited collections of documents, especially the following: Bert Andréas, ed., *La Ligue des Communistes* (Paris: Aubier, 1972); Bert Andréas, ed., *Association démocratique ayant pour but l'union et la fraternité de tous les peuples: Eine fruhe demokratische Vereingung in Brussel 1847–1848* (Trier: Schriften aus dem Karl-Marx-Haus, 2004); Herwig Förder, Martin Hundt, Jefim Kandel, and Sofia Lewiowa, eds., *Der Bund der Kommunisten. Dokumente und Materialien*, vol. 1: *1836–1849* (Berlin: Dietz Verlag, 1970); and Helmut Elsner, Jacques Grandjonc, Elisabeth Neu, and Hans Pelger, eds., *Fragment zu internationalen demokratischen Aktivitäten um 1848* (Trier: Schriften aus dem Karl-Marx-Haus, 2000).

For exhaustive collections of documents on Belgian democrats, liberals, republicans, and radicals, see the following: Louis Bertrand, *Histoire de la démocratie et du socialisme en Belgique depuis 1830* (Brussels: Dechenne, 1907); Ernest Discailles, *Charles Rogier (1800–1885), d'après des documents inédits*, 4 vols. (Brussels: J. Lebegue, 1894); and Hubert Wouters, *Documenten betreffende de Geschiedenis der Arbeidersbeweging (1831–53)*, 3 vols. (Louvain and Paris: Editions Nauwelaerts, 1963). In addition, see the many articles by Francis Sartorius, including "L'Association démocratique (1787–1848)," *Socialisme* 136 (August 1976), and "L'importance, composition et évolution du mouvement migratoire des artisans et ouvriers allemands vers Bruxelles durant les années 1840: L'exemple de 1847," *Cahiers de CLIO* 71 (1982): 84–99. See also the detailed recently published guide to the left in Belgium in the first decades after independence by the Belgian historian most at home in the archives and most familiar with all subjects Belgian: Els Witte, *Belgische Republikeinen: Radicalen tussen twee Revoluties (1830–1850)* (Brussels: Pollis, 2020).

For the two most famous exiles in Brussels before the outbreak of the 1848 Revolutions, see the short but information article by Julien Kuypers, "Les liens d'amitié de Karl Marx en Belgique," *Socialisme* 58 (July 1963): 410–421. Written to accompany a Belgian television program, the best guide to the period of Marx's exile is Edward de Maesschalck, *Marx in Brussel: 1845–1848* (Louvain: Davidsfonds, 2005). The thoughtful study by Luc Somerhausen, *L'humanisme agissant de Karl Marx* (Paris: Richard-Masse, 1946), is not to be missed. Finally, many, if not all, of Marx's and Engels's publications focusing on Belgium are collected in one small volume: *Karl Marx and Friedrich Engels, La Belgique: État constitutionnel modèle* (Paris: Éditions Fil du Temps, 1977).

Scattered issues from newspapers, including *Le Débat social* and the *Deutsche Brüsseler-Zeitung*, are available in various collections around Belgium, especially accessible and more complete at AMSAB, Instituut voor Sociale Geschiedenis Gent, and the Periodicals Room of the KBR, the Royal Library of Belgium. See also Jacques Grandjonc, "Deutsche Emigrationspresse in Europa wahrend des Vormarz 1830–1848," in *Heinrich Heine und die Zeitgenossen. Geschichtliche und literarische Befunde* (Berlin: Aufbau-Verlag, 1979), 229–297, and Guido Ros, "De Pers van de Duitse radicale en communistische Emigranten te Parijs en te Brussel 1844–1848: Van Deutsch-Französisische Jahrbücher tot Deutsche-Brüsseler-Zeitung" (dissertation, Universiteit Gent, 1980).

For readers interested in the arrival of the Forty-Eighters in America, there has been a recent outpouring of thoughtful scholarly publications, including, notably, the following: Alison Clark Efford, *German Immigrants, Race, and Citizenship in the Civil War Era* (Cambridge: Cambridge University Press, 2013); Mischa Honeck, *We Are the Revolutionists: German-Speaking Immigrants and American Abolitionists after 1848* (Athens: University of Georgia Press, 2011); and Heléna Tóth, *An Exiled Generation: German and Hungarian Refugees of Revolution 1848–1871* (Cambridge: Cambridge University Press, 2014). See also the older standards: Carl Wittke, *Refugees of Revolution: The German Forty-Eighters in America* (Philadelphia: University of Pennsylvania Press, 1952); A. E. Zucker, ed., *The Forty-Eighters: Political Refugees of the German Revolution of 1848* (New York: Columbia University Press, 1950); and the many locally focused articles and essays based on meticulous archival research.

Acknowledgments

MY STUDENTS AT THE University of New Hampshire, especially those in my seminar on Global Citizenship, inspired me to write this book. They persistently raised questions that pushed me to think about citizenship, refugees, borders, hospitality, and asylum in new ways. This book is for them.

My first guides to Hamburg at the end of the eighteenth century were Mary Lindemann and Katherine Aaslestadt. Through their published works but also in conversations over dinners and on walks in Berlin and The Hague and at conferences, they introduced me to the civic consciousness of Hamburg and Altona and to its historians in Hamburg. Franklin Kopitzsch, director of the Arbeitstelle für Hamburgische Geschichte, and his wife, Ursula Stephan, could not have been more gracious in welcoming me and sharing their vast knowledge. Two other historians who know the central figures in the Hamburg chapters as if they were longtime friends are Almut and Paul Spalding. They welcomed me into their scholarly world and generously read chapter drafts, as did Kirsty Carpenter, the expert on the émigrés.

Professor Dr. Angelika Schaser secured privileges for me at Hamburg University, welcoming me to the university and to her home. I am also indebted to Friedemann Pestel at Freiburg for sharing his perspective. Frank Hatje introduced me not only to Ferdinand Beneke, but also to a wonderful café in the neighborhood, and Claudia Schnurmann shared her knowledge of commerce, in particular of the trading world of John Parish. Visits with Dirk Biretzke in the Hamburg history center at the university bookended my visit.

In the Staatsarchiv Hamburg, I am grateful to Volker Reissmann and Barbara Koschlig for their assistance. Dr. Heinrich Sieveking gave me permission to read the family papers and also shared information with me on a number of phone calls. The family of Jacques Chapeaurouge also opened the family papers to me. In the Hanseatische Wirtschaftsarchiv at the Handelskammer in Hamburg, Kathrin Enzel eased my way and provided scans of documents. The staff at the University Library in Hamburg, including Mark Emanuel Amstätter, lent me not only books, but also a quiet place to read. I am grateful to Sonja Annacker for her help in tracking French émigrés at the Kirchenkreis archives in Pinneberg. Britta Niebuhr lent me assistance at the Altonaer Museum für Kunst und Kulturgeschichte.

The staff of the Konigelige Bibliotek and at the Rigsarkivet in Copenhagen tolerated my haste and inability to speak Danish.

I am truly thankful for the expertise and kindness of Esther Borner, the administrator in charge of the Hamburg collection at Hamburg University. She found me a place to work in the center and was never too busy to answer a question or offer assistance. The onset of Covid meant that she is still the guardian of my bike helmet and teapot, shelved in the corner of her collection. Thanks as well to Eckart Krause and Rainer Nicolaysen for their open office door, tea, and introduction to the university and its history.

My home-away-from-home whenever I was in Hamburg was the Gaesterhaus der Universtät Hamburg. The staff, including General Manager Anna-Maria Karl, Sonja Lorenzaren-Sapori, and Meike Frank, made all scholars more than welcome and created a camaraderie among us. Kerstin Bartling and so many others at Universität Hamburg made me see the advantages of studying cities that opened doors in the past.

For help and introductions to Genevan sources, I am very grateful to Richard Whatmore and Marc Lerner, who also read my Swiss chapter when Covid made a return to the archives impossible in 2020. Consequently, I really appreciate the suggestions of Béla Kapossy, Michael Suter, and Markus Buergi, who lent their expertise and shared sources with me.

In Brussels, Els Witte has listened to descriptions of this project for years over dinners and coffees. Her newest book, *Belgische Republikeinen*, came out just as I was about to send mine to my editor. She helped me to see connections I had missed and to rethink others. Lunches with Guy Vanthemsche and Brecht Deseure and our continuing conversations through correspondence remind me why I was drawn to Belgian history from the beginning. Brecht and Jonathan Sperber helped me think through the difficult question of labeling for activists on the continuum from liberals to communists, and they read the Brussels chapters

I returned to my familiar desk at the Werkzaal/Salle de Travail at the Belgian Royal Library. Didier Amaury and Alain Gérard gave me access to the diplomatic archives of Foreign Affairs, Foreign Trade, and Development. At the Algemeen Rijksarchief/Archives générales du Royaume, Filip Strubbe helped me to locate files of refugees. The Archives de la Ville de Bruxelles/Archief van de Stad Brussel made it possible for me to read through enormous stacks of police archives.

In Ghent, I have come to rely on the knowledgeable staff and carefully curated collections at the Archief en Museum van de Socialistische Arbeidersbeweging. In Antwerp, access to the University Library and office space was graciously provided by the History Department. My thanks to Greet de Block and her colleagues, Hilda Greefs and Maarten Van Ginderachter, for those arrangements, as well as the many discussions of questions of immigration, urban planning, and beyond. Librarians and former librarians, including Melvin Collier at the Katholieke Universiteit Leuven, and faculty in the KUL History Department, including Leen van Molle, again provided access to their rich collections, as they have over many decades.

As always, my research would not have been nearly as enjoyable without the comradeship of Het Quint in Louvain. Thanks for their friendship, meals, lodging, hikes, concerts, and bike rides to Robert Brusten, Hedwig Schwall, Mel Collier, Leo Garcia, and to the friends from around the block, Rita Schepers and Els Roeykens and Eric Min and their children.

In addition, I am grateful to Professor Anne Morelli, who knows Belgian refugees better than anyone, for taking the time to share her knowledge. Francis Sartorius met me in the Université libre de Bruxelles, hidden at the end of a very elaborate maze. Anne Winter helped guide my research through the Belgian archives.

Grant Harris at the Library of Congress provided me study space to work with the library's amazing collection. The staff of the Houghton Library at Harvard University has been gracious to me and my students. I also appreciate the access to the collection at the Widener Library and a well-worn tradition of lunches with Laurel Ulrich.

Finally, the UNH library ILL staff went above and beyond. When Covid closed off the possibility of return trips to the archives, the staff somehow located obscure publications and mailed them to me.

Eleta Exline expertly scanned my photos at the UNH library. Birgit Staak and Elka Schneider from the Altonaer Museum, Nils Moeller and Meike Borgert from the Elbe Werkstatten, and Volker Reissmann from the Hamburg Staatsarchiv helped to locate photographs. The Harvard Library and Boston Public Library map collections were invaluable. Bill Nelson again prepared the maps with aplomb.

Many of my ideas in this volume grew out of workshops, networks, and conferences organized by Delphine Diaz in Reims, Hilda Greefs and Greet de Blok in Antwerp and Leipzig, Mareike König and Delphine Diaz in Paris, and Henk te Velde in Leiden. Especially helpful have been seminars and conferences at the University of Minnesota, Washington University, Ohio University, Emmanuel College, King's College London, the Consortium for the Revolutionary Era in Atlanta, French Historical Studies, and, of course, the University of New Hampshire.

My first and most committed reader for this manuscript was Lila Teeters, then a PhD candidate at UNH who read, edited, and asked really smart questions about chapters throughout the summer of 2020. Other readers subjected to the entire manuscript include Jeff Bolster, Marilyn Hoskin, Bill Lyons, and my students Daniel Frehner, Abby Colby, and Benjamin Bernier. David Lyons, Laurel Ulrich, John Voll, Ellen Fitzpatrick, Jess Lepler, Lucy Salyer, Mary Rhiel, and members of the History Department faculty seminar read chapters, sometimes more than once, and helped me rethink them at critical moments. Marcella Paez helped with the final formatting.

Finally, my department chairs, Eliga Gould and Kurk Dorsey; department administrative assistants Lara Demarest, Laura Simard, and Sto Alexander; and Deans Ken Fuld and Michele Dillon have been supportive from beginning to end. Above all, thanks to my family, to my husband Bill Lyons, who has welcomed travel organized around archives, read chapters, and discussed ideas, and to my children and their partners, Dave Lyons and Ashley Kranz, and Marta Lyons and Ishraf Ahmad, all writers and researchers, for listening and adding their expertise and love.

Adina Berk has been an enthusiastic and supportive editor. I sincerely appreciate her interest in refugees. Ash Lago and Eva Skewes have supplied answers to all of my day-to-day questions about book production. In the final phases, I have benefitted greatly from the support of Margaret Otzel and the attentive copyediting of Bojana Ristich. Chris Rogers is the best agent ever, reading a full manuscript and getting back to me within a day.

Index

Italicized page numbers indicate figures and illustrations.